# IN THE NAME OF PEACE

### HOW HISTORY'S GREAT PACIFISTS CHANGED THE WORLD

### ERIN LADD SANDERS

FOR THE PAST AND THE FUTURE:
MY PARENTS, ED AND MARIAN,
AND MY CHILDREN, NELL AND YOSHI

# CONTENTS

# INTRODUCTION

IN THE FIRST HALF OF THE TWENTIETH CENTURY, THE GREAT HINDU sage and Indian independence leader Mohandas K. Gandhi led hundreds of thousands of protesters in peaceful civil disobedience against British rule. Facing massacres, mass arrests and oppression from unrestrained British troops, Gandhi told his followers: 'I cannot teach you violence, as I do not myself believe in it. I can only teach you not to bow your heads before any one even at the cost of your life.' Gandhi's willingness to lay down his own life before resorting to violence is the essence of pacifism. I have sought to show how he, along with many other familiar and overlooked pacifists portrayed in the following chapters, reveal how the major threads of pacifism—from the Eastern concept of *ahimsa* (non-violence), to pacifist Christian teachings, to the social outcry against the twentieth century's modern wars—have affected and changed the course of world history.

So, who were these people of peace? Who were these individuals who opposed the use of war or violence for gaining advantage, settling disputes or leading their people out of oppression? And what drove the choices they made? I found, as I immersed myself in the lives of these extraordinary individuals, that they were fundamentally the shapers of civilisation from earliest antiquity right up to the beginning of the twenty-first century.

Yet throughout history, wars have raged worldwide and unspeakable violence has been visited on mankind daily. Does this mean that their efforts have failed? Has pacifism always been the best course of action? And what were the expectations and experiences that shaped these pacifists' beliefs and thrust them into action?

Through a broad collection of profiles and stories, *In the Name of Peace* uncovers the fundamental motives for what drove these great and unsung adherents of non-violence. The book's initial section touches on the earliest roots of non-violence and the originators of pacifist doctrine who offered the first examples of peace as a way of life. The next section looks at those who set out to communicate and orchestrate a legacy of non-violent thought and action. The third section explores those who actively opposed and worked to deter the devastating wars of the twentieth century. And the final section brings to life those great leaders who courageously chose a non-violent path for liberating their followers. I hope I have done justice to their courage: of the five profiled in this last section, three have been assassinated and the other two remain in exile or under arrest.

What I found most remarkable as I wrote this book was the unrelenting optimism of these individuals about the fundamental goodness in all people. One example was the Christian pacifist and social revolutionary A.J. Muste. In the late 1920s he led some of the largest peaceful worker strikes in the history of the United States. He had instructed his beaten and abused textile-mill picketers to resist being baited by baton- and gun-wielding police. 'Our real power was in our solidarity and our capacity to endure suffering,' he later recalled. 'No one could "weave wool with machine guns"; that cheerfulness was better for morale than bitterness and that therefore we would smile as we passed the machine guns and the police on the way from the hall to the picket lines around the mills.'

I hope these many stories offer a gripping narrative about how conscience, courage and conduct played a pivotal role in these pacifists' lives. All, in ways large and small, have made their mark on history in the name of peace.

*'There is no quality of soul more subtle than non-violence
and no virtue of spirit greater than reverence for life.'*
**LORD MAHAVIRA**

# PART I

# IN THE BEGINNING

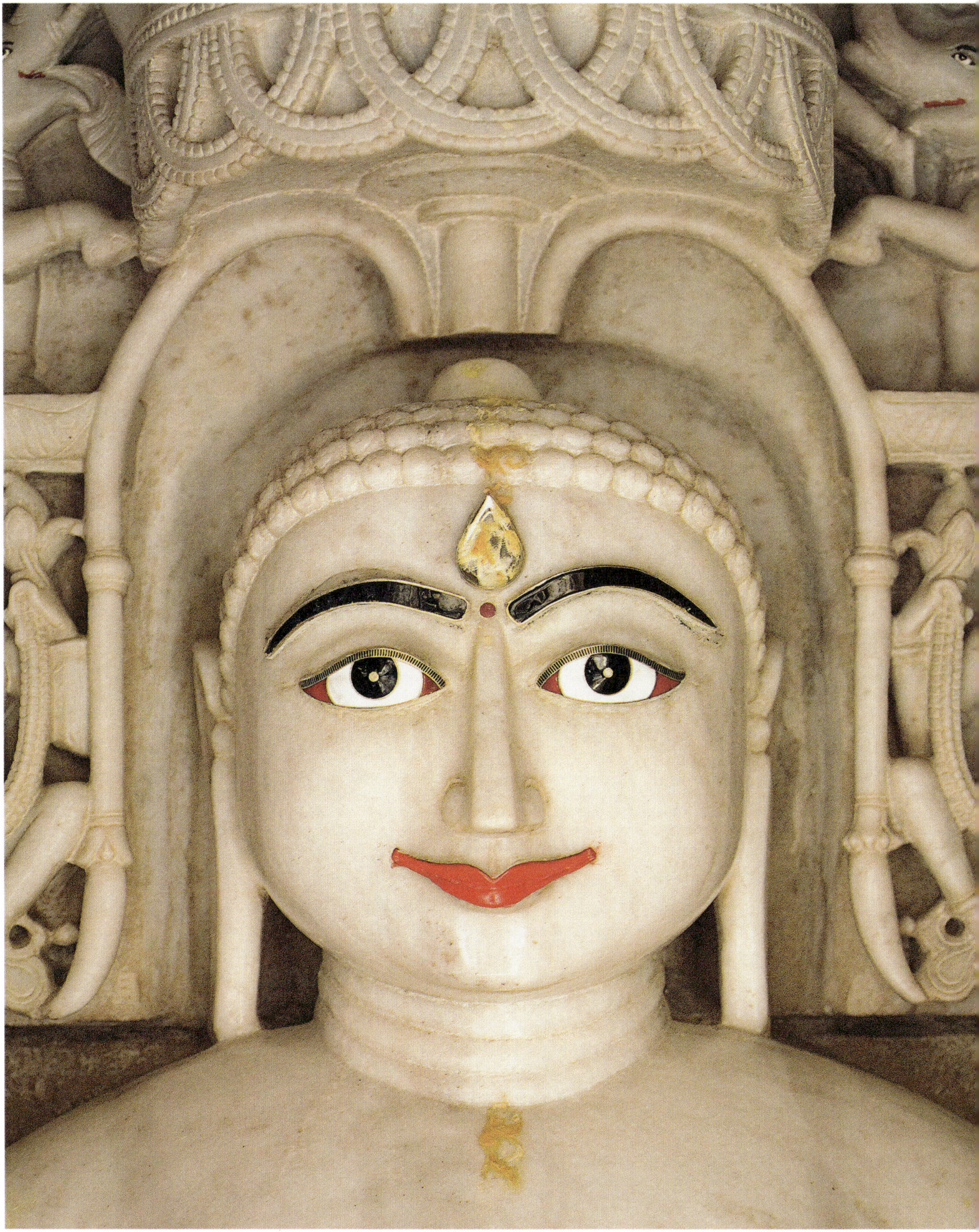

# LORD MAHAVIRA: JAINISM AND A RELIGION OF NON-VIOLENCE

DROUGHT WAS SLOWLY LAYING WASTE TO THE FERTILE PLAINS OF Kshatriyastan in the ancient republic of Vaishali. King Siddhartha had sat for hours meditating on the teachings of Parshva, the 23rd Jain Tirthankara (see 'Important Jain terms', page 6). He'd made countless sacrifices to Indra, the great diva of weather. But still the rains would not come. Food was growing scarce and soon there would be unrest. He wasn't sure how long he could restrain his Kshatriya warriors. It did not matter that his was a lesser kingdom of Vaishali—it was still a centre of commerce and learning and he could not allow it to dissolve into anarchy. Another season of drought would be ruinous.

But the fortunes of the king, his kingdom, and the entire Vaishali republic were about to change. That morning, Queen Trishala had woken from a fitful night in which she'd had the most wondrous dreams, and rushed to tell her husband. He summoned his scholars, whose interpretation of the dreams was unanimous—the queen would bear him a son and prosperity would return to the kingdom.

So begins the legend of Lord Mahavira. The year was 599 BCE and the prince was born in one of history's earliest democratic republics, now India's Bihar state. India's great Vedic traditions were coalescing into Hinduism, and Mahavira's birth came only a few years before that of his contemporary,

The serene face of Lord Mahavira: a white marble statue in a Jain temple inside the extensive twelfth century Jaisalmer Fort in India's north-western state of Rajasthan.

Gautama Buddha. The events of his childhood and his years as an ascetic would not only lead him to fulfil his destiny as the 24th and final Jain Tirthankara but would also shape the way he reframed Jainism as a world religion. This is the story of a prince groomed to be a warrior who would instead remould his privileged upbringing to embrace *ahimsa*, the concept of inner and outer peace, and establish one of the great spiritual philosophies as an enduring 'religion of non-violence'.

⸺

## THE AUSPICIOUS DREAMS OF A QUEEN

MAHAVIRA WAS BORN INTO THE WARRIOR KSHATRIYA CASTE. HIS MOTHER, Queen Trishala, was the eldest of eight daughters of King Chetaka, who ruled the republic of Vaishali. As a young girl, she was married to King Siddhartha of the Licchavi royal family whose kingdom, a stronghold of the Kshatriyas, lay on the outskirts of the ancient Vaishali metropolis, the seat of power of the republic.

As king of Vaishali, Queen Trishala's father ruled over the Vajjian Confederacy, a democratic alliance of regional kingdoms that predated the ancient Greeks. Shielded on the northeast by the majestic Mahavana forest, a dense, broadleaf blanket stretching straight up into the Himalayas, and to the south by the equally untamed Gosingalasala forest, the republic sat in the midst of the fertile central plains of the Ganges River. The ancient metropolis was rich and flourishing, crowded with haggling merchants, bejewelled courtesans, revered scholars and stolid soldiers. Sentries manned the watchtowers along the city's walls and the three reinforced gates. Beyond, throughout the Gangetic–Himalayan region were the smaller kingdoms of the seven thousand and seven rajas that came under Vajjian administration. Each raja, no matter how small his state, allocated himself a large retinue of courtesans, and built palaces, pleasure parks and fragrant lotus ponds.

Eight great families ruled the Vajj. The Licchavis, Jnatrikass and Videhas families were the most prominent, each with their own semi-autonomous territory. Ruling representatives were chosen from each territory as members of a 'people's council,' the head of which was King Chetaka, the maharaja or 'great king.' The post was not dynastic, but selected by the council of lesser rajas, who not only ruled their own considerable kingdoms but also oversaw various republic ministries such as internal security, defence, justice and local administration.

The time leading up to Mahavira's birth had been plagued by droughts. Food was in short supply. People were dying in great numbers and their rotting corpses 'attracted evil spirits'. So news spread quickly of Queen Trishala's sixteen auspicious dreams, especially of the collective interpretation of the great deeds that would be accomplished by her son. The dreams predicted a noble son, strong and virtuous, who would command a 'vast spiritual realm' and would be liberated from his own karmic limitations. Legend has it that almost immediately upon the news, the rains came. Flowers bloomed in abundance and the Ganges plain again grew fruitful. Such was the sudden prosperity of the kingdom that the child became known as Vardhamana, Sanskrit for 'increase.'

On the thirteenth day of the month of Chaitra in the Hindu calendar (12 April), Queen Trishala gave birth. On that day, according to Jain lore, Indra, the king of the divas (gods), came down from his celestial throne and cast a spell over the kingdom. While everyone slept, he took baby Vardhamana away to the mythical Mount Meru, the spiritual centre of the universe. There, he bathed the infant in celestial milk and recited the *Bruhat Shanti*, the ritual of peace and tranquillity, laying the path for Vardhamana to one day take his place as a Jain saint, the 24th and final Tirthankara.

King Siddhartha and Queen Trishala were followers of Parshva, the 23rd Tirthankara. Vardhamana grew up exposed to his teachings, and also studied the Kshatriya military tradition of his mother's family. He became adept in all forms of weaponry and was an excellent horseman, fighter and swimmer. He showed unusual courage and ability, 'trusting in a force deep within himself'. Stories abounded of his courage: he saved a childhood friend from a poisonous snake and 'defied an angel disguised as a monster'.

But the event that shaped his life took place when he was only five years old. He and his childhood friends were playing on the palace grounds when an elephant of the guard suddenly became spooked. Crushing everything in its path, the elephant careened towards the trembling children. As the guards shielded the children and prepared to kill the beast, Vardhamana stood his ground. The charging elephant lowered its head, aiming its lethal tusks at the boy, but Vardhamana deftly grabbed its trunk, planted his foot on the animal's knee and hurled himself onto its neck. He patted the elephant's cheek, whispered in its ear and brought it under control, saving both the noble animal and the children. When he rode the pacified elephant into the palace, the entire court turned out to marvel. Vardhamana was hailed as a 'great hero', and so the name Mahavira came to be.

# IMPORTANT JAIN TERMS

**AGAM SUTRAS** the collected teachings of Lord Mahavira

**AHIMSA** one of Jainism's five ethical expectations of 'right behaviour': the dedication to complete non-violence of thought, action and deed

**ANEKANTAVADA** one of the complex tenets of Jainism that proffers the validity of perceiving reality from differing points of view

**APARIGRAHA** one of the five ethical expectations of 'right behaviour': the detachment from all possessions and material things

**ASTEYA** one of the five ethical expectations of 'right behaviour': the refusal to take anything not freely given

**BRAHMACHARYA** one of the five ethical expectations of 'right behaviour': the conducting of a chaste life

**JAIN** a follower of Jainism, from the Sanskrit word *jina*, meaning 'one who has conquered'

**KARMA** actions or deeds within the cycle of life's cause and effect that shape past, present and future experiences

**MAHARAJA** Sanskrit term for 'high king' who rules over lesser kings (rajas)

**MAHAVIRA** literally, 'great hero' and the name of the 24th Jain Tirthankara, bestowed at a young age because of his heroic feats

**MOKSHA** the 'release' from the endless cycle of death and rebirth known as *samsara*. It is achieved by the annihilation of all karmas and the attainment of the 'purest self' known as *siddha*.

**PURVAS** fourteen *purvas*, or bodies of scripture, collected and taught by Jain Tirthankaras containing all the knowledge of this universe

**SAMSARA** the process of reincarnation in the endless cycle of death and rebirth

**SATYA** one of the five ethical expectations of 'right behaviour': being truthful in all thoughts and actions

**SYADVADA** essential Jain tenet of the 'assertion of what may be', a complex postulation on the relativity of all things

**TIRTHANKARA** literally, 'ford builder' or 'crossing maker'; one of the twenty-four Jain saints who offer spiritual guidance for enlightenment and achieve moksha, ending the cycle of reincarnation

**VARDHAMANA** original name of Lord Mahavira, translated as 'increase' and given because of the prosperity brought on by his birth

In time, the king and queen turned their attentions to finding their prince a suitable princess. Rajas and nobles sent luscious paintings of their daughters in the hopes of luring his attention. And though Mahavira acquiesced in his parents' wishes, married and had a daughter, he was already detaching from the lavish world around him. In time, he lost all interest in the luxuries of his birthright, which he saw as fleeting delights. He wished instead to turn his physical strengths against his inner enemies: anger, greed, material needs and the illusion of reality. Disillusioned by the cruelty and violence around him, Mahavira was troubled by the Hindu caste system, the unbalanced treatment of women and the ritual sacrifice of animals. He believed that all souls were able to attain enlightenment, that every soul could be shown the way.

When two great sages of the era, Sanjaya and Vijaya, arrived in the kingdom, in deep dispute over the Jain scripture *Purva*, Mahavira was able to clarify their questions. Sanjaya and Vijaya immediately recognised the young man as an evolved soul and pleaded with the king to send Mahavira out to begin his spiritual journey. King Siddhartha could see his son's unrest, and asked him what he wished to do. Mahavira asked to be released from his royal duties.

## THE 'SKY-CLAD' CONQUEROR

Thus it was that at the age of thirty, Mahavira gave up his wealth and his birthright. In the garden of Shandavana, under an ashoka tree, Mahavira removed his princely robes. He pulled out all his hair by his own hands. Naked, or 'sky-clad', he began his life as a Jain monk by fasting for two days.

For the next twelve years he wandered. His life as an ascetic included regular fasting, strenuous yoga and endless meditation. He ate only what was given him, wore no clothes, harmed no animals and respected all souls. He kept no worldly attachments and maintained no self-indulgences. Nothing disturbed his mind, not thunder, wild animals, snakes or any manner of evils. He never resisted or protested when he was scorned, beaten or stoned. He forgave anyone who did him harm, even his tormenter, the trickster Sanghamakha, who bedevilled him for years. Sanghamakha pretended to be a follower and would steal from Mahavira's benefactors and blame it on 'his master'. In time, however, Sanghamakha came to see the error of his ways.

In his thirteenth year of abstinence, Mahavira came to the village of Jrumbhika beside the flowing waters of the Rujukoola River. As he had when his spiritual journey began years before, Mahavira sat beneath an ashoka tree.

॥डिए॒ष्टस्या॒तवासिनइतिया॒डुंॗ॥गो॒नमस्यगा॒वएा॥ इं॒इ॒चूर्तिनीस्या॥ञा॒नत॒
वीरविषायपिॐबें॒धाम॒नि॒सिद्धबेंधनव्यवञ्जिन॒इञितस॒निॢकवलब्ञर॒चें
गा॒ञा॒मा॒नगव्यापइ॒बि॒इ॒ञखग॒गा॒म॒ञगें॒बाददि॒न॒दि॒गउविञआ॒लॢ

र काल गए ड॒ावस ब डु क क प॒दी॒एा
तं॒रय॒एॢीब॒कॢदिॢदवदिय दवीदिय
यमा॒एॢादिय उथ्थयमा॒एॢादिय
लगरुया॒ कदकद गरुया॒आ॒
बा॒१७॥ डंरय॒एॢिंबॢास
मा॒एॢलगवेमहावीर डॢाव
बडुक्कप॒दीॢएा तेरय॒एॢिंचॢां
स्मा॒एॢञमस्म इंदडुॢइसॢञागर
तिवासिस्म ता॒एॢपिॐबें॒धाएाडुॢहि

स्मा॒गएॢदावंसिॢदिॢगउएॢिबॢक्ष्याॢदाई॒ष्वाॢरसंॠवादसविद॒रिॢसइतिहॢ
 विंत्या॒॥आवश्यपकादिनिॢर्विॢराॢक्त्ना॥

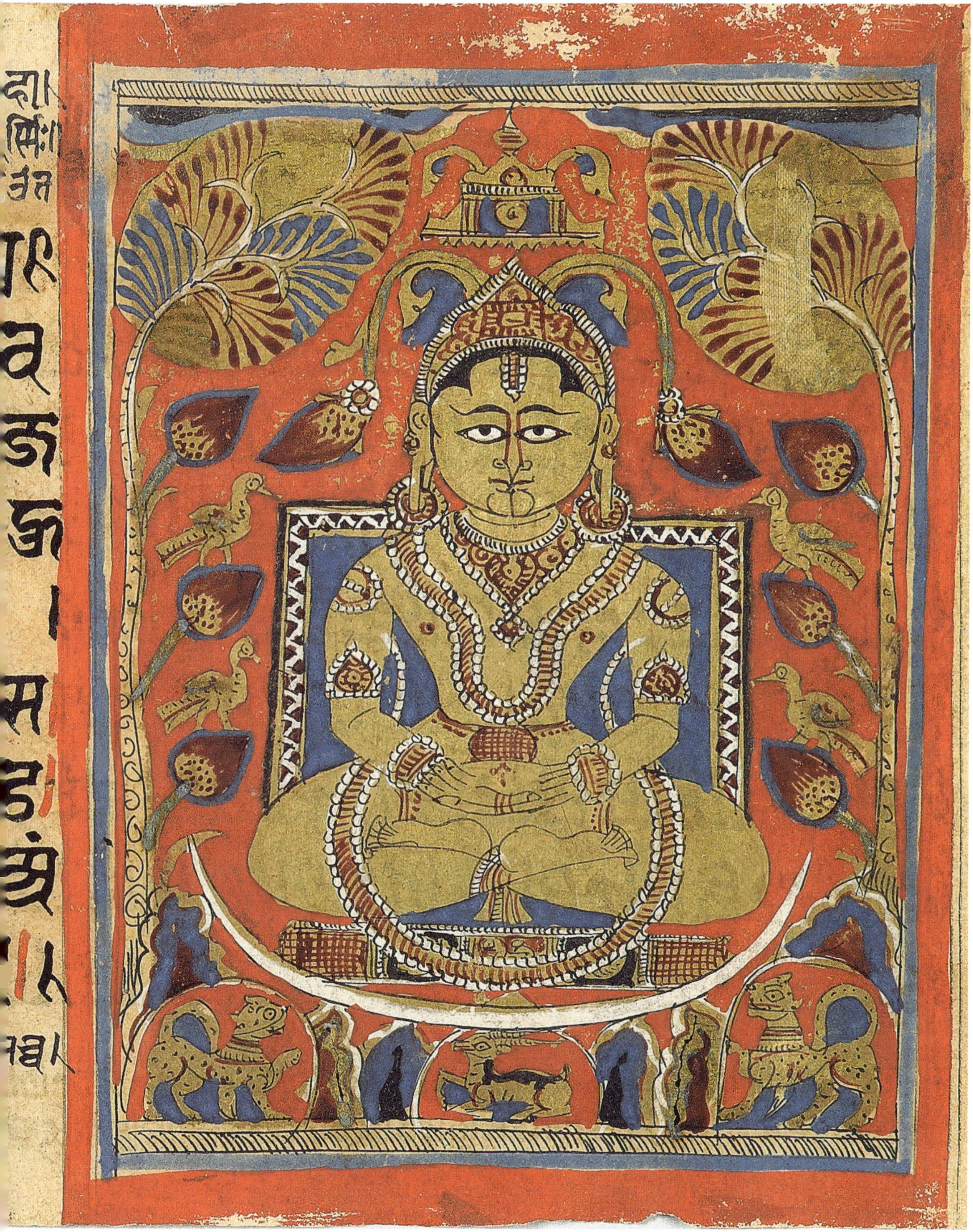

Previous pages:
An image of Lord
Mahavira's initiation
from a fifteenth
century illuminated
manuscript of
the *Kalpa Sutra*,
the most sacred
text in Jainism,
which recounts the
biographies of the
Tirthankaras.

He leaned backwards until his body was fully reclined, his legs tucked beneath him in the arduous paryankasana posture, and fell into deep meditation. The afternoon shadows stretched towards the east as darkness gathered around him but Mahavira was oblivious to the world. Here, at last, he conquered his earthly constraints and achieved divine knowledge. The transformation was said to be instantly recognisable: he 'shone like a crystal' and celestial music was heard emanating from him.

[He] moves so as not to hurt any living creature. He has only one face, but people looking at him see four faces on all four sides. He knows all branches of knowledge. His body does not throw a shadow. His eyelids do not move. His nails and hair do not grow.

The Sanskrit terms *jina* and *tirthankara* both mean 'one who has conquered', referring to the ability to conquer karmic constraints. To fulfil his destiny as a Tirthankara, Mahavira would devote the remainder of his earthly life to teaching others the way to spiritual freedom. Using the administrative skills he learned as a young man, he organised and strengthened the tenets of Jainism to greatly expand his following. For the next twenty-three years, he spread the Jain philosophy into the mainstream of Indian life.

At last, in an area known then as Pawapuri, Mahavira attained moksha, liberation from the endless cycle of reincarnation, on the last day of Dipavali, the festival of the lights. In the year 519 BCE, at seventy-two years of age, legend and history merged and Mahavira left his earthly vessel.

—

## 'FORDING THE RIVER OF HUMAN MISERY'

MAHAVIRA IS OFTEN CREDITED WITH 'FOUNDING' JAINISM BUT THE religion existed long before. The succession of Jinas trace their roots back to the first Tirthankara, Rishabha, a mythological giant who is said to have lived over eight million years ago. Some accounts suggest that the soul of Rishabhda's grandson Marichi reincarnated as Vardhamana. Most of the early Tirthankaras are steeped in mythology, with fantastic histories similar to the early heroes of the Old Testament. But there is enough historic evidence to substantiate that both Parshva, the 23rd Tirthankara, who lived about 250 years before Mahavira, and Neminatha, the 22nd Tirthankara, were real. Some even argue that there is evidence to prove the likelihood of pre-historic Tirthankaras.

# THE SWASTIKA: A SYMBOL OF PEACE AND HARMONY

Although the swastika has dark connotations today because of its association with Nazi Germany, it is one of the oldest and holiest icons in the Jain, Buddhist and Hindu religions. The term 'swastika' comes from the Sanskrit *svasti*, 'well-being' and in turn *svastika*, combined from *su* (good) + *astika* (to be). In other words, it was the original good luck charm. The symbol's unique shape, either left- or right-facing, may have come from the combined Brahmi characters abbreviating the word *su-asti*. But the Jains endowed the symbol with special significance: associated with the concept of *ahimsa*, it came to represent peace and non-violence towards all beings. It was the chosen symbol of the seventh Tirthankara, Suparsva, and was used to decorate his solid gold temple in India's Bihar state. Nearly all Jain temples and spiritual texts contain swastika decorations and monks would commonly begin and end holy rituals by drawing swastikas in rice around their altars. However, from archaeological evidence the symbol goes back much further, and can be dated to the Neolithic period. It appears to have been in common use 3000 years ago in the ancient cities of Lothal and Harappa in the Indus Valley region of India.

The swastika appeared independently in many far-flung civilisations, including Chinese, Ancient Greek, Celtic, Slavic and Native American cultures. There are several theories as to why this symbol was so ubiquitous among peoples who could not possibly have influenced one another. It may be common because it's a simple interlocking shape found in square basket-weave. The shape may have entered the common consciousness from the appearance of the Big Dipper constellation rotating around the Pole Star in the night sky. Scientist Carl Sagan speculated that a comet that passed close to Earth may have been seen around the world. As its rotation became visible through the bending of its jets of gas, the swastika shape was born. However the shape came to be, each culture independently imbued it with a sense of good fortune.

Of course this shifted dramatically when the swastika was appropriated by the Nazis in 1920. Heinrich Schliemann, a German archaeologist, had 'discovered' the symbol while excavating the site of ancient Troy late in the nineteenth century and made the connection to similar designs on primitive pottery found in Germany. He concluded that the swastika was a significant religious symbol associated with German 'Proto-Indo-European' ancestors, collectively known as Aryans (another Sanskrit word, meaning 'noble'). Schliemann's work was manipulated by Alfred Rosenberg, a German nationalist and influential member of the Nazi Party, into the self-serving theory of a Nordic Aryan 'master race'. And so the swastika was adopted as their icon. Adolf Hitler described the importance of the symbol in his book *Mein Kampf*: 'In the swastika the mission of the struggle for the victory of the Aryan man, and by the same token, the victory of the idea of creative work ... always will be anti-Semitic.' It's a sad irony that the swastika, universally recognised as a symbol of peace and good fortune for so many centuries, is now most associated with hate, anti-Semitism, violence and death.

Tirthankaras are Jain saints who have achieved enlightenment by conquering their emotions and desires. By leading others to enlightenment, they achieve their stature and bring to an end *samsara*, the cycle of reincarnation. *Tirthankara* translates literally as 'ford builder'—the Tirthankara's spiritual guidance helps souls cross the 'river of human suffering'. Tirthankaras are very rare. Supposedly, only twenty-four beings in the past eight million years have achieved moksha and ascended to the supreme throne at the top of the universe.

According to Jain cosmology, there was no beginning to the universe, nor will there be an end. Time moves in infinite cycles, 'like the wheel of a cart'. The cyclic nature of the universe is a consistent motif in Jainism. Circular images, like a wheel in the palm of a hand or a decorative rotating swastika, provide some of the oldest and holiest symbols of the Tirthankaras (see 'The swastika: a symbol of peace and harmony', page 11). Forty-eight Tirthankaras are born in each full cycle of time—two half-cycles of twenty-four—before the cycle repeats indefinitely. One half-cycle is 'ascending', where society, through its ethics, happiness, health, progress and religion, develops from its lowest state to its highest. The next cycle is 'descending', and society deteriorates towards its most base state. Each half-cycle is made up of six uneven time periods called *Aras*. Currently, our universe is in the fifth Ara of a descending half-cycle, with about 19,000 years left. The next Tirthankara will ostensibly be born at the beginning of the new ascending half-cycle, in approximately 81,500 years.

The Jain cosmos exists in a set of layers or states: Siddha is the supreme condition, resting 'at the top of the universe' where the souls who achieve moksha reside; the upper world is made up of thirty heavens all occupied by celestial beings; the middle world consists of our world and universe; the nether region is comprised of seven hells of various miseries and punishments; the Nigoda is where the lowest forms of life reside; and the void beyond is merely infinite space without soul, time or matter.

In order to overcome their worldly limitations, Jains seek to attain the state of *Kevala Jnana* (absolute knowledge), transcending the cycle of cause and effect known as *karma*. A sort of spiritual tally of positive and negative actions, the concept of karma is interpreted differently by Jains, Buddhists and Hindus. Jains believe every soul's original state is pure but becomes contaminated by karmic particles (what Mahavira called 'karmic dust') through contact with the world. They see the ultimate spiritual goal as the liberation of the soul from all these particles. This is achieved through absolute detachment from the illusion of reality, the bondage of pleasure and material things, and the self-centred limitations of anger, hatred and greed. By destroying all karmas, Jains believe an enlightened soul achieves a state of perfect being and supreme knowledge that transcends matter, energy, time, space and causation. This is how they end the cycle of *samsara*.

The concept of karma is the first of three core metaphysical precepts accepted by Jains. To break this karmic cycle, Mahavira taught that a soul must embrace 'right faith', 'right knowledge' and 'right conduct' through spiritual practice and ethical behaviour. The second is *anekantavada* ('non-one-sidedness'), a spiritually complex belief based on the recognition that an unenlightened soul is not able to understand universal wisdom from a single vantage point. It is, in essence, a belief in the validity of multiple viewpoints, that no one religion can offer all the answers and that truth and reality are perceived differently from varying perspectives. The third metaphysical underpinning of Jainism is the concept of *syadvada*. This idea is not easily translated but refers to Mahavira's 'assertions of what may be', and provides teachings for postulating about the relativity of all things. It provides the means for putting *anekantavada* into practice. Central to Jain practice are the five ethical expectations of *mahavratas* or 'right conduct'. These include *satya*, truthfulness in all thoughts and actions; *asteya*, refusal to take anything not freely given; *brahmacharya*, the conducting of a chaste life, devoid of sensual pleasures; and *aparigraha*, the complete detachment from possession, people, places and material objects. However, the first and foremost ethical commandment is that of *ahimsa*, non-violence of thought, action, deed and speech.

Mahavira put the concept of *ahimsa* at the very front of the Jain religion. Implicit in his belief is the sanctity of all life, evident in his teaching of non-violence, his abolition of animal sacrifice and his near-fanatical devotion to vegetarianism. But it's perhaps best reflected in his outreach to all peoples. Mahavira attracted men and women from all walks of life, castes and orders as he expanded the Jain belief. Even the untouchables were welcomed. He organised the religion into four levels in the order of monk (*sadhu*), nun (*sadhvi*), layman (*shravak*) and laywoman (*shravika*). And perhaps most radical for his era was the strict command that women were to be considered spiritual equals and that all may seek moksha. By the end of his lifetime, Mahavira had over 400,000 followers, who vowed an ethical, open life committed to non-violence.

*A*HIMSA IS A SANSKRIT TERM THAT LITERALLY TRANSLATES AS 'AVOIDANCE of violence' (*a* + *himsa*). It is a concept that originated in ancient India, perhaps as far back as the third millennium BCE, but is certainly found in early Vedic texts from around the eighth century BCE. It's a central tenet of Jainism but is also an essential component of Hinduism and Buddhism. Mahavira's slightly younger contemporary, Gautama Buddha, found common threads in his approach to non-violent practices (see 'Siddhartha Gautama Buddha: a contemporary', opposite). Simply, *ahimsa* is a commandment against killing or harming any living beings. Violence—intentional or accidental—carries with it the effects and consequences of negative karma. Jainism elevates *ahimsa* to one of its core tenets, and Mahavira organised much of the ethical and metaphysical aspects of Jainism around it.

Non-violence is seen as an indispensable spiritual duty of everyone. Before Mahavira, who took it to a more radical and comprehensive extreme, *ahimsa* was an essential part of the 'Fourfold Restraints' dictated by Tirthankara Parshva. Beyond causing any harm to humans, Mahavira made every effort to extend *ahimsa* to the protection of all life, including animals, plants and even micro-organisms. He shunned cultivating crops for the harm done to earth-borne beings, and required strict vegetarianism. He asserted all life must be sacred because every living organism has the potential for enlightenment through reincarnation, the destruction of its karma, and eventual spiritual liberation. Every being has the potential of reaching god-like elevation of pure soul through moksha and equality under the universal *dharma* ('law'). As each soul has 'transmigrated' as an animal, plant or micro-organism innumerable times, a karmic kinship is created between all life forms. Since all souls are on a spiritual quest towards liberation, Jains see any hindering of this goal as an attractor of negative karmas. Essential to Jainism is '*parasparopagraho jivanam*', which declares 'all life is interrelated and it is the duty of all souls to assist each other'.

But it would be inconsistent with Jain philosophy to attach any sentimentality to this. Dharma is based on rational consciousness and personal responsibility to the self. Seeing all humanity as linked and related means that any injury done to another is also an injury done to oneself. Simply, only through non-violence in every action—avoidance of violent intention, carelessness or harmful thoughts—does one harbour peace and allow for karmic evolution. Any outward or inward violence retards this

Siddhartha Gautama, the Buddha, was a younger contemporary of Mahavira, living around 563–483 BCE. Their stories are strangely similar: both were born in the region of the Vaishali republic, privileged princes of the Kshatriya warrior caste. Both renounced their upbringings, spent years in ascetic detachment, achieved enlightenment and spent the remainder of their earthly days teaching and spreading their faiths.

Like Mahavira, Gautama became disillusioned with the excesses of his courtly life. In escaping his princely isolation, he encountered the old, the dying, the dead and the pious, which convinced him that on his current path he could only look ahead to suffering. So he renounced his title, became a monk, and dedicated himself to becoming free of suffering. Much like Mahavira, he became enlightened to the supreme knowledge after years of asceticism, while meditating under a tree. He took the title Buddha, meaning simply 'the awakened one'.

Gautama Buddha spent the rest of his life teaching what he'd come to understand. Of this he said, 'I teach suffering and the end of suffering.' His epiphany was that of 'the middle path', a way to enlightenment based on moderation, from the extremes of sensual indulgence and the self-deprivation of the most rigorous ascetic. He crystallised this view in the Four Noble Truths: suffering is common to all life and is inherent in existence; the cause of suffering is ignorance and the symptoms are attachment and desire; suffering will stop when desire is conquered; the only way to be free of desire and attachment is to follow the Noble Eightfold Path, a set of ethical behaviours similar to those taught by Mahavira.

Jainism preceded Buddhism; it was already an established faith in the time of India's two greatest sages. Both agreed on the necessity of individuals developing their minds through spiritual effort, and that enlightenment comes from that effort rather than any divine intervention. The concepts of karma, nirvana and *ahimsa* belong to both faiths, meaning that both track their roots to early Jainism. The Buddha and Lord Mahavira visited and taught at many of the same historical sites throughout their concurrent lives, and although there is no textual evidence of their meeting it is generally assumed that they exchanged ideas and influenced one another.

The main difference between Jain and Buddhist practice is the extreme to which Mahavira imposed his dictates of total abstinence. Jain monks practise an absolute form of *ahimsa*, taking great care not to harm or kill even the smallest of insects. The Buddhist way is far more temperate. This is perhaps an indication of why Buddhism today numbers upwards of 500 million followers, whereas the Jain religion has 'only' between ten and twelve million. The Buddhist interpretation of *ahimsa*—condemning the taking of human and animal life and the aversion to animal sacrifice—is likewise more moderate, for it allows for the eating of some meat and the cultivation of root crops. Though they differ in the way *ahimsa* should be applied in daily life, Jainism and Buddhism both accept the sanctity of all life. Both believe *ahimsa* is the principle of universal love for the primary purpose of transforming human nature from the animal plane to the spiritual plane. The methods vary but the ideal is the same.

effort. So *ahimsa* is not only about the absence of physical violence but also the absence of any desire to take part in violence. This culminates in the non-injury to the inner spiritual welfare of the soul and leads to the karmic result of spiritual evolution.

Beyond personal non-violence, Jains extend the belief to their view of other faiths. *Anekantavada*, the Jain concept of plurality of perception, also described as 'ahimsa of the mind', calls for the peaceful coexistence of conflicting religious beliefs. Jains would never declare their belief to be the one true religion—they believe that absolute truth cannot be achieved by one path but through the acceptance of multiple points of view. This acceptance of the validity of all other religious beliefs is, in essence, the antidote to religious extremism. *Anekantavada* was perhaps best summed up by the nineteenth century Jain monk Vijaya Dharma Suri (1868–1922), who said, 'I am neither a Jain nor a Buddhist … a Hindu nor a Muslim, but a traveller on the path of peace shown by the supreme soul, the god who is free from passion.'

## 'PEACE EVERYWHERE AND IN ALL THINGS'

MAHAVIRA INHERITED THE MANTLE OF JAIN LEADERSHIP, BUT HIS DEEP spiritual awakening was matched by his organisational genius. He structured the tenets of the religion into a cohesive whole and founded both a religious and secular side. His teachings were gathered together in the *Agam Sutras*, which were passed on orally for centuries. Over the course of time, many of these teachings were lost. But about a thousand years after Mahavira's death, the *Agam Sutras* were recorded on rudimentary, leafy paper known as *tadpatris* and kept for all posterity. Like the Buddhist scriptures, the earlier Jain books were written in a dialect of their own, called Jaina Prakrit; it wasn't until around 1000 CE that the Jains adopted Sanskrit as their literary language.

Mahavira transcended his warrior upbringing to restructure the religion around non-violence, putting a new emphasis on the sanctity and equality of all life. His emphasis on the importance of both self-control and tolerance for other points of view has had a major impact on Indian culture. The concepts of karma, moksha, reincarnation and *ahimsa*—seen as 'typically Indian' today—either originated with or evolved through Jain teachings.

In India today, Jains are among the wealthiest and best-educated citizens. They make up less than one-half of 1 per cent of the Indian population—between ten and twelve million people—yet they contribute nearly 25 per cent of Indian taxation. They are India's most literate demographic and run many of the nation's best schools, colleges, temples and hospitals. They are preservers of India's oldest libraries, at Patan and Jaisalmer. They have propagated a vegetarian and vegan diet and influenced world cuisine through their mild Gujarati diet.

Mahavira's teachings form the basis of Eastern non-violent thought and action. The tenets of Jainism have either directly led or influenced most, if not all, of India's great thinkers, leaders and artists throughout history—a series of leaders, activists, scholars and teachers who have taken those ideals and put them into practice. The twin beliefs of truth and non-violence were crucial influences on India's Home Rule movement of the early twentieth century. In fact, Mohandas K. Gandhi's mother was descended from Jains, and *ahimsa* formed the central component of his strategy of *Satyagraha*, the non-violent civil disobedience movement that ultimately led to India's independence from Great Britain. These actions all come from the essence of Jainism, best summed up in a single passage from the *Sutra-Kritanga* (3.20): 'Man, by injuring no living being, reaches the enlightenment which is peace.'

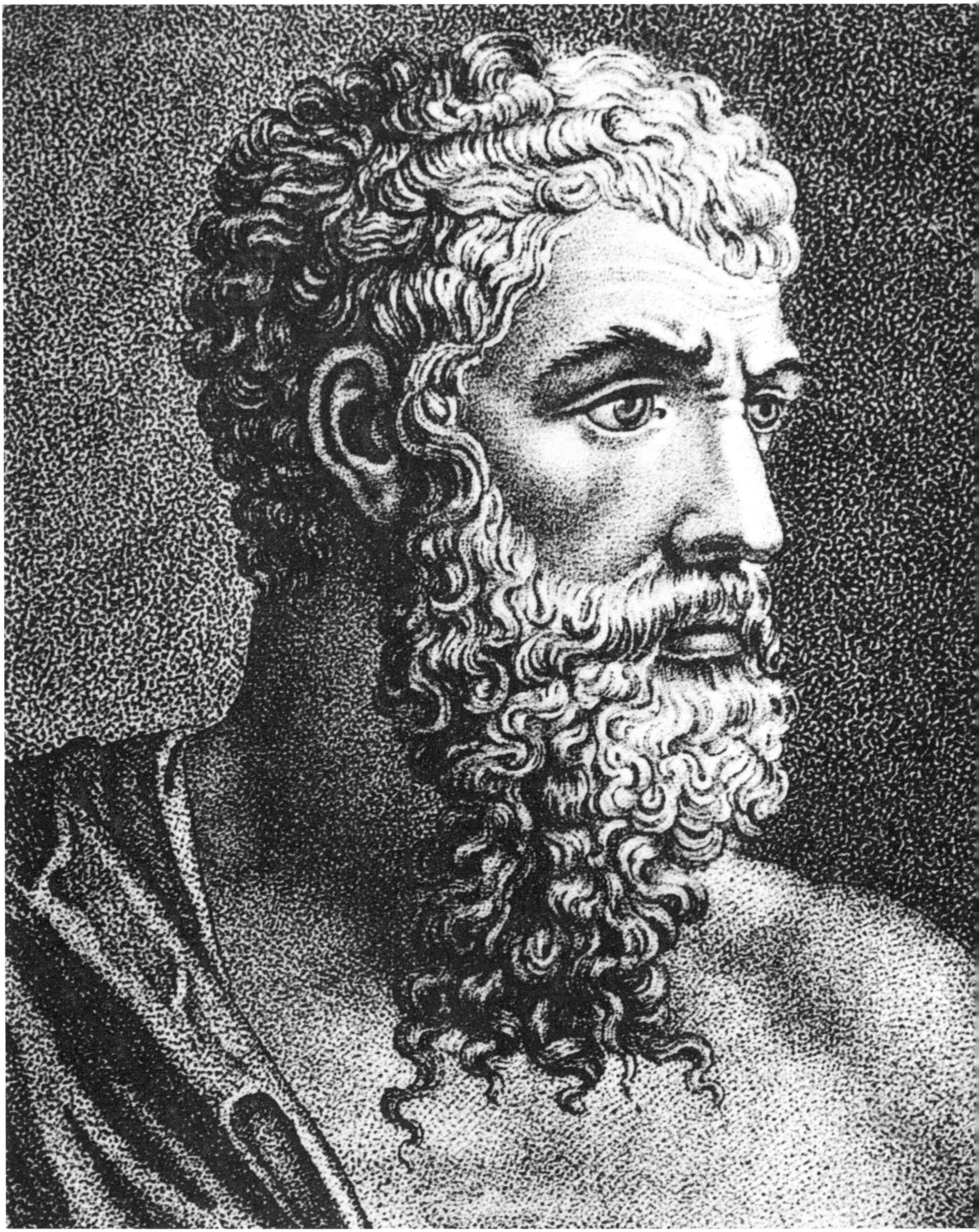

# *LYSISTRATA*: MAKE LOVE, NOT WAR

A NATION IS MIRED IN A LOATHSOME FOREIGN WAR. A CHANGE IN government has brought the hawks to power. A whole generation of young men has been consigned to the military, many never to return. A popular, but controversial, playwright pens a blistering anti-war comedy full of sexual burlesque, scathing personal attacks and a call to end the war. And when the play is performed before the country's most powerful and influential leaders, including members of the senate and foreign dignitaries, the populace seems poised for revolt.

The United States during the Vietnam War? Not quite. Greece, 411 BCE. The playwright was named Aristophanes, the play was called *Lysistrata* and the unpopular conflict was the Peloponnesian War. Now in its twentieth year, the war had gone from bad to worse, and Athens' golden age had been sadly tarnished. Aristophanes was a feared satirist who had already written two other comedies that supported peace. Chastened by litigation at the hands of one of the most powerful men in the country, Aristophanes was back from a seven-year absence from the theatre, mustering all the power of his considerable talents.

A conservative in the mould of Pericles, Aristophanes rightly feared that his beloved Athens was doomed by this war. Others of his era had written tragedies with anti-war themes, among them Aeschylus, Sophocles and Euripides—but

This idealised engraving of a deeply thoughtful Aristophanes, probably from the eighteenth or nineteenth century, may be based on one of the few extant Greek busts of the playwright.

theirs were dense, complex plays whose themes failed to pierce the popular conscience of the time. Aristophanes was first and foremost a comedian—and with *Lysistrata* he created a comedy that, while uproarious to statesmen and the masses alike, would strive to alter the outcome of the war. It would also prove to be a model for anti-war activism throughout time.

—

## 'THE GRACES CHOSE HIS SOUL'

ARISTOPHANES GREW UP AT THE TAIL END OF ATHENS' GOLDEN age and the thirty years of peace under the great Greek general Pericles. The son of Philippus, a wealthy Athenian, Aristophanes was most likely born in Attica and spent much of his youth at his family estate on the island of Aegina. When he was fifteen, the threat of war with Sparta forced his family to move permanently into the fortified *polis*, or city-state, of Athens. With its reinforced 'long walls' surrounding both the city and the port of Piraeus 8 kilometres (5 miles) to the west, the Athenian citizenry was protected from the invading forces of the mightier Spartan armies.

Since the wars with Persia, Pericles had ruled over a peaceful Athenian empire which had grown so powerful that its legislation could dictate trade restrictions, levies and political allegiances throughout the lesser *polises* of Peloponnesian Greece. But in 432 BCE, when the Spartans convened a council with the Peloponnesian League of autonomous city-states, Pericles took it as preparation for war. So Athens also readied 'with a sort of arrogance and a love of strife', the ancient historian Thucydides recorded.

Initially, Pericles avoided open warfare with the far better trained Spartan army. Their *hoplite* warrior class was the best-trained fighting force in Greece, expert in the ways of large ground invasions. Pericles instead relied on his navy, protected at the port of Piraeus. The fleet was far superior to any others in the region, allowing for the tactical advantage of ferrying troops that could attack from the safety of the open seas, striking and retreating quickly. The navy thus struck early and scored several significant victories. The Spartan forces laid siege throughout the peninsula, but were unable to breach the strong walls surrounding Athens.

Everything changed the following year, when Athens was hit with an outbreak of the plague. In the densely populated city, its numbers swollen by refugees from outlying areas, the disease spread rapidly. More than 30,000 people died, nearly half the population, wiping out much of the Athenian fighting force. Foreign mercenaries refused to join Athenian ranks for fear of becoming ill. So widespread was the outbreak that the invading Spartan forces abandoned their campaign for fear of coming in contact with plague-ridden Athenian warriors. But just as the Spartan forces retreated, Athens lost its leader Pericles to the disease.

The death of Pericles led to a vacuum of leadership. Cleon, the son of a tanner and a shrewd orator and politician, had made an earlier coup attempt against the Pericles reign. A populist, or demagogue, his hawkish style suited the prevailing backlash against Sparta, the terror of the plague and the cautious naval skirmishes that had done little to thwart the invasion. Cleon increased the naval attacks and prepared ground forces to take the fight to the Spartans in the Peloponnesus.

Shortly after Cleon's ascension in the Athenian legislature, and only four years into the war, Aristophanes debuted his first comedy at the rural Dionysian festival. The war had turned in Athens' favour as the military secured solid footing with fortified posts throughout the region. Yet there was still great dissension within the Assembly. Aristophanes' comedy was called *The Banqueters*. Although it is now lost, records show the play took full advantage of the freedoms of the time to satirise and ridicule the war profiteers, of whom Cleon was one. The following year, when *The Babylonians* was presented at the larger City Dionysian festival, this second comedy was seen not only by the general populace of Athens but also by foreign dignitaries. In his attack on Athenian mores, Aristophanes singled out Cleon and his execution of the war. Cleon was incensed. He brought charges of slander and Aristophanes, not yet eighteen, was dragged before the ruling council of Athens.

The young poet had a brazen flair for the style of Old Comedy. Aristophanes had attended the best schools and studied poetics and philosophy with the greats: Socrates and his mentor Plato, who said of him: 'The Graces chose his soul for their abode.' Coming from a wealthy background, Aristophanes was aligned with the conservative, aristocratic, pro-democracy faction that advocated for peace. When he threw his considerable talents into lampooning the hypocrisies of those who profited by war, he put himself at odds with the populist Cleon.

———

## AN ENEMY OF CLEON

IN RESPONSE TO ARISTOPHANES' SLIGHTS, CLEON LITIGATED—A FAVOURED way of dispatching one's enemy at the time. It was typical that those who lost in litigation faced a ten-year banishment from the republic. For Cleon to seek satisfaction from the Assembly, the play must have had quite a popular

# THE FESTIVALS OF DIONYSUS

The Dionysia were religious festivals that honoured the god of wine, Dionysus. The main festival, held in the spring, was the Dionysia ta en Astei, the 'City Dionysia', which took place within the walls of Athens. The smaller festival at the end of January, the Dionysia ta kat' agrous, the 'Rural Dionysia', took place out in the countryside. Competitive performances of comedies and tragedies were a central part of these festivals. The open and celebratory nature of the events meant that playwrights could get away with things they might not be able to say at other times. Comedy offered the opportunity to lampoon and satirise current events, social mores, political activities, and the foibles of powerful leaders and celebrities. The plays were judged by a panel of five, their selection narrowed through a series of lotteries to avoid prejudice or corruption. The panel judged the plays on merit but also by popular reaction, which was often overwhelming. The winner received recognition and fame.

The first Dionysian performance was in 534 BCE, of a play written by the tragedian Thespis, from whom we have the word 'thespian' (comedies would not be allowed for another fifty years), and his prize was a goat, the symbol of Dionysus. This prize is where we get the word 'tragedy', which translates from the Greek *tragoidia* as 'goat song'.

The festival opened with the *pompe*, a procession of men carrying large phalluses and women carrying open baskets. The revelry of the *pompe* allowed for a degree of role-reversal as the lower classes got to jeer and mock the upper classes, and women could openly insult their male counterparts. The Theatre of Dionysus, which could seat 10,000, was then 'purified' by sacrificing a young goat. The following three days were dedicated to the performances of tragic plays. Playwrights would perform a set of three tragedies and one satyr play (a tragi-comic burlesque) each day. The judges, called *agonothetai*, and other notables were seated in the front row. The sixth day was dedicated to performing five comedies. These were of secondary importance, as the Lenaia Festival was the main venue for comedies, but nevertheless it was considered a great honour to win a comedy prize at the Dionysia. The festival concluded with a procession and celebration when the judges chose the winning playwrights, who received a wreath of ivy as a symbol of the honour.

impact. Playwrights of that time more resembled modern journalists than today's dramatists—more specifically, their plays were treated more like today's political and social commentaries. These works were judged at the annual festivals by their ability to reveal the issues, get the laughs and tweak the mores. Athenian society was remarkably open, but the courts could still check the freedom of public expression.

Cleon's claim against Aristophanes was not limited to personal slander. He elevated the charge to slander against the entire Athenian *polis* and even challenged Aristophanes' loyalties as a legitimate 'son of Athens'. Since the young man was not born in Athens, his citizenship could only be upheld if both his parents were Athenian. This was apparently proved true, but not without a good amount of nationalistic doubt being cast his way. In the end, Cleon's attempt to deny Aristophanes his civic rights was thwarted—and because the plays were award winners at the festivals, the slander case was thrown out.

If Cleon thought that the young playwright would be cowed by such treatment, he was mistaken, for Aristophanes took the attacks on both his writing and his character as a call to arms. Because he was underage, he was required to present his plays under the names of his lead actors, Callistratus and Philoneides. The same was true of his next play, *The Acharnians*, produced in 425 BCE, in which Aristophanes complained that Cleon had lied, slandered him and abused him nearly to death. This was also the first work that dealt directly with the war with Sparta and the trade embargo with Sparta's ally, Megara. The comedy centres on a 'typical Athenian' who, tired of the war's impact on commerce, fails to convince the Assembly to end the conflict. He decries how the war is being waged for the benefit of the ruling class and so declares his own truce with the enemy and opens his home to trade.

Aristophanes' next play, *The Knights*, was the first presented under his own name, in 424 BCE. The comedy so brutally parodied Cleon and his populist rhetoric that no actor was willing to play the part. So Aristophanes, only twenty-one and still resentful of Cleon's accusations, donned the performer's robes and recited the part of Cleon himself. The play's popularity, no doubt, fed on the open hostility between Cleon and Aristophanes and won first prize at the Lenaia Festival that year (see 'The festivals of Dionysus', opposite). The direct challenge to Cleon had won favour with the judges, but the populace and the Senate still sided with Cleon.

On the back of a great victory at the Battle of Pylos, Cleon and his indispensable general Demosthenes returned to Athens with over 400 captured Spartan warriors. But the advantage was short-lived. The Spartan general

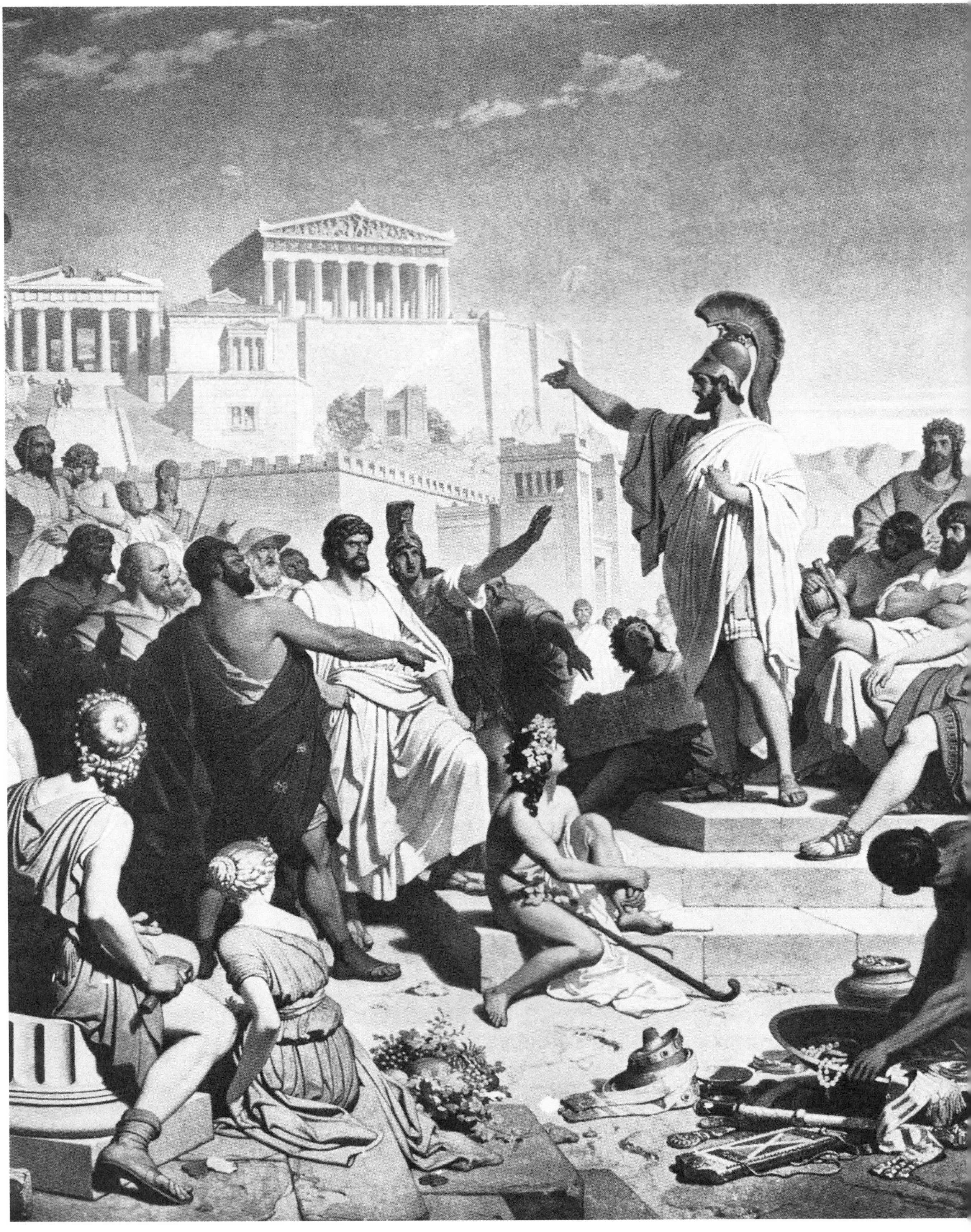

Brasidas marched a massive army to Amphopolis in Thrace and took several silver mines that produced the wealth funding Athens' campaigns. Now Cleon was forced to meet Brasidas in defence of Amphopolis. The pitched battle, fought by thousands of mostly *hoplite* warriors on both sides, ended in a rout by the Spartans. Both Brasidas and Cleon were killed in battle, and Athens' new leader Nicias sued for peace.

Aristophanes' next play, *The Peace*, produced in the following year, supported Nicias' negotiations. The comedy's upbeat tone celebrated the truce between Athens and Sparta but Aristophanes also took the opportunity to once more lampoon the fallen Cleon. No doubt Aristophanes found great joy in the demise of his nemesis.

The Peace of Nicias brought a six-year lull in the war, but the Athenian Assembly passed new laws curtailing freedoms of expression. Perhaps in reaction to Aristophanes' plays, the new laws outlawed the actual naming of individuals and the satirising of political or military issues in the festival plays, and effectively silenced Aristophanes. Perhaps he was protesting the restrictions on artistic liberty, or again faced the blood sport of Athenian litigation and found himself threatened with banishment. Whatever the reason, Aristophanes' prolific output of ten works in six years was ended. Cleon may very well have had the last laugh from the grave, for it would be another seven years before a new work by Aristophanes would be performed.

—

## THE STORY OF *LYSISTRATA*

ARISTOPHANES WAS A MASTER OF OLD COMEDY. BORN OF DRUNKEN revelry and bawdry songs, the form originated in the *pompe*, a rollicking procession not unlike today's Mardi Gras parades. In fact the word 'comedy' comes from the Greek for 'revel', *komos*, and 'song', *ode*. Aristophanes elevated the form by infusing it with raw political and social insight, turning his wit on every aspect of Athenian life that deserved satire: statesmanship, political and private lives, education, the arts or anything else that concerned the *polis* and amused the citizenry. This kind of uncensored criticism would not have been possible without an open and democratic society. In fact, it still isn't possible in many societies.

*Lysistrata* is now regularly grouped with *The Achamians* and *Peace* as Aristophanes' triptych of 'peace plays'. But *Lysistrata* has clearly lasted the test of time. Produced ten years after *Peace*, in the twenty-first year of the

*The Age of Pericles by Philipp von Folz: below the acropolis, Pericles gives the funeral oration for the dead at the end of the First Peloponnesian War.*

Peloponnesian War, the play reflects Aristophanes' mature understanding of the Athenians' fatigue with the war's futility. And so, he suggests a solution to end the war, albeit a burlesque one …

The scene is the Acropolis, Athens' citadel and shrine atop a hill looking out over the blue Aegean Sea. At its centre is the Parthenon, the majestic Doric temple surrounding an ivory and gold statue of Athena, the goddess of wisdom and war. Also kept here was the treasury of the Delian League, the alliance of Greek *polises*. As the action opens, characters in the play are arriving from various locations in Greece and the southerly peninsula of Peloponnesus.

The main character is Lysistrata—the name loosely translates as 'she who disbands armies'—a beautiful Athenian noblewoman who has orchestrated a meeting of all the young women of Greece. She has a plan to end the war. She and all her sisters of Greece are to refuse sex with their husbands or lovers until a peace treaty is signed. She says, 'If the women join us from Peloponnesus and Boeotia, then hand in hand we'll rescue Greece.' To do this, she has already set in motion a plan to seize the Acropolis and confiscate the treasury. As women from various regions assemble, Lysistrata lays out her plan and convinces them all to swear an oath of abstinence until a peace treaty is signed. She coos:

> By the two Goddesses, now can't you see all we have to do is idly sit indoors with smooth roses powdered on our cheeks, our bodies burning naked through the folds of shining Amorgos' silk, and meet the men with our dear Venus-plats plucked trim and neat. Their stirring love will rise up furiously, they'll beg our arms to open. That's our time! We'll disregard their knocking, beat them off. And they will soon be rabid for a Peace. I'm sure of it.

They drink to their oath as the Chorus of Women celebrates the capture of the Acropolis.

A Chorus of Men appears and feebly attempts to retake the Acropolis. They're followed by a thick-headed Magistrate trying to secure funds for the navy, who is startled to find the Acropolis taken. He orders his policemen to arrest the women but, in a slapstick battle, the women drive off the incompetent police. The Magistrate, now fending for himself, attempts to lecture the women on how they have been allowed too much freedom. Incensed, Lysistrata explains how things would be better if women were in charge, using the analogy of spinning wool:

## COLOMBIA'S GANGLAND SEX STRIKE

The city of Pereira, Colombia, a centre of the Colombian drug trade, is one of the most violent in Latin America. With a population of just over 500,000, Pereira has a staggering crime rate. In 2006, murders among gang members spiked to a record high of nearly 500, 90 per cent of them males between the ages of fourteen and twenty-five. In response, the city's mayor attempted a disarmament campaign, which unsurprisingly didn't work. That was when the gang members' wives and girlfriends borrowed a lesson from the women in Lysistrata and took matters into their own hands.

For ten days they refused to have sex with their boyfriends, lovers or husbands unless they swore to give up violence. The Colombian media dubbed the action 'the crossed-leg strike'. The younger women even composed a rap song that became a hit on the radio. The chorus went:

I choose how, where and when I give in.
Women united against violent men.
Let's close our legs.

The action succeeded in reducing violent crime by a measurable amount. Sociologists found that rather than economic necessity, one of the main reasons that young men were lured by a life of crime was because they thought it gave them status with women. When this proved not to be the case, the criminal life seemed quite a bit less attractive, something the gangsters' wives and girlfriends had already figured out. Their message: violence is not sexy. And, as one young gang member summed it up: 'You listen to your woman.'

If, when yarn we are winding, it chances to tangle, then, as perchance you may know, through the skein this way and that still the spool we keep passing till it is finally clear all again. So to untangle the War and its errors, ambassadors out on all sides we will send this way and that, here, there and round about—soon you will find that the War has an end.

War is a concern for women, she argues, because they must suffer the loss of husbands and sons. She berates the Magistrate about how hard it is for women to find a husband when all the men are dying in the wars. To drive home the point, they seize the Magistrate and dress him as a woman.

Some time later, the sex strike is working. The husband of one of the young women is found skulking around with a painful erection. He's desperate for his wife, crying: 'O Zeus, what throbbing suffering!' But she is steadfast, refusing to 'ease his burden' until there is peace between Greece and Sparta. He pleads with her, saying how much he needs her. So she toys with him, pretending she may give in, and repeatedly returns to the Acropolis to fetch things for their lovemaking. Finally her husband can take no more, and promises to agree to a peace treaty. His wife disappears for the last time, leaving him in frustrated agony.

Soon a Spartan Herald arrives at the Acropolis, equally afflicted, with an erection so grand the Magistrate thinks he's hiding a lance: 'Then why do you hide that lance that sticks out under your arms?' The Herald tells of the desperate situation his country is in and pleads for a treaty. Delegations are assembled and meet at the Acropolis to discuss terms for peace. They all suffer from the same affliction; the Athenian delegations declare, all puns intended: 'What allies? There's no distinction in our politics: we've risen as one man to this conclusion; every ally is jumping-mad to drive it home.'

Lysistrata appears with her naked handmaiden, the gorgeous Peace. While the men are distractedly ogling Peace, Lysistrata tells them why reconciliation is so essential: Athens and Sparta share a common heritage and were once allies. They should end the war. Enraptured, the men use Peace as a map of Greece, and the leaders of Sparta and Athens negotiate a division of territories to end the war. Lysistrata then releases the women from their oath and the play ends with song and celebration:

> Earth is delighted now, peace is the voice of earth. Spartans, sort out your wives; Athenians, yours. Let each catch hands with his wife and dance his joy, Dance out his thanks, be grateful in music, And promise reformation with his heels.

—

## NOT THE END AS WRITTEN

PEACE DID COME, BUT NOT IN THE WAY IMAGINED BY ARISTOPHANES. Small skirmishes in the years following the Peace of Nicias gradually escalated. The new Athenian government, led now by Alcibiades, convinced the nation that they'd accepted a dishonourable peace. War came again to the Peloponnesus, and Athens sent a huge expeditionary force to engage Syracuse in Sicily. The attack went badly, the entire Athenian force was wiped out, and then Sparta went on the offensive. With support from Persia, Sparta encouraged rebellion among Athens' subject states in the Aegean Sea and Ionia. Athens was losing control of its empire. When its one advantage, its superior navy, became bogged down and was destroyed at Aegospotami in a final confrontation, Athens was stripped of

# THE *LYSISTRATA* PROJECT

One of the most ambitious presentations of *Lysistrata* took place in 2003. In response to the US-led invasion of Iraq, two American actresses decided to protest the war with a reading of the play. Inspired by a New York theatre group called Theaters Against War, the young actress and playwright Kathryn Blume set out to produce a reading of the play, aided by fellow actress Sharon Bower. They began a grassroots email campaign to use the reading as a charity benefit, and the idea spread like wildfire.

Within days, theatres in cities as far apart as Seattle on the West Coast and Austin, Texas were signing on to do readings. A website extended the reach internationally, providing downloadable scripts, press releases and instructions for producing the reading. Playwrights with adaptations and translations joined up and volunteered their scripts. Before they knew it, the press caught on. Calls and emails by the thousands began coming in from all over the world. The result was the '*Lysistrata* Project: The First-Ever Worldwide Theatrical Act of Dissent'.

On 3 March 2003, the ancient Greek play was performed 1029 times, in all fifty US states and in fifty-nine countries worldwide. An estimated 225,000 people attended or took part in the readings. In New York, at the Brooklyn Academy of Music, the reading was directed by Blume and Bower and performed by such notable actors as Kevin Bacon, Kyra Sedgwick, Mercedes Ruehl and F. Murray Abraham. In Washington, DC, actors donned togas and performed outdoors despite unusually frigid temperatures. A reading in northern Iraq was organised by the members of the international press corps, despite being under threat of losing their jobs. And at Patras in Greece, the play's homeland, a group of Greek and Kurdish refugees performed the play together.

The *Lysistrata* Project raised awareness about the controversial reasons for the American involvement in Iraq. Moneys earned by the readings were donated to various peace charities and humanitarian relief organisations. A documentary entitled *Operation Lysistrata* was produced and screened at festivals in the United States and India.

its ability to wage war and was besieged. Eventually starvation and despair drove the Athenians to surrender—they had lost their empire, their allies, even the walls surrounding the *polis*. Seven years after *Lysistrata* was first performed, the war ended, not with an honourable peace but through defeat and subjugation.

The Peloponnesian War forever changed Ancient Greece. Athens, once the dominant city-state, now was ruled by Sparta, devastated, never to regain its prosperity. Poverty engendered by the economic toll of years of war was widespread throughout Greece, but especially in the Peloponnesus. The region was thrown into a period of near-constant civil war as political factions supported by democratic Athens sparred with the oligarchic Spartans. Warfare previously had been formalised and limited, now it became an all-out scramble. Religious and cultural mores were destroyed, atrocities were committed on all sides and the major cities were destroyed, pillaged or overrun by the indigent.

Under Spartan rule, the civil liberties that Athenians once enjoyed were significantly curtailed. The times were turbulent: with the execution of Socrates and the loss of free expression, it became too dangerous to make political attacks. After *Lysistrata* Aristophanes gave up on politics, sticking to social comedies instead. Eventually some freedoms would return, but he would not live to see them.

Aristophanes died in 386 BCE and left behind some forty plays, eleven of which are still in existence. His Old Comedy was transformed into a New Comedy of manners that flourished for eighty years, but nearly all plays in this later form have been lost.

—

## LYSISTRATA'S LEGACY

CRITICS HAVE LONG FAULTED ARISTOPHANES FOR DENIGRATING WHAT he might instead have bolstered. But his dogmatic views were never to be taken as literal Athenian history. His satire came out of an earnest love of country and the liberties that the golden age of Athens bred. *Lysistrata* did not affect the outcome of the war, but it did give voice to the collective frustration of the nation. And the seemingly outrageous idea that women, by banding together to withhold sex, could force peace has captured the collective imagination throughout the centuries (see 'Colombia's gangland sex strike', page 27).

Modern Western drama can trace its roots to the great works of the Ancient Greek playwrights, and *Lysistrata* served as an early template for plays of political discourse and dissension. That Aristophanes influenced modern dramatists through his poetics, structure and use of satire is well documented—less well documented is his influence as a writer of political commentary, seen especially in the impact of his anti-war plays. His influence at the time was great, partly because the satiric nature of his works allowed him to remain both within the political community and outside as a commentator.

Aristophanes wanted first and foremost to make people laugh—and *Lysistrata* has made people laugh for some 2500 years. If nothing else, he has shown that people can laugh and think at the same time. Through the centuries, Aristophanes has influenced many satirists and political humorists, among them Jonathan Swift in the eighteenth century, and the nineteenth century's Percy Shelley, whose comic drama *Swellfoot the Tyrant* was written in imitation of Aristophanes. But it was the twentieth century that saw fully renewed interest in *Lysistrata*, with multiple readings, stagings and productions. The *New York Times* recorded on 18 February 1913: 'The first militant suffragettes, Aristophanes's conception of them in his comedy "Lysistrata," were shown at Maxine Elliott's Theater yesterday afternoon for the benefit of the Woman's Political Union.' In 1936 the Washington State WPA administrator closed a 'Negro' unit's adaptation of *Lysistrata* after a hugely successful opening, calling the play 'indecent and bawdy'. Most likely the play caused consternation because black people were performing sexually suggestive comedy. Even though the head of the Federal Theatre Project called for the production to be re-opened, the local authority refused. Another all-black production in New York took place in 1946, just after the end of World War II, in which well-known actress Etta Moten Barnett starred. The play had particular resonance for African-American soldiers returning from the war to legal segregation and few opportunities.

In the 1960s a musical adaptation called *The Happiest Girl in the World* was presented on Broadway, and the radical feminist film *Flickorna*, featuring scenes from *Lysistrata* performed by Swedish sirens Bibi Andersson, Harriet Andersson and Gunnel Lindblom, was released; both emphasised the 'free love', anti-war atmosphere of the time. And in 2003, in response to the US invasion of Iraq, a peace protest initiative called the *Lysistrata* Project organised over 1000 simultaneous readings of the play in fifty-nine countries (see 'The *Lysistrata* Project', page 29).

Aristophanes was, at heart, a reactionary. But his was a conscientious conservatism: he believed in able leaders, strong women, education and, above all, peace. He lived in a time of strife when democratic principles, from majority rule to free and open debate, were being challenged by leaders caught up in a prolonged war. Aristophanes as moral pundit, acutely aware of Athens' decline and always ready to lampoon his way to justice and truth, took them all on.

# THE PRINCE OF PEACE:
# THE SERMON ON THE MOUNT

THE CATHOLIC PEACE ACTIVIST DOROTHY DAY WAS ASKED TO WRITE a 'pacifist manifesto' in 1942, shortly after the Japanese attack on Pearl Harbor and America's entrance into World War II. In response, she wrote: 'We will print the words of Christ who is with us always. Our manifesto is the Sermon on the Mount.' For 2000 years, this short three-chapter section of the Gospel of Matthew has been the mortar in the foundation of Christian pacifism. Even to the novice parishioner it is one of the best-known parts of the Bible, containing the Beatitudes, the Lord's Prayer, the 'golden rule' and the Christian adages 'turn the other cheek' and 'love thy enemy'. The Sermon on the Mount has been so thoroughly studied, dissected, interpreted, debated and distorted over the centuries that ultimately more questions have been raised than have been answered.

Much of the message is also found in the Gospel of Luke as the Sermon on the Plain. Were Matthew and Luke describing the same sermon? Or were they merely recording compilations of Jesus' sayings? Did the historical Jesus really expect his followers to end violence and start loving one another? And if he did, how has the Church justified its many wars when he spoke so plainly against violence, retribution and war? Questions like these have inspired theological debate for centuries, but perhaps one thing can be agreed upon:

the Prince of Peace was speaking to a following that would hardly recognise today's Church or how his teachings have been interpreted over time.

### MATTHEW THE *PUBLICAN*

IN THE EARLY 1480s THE CONSTRUCTION OF THE SISTINE CHAPEL WAS nearly complete. Pope Sixtus IV, for whom the chapel is named, had commissioned new frescoes of the lives of Moses and Jesus by some of the masters of the early Renaissance. Along the chapel's north wall was the newly completed fresco *The Sermon on the Mount and the Healing of the Leper* by the Florentine painter Cosimo Rosselli and his son-in-law Piero di Cosimo. This narrative rendering, full of

A Byzantine mosaic in St Mark's Basilica in Venice portrays Constantine the Great (c. 274–337), the first Roman emperor to embrace Christianity.

allegorical significance, depicts Jesus with his hand raised in blessing, dressed in a red robe and blue mantle, a large crowd spilling out of the painting. But whether intentionally or not, Rosselli not only captured the splendour of Jesus' sermon but hints at the conflict and debate it spawned from the beginning.

At about thirty years of age, Jesus was by then famous 'throughout all Syria' when he gave his famous sermon. Because he had cured 'all the sick, those who were afflicted with various diseases and pains, demoniacs, epileptics, and paralytics', followers had flocked to him from all corners (Matthew 4:24–25). Ascending a mound in the hills of Galilee, perhaps even ancient Mount Eremos, where now sits the Church of the Beatitudes, he addressed his twelve disciples and the gathered crowd. Rosselli's painting depicts his disciples off in the distance, attentive to his words, while some in the crowd are clearly distracted. This is especially true of two prominent figures in the lower left foreground, standing arguing, nearly oblivious to the sermon, facing side-on to Jesus. Was this Rosselli's attempt to show how even in the midst of the original sermon, the words of Jesus were sure to be hotly debated? Could these figures be the writers of Matthew and Luke's gospels already discussing how best to capture, convey and even amend the words of this startling dissertation?

Rosselli painted one of these figures with Romanesque features, dressed in a rich burgundy robe and hat; the other wears black velvet, a headscarf, full beard, with the Star of David hanging from his cowl. Is this an allusion to Moses and a hint of the sermon's significance to Jewish tradition and the break the Catholic Church had made? Jesus is also portrayed standing, as a Catholic priest would address his congregation. But this was an open-air sermon and Matthew makes it clear that Jesus 'went up the mountain and … *sat down*' (5:1) to address his disciples. This would have been more in keeping with the rabbinical tradition of lessons conveyed by a master teacher to a small group of disciples. But clearly, because of the size of the crowd, the sermon was meant for a wider audience. So who recorded it? Was it a disciple, a member of the crowd or a collective effort by the many present?

The sermon is the centrepiece of Matthew's gospel. As Matthew was one of the Twelve Apostles, that would suggest he recorded it. But no one is certain. In fact, little is known about this apostle. We can discern from the New Testament that Matthew was a *publican* (tax collector), the son of Alphaeus, known also as Levi. Understandably, tax collectors were unpopular figures, suspected by the Jewish establishment to be sinners and conspirators with the Romans. Mark records that after Matthew became an apostle, Jesus was confronted by the Pharisees because he 'sat at dinner' in Matthew's house with other *publicans*. In defence of Matthew's conversion, Jesus replied to the Pharisees: 'Those who are well have no need of a physician, but those who are sick; I have came to call not the righteous but sinners' (Mark 2:17).

A *publican* would have had the education necessary to record the sermon, and Matthew was literate in both Aramaic and Greek. The gospel mentions money and uses monetary terms—something a tax collector certainly would know about. But the evidence seems more weighted towards an anonymous author, writing later, who attributed the gospel to Matthew. The recognised version of the gospel was written in a style of Greek that uses idioms dating it after the age of the apostles. It's also written in the third person and lacks the kind of detail expected in an eyewitness account. The author may even have been a scribe of one of the Jewish–Christian communities that grew out of the teachings of the disciple Matthew. This may even be hinted at when the author says 'every scribe who has been trained for the kingdom of heaven is like the master of a household who brings out of his treasure what is new and what is old' (Matthew 13:52).

—

## 'ONE WHO HAD AUTHORITY'

THE SINGULAR OR COLLECTIVE MATTHEW OPENS HIS GOSPEL BY DESCRIBING how Jesus ascended the mountain, followed by a large crowd, and began his sermon with a litany of blessings called the Beatitudes (Matthew 5:3–12). Promising entrance into the Kingdom of God for those who followed his teachings, Jesus' blessings must have seemed shocking at the time. They offered such progressive and novel notions as the meek inheriting the Earth and the poor of spirit entering Heaven. Of particular significance to Christian pacifist is the seventh blessing:

> Blessed are the peacemakers, for they will be called children of God (Matthew 5:9).

Clearly, this is high praise for those who seek peace. But the passage would also be used to help justify warfare in the name of the Church. Following the campaigns of Constantine, the first Roman emperor to convert to Christianity, Bishop Augustine of Hippo developed a theology of 'just war' allowing for conflict that could bring about a greater peace.

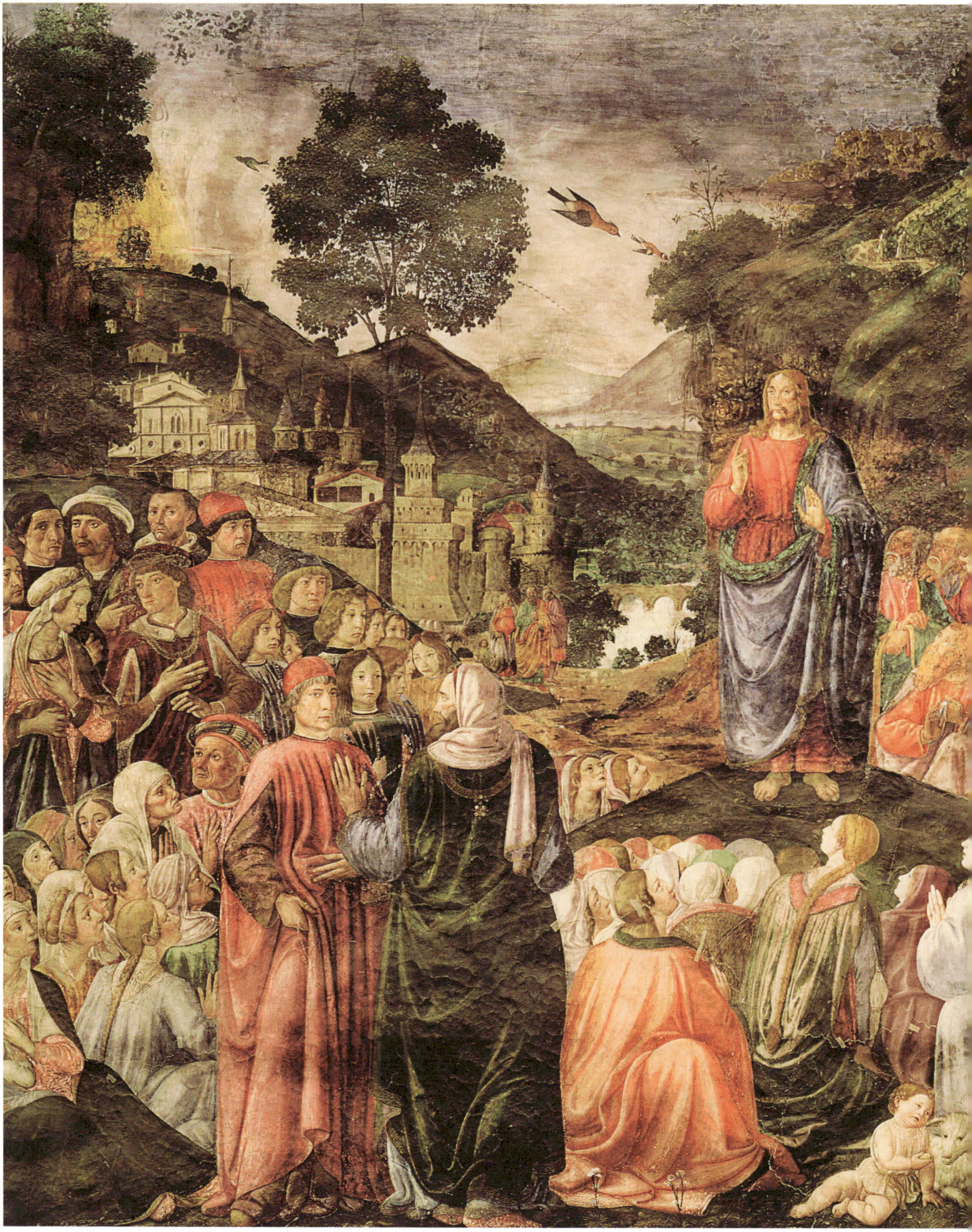

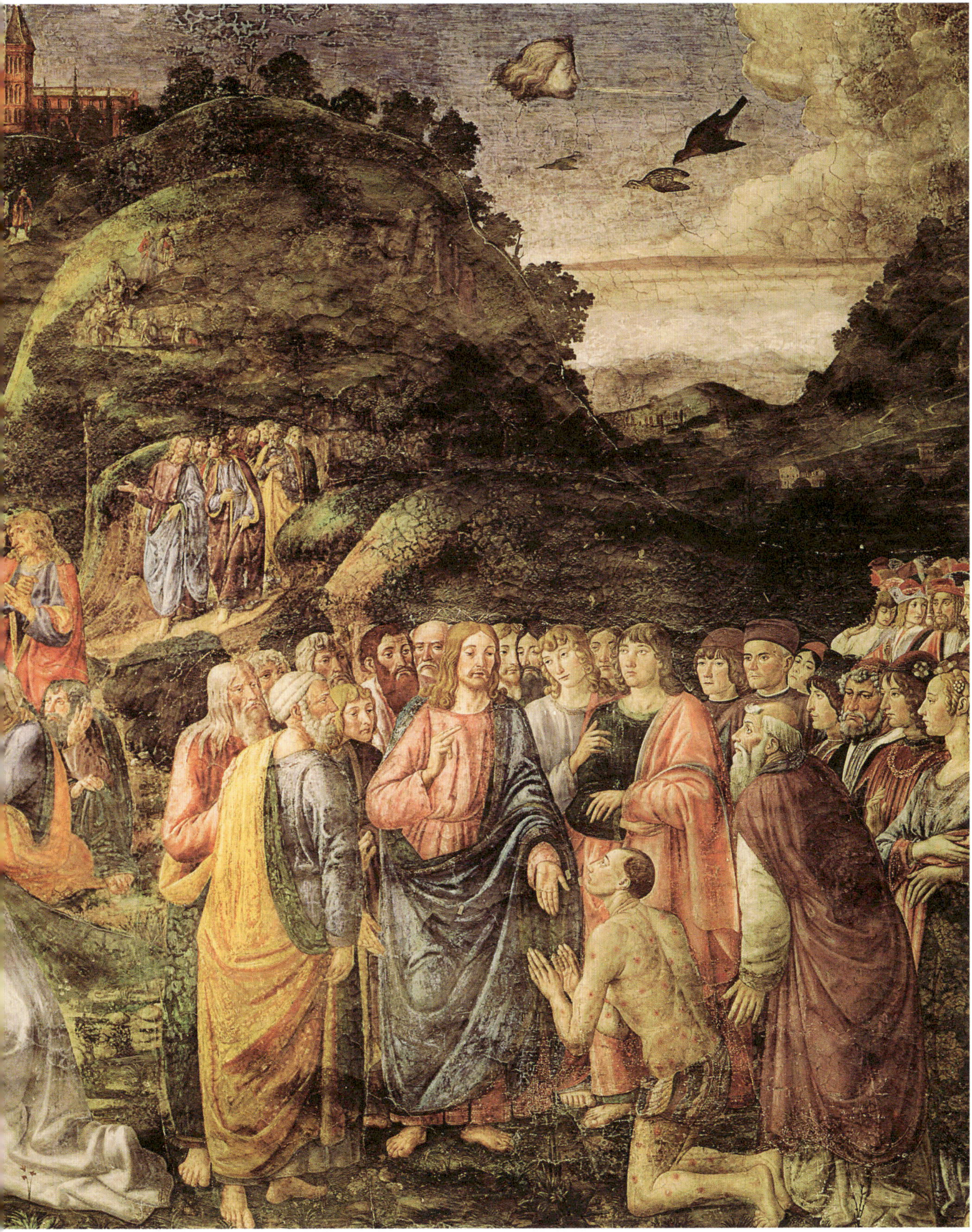

# THE GOLDEN RULE

*In everything do to others what you would have them do to you; for this is the law and the prophets* (Matthew 7:12).

This seemingly simple passage from the Sermon on the Mount encapsulates the 'golden rule' of universal morality, otherwise known as the 'ethic of reciprocity'. This precept states that everyone has the right to just treatment, and likewise a responsibility to ensure the just treatment of others. At its core, this is a universal statement of reciprocal respect, peace and the foundation for basic human right. But Jesus was hardly the first to make this statement. Most every, if not all, philosophies and religions throughout history have some variant on this theme. Here are a few:

**ANCIENT EGYPT** 'Do for one who may do for you, that you may cause him thus to do' (*The Tale of the Eloquent Peasant*, 109–110, c. 2000 BCE).

**ANCIENT GREECE** 'Do not to your neighbour what you would take ill from him' (Pittacus of Mytilene, sixth century BCE) and 'Do not do to others that which would anger you if others did it to you' (Socrates, fifth century BCE).

**BUDDHISM** 'A state that is not pleasing or delightful to me, how could I inflict that upon another?' (Samyutta Nikaya v. 353, sixth century BCE).

**CONFUCIANISM** 'Do not do to others what you do not want them to do to you' (Analects 15:23, sixth century BCE).

**HINDUISM** 'This is the sum of Dharma: Do naught unto others which would cause you pain if done to you' (*Mahabharata*, 5:1517, eight century BCE).

**ISLAM** 'None of you [truly] believes until he wishes for his brother what he wishes for himself' (*Forty Hadiths of Al-N awawi*, seventh century CE).

**JAINISM** 'In happiness and suffering, in joy and grief, we should regard all creatures as we regard our own self' (Lord Mahavira, sixth century BCE).

**JUDAISM** 'Thou shalt love thy neighbour as thyself' (Leviticus 19:18) and 'What is hateful to you, do not do to your fellow: this is the whole Torah; the rest is the explanation; go and learn' (Hillel the Elder, Pirkei Avot, Shab. 31a, first century BCE).

**SHINTO** 'The heart of the person before you is a mirror. See there your own form' (Kojiki, seventh century CE).

**TAOISM** 'The sage has no interest of his own, but takes the interests of the people as his own. He is kind to the kind; he is also kind to the unkind: for Virtue is kind. He is faithful to the faithful; he is also faithful to the unfaithful: for Virtue is faithful' (*Tao Teh Ching*, Chapter 49, sixth to third centuries BCE).

In the next section of the sermon, Jesus calls his followers the 'salt of the earth' and the 'light of the world' (Matthew 5:13–14). Salt has many possible meanings: it was used at the time as a purifying agent and as a preservative, and as an analogy for 'wisdom' in rabbinical teachings. Together, Jesus may be offering his followers the wisdom to preserve the purity of the world. Even today we use 'salt of the earth' to describe someone who is fundamentally good, honest and 'down to earth'. The use of 'light' suggests that Jesus' followers would serve as a beacon both inside and outside the church.

The bulk of his sermon is dedicated to the expounding of the law (Matthew 5:17–48) and the fulfilment of Moses' commandments. Also known as the *antithesis*, this section may be seen as a counterpoint to Mosaic Law or as a reinterpretation for his contemporary audience. Jesus' own words seem to support this: 'Do not think that I have come to abolish the law or the prophets; I have not come to abolish but to fulfil' (Matthew 5:17). Whether fulfil means 'make real' or 'reinterpret' has been argued for centuries. The sermon follows, with a structured 'you have heard … but I say to you' exposition on anger, adultery, divorce, oaths, retaliation and the love of one's enemies.

In the first of these passages, Jesus quotes the commandment 'Thou shalt not kill', and argues that anger itself may be as bad as murder. He encourages his followers to settle disputes quickly so the disputes won't grow, even putting the task ahead of making time at the altar.

Adultery comes next, quoting the ethical decalogue in Exodus 20:14. Here Jesus appears to suggest that the admonition against lusting after another man's wife does not go far enough: do not even 'look at a woman lustfully'. He then uses some of the most extreme language in the sermon when he calls on his followers to gouge out their eye and cut off their hand rather than be tempted by sin. Fortunately, no Christian denominations have taken these suggestions literally. In fact, this part of the sermon is often seen as purposefully hyperbolic, or exaggerated, and used by non-pacifist Christians to argue that Jesus' peaceful proclamations are equally hyperbolic.

On divorce, Jesus extends his admonition of adultery. He requires a man give his wife a formal divorce certificate, borrowing from Deuteronomy 24:1. At the time, a husband could divorce his wife on almost any grounds, from infidelity to bad cooking. But elaborate pre-nuptial arrangements were common, so a certificate gave proof for a woman to collect on promised payments. One interpretation suggests that Jesus meant to help protect a married woman's rights and make it harder for a husband to abandon one wife to find another.

Previous pages: The beautiful fresco, *The Sermon on the Mount and the Healing of the Leper* by Rosselli, in the fifteenth-century Sistine Chapel in Rome presents two portraits of Jesus—preacher and healer.

39

Regarding oaths, Jesus states: 'Let your words be "Yes, Yes" or "No, No"; anything more than this comes from the evil one.' He could be saying, simply, make your word good and don't swear oaths on God, Jerusalem or even on your own head. Some have interpreted this as a strict mandate against swearing oaths at all; others offer it as another example of the sermon's hyperbole. In the seventeenth century, the Religious Society of Friends (Quakers) did interpret this passage literally and refused, as some do to this day, to swear oaths of any sort.

In the penultimate passage, Jesus deals with the issue of punishment, specifically refuting the Mosaic premise of 'an eye for an eye'. In a much-quoted saying, Jesus admonishes his followers not to retaliate: 'if anyone strikes you on the right cheek, turn the other also'. Most who see the sermon as validating pacifism point to this passage as a sure sign of meeting violence with love and non-resistance.

The final passage also deals with love and is central to pacifist beliefs. Jesus reminds his followers of Leviticus' instruction to 'Love thy neighbour as thyself', and refutes 'hate thine enemy' (which has no antecedent in the Old Testament) with the immortal words, 'Love thine enemy'. The Greek version of the Gospel of Matthew used the word *agape*, which had a very specific meaning at the time, for love—a kind of unconditional, self-sacrificing love of God for all humanity. Thus the early pacifist Christians saw this love as the highest ideal, a love in the 'imitation of God'. In later centuries, the passage became a problem for the Church. 'Love' was reinterpreted to mean that which is between individuals, not between peoples, faiths or nations.

In the discourse on ostentation (Matthew 6), Jesus offered guidance about giving to the poor, proper prayer (the Lord's Prayer), fasting and materialism, declaring that alms should be given in secret, without self-promotion or ostentation, and that prayer should be offered privately, without public display or rote repetition. The Lord's Prayer, which provides an example of proper devotion, has over the years become one of the most noted passages of the New Testament. Fasting should be done modestly. The passage on materialism supports the piety of poverty and recommends treasuring what can be held by the spirit rather than what can be stolen or destroyed by moths and rust, concluding with the admonition that no one can serve 'two masters'—God and money.

In the discourse on judgmentalism (Matthew 7:1–6), Jesus admonishes his followers not to judge others before judging themselves. He uses the metaphor of trying to remove a 'speck' from a brother's eye before removing a 'log' from one's own. Clarity will come, literally and metaphorically, from attending to one's own flaws before trying to fix others'.

In the final section, on holiness (Matthew 7:7–23), Jesus warns about avoiding 'false prophets', and about trying to 'bear fruit' without the grace of God. He suggests we 'ask' for what we want, 'seek' out answers from God, and 'knock' on the door of heaven for admittance. Borrowing from many earlier, great traditions, Jesus offers 'the golden rule' as a summation of his sermon and the Law, commanding that we 'do unto others as we would have them do unto us' (see 'The golden rule', page 38). Many Christian pacifists hold this rule of ethical reciprocity as the central message of the sermon and see in it the guidance required for peaceful coexistence.

Jesus concludes his sermon by telling his disciples that should they heed his advice, they will be wise like the man who builds his 'house on the rock' rather than on sand. Clearly, Matthew is stressing that the message of the sermon is the foundation on which the house of the Lord was built. Then Jesus comes off the mount, and the crowd is described as 'amazed' by the way he 'taught as one who had authority'. Although directed at his disciples, the sermon was likely intended for posterity as well. Matthew seemed to understand this, and the power of his record held sway as the gospel of primacy for the early followers.

---

## THE SYNOPTIC PROBLEM

IF MATTHEW WAS NOT SITTING AT THE FEET OF JESUS TAKING DICTATION, how did the sermon come to be recorded? As may have occurred with much of the teachings of Jesus, his words most likely were passed along orally until someone wrote them down. This would explain similarities within the gospels and other sections of the New Testament. The Sermon on the Mount bears a striking resemblance to the Sermon on the Plain in the Gospel of Luke. Could they be one and the same? Or were they, at least, derived from the same source? The Gospels of Matthew, Mark and Luke make up the synoptic gospels, named from the Greek *synopsis*, 'one view'. Beyond sharing a point of view, they are similar in language, structure and narrative. The fourth canonical gospel of the New Testament, the Gospel of John, is quite different, focusing more on the miracles of Jesus than his sermons and narrative.

Matthew's gospel was probably written after the destruction of Jerusalem by the Romans around 70 CE (Matthew 22:7) and before the death of St Ignatius, who wrote of the gospels before 117 CE. But whether it was the first of the three synoptic gospels to be written has been hotly debated. Competing theories have developed over the centuries that attempt to explain their origins and the reasons behind their overlapping material. With only about 20 per cent of the material in Matthew unique to either Mark or Luke, the 'synoptic problem' seeks to answer which gospel came first and whether a single author or multiple authors may have used the other gospels, along with other lost sources, to tell their tales.

Augustine of Hippo, the early fifth century theologian, bishop and saint, was the first to propose a theory about the relationship of the three gospels. His 'Augustinian hypothesis', which stood as canonical dogma for centuries, argues that the Gospel of Matthew was the first written, by Matthew the apostle of Jesus. The Gospel of Mark was written second by Mark the Evangelist, a disciple of the apostle Simon, using both Matthew and the teachings of Peter as its source. A disciple of Paul of Tarsus, Luke, wrote the Gospel of Luke third, using the previous two as his sources. This simple, coherent solution to the synoptic problem relies mostly on historic testimony from early Church leaders dating back to the beginning of the second century but ignores several key weaknesses, especially the preponderance of source material in Mark. In fact, Augustine dismissed Mark as 'an abbreviator of Matthew'.

This theory held for more than a millennium, until the Protestant Reformation, when German biblical scholar Johann Jakob Griesbach shifted the order somewhat. The Griesbach hypothesis, published in 1783, agreed that Matthew was written first but argued that Luke was second, based on Matthew and other sources, and Mark was last, based on the other two. Similar to Augustine's theory, Griesbach's theory preserved the idea of Matthean priority and suggested direct literary dependence between the gospels.

Half a century later, in 1838, another German scholar, Christian Hermann Weisse, articulated a radical bit of theorising on their origins. Made popular by fellow German Heinrich Julius Holtzmann, this theory became known as the 'two-source hypothesis' and argued that Mark came first, and that Matthew and Luke used it for the basis for their narratives and the core elements of Jesus' life. To explain the material in Mark not found in Matthew and Luke, the two-source hypothesis argues that a mysterious, now-lost second source must have been copied. This lost text is referred to as the 'Q document', from the German word *Quelle*, 'source' (see 'The question of Q', opposite). Shifting the priority to Mark and suggesting a second source has become the dominant theory, although it has some flaws in explaining the few instances where Matthew and Luke agree against Mark. These 'minor agreements' are compounded by a lack of textual evidence for the existence of the Q document and could have been caused by the copying mistakes of scribes. However, a number of document

Ever since the time of Papias, an early Christian writer and leader in the first half of the second century, there have been questions about lost textual sources and the nature of the original Gospel of Matthew. Papias may have recorded much of the oral history about Jesus' teachings in his now lost *Interpretations of the Sayings of the Lord*. Could this five-volume collection be the Q Document, a hypothetical lost source of the Gospels of Matthew and Luke?

First proposed in the nineteenth century, the Q Document helped explain the 'two-source' theory of German theologian Christian Hermann Weisse, popularised by his countryman Heinrich Julius Holtzmann. Papias refers to an early version of Matthew's gospel written in Hebrew (most scholars believe the gospel was written in Greek). If Papias didn't write the Q Document, he may have copied portions of it, but no one can be certain because there is no extant document or fragment to support the hypothesis.

Scholars have combed over the gospels, over ancient gospel fragments and related texts for similarities. The results are surprising. The two-source hypothesis, now widely accepted, argues that Matthew and Luke both used Mark. This explains the material that is in both Matthew and Luke and common to Mark. But what of the material not in Mark that is common to Matthew and Luke? This is where the hypothetical second source comes into play. While some have argued that shared oral traditions could explain this material, it doesn't explain the near word-for-word passages and the identical Greek idioms.

If Q existed, what was it? Many assume it to be a reconstructed gospel, perhaps one of the forty or so 'apocryphal gospels' written for use in the early churches. Most agree it was a collection of Jesus' sayings that did not include the narrative of the virgin birth, the twelve disciples, miracles, the crucifixion, resurrection and ascension. Lacking the magical or supernatural beliefs later added (and perhaps imported from other religions), it must have been written much earlier than Matthew, Mark, Luke and John, perhaps only twenty years after the death of Jesus. It might have presented Jesus as a captivating teacher, learned healer and simple man of God, and certainly must have been written by an eyewitness to his teaching.

Were we able to go back in time and view this document and the nascent Church, we might see few similarities to the Christian beliefs of today. Christianity was an evolving movement, devoutly Jewish, but dedicated to the message of the charismatic philosopher and teacher, Yeshua. To survive and grow, it would require a new theological structure. Once the four canonical gospels had the blessing of the Church, Q would have become redundant, possibly even heretical. No longer sanctioned, the mysterious Q would have faded and eventually disappeared from record and memory.

fragments do suggest the existence of Q, which has led to hypotheses for other variations.

Does all this agonising over the order and source of the gospels get us any closer to understanding the message Jesus meant to convey? Clearly there were versions of the gospels before those that became canonical scripture, suggesting that the gospels were 'living documents' passed along by writers within various communities of Jesus' followers.

—

## A PACIFIST CHURCH

THE QUESTION OF PRIORITY HAS ONLY BEEN DEBATED SERIOUSLY SINCE the nineteenth century. The earliest Christian scholars were unanimous in their belief that Matthew's gospel came first. Long before Augustine of Hippo wrote of Matthew's priority, the early writings of Papias in 125 CE, Justin Martyr later in that century and Clement of Alexandria around 200 CE all supported the priority of Matthew. Much of the material can be traced to the Old Testament and Rabbinic literature.

The only writer of a synoptic gospel who was also one of the Twelve Apostles, Matthew clearly saw the Sermon on the Mount as a charter for the Church. Early Christians were far more pacifistic than many of today's followers of Christ, for the teachings of Jesus were interpreted to rule out violence even in cases of self-defence. This view was held by most of the early Christian sects, among them the Ebionites, a Jewish–Christian group who lived in cooperative, non-violent communities, were vegetarians, adherents of Matthew's gospel and followers of Jesus' brother James and the Church of Jerusalem (see 'The Ebionites, and a vegetarian Jesus', opposite). Nearly all the earliest Christian theologians and philosophers promoted non-violence, even in the face of death. Clement of Alexandria, 200 years after the death of Jesus, summed up the attitude towards aggression: 'Above all, Christians are not allowed to correct with violence.'

How was it that this emphasis on Jesus' teachings of non-violence began to erode? Some critics cite the influence of Paul of Tarsus, who broke with the Jewish–Christians of the Church of Jerusalem and moved the Church irrevocably towards the conversion of Gentiles. The influence of Pauline Christianity has been much debated, with interpretations ranging from the radical (Christ was a mythological figure created by Paul) to the insignificant (Paul was just one of many interpreters of the word of Jesus). His role in

# THE EBIONITES, AND A VEGETARIAN JESUS

The Greek-speaking Ebionites were an early Jewish–Christian sect, active for several centuries after Jesus, who insisted on the necessity of following Jewish religious law and rites, which they interpreted in light of Jesus' exposition of the Law. The name comes from *ebionim*, a Greek term for 'the poor', because the sect viewed self-imposed poverty as the most virtuous way to prepare for Jesus' messianic return. The Ebionites were protectors of the *desposynoi*, the blood-relatives of Jesus who lived in their communities, and they revered his brother James as the head of the Jerusalem Church. Their gospel may have been an early draft of Matthew's gospel. They originally lived in cooperative communities east of the Jordan River, but migration as a result of the Jewish–Roman wars pushed them north and further east. The Ebionites rejected Paul as a false prophet, seeing his form of Christianity as controversial at the least. They believed Paul was anti-Semitic, and that he was responsible for igniting the anti-Jewish hostility that ultimately Romanised the Christian faith.

According to the Ebionites, Jesus was a human being, not divine, born by natural processes to Joseph and Mary, and the 'true prophet' chosen by God at his baptism. They believed in the validity of the Torah, but were pacifists and vegetarians who rejected animal sacrifice and the 'false texts' of the Old Testament that required sacrifices or questioned God's omnipotence and peaceful nature.

The Ebionite Gospel, which now exists only in fragments, was most likely suppressed by the Pauline Church. A harmony of all the synoptic gospels, it gave prominence to an early version of Matthew's gospel. The Ebionites especially revered the Sermon on the Mount for its interpretation of Mosaic Law and saw Jesus as an inspired teacher, like Isaiah and Jeremiah. They condemned warfare, as evident in passages of the *Recognitions*, citing Christian non-violence and Peter's opposition to war. They opposed slavery and oppression and possibly helped defuse growing Christian anti-Semitism. They believed Jesus, a prince of peace, would return to reign over the Earth for a thousand years as the King of the Jews, that he was the spiritual king of the entire world and the successor to David and Solomon. For this they were branded a heretical Jewish sect.

By the end of the third century their influence had largely died out. Having to hide their beliefs from increasing persecution from the Catholic Church, and finding little support from the Jewish establishment, most Ebionites were ultimately absorbed back into the normative Jewish faith. Some factions persisted for several centuries, however, and a number of historians believe they may have eventually come into contact with the origins of Islam.

the formation of the early Church cannot be minimised, though, and as the Church grew increasingly anti-Semitic, Paul's influence held sway.

By the fourth century, most, if not all, pacifistic Christian sects, including the Ebionites, Gnostics and Nazarenes had been marginalised and tagged as heretical. With the conversion of the Roman emperor Constantine, Christianity became entwined with the state and with conquest, and the need arose to reconcile Jesus' pacifistic teachings with the right to wage war. This was provided by Augustine's writings on 'just war', which offered conditions under which war was acceptable. Constantine's many campaigns were thus rationalised as occurring for a greater purpose, conducted with God's blessing and 'motivated by love'.

—

## VIEWS FROM THE SERMON ON THE MOUNT

FOR CENTURIES, CHRISTIANS HAVE ADVOCATED FOR THE CHURCH'S right to wage war against its enemies, and the Church has witnessed, condoned and carried out widespread killing in the name of God and against contrary philosophies. Does this mean that the pacifism promoted in the Sermon on the Mount is an unattainable ideal? All Christian denominations have written extensively on this question, giving rise to several schools of thought in the process, and finding justification for both non-violent and pro-war positions.

The 'Absolutist View' interprets the Sermon on the Mount literally, holding that it applies universally, and that salvation comes only from obeying the scripture, even if the welfare of the believer is at stake. Early Anabaptists embraced this view, and it's still held by the Mennonite and Hutterite sects. Advocates of the Absolutist View include St Francis of Assisi, the German theologian Dietrich Bonhoeffer and Leo Tolstoy, who embraced Christian non-violence later in life.

The official position of the Roman Catholic Church is referred to as the 'Double Standard View'; it requires the clergy to obey the sermon as part of Jesus' specific counsels for perfection while allowing the general populace to follow the words as general precepts for salvation. This view, originated by Augustine of Hippo and later developed by St Thomas Aquinas, holds that the New Testament distinguishes between the clergy and the laity in moral matters and sets a higher standard for clergy, monks and the most pious of the Church to obey the counsels, which included poverty, chastity and a vow of obedience.

With the Protestant Reformation a new interpretation evolved, the 'Analogy of Scripture View'. This found that the harshest examples within the sermon could be softened by other passages of the New Testament upon careful reading. This in turn led to the most common reading of the sermon, the 'Hyperbole View', which holds that some of what Jesus said was simply exaggeration to make a point and could be moderated as it applied to the real world. Most would agree that there is some hyperbole involved. But there the agreement ends. No standard agreement has been developed to distinguish which passages should and should not be taken literally. The 'General Principles View' is similar to this, suggesting that Jesus wasn't offering specific directions but merely providing examples of more general precepts of behaviour.

With changing times have come more interpretations, several of which became popular in the nineteenth century. Tracing back to Augustine, the concept of 'Attitudes not Acts' suggests that the sermon speaks more about the attitudes of good Christians than about physical actions. The 'Interim Ethic View' of Albert Schweitzer argues that Jesus was sure the world would soon end (that the Apocalypse was nigh was believed by many Jews of his time) and so in the end-times all material concerns would be irrelevant.

The twentieth century brought further theories based on eschatology, concerned with the final judgment and preparation for the Kingdom of God. Martin Dibelius' 'Unconditional Divine Will View' argues that the ethics behind the sermon are absolute, but allows that humanity's fallen state has made them impossible to uphold. The related 'Repentance View' suggests that the sermon's precepts were meant to be unattainable and that in failing to obey them, humanity would be driven to repent. 'Dispensationalism', first proposed by the Plymouth Brethren, breaks human history into periods or 'dispensations' and finds that we are living now in a state of grace. This means that fulfilling all the teachings of the sermon is impossible, but that in the future humanity will see an age when following the precepts will lead to salvation.

So, should Christians obey all the precepts of the Sermon on the Mount unconditionally, or should they not even try, so they can repent? Should they treat the text as exaggeration or follow it literally? Should they let the most pious take the brunt of the work or accept its standards as part of their everyday expectations? More questions, more interpretations. But perhaps that was Jesus' true purpose all along—to get his followers to question and to answer these questions individually. Maybe this is what the two scholars in Rosselli's painting are arguing about. Everyone can approach the words from their own understanding and, as we will see, most Christian pacifists did just that.

47

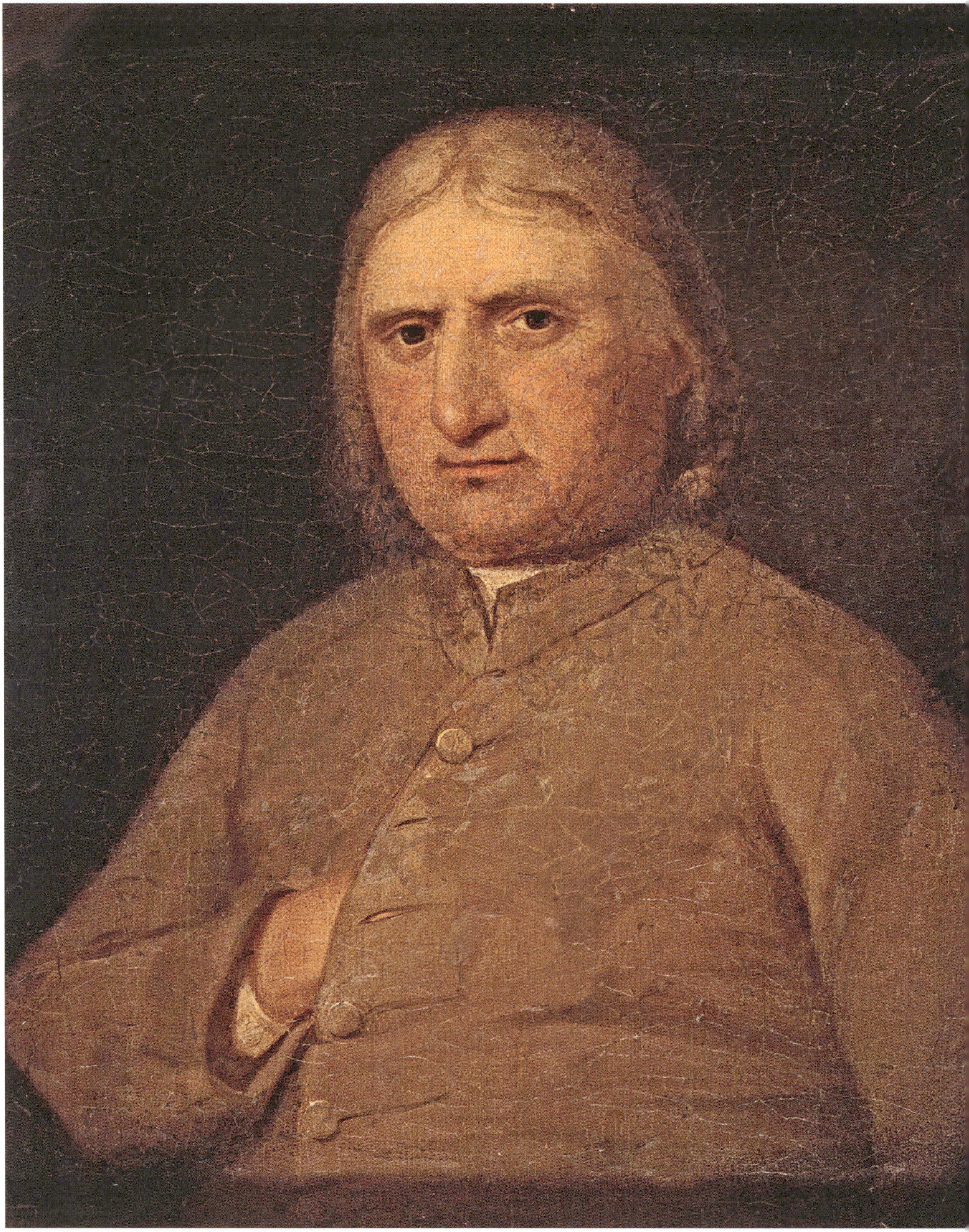

# GEORGE FOX: A SEEKER OF PEACE

A PACIFIST AND SEVENTEENTH CENTURY DISSENTER FROM THE CHURCH of England, George Fox outlasted four monarchs, endured the English Civil War and influenced the Commonwealth of Oliver Cromwell. He was a man of modest education, who suffered prosecution for heresy by both Catholics and Puritans, and years of imprisonment under some terrible conditions. Convinced his calling came directly from God, he led a new age of 'seekers of truth' in a radical form of Christianity that professed the equality of all people, sought the 'inner light' of God in every person, and stood in non-violent opposition to the abuses and intolerance of state and Church authority.

Fox founded the Religious Society of Friends—Quakers—as a direct result of his experiences of ministry during one of the most tumultuous periods in English history, a time of political upheaval and religious experimentation that coincided with the early days of the European Enlightenment, highlighted in England by the luminaries Isaac Newton, John Locke and John Milton. But Fox was both a man of his time and strangely apart from it. As a pacifist, he refused to take up arms with either the Royalists or the Parliamentarians of Cromwell during England's Civil War. As a staunch adherent to Jesus' teachings in the Sermon on the Mount, he avoided taking oaths of any kind. A romantic, and a man of inner conflicts, he felt his religious conviction more deeply in the simplicity of the woods than in the 'steeple houses' of the

George Fox, founder of the Quakers, in sombre, thoughtful mood. This portrait is believed to have been executed by the Dutch artist Sir Peter Lely (1618–1680).

Church. His otherworldly stamina, oratorical fire and immodest sense of self-destiny led him on an adventure of spirit and rebellion that resulted in the establishment of history's most enduring sect of Christian pacifism.

—

## 'GRAVITY AND STAYEDNESS OF MIND AND SPIRIT'

> That all may know the dealings of the Lord with me, and the various exercises, trials, and troubles through which He led me, in order to prepare and fit me for the work unto which He had appointed, and may thereby be drawn to admire and glorify His infinite wisdom and goodness, I think fit (before I proceed to set forth my public travels in the service of Truth) briefly to mention how it was with me in my youth, and how the work of the Lord was begun …

So BEGINS GEORGE FOX'S JOURNAL, THE RECORD OF HIS UNUSUAL AND exemplary life. Born in 1624 in a small Leicestershire hamlet, George was the son of a weaver named Christopher Fox but known as 'Righteous Christer'. His mother Mary Lago was a descendant of Robert Glover, a 'Mancetter Martyr' who was burned at the stake for opposing the Catholic Church under Queen Mary's reign. From such stock, it's no surprise that he was a serious lad who possessed 'a gravity and stayedness of mind and spirit not usual in children'. Considered for the priesthood, his father instead apprenticed him to a shoemaker, where he gained a reputation for 'innocency and honesty'.

When George Fox was nineteen, a seemingly minor event changed his life. Already known in his village as a serious critic of the clergy, he clearly suffered spiritually from what he saw as the hypocrisy between their words and deeds. When a young cousin asked George to join him and an older priest for a 'jug of beer', Fox reluctantly accepted. One beer turned into many as the cousin and the priest played a drinking game to see who'd end up with the bar tab. George was put off by the whole experience and stormed out. That evening he had a spiritual awakening, later writing in his journal: '[I] prayed and cried to the Lord, who said unto me: "Thou seest how young people go together into vanity, and old people into the earth; thou must forsake all, young and old, keep out of all, and be as a stranger unto all."'

Taking this message from God as a summons to action, Fox decided to leave his village and seek answers to the call. So began a journey that would span fifty years and take him to nearly every corner of Great Britain, the West Indies, the American colonies, Germany and Holland. Initially on a quest for guidance, he sought out all manner of clergy in the English Midlands. Some took the young man's intensity seriously, but most were simply irritated by his argumentative nature. They recommended he marry, or enlist in the military, or even seek treatment with the dubious practice of bloodletting.

Fox became convinced he wasn't going to find any comfort or useful instruction from the established clergy—in fact, he came to view any Oxford-educated minister as suspect, and questioned whether God might be better experienced directly, without any intermediary. This was the beginning of his own ministry. Soon he became convinced that the Holy Spirit was found within the hearts of all people. Anyone—man, woman or child—could minister out of the kinds of experiences that 'turn people to that inner light, spirit and grace by which all might know their salvation and their way to God'.

—

## THE MAN IN THE LEATHER BREECHES

FOX WAS NOT A TALL MAN NOR WAS HE PARTICULARLY HANDSOME. HE had a long nose, was stout and muscular, and wore his hair long, a style out of favour at the time. He was said to have 'penetrating' eyes and a kind of intensity that seemed to draw allegiance or aversion. His self-styled 'common man's' uniform of leather pants, which he may have made himself, close-fitting doublet and wide-brimmed hat became his trademark. When he arrived in a town, it was common to hear, ''Tis the man in the leather breeches!'

His first attempts at ministering were faltering; but what he lacked in oratorical skill, he made up for in gumption. He preached anywhere people would gather—churchyard, marketplace, field or woods. He would speak out at the end of church services—a common practice among dissenting ministers— even interrupting a service when he could no longer tolerate what he was hearing. He would reprimand, threaten, entreat and cajole. His near-encyclopaedic knowledge of the Bible was self-taught, as were his interpretations, which he thrust on people with the arrogance of one convinced that God had chosen him singularly. William Penn: an early convert to Quakerism, wrote of Fox:

[God] took one that was not of high degree, or elegant speech, or learned after the way of this world, that his message and work He sent him to do might come with less suspicion or jealousy of human wisdom and interest and with more force and clearness upon the consciences of those that sincerely sought the way of truth ... (see 'William Penn: colonial Quaker', pages 58–59).

51

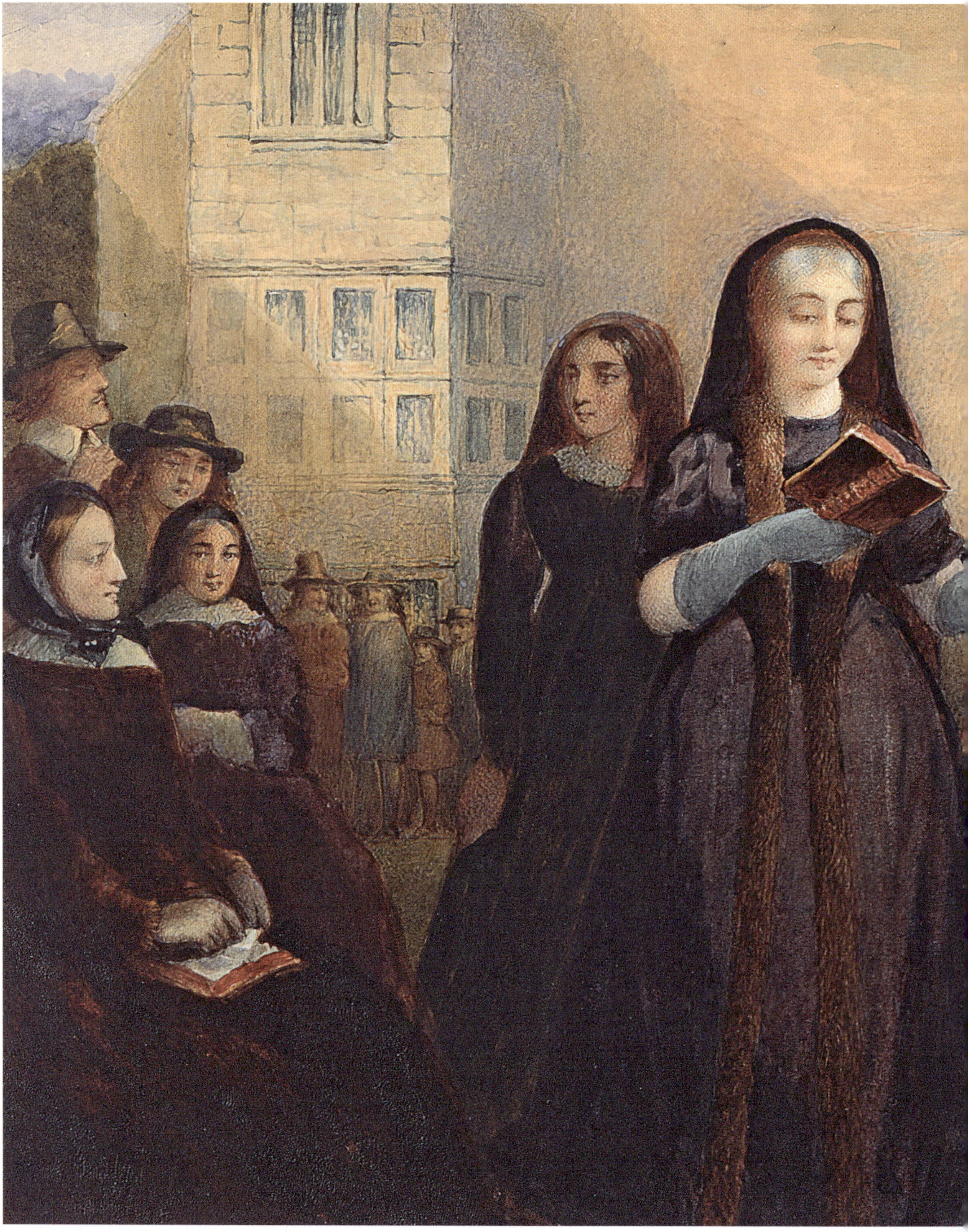

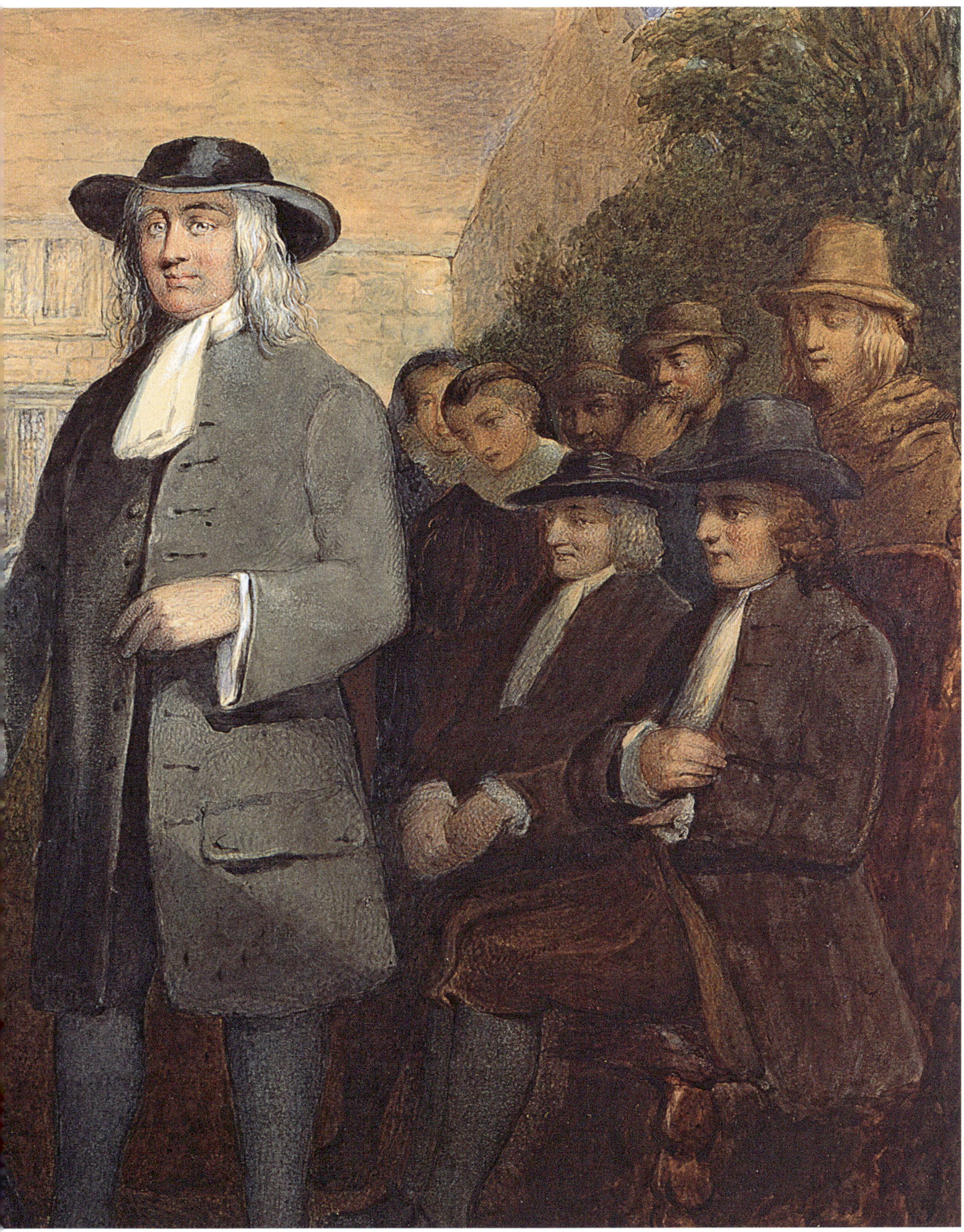

When George Fox climbed Lancashire's majestic, mist-shrouded Pendle Hill in 1652 and had his vision of bringing all Quakers together, the 560 metre (1837 foot) high landmark had long been notorious. Sensational tales of witches, evil spells, ghastly murders, cannibalism and the summoning of the dead were well known at the time. The Pendle Witch Trials of 1612, in which ten people were found guilty of witchcraft and hanged, were recorded in great detail and published in a lurid tell-all called *The Wonderfull Discoverie of Witches in the Countie of Lancaster*. Credited to the Court of Assizes clerk, a man named Thomas Potts, the book's favourable impression of the two judges was no doubt manipulated to further their careers.

Ten women and two men had been accused, most of them belonging to two families headed by matriarchs in their eighties, Elizabeth Southerns, known as Demdike, and Anne Whittle, called Chattox. Through potion-making, extortion and begging, witchcraft was a lucrative, if dangerous, profession. The two families were in competition and made accusations of conjuring and murder against each other. Of the twelve, one woman died in prison, one woman was found innocent, and the other ten were hanged.

Fox would have been familiar with the stories surrounding Pendle Hill. Given the superstitious nature of the time, climbing the hill was more a matter of spiritual courage than physical challenge. And whether the frightening tales or the ancient burial ground on the summit influenced Fox's heavenly vision are purely matters of conjecture. But to this day Pendle Hill is thought to be one of the most haunted places in the world. Many ghost-hunting television programs have featured the small mountain and crowds gather every Halloween for a midnight fete on its summit.

As for Potts, he parlayed his fifteen minutes of fame into favour with the court of King James and in 1615 was given the keepership of Skalme Park as the breeder of the king's hounds.

But before he built a following, Fox spent much of his time in lonely contemplation. He wrote in his journal of those early days:

> I fasted much, walked abroad in solitary places many days, and often took my Bible, and sat in hollow trees and lonesome places till night came on; and frequently in the night walked mournfully about by myself; for I was a man of sorrows in the time of the first working of the Lord in me.

Fox was especially drawn to Jesus' Sermon on the Mount, in the Gospel of Matthew, and the Gospel of John. He rejected the outer trappings of the

Church and embraced the inward workings of the Divine. 'The Light within' became his way of describing his radical view of the spirit of Christ. He argued that the Bible supported this direct experience of that light, quoting from the Sermon on the Mount, 'You are the light of the world' and 'let your light shine before men, so that they may see your good deeds and praise your Father in heaven' (Matthew 5:14–16). From the Gospel of John, which would become known informally as 'the Quaker text' because of its frequent mention, Fox cited the passage: 'That was the true Light, which lighteth every man that cometh into the world' (John 1:9). He took this light to be the essence of God that permeates everything; in a later epistle to his followers, he wrote: 'While ye have the Light, walk in the Light, and live in the Light, Christ the Truth.'

From this conviction Fox built his fellowship. He stressed that everyone, including women and children, had the right to minister since the qualifications for ministry came directly from God. He believed all rituals could be ignored as elements that interfered with the experience of true spiritual conversion. He preferred to worship out in the open, as Jesus did on the mount, because the Lord 'dwelleth in the hearts of his obedient people', and was not confined to houses of worship. And, particularly irksome to Protestants, Fox argued that Truth was to be found in the experience of God rather than in the Bible.

Fox's ministry angered the established clergy, who saw it as blasphemous; as his fame grew among the commoners and farmers, so did his infamy within the Church. By 1648 he had a substantial following and was leading large meetings throughout the north of England. Although he was not particularly eloquent—speaking as a Leicestershire countryman 'uncouth and unfashionable to nice ears'—he was forceful. And most certainly loud: his voice could carry to the back of an outdoors crowd a thousand deep. With such divisive popularity, it was only a matter of time before Fox would attract the scrutiny of the government.

## GOALS AND GAOLS

By 1649 England, in the grip of political and religious turmoil caused by the deep intertwining of Church and state, had endured seven years of civil war. Charles I, refusing to relinquish his right to rule and accept the decisions made by Parliament, had aligned himself more closely with Roman Catholicism. His reign came to an end when he was captured by the (Roundhead) forces commanded by Oliver Cromwell, tried, and executed for treason.

GEORGE FOX

55

Following the fall of the monarchy, England became a Commonwealth under the Puritanical leadership of Cromwell. An astute military commander, Cromwell brutally suppressed Catholics in Ireland and consolidated his power by successfully invading Scotland and defeating the Royalists. The Commonwealth was short-lived—in 1653 Cromwell fashioned a Protectorate and established himself as Lord Protector for life. But his rule as Lord Protector was also short—in 1658 Cromwell died and was buried in Westminster Abbey. His son Richard was unable to hold power as Lord Protector, and in 1660 Parliamentary forces paved the way for a restoration of the monarchy under Charles II. Oliver Cromwell's remains were dug up and posthumously 'executed'.

Unrest, radical transformation and religious fervour were the norm in this period, and religious freedoms rose and fell with the shifting political winds. During the reign of Charles I, the Church of England had opposed any non-conformist worship, resulting in wholesale incarceration of dissenters. Under Cromwell, a Puritan convert, religious dissent was tolerated but social conventions were equally oppressive, with various Acts of Parliament requiring oaths of allegiance and military conscription. With the Restoration of the monarchy under Charles II, Parliament passed the *Conventicle Act*, which further suppressed religious dissent by classifying it as sedition. The Act restricted nearly all of the dissenting groups of the time, most now forgotten: among them the Adamites, Anabaptists, Levellers, Diggers, Grindletonians, Muggletonians and Seekers (who would later merge with the Quakers), to name but a few. The laws hit Fox's followers hardest, maybe because they were the most outspoken about equality, and their refusal to take oaths or pledge allegiance—or perhaps because most of the thousands of Quaker converts were simple country folk who lacked the political connections to keep themselves out of prison or to secure their property from seizure.

Over his lifetime, Fox spent nearly six years imprisoned. His first incarceration came at Nottingham in 1649 after he'd stormed into a large congregation of members of the Parliamentarian military and sought to convert them. He was imprisoned for six months, during which, with a kind of Robin Hood flair, he converted one of the sheriffs of Nottingham. The following year he was arrested on charges of blasphemy and brought before Justice Bennett. Fox launched into his defence, full of fury and rapture, booming at the Justice 'to tremble and quake at the name of the Lord!' Bennett was not impressed, mocking Fox's admonitions by labelling him and his followers 'Quakers'. Although the name was meant as a term of derision, it stuck. Bennett gave Fox six months but offered to reduce the sentence if he would join the Royalist military. Fox refused. His sentence was promptly doubled and he endured over a year of harsh treatment.

Upon his release, Fox continued his travelling ministry, mostly on foot, throughout the English Midlands, concerned only with spreading his message of the direct experience of God. In his wake, he left groups of people changed by his ministry; others abandoned their former lives and joined him on his travels. He did not claim to be the leader of any organised new movement or religion. But this changed in 1652.

Preaching and covering ground at a furious rate, Fox made his way through Yorkshire and on to Cumberland, Westmorland and south into the Yorkshire Dales and Lancashire. There he came upon Pendle Hill, a misty flat-top hillock rising above the Forest of Bowland. Fox described what happened there:

> As we travelled, we came near a very great hill, called Pendle Hill, and I was moved of the Lord to go up to the top of it; which I did with difficulty, it was so very steep and high. When I was come to the top, I saw the sea bordering upon Lancashire. From the top of this hill the Lord let me see in what places he had a great people to be gathered.

Pendle Hill had long been steeped in superstition as a haven for witches (see 'The witches of Pendle Hill', page 54). When Fox returned from the summit, his reputation as a mystic with uncanny powers only increased. He was rumoured to charm people by tying ribbons around their wrists, and to tear around the countryside on a magical black stallion. In truth, it was his restlessness, purposefulness and need to stay one step ahead of the local magistrates that led him to move about the countryside as fast as possible.

With a new urgency to his mission, Fox and his Quaker followers headed further north where they met up with the Seekers, another dissenting group with similar beliefs. Fox united the two groups through his preaching of the Light, and began the work of organising a cohesive movement, the Religious Society of Friends. He began delegating work to his 'Valiant Sixty' core followers, pressing them to be 'publishers of Truth', when his own work was again interrupted by his arrest at Carlisle in 1653.

The High Sheriff of Carlisle called for his immediate execution, but because of Fox's notoriety first sought permission from London. Fox recorded in his journal that fifteen armed guards were set on him the first night, 'some of whom sat in the chimney, for fear I should go up it; such dark imaginings possessed them'. While Fox awaited his fate, he was moved to a single dank chamber packed with sick and abused convicts, both men and women. One woman, whom Fox converted before her death, was so ravaged by lice as to

# WILLIAM PENN: COLONIAL QUAKER

William Penn was one of the most influential Quakers of his, or any, time; some even say it's his likeness that appears on the Quaker Oats™ box. He founded the Commonwealth of Pennsylvania in 1681 as a safe haven for all religions, and it became the first true 'melting pot' of the American colonies. His 'First Frame of Government' for Pennsylvania was arguably the blueprint for the US Constitution. Penn was a close friend of George Fox and one of the first gentry-class converts to Quakerism.

Born in 1644, the son of Admiral Sir William Penn, later Commissioner of the Navy under Charles II, Penn grew up in London and Ireland during the Commonwealth of Cromwell. A notable student, he fell foul of the authorities at Oxford when he bucked the enforced religious worship and was expelled. Some years later, when he embraced the beliefs of the Religious Society of Friends, his father disinherited him, and Penn spent a long period penniless, living with Quaker families. An early Quaker apologist, Penn eventually began to preach and publish his views. Fox became his mentor, and they travelled frequently together. Arrested after the publication of his inflammatory tract *The Sandy Foundation Shaken*, Penn spent nearly a year in prison, where he wrote his seminal work *No Cross, No Crown*, complete with analysis and quotes drawn accurately from memory.

Upon his release Penn reconciled with his father but continued to preach, publish and agitate against the persecution of Quakers. In a landmark case, he challenged the oppressive *Conventicle Act* in 1670 upon his arrest for sedition. He argued that without a formal indictment he could not be found guilty. The jury agreed and he was acquitted. The Lord Mayor of London refused to accept the verdict, fined the jury and imprisoned them in Newgate for two months. Finally, the Court of Common Pleas issued a writ of habeas corpus setting the jury and Penn free. The Lord Chief Justice of England ruled that juries could not be coerced or punished for their verdicts, establishing a key right of jury trial that stands today.

The trial raised Penn's stature as an advocate for the oppressed but did little to staunch the persecution of Quakers. Seeing that conditions were unlikely to improve in Great Britain, Penn took his appeal directly to the king and proposed a plan to relocate Quakers to the colonies. To his surprise, in 1681 King Charles II granted him sovereignty over 117,000 square kilometres (45, 174 square miles) south of New York. Penn was now the largest landowner in the world. He named his new colony 'Sylvania', the Latin word for 'forest', but Charles changed it to 'Pennsylvania' in honour of Penn's father.

Penn's new Commonwealth was inspired by Quaker principles and infused with the enlightened principles of the day. His 'First Frame of Government' proclaimed: 'Men being born with a title to perfect freedom and uncontrolled enjoyment of all the rights and privileges of the law of nature … no one can be put out of his estate and subjected to the political view of another, without his consent.' The language bears a striking resemblance to that of Jefferson in the Declaration of Independence. Penn's document was also the first constitution that allowed for amendments to be proposed and ratified, providing a means for peaceful opposition and change. The Commonwealth of Pennsylvania would have a democratic government under which religious tolerance was secured, the military was barred, a free press and trial by jury were assured, private property was protected and unlimited free enterprise was to be advanced.

But despite his Quaker convictions and the application of his friend John Locke's ideas of natural rights, Penn had a blind spot when it came to slavery. He, along with other Quakers, owned and sold slaves in the colonies for decades. He also proved to be a better theorist than administrator, losing all of the considerable fortune he put into his 'Holy Experiment'. Swindled by his business manager, fellow Quaker Philip Ford, Penn briefly lost possession of Pennsylvania and in 1706, at the age of sixty-two, landed in debtor's prison. He regained title to the colony but suffered the first of several strokes in 1712 while trying to negotiate its sale back to the Crown. Penn slowly lost his memory and died penniless in 1718 at his home in Berkshire.

have had half her face eaten away. After months, word finally came back from Cromwell's 'Rump Parliament', to the High Sheriff's chagrin calling for Fox's release, and adamant that 'a young man [should not] die for religion'.

By 1655, Fox was regularly preaching before crowds a thousand strong, and Cromwell's government grew suspicious that he might throw his influence behind the Royalists looking to restore Charles II. Fox was arrested in Leicestershire and taken under armed guard to London, where he was brought before the Lord Protector. This first meeting lasted an entire morning and established a bond between the two. Fox convinced Cromwell of his pacifist nature, promising that he would not take up arms in the support of monarchists or Parliamentarians. When their conversation turned to the pacifist and egalitarian beliefs of the Friends, Fox encouraged the Lord Protector to listen to God's voice. His words had a powerful impact on Cromwell. Fox wrote in his journal, 'with tears in his eyes [Cromwell] said, "Come again to my house; for if thou and I were but an hour of a day together, we should be nearer one to the other"; added that he wished me no more ill than he did to his own soul'.

Fox was again freed. Throughout the year he petitioned Cromwell to help ease the persecution of Quakers, returning to Whitehall later in the year and twice the following year. Although the two disagreed on many issues, they had enough rapport for Fox to advise Cromwell to 'lay down his crown at the feet of Jesus'. Cromwell declined, but Fox's words would become part of Quaker lore, a tenet of Quaker belief known as 'Speaking Truth to Power' which stands today.

Despite Fox's rapport with Cromwell, his continued frenetic evangelising landed him in prison again in 1656. The appropriately named Doomsdale dungeon at Launceston was a miserable hellhole where prisoners were chained and forced to stand ankle-deep in their own excrement. Fox wrote in his journal: 'At night some friendly people of the town brought us a candle and a little straw, and we burnt some of it to take away the stink.' He endured six months of abuse, beatings and starvation before his eventual release, when he requested another audience with Cromwell. In a brief meeting at Hampton Court only months before Cromwell's death in 1658, Fox again pressed his case for religious tolerance.

Following the restoration of Charles II, persecution for non-conformity and acts deemed subversive only increased. While again imprisoned, at Lancaster in 1660, Fox wrote Charles a detailed argument against war and the persecution of dissenting faiths. His letter had an impact, for Charles released not only Fox but nearly 1000 other Quakers. But the next year, after a dissenting group called the Fifth Monarchists attempted a coup, the court clamped down on all non-conformists. This turn of events prompted Fox, along with other prominent

# MARGARET FELL: THE MOTHER OF QUAKERISM

Margaret Askew was born in 1614 in Dalton-in-Furness, Cumbria, and married barrister Thomas Fell at eighteen. Twenty years later, Askew converted to Quakerism and became a founding member and ardent organiser of the early Society of Friends. Her preaching, missionary work, writings, loyalty to Fox and endless efforts on behalf of all persecuted Friends earned her the title 'the nurturing mother of Quakerism'.

Margaret Fell first heard Fox's ministry in 1652. She recalled her reaction: 'I sat down in my pew again and cried bitterly: and I cried in my spirit to the Lord, "We are all thieves; we have taken the Scripture in words, and know nothing of them in ourselves."' Her husband Thomas Fell was a supporter of the Friends but never converted. When Fell passed away in 1658, Margaret inherited control of their Elizabethan manor, Swarthmoor Hall. The manor became the centre of the Quakers and throughout the 1660s was raided repeatedly by the authorities. In 1664 Margaret was arrested for allowing illegal Quaker meetings and refusing the Oath of Obedience to the king. She said at her trial:

> This I shall say, as for my allegiance, I love, own, and honour the King and desire his peace and welfare; and that we may live a peaceable, a quiet and a godly life under his government ... And as for the oath itself ... Jesus ... hath commanded me not to swear at all, neither by heaven, nor by earth, nor by any other Oath.

But to no avail; she was sentenced to life in prison and the forfeiture of all her lands and property.

While imprisoned at Lancaster, she wrote a number of epistles—her most famous, 'Women's Speaking Justified', a seminal and articulate argument for the right of women to minister.

In 1665 the King granted her forfeited estate to her son George Fell, who had renounced Quakerism. In the fourth year of her sentence, the King ordered her release. She married Fox, ten years her junior, in 1669, in a ceremony witnessed by the Quaker meeting at Bristol. Almost immediately they returned to their work, she at Swarthmoor Hall and George in the south of England. Margaret was again arrested in Lancaster for breaking the *Conventicle Act* and George, separated from his new wife, became so ill and depressed that he lost his sight for awhile.

Upon her release a year later, Fox departed for the colonies. Gone for two years, he returned in 1673 and was again arrested and held for another two years. In their first five years of marriage, George and Margaret spent only a few months together. Between prison sentences, missionary travel and separate organising efforts, this was to be the pattern for the twenty-two years of their union, hardly a typical marriage. Nevertheless, it would be unfair to say their passion was more directed at evangelising than one another, for their mutual love was well known.

After Fox's death in 1691, Margaret spent her remaining years at Swarthmoor, overseeing the publication of his journal and epistles and later the construction of a meeting house. Well into her eighties, Margaret Fell Fox died in 1702, having outlived two husbands. Her final words were 'I am in Peace', and she was buried in an unmarked grave beside the Swarthmoor Meeting House.

Quakers, to issue a broadsheet, a printed tract committing themselves to opposing all armed rebellion and war as contrary to the will of God. This would become known as the Quaker 'peace testimony' and solidify the denomination as one of the world's earliest and most influential historic peace churches.

—

## THE NEW WORLD

As the Quaker faith took shape, some of what started as Fox's eccentricities became the rational etiquette of this new religion. Quakers refused to take off their hats or bow to social 'superiors', believing all people were equal. They refused to swear oaths, in accordance with Jesus' teachings (Matthew 5:34), or to pay tithes. Their ceremony of silent contemplation, sometimes for hours on end, broken only by the rapturous ministry of any individual in the group, saw them branded as heretics. Their denial of original sin and their belief in the direct experience of God, without the intermediation of ritual or clergy, was seen as dangerously radical and blasphemous. Quakers suffered daily harassment, beatings, stonings and abuse from Catholics, Protestants and other dissenting groups alike. As a pacifist Fox bore these assaults, but he never shied away from conflict. In fact, his near-fanatical intensity mostly encouraged it. With his size and strength, Fox could have exchanged blow for blow, but he would, instead, literally 'turn the other cheek'.

Fox required his followers to do the same. His journal is full of instances of the beatings Quakers took, often from repeat offenders:

> The same man set upon six Friends that were going to a meeting at Yelland, and beat and abused them so, that he bruised their faces and shed much of their blood, wounding them very sore, and one of them in several parts of his body; yet they lifted not a hand against him, but gave him their backs and cheeks to beat.

In 1664 Fox again landed in prison, this time for nearly two years, at Scarborough Castle. His gaoler was particularly ruthless. Had Fox possessed less fortitude, he would never have lasted the distance: his cell was so exposed to the elements that he was repeatedly drenched with rain and chilled by the wind, leaving him afire with fever. Sympathetic visitors tried to help him light fires to warm himself, but his gaoler beat them away. Such treatment was not uncommon, however; of the approximately 12,000 Quakers imprisoned over a twenty-year period, over 300 died.

Through all the persecutions and imprisonments, Fox continued to organise and build his movement with the help of his Valiant Forty. The organisation had grown and now attracted members of the merchant class and the gentry, including William Penn, Robert Barclay and Isaac Penington, the son of the Lord Mayor of London. But perhaps most important to Fox and Quakerism was Margaret Fell, the wife of Judge Thomas Fell, the wealthy Vice-Chancellor of the Duchy of Lancaster. Cultured, beautiful, the mother of seven, she would fall under Fox's spell and become a dedicated organiser and evangeliser, suffering persecution and years of imprisonment. She would also become Fox's wife after her husband's death (see 'Margaret Fell: the mother of Quakerism', page 61).

Fox married Margaret Fell in 1669, and set his sights on the colonies in the Americas. Shortly after their marriage, however, Margaret was arrested and imprisoned for nearly a year at Lancaster, and Fox became deathly ill and depressed, for a period losing his eyesight. The years of rough travel, personal deprivation and imprisonment had taken their toll. But upon Margaret's release, he again resolved to travel abroad. He set sail in 1671 for Barbados, a voyage of seven weeks, and barely made it to the island. He was so ill on his arrival that he had to be carried from the ship. After three weeks, he wrote to Margaret before setting sail for Jamaica: 'My Dear Heart … I have undergone great sufferings in my body and spirit, beyond words; but the God of heaven be praised, His Truth is over all. I am now well.'

From Jamaica he took ship to Maryland, where he set about organising meetings throughout the colonies. He also met with Native Americans in an 'Indian town where … the king came to us, and he could speak some English. I spoke to him much and also to his people; they were very loving to us.' Some of the Indians joined in the meeting. He went north to New England, where Friends continued to suffer under Puritan persecution but still held their 'glorious meetings'. For two years, he travelled around New Jersey, Virginia and Carolina, organising in the same way he had in England, preaching and converting many. Convinced that Quakerism was now well established, he set sail for England.

Upon his return in 1673, Fox faced both internal revolt within the organisation and further persecution from Parliament. A rift had developed over 'women's meetings', which were opposed by provincial Quakers and championed by the London-based Friends led by William Penn and Robert Barclay, with whom Fox threw in his lot. Before the issue was resolved, however, Fox was arrested and imprisoned once again for refusing to take an oath of allegiance to Parliament. He was gaoled for two years at Worcester, where he became so ill many of his followers were sure he would die. Scotsman Robert

Barclay, a dedicated follower of Fox and an educated leader, now took on much more of the organising, and would prove to be one of the most eminent writers belonging to the Religious Society of Friends. His influential *Apologia* of 1675, described as an 'Explanation and Vindication of the Principles and Doctrines of the People called Quakers', was written in Latin and translated into English, Dutch, German, French and Spanish. It was even studied at the Vatican. Barclay purchased, along with other wealthy Quakers, a swathe of territory in North America and briefly took the ceremonial role of governor of East New Jersey. Barclay's acquisitions, along with William Penn's grant of lands, resulted in a wave of Quaker immigration. Penn, a loyal aide to Fox, would become the best known Quaker leader in America when he founded Pennsylvania in the 1680s as a safe haven for Quakers and other dissenters and non-conformists (see 'William Penn: colonial Quaker', pages 58–59).

Fox continued his missionary work with trips to Holland and Germany to establish meetings and extend his ministry, dangerous ventures given the ongoing suspicion of the English and England's oppression of Catholic rule. He wrote prolifically, sending letters to the leaders of Poland, Denmark and Germany and elsewhere in support of Quakers. Although many thought of him as indestructible, Fox was now in his sixties and his health began to break down. He was forced to delegate, but as the Quaker movement came increasingly under the leadership of Penn and Barclay, it gained in acceptance.

## A TESTIMONY OF PEACE

IN THE WANING YEARS OF HIS LIFE, FOX spent most of his time in London while Margaret coordinated efforts from Swarthmoor Hall in Cumbria, which she had inherited from her former husband and which had become the de facto Quaker centre. Fox argued before Parliament on behalf of Friends and eventually helped convince James II to pardon nearly 1500 gaoled Quakers. With the 'Glorious Revolution' and the ascension of the Protestant monarchs William and Mary, religious persecution eased. In 1689, 'An Act for Exempting their Majestyes Protestant Subjects dissenting from the Church of England from the Penalties of certaine Lawes'—the *Act of Toleration*—was passed and many dissenting faiths were finally allowed freedom of assembly. Although the Act required oaths of allegiance and recognised the supremacy of the Crown, still odious to most Quakers, and even given its many provisions targeting Catholics and Quakers, Fox saw it as a great triumph.

In the last decade of the seventeenth century, religious persecution eased. Quakers were well established in England and on the way to becoming a dominant faith in Pennsylvania. The hierarchy of local Monthly Meetings and regional Yearly Meetings was established throughout Great Britain and rapidly taking hold in North America. The Friends' 'testimonies' of peace, equality, simplicity and truth were solidifying into established rules. Although Friends have no hard and fast 'creeds', these testimonials provided a common view of how to relate to God and the world. Primary among them was the Peace Testimony, which stated that war and violence were contrary to the teachings of Jesus. The Testimony of Equality held that within every person could be found 'the seed of God' and thus all deserve equal rights. The Testimony of Simplicity encouraged simple dress and the limiting of material possessions. The Truth Testimony was essentially a vow of integrity, promising to follow God's guidance over the urging of others.

Breaking these testimonies or the norms of a Monthly Meeting could result in being 'eldered' or reprimanded or, in the worst cases, 'read out of meeting', a uniquely Quaker form of excommunication. This was particularly true of Quakers who chose to participate in the wars of the eighteenth century, including the French, Indian and Revolutionary wars. Some Quakers chose to marry outside the faith, which also led to their 'disownment' from meeting.

But Fox would not live to see much of this coalescing of Quaker doctrine. He died on 13 January 1691, two days after preaching at the Gracechurch Street Meeting in London. Yet he must have felt great comfort in the firm footing the Society of Friends had secured. Just days before his death, he told his followers; 'Now I am fully clear! … All is well; the Seed of God reigns over all and over death itself. And though I am weak in body, yet the power of God is over all.' Thousands of mourners attended his funeral. In 1694, his journal, compiled by Margaret Fell Fox and edited by Thomas Ellwood, was published. It stands today as one of a handful of classic religious autobiographies.

Fox's ministry radically extended the reach of the Protestant Reformation by, in essence, freeing the congregation from the authority of the church. He championed the rights of the individual and set the bar for how modern democracies might be founded. He created a living model of non-violent dissent and established a religion of pacifism that is still vital today. William Penn, writing in the preface to Fox's *Journal*, offered a simple description of his friend, mentor; his 'dear George':

I have done, as to this part of my preface, when I have let this short epitaph to his name: 'Many sons have done virtuously in this day, but, dear George, thou excellest them all.'

*'Listen all! From now and forever,*
*never again let there be war as this day has been!'*
**NUNUKU-WHENUA**

# PART II

# WORDS TO LIVE BY

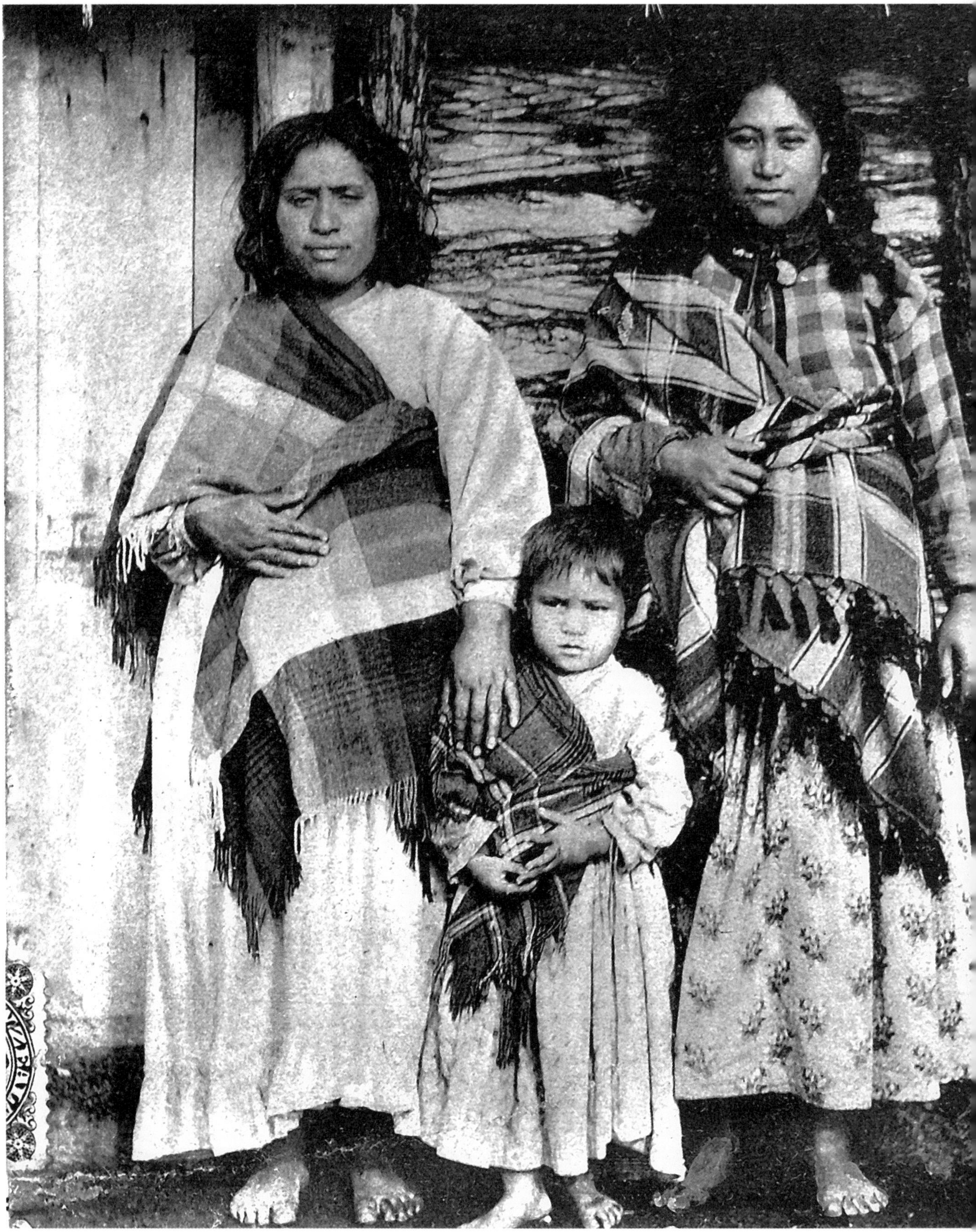

# THE MORIORI: NUNUKU-WHENUA'S LAW

SHROUDED IN SECRECY FOR CENTURIES, VERDANT CHATHAM ISLAND SITS some 870 kilometres (540 miles) southeast of Christchurch, New Zealand. Buffeted by the southerly confluence of Antarctic waters and warm northerly currents, the island produces raw winters, sweltering summers and a relentless wet wind. One of a cluster of small islands cresting the ancient submarine mountain range known as the East Chatham Rise, Chatham Island's imposing peaks loom out of the mist. Only a resilient and steely people could have braved the rugged coastline, dense broadleaf forests and murky salt-marsh lagoons.

The original inhabitants, the Moriori, called their island Rekohu, meaning 'misty sun', for its ethereal near-constant cloud cover. Veiled in mystery and hidden by isolation, the full story of the Moriori has only recently come to light. Their lives were harsh and short, but far from dismal. By all accounts, they were a cheerful, gentle people who lived for half a millennium in undisturbed seclusion, adamant in their rejection of aggression and determined to live in harmony with their formidable natural environment. Where did they come from? What led them to abandon bloodshed and remould their society into a model of self-sustaining cooperation? And what happened to leave them so vulnerable to the usurping Europeans and, ultimately, the conquering Maori?

By the turn of the twentieth century, the Moriori had abandoned traditional dress for the all-enveloping garments deemed acceptable by Christian missionaries.

Most answers trace back to an early Moriori ancestral chief, Nunuku-whenua, who probably lived in the fourteenth or fifteenth century. His decree that warfare and cannibalism should end ushered in a period of non-violent cohabitation unrivalled in recorded history. And yet, what led to the creation of a peaceful epoch would also prove to be the Moriori's undoing.

---

## THE 'ORDINARY PEOPLE' OF REKOHU

THE MORIORI NEVER HAD A NAME FOR THEMSELVES. FOR MORE than 500 years, they simply *were*. It was the Maori, their conquering cousins from New Zealand, who imposed the name. Shortened from *tchakat moriori*, the name debased them as inferior and primitive 'ordinary people'. But the Moriori were clearly descended from the same seafaring Polynesian lineage as the Maori—a fact that the Maori disputed for decades to help justify their occupation of the island. Part of a great Polynesian migration, the Moriori ancestors came to the South Pacific during the thirteenth or fourteenth centuries from Southeast Asia and the South China Sea. Early migratory waves settled the Melanesian islands, Fiji, Tonga and Samoa, ventured on to the Cook, Society and Marquesas groups, north to Hawaii, further east to Easter Island and from there southwest to New Zealand. Whether intentionally or accidentally, from the east coast of New Zealand the Moriori arrived at the Chathams on prevailing currents flowing southeast from Cook Strait. Archaeological findings suggest they first settled on smaller Rangiauria (Pitt Island today), 20 kilometres (12 miles) to the southeast of Rekohu.

Several versions of Moriori creation mythology exist; one in particular resonates with clues to the Moriori identity. These earliest inhabitants, the Tuiti, were peaceful sun worshippers from Rangiauria's vertiginous mountain peaks. They 'warred neither with the Maker nor his children; they fed on fruit and shed no blood'. In the myth, a young boy wandered down to the shore one day, where he came upon a sea eagle. The 'king of the birds' could no longer fly, bound by a spell. He begged the boy to release him. But the young Tuiti knew the Maker had taken away the eagle's flight because he lorded over all the other island birds, so he at first refused. Then the crafty eagle promised the boy that if he were released, he would show him how to 'soar' to an uninhabited, bountiful land that 'called aloud for a master':

A continent in size, compared to Rangiauria; with undulating, fertile plains south and lofty mountains in the north, sparkling with lakes of dark transparent water, and vocal with the song and bright with the plumage of birds.

Conflicted, the boy fell to the sand, struggling with obedience to his Maker and the desire to lead his people to a better land. Finally, as the sun was setting, he consented; the eagle parted the mists, revealing the way to Rekohu.

But then the eagle took his revenge. Letting loose a war cry, he attacked and destroyed all the island birds during the night. In the morning, a Tuiti child fell dead. Despairing, the boy confessed his betrayal and was left to wander the shores alone, whereupon the eagle took pity on him. Fulfilling his promise, the eagle taught the boy how to make the *waka korari*, a wash-through raft of wicker and reeds. The young Tuiti could now 'soar' across the waves and lead his people to their new home.

By whatever means the Moriori came to Rekohu, it's sadly clear that warfare came with them. The Wheteina and Rauru tribes, two hostile Moriori factions, had been engaged in wars of vengeance for generations. The original bloodshed was sparked by an enraged Wheteina chief killing his Rauru wife for alleging he was impotent. Avenging conflict spread and the cycle of violence was perpetuated year after year, replete with the cannibalistic practice of eating the vanquished. But eventually the Moriori took a sudden and enduring detour from warfare. Crystallised on the battlefield, this bold pacifist stroke would become the legacy of an all-powerful Rauru chief named Nunuku-whenua.

—

## 'NEVER AGAIN LET THERE BE WAR!'

ON THE BATTLEFIELD, NUNUKU-WHENUA WAS AN IMPOSING FIGURE. He wore only a loincloth and a woven flax cape or sealskin cloak, fastened with a bone pendant. His chiefly stature was signified by a topknot in his hair, capped with a red parakeet feather headdress called a *kura*; his thick beard was studded with tufts of white albatross feathers. Stout, muscular and barrel-chested, his dark skin glistening with sweat and mist, Nunuku led his Rauru warriors into battle by raising his formidable *tupuari*, his fighting staff. But a day would come when he would instead lead them away from war.

One day, legend has it, the Wheteina and Rauru prepared for yet another battle in a clearing on the western side of the murky Te Whanga lagoon. The Wheteina emerged from the forest thickets, crouching and wielding their spears

## KOCHE: KING OF PITT

Koche, a young Moriori folk hero, was 'a man of undaunted spirit, which no adverse fortune could bend, much less break'. He survived invasion and enslavement, became the nemesis of the ruthless Maori chief Matioro, and eventually escaped to tell his tale. Published in 1873, *Koche, King of Pitt* is credited to Hugh Boyle Ewing, an American lawyer, diplomat and Civil War general. But how Ewing and Koche ever crossed paths remains a mystery, fascinating to this day.

Ewing's life story was no less adventurous. He was the third son of Thomas Ewing, a prominent lawyer and senator from Ohio who served in the cabinets of three presidents. In 1866, President Andrew Johnson appointed Hugh Boyle Ewing Minister to The Hague.

Ewing's travels must have taken him to the Pacific, where he either met Koche or someone who had recorded the Moriori's tale. Upon his return to America, Ewing settled in Lancaster, Ohio, where he penned Koche's memoir and went on to become an author of some regard.

Koche's story begins with the arrival of the merciless Matioro. In an early test of Moriori mettle, Matioro defiled a sacred Rekohu site. Koche was one of the first to respond, but was quickly overwhelmed. He and others were 'bound and hung by the feet from a tree, head downward, until nearly dead'. Koche survived and was taken as a slave by Matioro. Because he was 'deep-chested, with sinews of iron, and capable of immense exertion', he was put to work fishing. Koche patiently awaited his opportunity for revenge; it came when he landed a rare poisonous fish called a *moeeka*. He snuck the deadly catch into Matioro's dinner, stole a canoe and escaped

to uninhabited Pitt Island. However, Matioro had escaped death because his cook became suspicious of the fish. Enraged, Matioro scoured the island for his runaway slave until he was convinced that Koche must have killed himself rather than face his wrath.

For the next several years Koche lived a solitary life of peace and plenty on Pitt Island until an unscrupulous botanist made a pact with Matioro and took possession of the island, whereupon Koche was captured. Beaten and paraded as the defiled 'King of Pitt', Koche was returned to slavery. But Matioro, who had killed so many before, spared Koche's life; he 'felt his honour enlisted in the contest, had resolved to break, not kill him'. For four more years Koche laboured until he won Matioro's confidence. Then he again escaped to Pitt Island.

For nearly two years he hid deep within Pitt's interior. But Matioro hired a European slave hunter who tracked and captured Koche. He was enslaved again, but by now his exploits had brought secret respect from the Maori. Even Matioro couldn't deny the power of Koche's *mana* (respect or self-worth). Most importantly, the Moriori people took strength from their hero: 'he was regarded as one who, had their lot been less hopeless, would have proven the leader and saviour of the nation'.

In no time Koche again escaped, this time to a harbouring whaler. Matioro searched the ship in vain, even forcing the whaler captain to remain in port. When the ship was finally allowed to set sail, Koche came out of his 'mysterious' hiding place. His fate is unknown, but many believe that the heroic Moriori eventually made his way to America.

and crude wooden clubs. The Rauru held their ground, flanked on one side by the dark waters of the lagoon, Nunuku's imposing figure taking the measure of the advancing Wheteina. With a single war cry, the factions clashed. Many warriors were killed, cut down on the field or driven into the waters. Nunuku was suddenly sickened by the endless bloodshed. He could stand it no more. Marshalling his full fury, he forced his way between the warring ranks and commanded that the fighting cease. Overawed by the power and the rage of this elder chief, the two tribes separated without another blow being exchanged.

Nunuku ordered that all weapons be stacked. 'Palsied with a fear of the unknown, they followed', and the warriors piled their weapons. Then Nunuku did what no Moriori could ever have imagined: he ordered that the weapons be set alight and burned. As the smoke billowed from the pyre, mingling with the mist off the lagoon, 'no word was spoken in protest'.

The legend of Nunuku was passed from generation to generation and became the fundamental testament of the Moriori people. Finally, in the mid-1800s, an American travelling on a whaling ship in the Pacific recorded the story in the memoir of Koche, a Moriori folk hero and escaped slave (see 'Koche: King of Pitt', opposite). Koche would tell of Nunuku's next command:

> 'Rauru! Wheteina! Arise and meet!' They arose and met. 'Touch nose to nose!'
> Nose to nose was touched. 'Listen all! From now and forever, never again let
> there be war as this day has been! From this day on forget the taste of human
> flesh! Are you fish that eat their young?'

This would become known as Nunuku's law and established the cornerstone of Moriori social order for the next 500 years. Historical, archaeological and oral records bear out that this was an unprecedented period of peaceful cohabitation. But Nunuku's proclamation was more than a purely moral reaction to unabated warfare. He understood that for the Moriori to survive, they would have to marshal all their resources. They could not split their energy between the efforts of gathering and cultivating food and of continuously waging clan warfare. In addition, Nunuku proved to be a wise statesman: if warfare were abolished, some other means for settling disputes would have to replace it. So how would he enforce his mandate? His solution was worthy of King Solomon. From Koche's memoir:

> So it was there agreed that because men get angry and during such anger feel
> the will to strike, that so they may, but only with a rod the thickness of a

thumb and one stretch of the arms in length, and thrash away, but that on an abrasion of the hide, or first sign of blood, all should consider honour satisfied. 'And,' said the teller 'all obeyed! Why? Because of the Nunuku curse: "May your bowels rot the day you disobey!"'

Undoubtedly the island's distance from other warring societies helped to keep Nunuku's Law intact, but some Moriori must have bucked the dictate. If the fear of Nunuku's curse was not enough, shaming and ostracism were sure to bring most into line. But for those who sought satisfaction outside Nunuku's ritualised combat, dissent would prove costly. For in this highly interdependent society, only the hardiest souls could survive apart.

—

## A CHEERFUL RACE

AGGRESSION WAS NO LONGER SEEN AS A MEANS FOR INCREASING ONE'S *mana*, respect or self-worth. Instead, acts of communal good became the touchstone of Moriori worthiness. Hunting, in parties of upwards of fifty men drawn from different family groups, was conducted communally. The hunters shared equally in bounty and deficiency. Bravery was displayed by hunting sea lions or by athletic feats while fishing from slick, sea-washed rocks. A would-be husband proved his merit by diving into rough seas and producing three crayfish—one in each hand and a third in his mouth. The Moriori grew wise in the ways of living harmoniously with their environs: they husbanded the seal herds and removed the carcasses so as not to deter breeding; they cultivated wild plants and herbs, especially fernwood and kopi; and they harvested the eggs of migratory sea birds.

Most ingenious was the innovative *waka korari*, a wash-through raft made of bound reeds and a buoyant base of inflated kelp. The odd-looking craft, which became partly submerged, was much steadier in the rough seas and strong winds characteristic of their location. Although not an ocean-faring craft like the large dugout canoes that brought the original settlers, the *waka korari* was perfectly suited to moving among the local fishing and hunting grounds.

Moriori social structure was surprisingly democratic. Chiefs worked side by side with their followers in all the subsistence tasks. Any local or island-wide issues were resolved through the persuasive powers of a counsel of 'notable men'. Their forty-odd settlements were shifted seasonally within seven distinct districts. Seasonal boundaries provided each group with rights

Kiti Karaka Rewai and members of her family at the meeting house at Wairua on Chatham Island in the 1890s. So numerous are her descendants that she is sometimes referred to as the founding mother of the present Moriori of the Chathams.

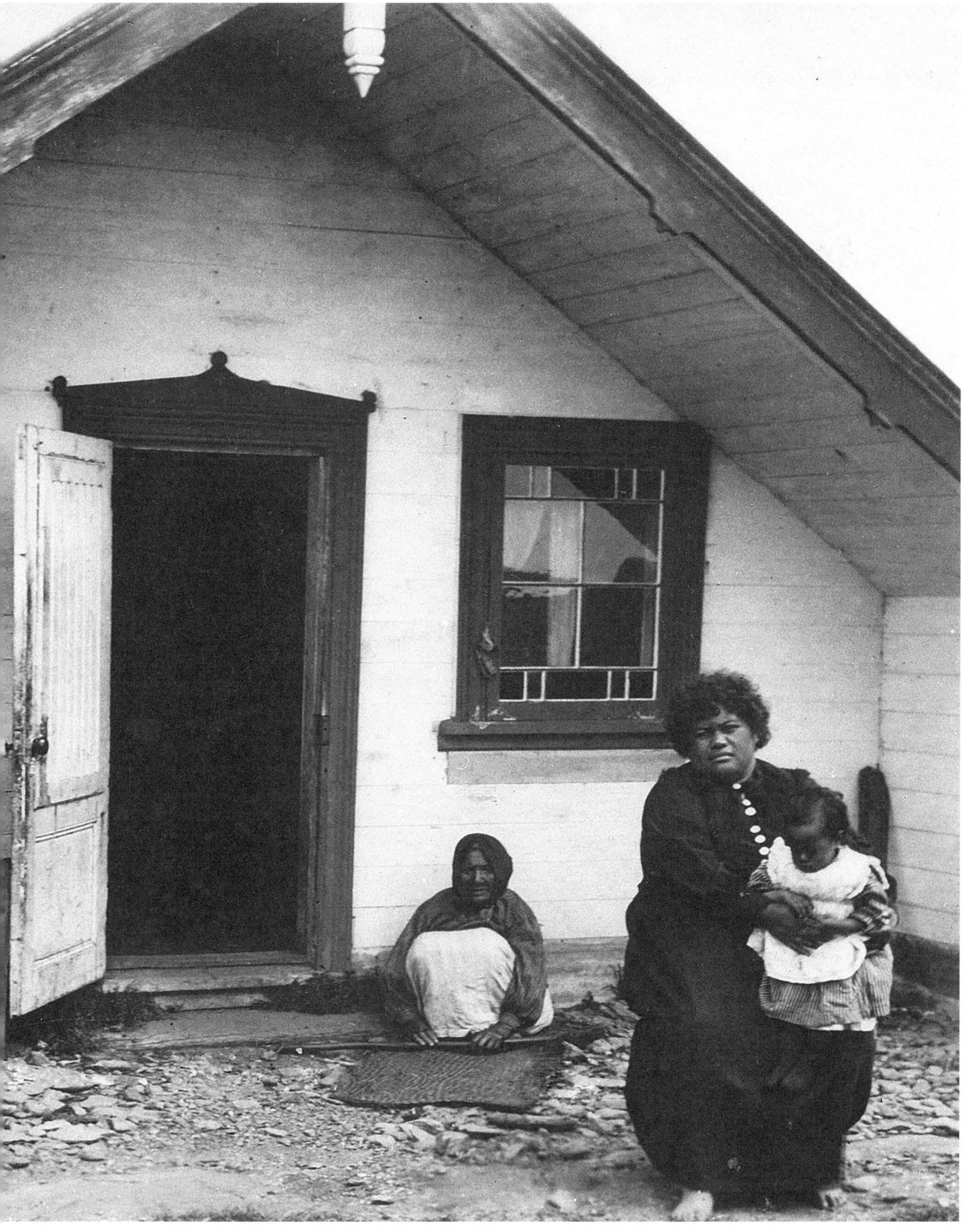

## KAI TANGATA: MAORI HUMAN FOOD

Cannibalism was a fundamental part of the ongoing warring life of the Maori. In fact, the eating of vanquished flesh was simply one component of *tikanga*, their 'way of doing things', that justified butchery. *Kai tangata*, or 'human food', was rarely eaten in peacetime. And though cannibalistic 'savages' have been much caricatured in popular history, the flesh-eating ways of the Maori were an essential aspect of their battle-hardened culture.

To the Maori, consuming human flesh offered an expedient solution to providing battle provisions. Between skirmishes, the attackers butchered and cooked the fallen. Sharp blades of obsidian were used to cut up the bodies and the meat was cooked in makeshift ovens, consisting of heated stones set in pits in the ground. Sometimes the flesh was prepared as a supply for the ongoing campaign; the meat de-boned and packed in small, individual flax baskets. Each warrior would receive his due ration.

Cannibalism also served a tactical role by raising the warrior frenzy for battle and by destroying their enemy's will to fight. Turning the enemy into so many cattle for slaughter dehumanised them and offered a primal motivation: hunger. The vanquished were often eaten in full view of the surviving enemy.

Consuming their enemies' flesh meant the Maori also consumed their *mana*. The Maori, like the Moriori, saw *mana* as the authority or respect an individual possessed. This could be gained by birthright or through bravery. To the Maori, cannibalism raised the victor's *mana* and decreased that of the vanquished. Victory, then, was not enough; butchering, cooking, consuming and turning their enemy into excrement was the ultimate humiliation and the most powerful means for strengthening their own *mana*.

to fishing, hunting and foraging. Their low-slung living structures, formed from bent saplings and thatched roofs, were spaced around a communal cooking area; these structures were easily disassembled and moved as weather and food-gathering needs dictated. Each settlement had no more than fifty close-knit inhabitants, with a total population consistently around 2000 people. Because of the high level of deadly infections, especially due to tooth decay, life expectancy was short, about twenty-two years. Even so, the Moriori practised a form of population control by castrating certain male babies.

Life, death and the protection of their gods were linked in their island home. The Moriori believed their gods lived in every element of Rekohu, from the plants and animals they ate, to the seasonal changes, to the very mountains they traversed. A first fish caught would always be offered to the fish gods Tangaroa and Pou. Out of respect, certain fowl could only be consumed indoors. They even believed in a kind of earthly reincarnation and so burned their dead and spread the ashes:

> Man springs from the earth as the flower springs: they return him to his mother … She drinks in with the rain the ashes of her children, man and flower, and sends them forth again after a season of repose to reign over and to beautify the land.

And so the demanding but peaceful life of the Moriori continued in isolation for centuries. 'They are a cheerful race,' reported Lieutenant William Broughton, commander of HMS *Chatham* and the first European to make contact with the Moriori, 'our conversation frequently exciting bursts of laughter among them'. Their way of life fostered an inborn sense of trust and cooperation. Their warring and cannibalistic ways were but a hazy memory, their days still structured by Nunuku's pacifist decree. Sadly, they would soon find themselves vulnerable to some of the worst atrocities visited on any race.

—

### 'THUNDER AND LIGHTNING DESCENDED THE MOUNTAIN'

THE ARRIVAL OF THE 'SUN PEOPLE' IN THEIR MAJESTIC 'WINGED CANOE' in 1791 was an accident of fate. Sailing in convoy with the explorer George Vancouver, in command of the warship *Discovery* on a mapping expedition of New Zealand's eastern coast, Lieutenant William Robert Broughton captained the British Navy brig *Chatham*. He was separated from the convoy and blown far south by a November squall. After weeks of trying to rejoin the *Discovery*, Broughton came upon 'a strange land' rising out of the mist. No such island existed on any Admiralty map, so Broughton dutifully surveyed the island, anchored and assembled a landing party of eight men.

Broughton and his crew, though apprehensive about the meeting, were at least familiar with Polynesian natives. The Moriori, however, in their centuries of cultural isolation, had never encountered people unlike themselves. They thought the imposing canoe in Kaingaroa Harbour had sailed down from the sun, its billowing sails like the wings of a giant albatross, its rigging an ensnaring fishing net. With Broughton's brass buttons glinting in the sun, these strange beings coming ashore generated mostly bemusement; the Moriori weren't even sure of the strangers' sex.

Accounts differ on what transpired when the landing party came ashore. There was immediate confusion: Broughton's men may have simply misunderstood the exuberant gestures of the Moriori; the Moriori may have become agitated by a sailor's handling of a prized fishing net. Whatever the reason, the outnumbered crewmen felt threatened and opened fire with their muskets. Tamakaroro, the nephew of a chief, was killed instantly by a musket ball through the heart. The remaining Moriori scattered into the forest. Emboldened, the British planted their flag, christened Kaingaroa Harbour 'Skirmish Bay', and retreated to their ship.

The Moriori convened a council where the elders admonished those who had taken part in the hostilities. They did not blame the sun people. They noted that since the body of Tamakaroro had been left behind, the visitors clearly were not cannibals. The elders decided that the Moriori's actions had dishonoured Nunuku's law and concluded that should their visitors return, they would be greeted with gestures of peace.

When Broughton and his crew next came ashore, they were presented with a green palm frond. The high chief removed his flax cape and placed it over Broughton's shoulders. The British reciprocated with gifts of trinkets and potatoes in the hope of atoning in some small measure for the death of Tamakaroro. But Broughton had performed the rite of taking possession of the island in the name of King George III, utterly ignoring the Moriori rights of ownership. From here on it would be known as Chatham Island, named for Broughton's ship, in turn named for the Earl of Chatham.

Years later, Koche would remember his father's account of watching the British sail off: 'The atmosphere became dark, sultry and gloomy and thunder and lightning descended the mountain and pursued the retreating strangers.' This dark vision was prescient. Within a few years, the reports from Broughton and his crew, and the availability of new charts of the area, led to an influx of whalers and seal hunters.

Seal furs were extremely lucrative on the Chinese market and there seemed no end to the supply on Chatham. Pelts fetched 15 shillings apiece in Canton; a boat was commonly loaded with over 2000 skins, worth £1,500, an unthinkable sum for the time. But the seal supply was in fact limited, as the Moriori had known for generations through their careful husbandry. By 1830 the seals were gone, slaughtered by the thousands; the Moriori had lost both a major food supply and, more importantly, their main source of warm clothing. Many of the sea birds whose eggs had long sustained the Moriori were killed, or driven off by a plague of cats and rats that had jumped ship from vessels in the harbour.

The whalers and sealers found the islands particularly attractive because of the peaceful and welcoming nature of the Moriori. But with them came the blights of these more 'advanced' interlopers: influenza, venereal diseases and alcohol. Exposure to flu alone would kill off nearly a quarter of the Moriori. Yet they remained true to their pacifist ideals. Unfortunately, their friendly and cheerful nature was interpreted as simplicity; they were branded as backward, simple-minded, and thus inferior. Their way of cooperation and generosity left them open to abuse, and their lands and their ability to sustain themselves were slowly stripped away.

Things were about to get much worse.

——

## INVASION

By 1835 there were about 1600 Moriori on Chatham Island. Most of their contacts with outsiders had been friendly. However, in the North Island of New Zealand, the Maori had been engaged in fierce trench warfare with their white invaders since 1833, an extension of a decade of tribal war and territorial skirmishes involving the Ngati Mutunga and Ngati Tama of the Taranaki region. Warfare had become habitual and the cause of countless forced migrations down the east coast. Now the Ngati Mutunga chief Matioro, forced from his ancestral lands by the Europeans, set his sights on Chatham Island.

On 19 November 1835, the brig *Lord Rodney*, out of Wellington, arrived on Chatham, chartered by Matioro and sailing heavy with 500 armed Taranaki Maori of both the Ngati Mutunga and Ngati Tama tribes. The eight-day crossing had been difficult with overcrowding and water scarce. Had the Moriori been a warlike people and suspected this sudden influx, they could have killed the weakened Maori with ease. However, true to their nature, they tended to the ill and led the desiccated to water. Within weeks, the *Lord Rodney* returned with an additional 400 Maori.

The Maori leader, Matioro, was a product of a battle-hardened warrior culture. Standing 155 centimetres (5 feet, 1 inch) and weighing 90 kilograms (198 pounds), his face pocked with tattoos, he was an imposing figure among the diminutive Moriori. Described by Europeans as ruthless and arrogant, 'a New Zealand chief armed to the teeth', he had led his forces in failed campaigns and costly retreats. Now his arrival on Chatham was met with dread:

His hair, carefully combed and oiled, was tied up on the crown of his head, and surrounded by a fillet of white feathers, and from his ears protruded bunches of soft down. Evidently a man of power, accustomed to command … The future darkened as he walked the beach.

Without warning, Matioro led his forces in the invasive *takahi*, the 'walking the land' ritual. War parties armed with muskets, clubs, spears and tomahawks spread out through the Moriori settlements. If the invaders wanted the land, they simply took it, declaring the inhabitants were now their subjects. At first, the Moriori hoped the interlopers would simply leave, as they had in the past. But then the killings started.

The Moriori had called a council to discuss their response to the Maori *takahi*. Many of the younger men wished to take up arms and defend their land. But the elders held sway, reminding them that their *mana* was not determined by force but by adherence to the ancient law of Nunuku. After much debate, it was decided they would welcome the Maori. They left the council intending to make a peace offering—but never got the chance. Suspecting that the Moriori gathering was a war council, the Maori lay in wait. Even if the Moriori had been able to sue for peace, the Maori would probably have taken it as weakness and savaged them all the same.

The ambush was coordinated, merciless and complete. Those who were not immediately slain were bound and held for later slaughter, many by being impaled on spikes and left to die slowly on the beach. In the massacre's first wave, 267 Moriori were butchered.

Nearly all the dead were eaten. Most were carved up where they lay, the best parts taken and cooked in makeshift ovens of hot rocks, the carcasses left to the dogs. Others were held as food stocks, to become meals on a later day (see '*Kai tangata*: Maori human food', page 76). The scene must have been one of surreal horror for a people who had abandoned violence for so long that it was hardly a part of their vocabulary. And yet they held fast to their non-violent convictions, even as they faced certain death.

Those who were not killed were taken as slaves. Others were held as food stocks, like so many pigs or cattle, carelessly tomahawked when they no longer served a purpose. Moriori children were particularly prized by the Maori chiefs for ceremonial meals. Many Moriori were overcome by grief, clearly convinced that their gods had abandoned them, and simply died of despair.

## TE WHITI-O-RONGOMAI AND THE
## MAORI NON-VIOLENT MOVEMENT

At the same time that the Taranaki Maori invaded Chatham Island and enslaved the Moriori people, they were engaged in escalating conflict with the British colonists in New Zealand. For decades they were caught up in a continuous cycle of combat throughout the Taranaki region. Now, as the European colonists seized more and more Maori land, the tribal warriors had dug in for a long siege, perfecting a kind of trench warfare that utilised reinforced stockades called *pa*. This extended conflict was costly on both sides. What the colonists would come to call the New Zealand Wars, the Maori more aptly called Te Rire Pakeha, or 'the White Man's Anger.'

But one Maori prophet and spiritual leader, Te Whiti-o-Rongomai, influenced equally by his Maori beliefs and the teachings of Christian missionaries, arrived at a different approach to the white man's anger. He began preaching non-violent opposition. 'Guns and powder,' he told his ever-growing number of followers, 'shall no longer be the protection of man. Our weapon is forbearance, patience, non-resistance. God is our refuge and our strength.' Peace, goodwill, and self-sacrifice became the principles of his life and he taught Maori warriors that defending their rights without using weapons was good *mana*.

Throughout the 1870s and 1880s, the village of Parihaka, in the Taranaki region of the North Island, was the focal point of Te Whiti-o-Rongomai's passive resistance movement. More than 400 followers were arrested and imprisoned without trial, some for as long as sixteen months, because they attempted to cultivate their own land. He convinced over 2000 Maori to welcome British soldiers, even offering them food and drink as they raided and destroyed their villages. The whites weren't sure what to make of this mystic leader. He was prone to indecipherable outbursts and labelled a fanatic and a lunatic. But his devout madness in the service of passive resistance prevented a Maori massacre and ultimately protected far more land than would have been saved by continued warfare.

Te Whiti-o-Rongomai must certainly have known of the peaceful Moriori of Chatham Island. And he was surely aware of the subjugation and misery they suffered under the cruel reign of his own people. Whether he was fully aware of its historical irony is unclear. But at least one small gesture of solidarity may be seen in the fact that Te Whiti-o-Rongomai always wore the white feathers of the albatross as a symbol of peace and hospitality.

FOR THE NEXT THREE DECADES, THE MORIORI SUFFERED TERRIBLY, THEIR population continually thinned by indiscriminate killings at the hands of their Maori masters. They were kept from marrying, or having children, with anyone other than Maori. Many women were taken back to New Zealand to become wives of Maori men. Disease, abuse and despair wiped out two-thirds of the remaining Moriori, hastened by the renewal of warfare between the Ngati Mutunga and Ngati Tama on the island. By 1842, this latest tribal war ended with the Treaty of Waitangi, brokered by missionaries from the Church of England who had converted nearly all of the Maori en masse. The treaty promised land rights to the Maori tribes but failed to address the concerns of the Moriori. Although their enslavement continued, the Christian conversions did at least bring to an end the random killings.

It would take another twenty years for the Moriori to gain their freedom. By 1862 only 101 Moriori of unmixed ancestry remained. But this diminished people remained vocal and adamant in their passive resistance. They continued to press the New Zealand government, which now had authority over the island, to take notice of their plight. Finally, in 1863, they did. This began with the arrival of Captain William Esdaile, the new resident magistrate. He announced formally that Moriori slavery would no longer be tolerated. It took several more years to enact fully, but all remaining Moriori finally gained their freedom.

Slowly the Moriori began to see a revival of their *mana*. Their condition was greatly improved by a large exodus of Taranaki Maori back to New Zealand in the later 1860s, for life in their homeland had become much more attractive. The New Zealand Land Court was conducting hearings and requiring attendance by Maori tribal members for any claims of territorial ownership. In addition, with an irony not lost on history, the advocacy of non-violent resistance to the New Zealand government by the Maori mystic and prophet Te Whiti-o-Rongomai was proving to both influence the Land Court and to revive Maori faith (see 'Te Whiti-o-Rongomai and the Maori non-violent movement', page 81). Maori were flocking to the Parihaka region, the Taranaki Maori's spiritual centre and seat of Te Whiti-o-Rongomai. Just as chartered ships had brought the invading Maori to Rekohu over thirty years earlier, they now carried them away.

Moriori numbers would continue to dwindle until the death of 'the last Moriori', Tommy Solomon, in 1933. But that is not how their story ends. Today there are over 7000 Moriori of mixed ancestry on Chatham Island.

Their culture, language and heritage are enjoying a renaissance and have become the focus of renewed international interest. The establishment of the Waitangi Tribunal, a permanent commission of inquiry, accelerated action to satisfy land claims against the New Zealand government. The Moriori refused to abandon their land. They never broke Nunuku's Law. And so, for centuries on end, their *mana* has remained intact. They are, once again, firmly established as *tchakat henu*, the indigenous, peaceful people of Rekohu.

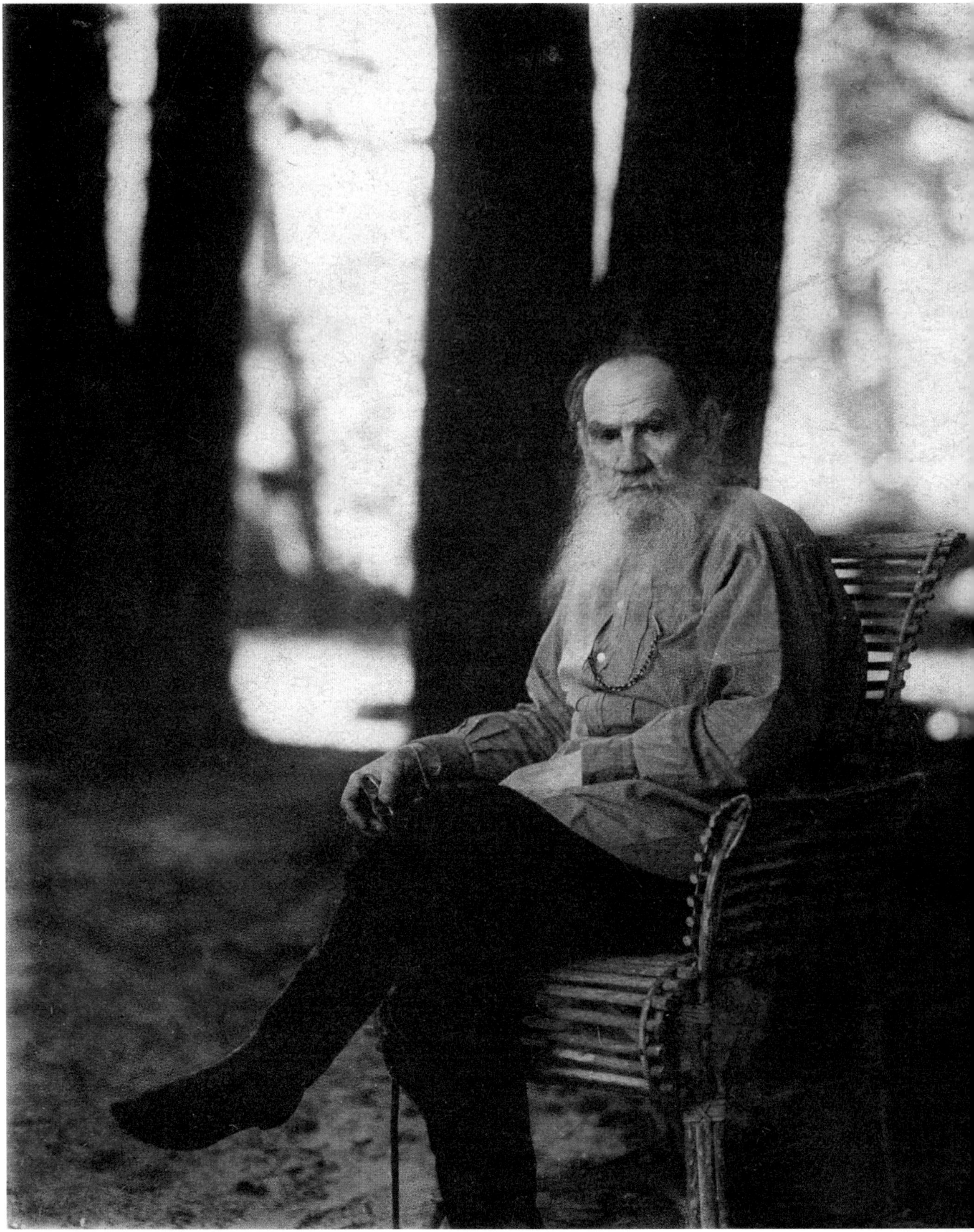

# LEO TOLSTOY: PEACE AND WAR

Count Lev Nikolayevich Tolstoy was not only one of the most important writers of all time but a moral philosopher and pacifist who influenced many of the major social reforms of the twentieth century. Author of the literary masterpieces *War and Peace* and *Anna Karenina*, he also published books, essays and articles on Christianity, passive resistance and human rights, as well as progressive educational materials, many of which were censored or banned. He renounced his titles and aristocratic rights, rejected the authority of any institution that used coercion, and established a personal religion based on the teachings of Jesus. He won worldwide respect but was also excommunicated by the Russian Orthodox Church.

A transformative figure in history, Leo Tolstoy's life was also one of great personal transformation. An indifferent and mediocre student, he emerged as Russia's greatest writer. A gambler and pleasure-seeking aristocrat who squandered his family wealth, he remoulded himself into a great moral philosopher and champion of the underprivileged. And, from being a hardened military man he underwent a spiritual conversion to become a Christian pacifist and one of the most influential founders of the modern peace movement.

Leo Tolstoy in the garden at Yasnaya Polyana in 1908.

# A MAGIC GREEN STICK

WHEN LEO TOLSTOY WAS A YOUNG BOY, HIS ADORED OLDER BROTHER Nikolay told him a fantastic tale. Nikolay had a hidden secret. Buried in a glen beside a roaring ravine on the Tolstoy estate of Yasnaya Polyana was a magic green stick. Carved into the stick were magical words that could destroy all the evil in men's hearts and bring peace to the world. Little Leo, born in 1828, searched high and low, and of course never found the magic stick. But the story inspired him, and his entire life he sought the secret to peace and virtue.

Nikolay may have told Leo the story to help ease his sorrow, for the boy had lost nearly everyone who cared for him as a child. With each illness and death, he and his siblings were passed from relative to relative. His mother died when he was just two years old and his grandmother Aleksandra and his distant cousin Toinette, who little Leo loved, stepped in to raise him. Soon afterward, both his father, Count Nikolay Ilyich Tolstoy, and his grandmother died. The count's older sister Aline became the children's guardian and split them up. The youngest, including Leo, were cared for by Toinette at Yasnaya Polyana; the older children, including Nikolay, stayed with Aunt Aline in Moscow. Within a few short years, Aline also passed away, and Pelagya, another of his father's sisters and lifelong enemy of Toinette, became guardian. Aunt Pelagya took the younger children away from Toinette to live at her home in Kazan, along the Volga River.

For Leo this was the hardest blow of all. Toinette had become his spiritual mother and he missed her terribly. Pelagya forced French and German tutors on him but he was a lacklustre student. Despite this, at fifteen, in 1843, he went to Kazan University. He started by studying languages, expecting to become a diplomat, but he found his studies difficult and switched to law, only to drop out a few years later. Once he came of age, he returned to Yasnaya Polyana, claimed his share of the inheritance, and invited Toinette to live with him once again.

In his earlier years, Tolstoy enjoyed all the privileges of the Russian nobility. But he also followed in the footsteps of his father and grandfather, who were both heavy gamblers, losing huge sums at cards. Leo was forced to pay off his gambling losses by selling large tracts of the estate and logging huge swathes of forest that had been promised to his serfs. Deeply conflicted by the hardships his debauchery was causing, he tried to become a model patron to the peasants under his authority, but soon fell back into his old habits, gambling, drinking and whoring.

His brother Nikolay was by now a decorated military lieutenant in the Russian army. In 1848, while on leave from service in the Caucasus, he returned to Yasnaya Polyana. Nikolay could see that Leo was wasting his life and convinced him to join the military. The brothers journeyed by train for days until they reached the front in the Caucasus Mountains, where Tolstoy signed on as a *Junker* or gentleman volunteer. All too soon, however, bored with the regimented life of a soldier, he found escape by drinking, chasing women and hunting—occasionally joining the battle as an artillery spotter.

Salvation was about to come from an unexpected direction. About this time, Tolstoy began a lifelong practice of recording highly personal and obsessively honest entries in his journal. He wrote in great detail of his deeply thought observations on the conditions of his life and all that took place around him. His diaries formed the basis of his master works and the record of his spiritual awakening. He later wrote in his book *Confessions*:

> I cannot recall those [early] years without horror, loathing, and heart-rending pain. I killed people in war, challenged men to duels with the purpose of killing them, and lost at cards; I squandered the fruits of the peasants' toil and then had them executed; I was a fornicator and a cheat. Lying, stealing, promiscuity of every kind, drunkenness, violence, murder—there was not a crime I did not commit … Thus I lived for ten years.

## SEVASTOPOL

Like that of most soldiers, Tolstoy's military life was one of great boredom, punctuated by moments of chilling violence. During the lulls, he wrote. His first completed work was the autobiographical sketch *Childhood*, published anonymously in 1852 to great acclaim. He started *The Cossacks*, writing about his experiences in war with an honesty that was uncommon for the time. He published the short story 'The Raid', which was heavily censored for its unambiguous anti-war sentiment, chronicling his experience with Nikolay's unit against Chechen tribesmen. He wrote: 'Can it be that there is not room for all men on this beautiful earth under these immeasurable starry heavens? Can it be possible that in the midst of this entrancing Nature feelings of hatred, vengeance, or the desire to exterminate their fellows can endure in the souls of men?'

The following year he transferred to Sevastopol in southern Ukraine, the scene of some of the most brutal and bloody fighting of the Crimean War, one of a series of long-running conflicts between various European powers jostling for control over the Holy Lands and the protection of Orthodox Christians as the Ottoman Empire declined.

On the Crimean Peninsula, Russian forces were bogged down by a yearlong siege of Sevastopol, where they took considerable losses to their navy. In the midst of some of the fiercest fighting, Tolstoy continued to write, capturing the war in a series of stories that would become *The Sevastopol Sketches*. The tales were unusual for the brutal honesty of their reportage and revealed the beginnings of Tolstoy's distinct vision of war as the expression of man's greatest and worst virtues, a state of confusion, heroism and utter waste. With their publication, Tolstoy's identity was revealed for the first time.

When Sevastopol fell, Tolstoy was asked to report on the final artillery assaults, which had included the scuttling of a number of Russia's cannon-laden ships of the line. He delivered his findings to the authorities in St Petersburg. Now famous for his war stories, he was received as a hero and celebrity at the highest ranks of Russian society. Tolstoy was ill at ease: troubled by his

## PACIFISM MEETS ANARCHY

The peasant movement Leo Tolstoy inspired was the first pacifist offshoot of anarchism, later labelled 'anarcho–pacifism', a term that describes a number of movements which support anarchism but reject the use of violence to achieve those goals. Anarchism is itself a widely defined movement opposed to state and government control, supporting societal organisation on a voluntary and cooperative basis. Tolstoy argued that any anti-government movement must be non-violent, because it is by definition opposed to the coercive tactics of the state. Tolstoyans were mostly made up of recently freed serfs who set up pacifist–anarchist communities, adhering to an absolutist interpretation of Christianity.

The refusal by Russian anarchists to recognise tsarist authority led to severe persecution and expulsion to Siberia. When the peasant revolts of 1905 turned violent, Tolstoy rejected their methods and refused to give his support. Anarcho–pacifists were subjected to further repression after the Bolshevik Revolution in 1917 for their continued opposition to the authority of the new Marxist government. Many were killed or exiled under the purges of Lenin and Stalin.

Tolstoy's non-resistant form of anarchism spawned other movements and inspired other pacifist–anarchists throughout the twentieth century. He was a great influence on Mohandas Gandhi's non-violent resistance movement in India. Ferdinand Domela Nieuwenhuis, the first socialist elected to the Dutch Parliament, espoused a form of pacifist anarchy and was a key proponent of his country's social reforms. Ammon Hennacy, the American pacifist, anarchist and social reformer, played a pivotal role in establishing the anti-war Catholic Worker Movement later in the twentieth century.

conflicting values, he continued to gamble, losing vast amounts. At the same time, however, he began to fight back against his own sense of 'criminal sloth'. He started to imagine a new 'practical religion' that could be 'divested of faith and mysteries'. These observations, along with a growing mistrust of the state, would form the seeds of 'Tolstoyism', his Christian anarcho–pacifist beliefs (see 'Pacifism meets anarchy', opposite).

❧

## MASTERPIECES

WITH THE END OF THE WAR, TOLSTOY TRAVELLED TO FRANCE, SWITZERLAND and Germany in 1857. His exposure to the West motivated him to help modernise Russia on his return. He saw education as the key. Before beginning his travels, in a fit of guilt over how his corrupt behaviour had harmed his serfs, he had made a half-hearted attempt to free them, but he had not won their trust and they refused his offer, sure it was a trick. So on his return he set to work establishing schools for the peasants. In all, he established thirteen schools on the Yasnaya Polyana estate, all with a cohesive libertarian bent. He wrote progressive language and maths texts and distributed them for free.

Entering the happiest period of his life, Tolstoy now met and fell in love with seventeen-year-old Sonya Behrs. Beautiful, intelligent, just half his age, she was a good match for Tolstoy's strong-willed aspirations. She was also enchanted by his growing reputation as a writer; he had just published *Youth*, the third volume after *Childhood* and *Boyhood* in his autobiographical trilogy. Before they married, Tolstoy insisted she read his personal diaries and know everything about his sullied past. He wished to keep no secrets from her. Although devastated by the revelations and frightened by his internal battles, Sonya was also forgiving. They married in 1862 and throughout their long marriage would allow each other to read their most personal diary entries, stirring jealousies and conflict right up until Tolstoy's death.

The first decade of their marriage was one of great happiness, and also proved to be Tolstoy's golden age as a writer. Within a year, Sonya gave birth to Sergey, the first of their twelve children. Still a teenager, Sonya took control of Tolstoy's life, proving to be an efficient manager of their estate. She also convinced him to close the schools he had set up for his serfs, for their libertarian emphasis had raised the suspicion of the tsar's secret police. Sonya persuaded Tolstoy to focus on his writing instead, and they settled into a routine: Tolstoy would write all day and Sonya would recopy his drafts at night. Later he would reveal how much he resented Sonya for convincing him to close the schools and abandon 'the supreme goal of his life'.

Over the next dozen years, Tolstoy composed his two greatest novels. The first drew on all the people, places, events and observations of his life, an epic tale of five families poured out against the backdrop of the Napoleonic invasion of Russia and serialised over four years in the magazine *Russian Messenger*. The first instalment of the novel, then called *1805*, was published in 1865. Tolstoy populated his story with some 559 historical and fictional characters, moving from the court of Alexander to the headquarters of Napoleon to the battlefields of Austerlitz and Borodino. Exploring the themes of predestination and free will, he threw in nearly everyone who had come into his life, including relations on both sides of his family. His detailed and realistic depictions of everything from societal balls to inexplicable battles, births, deaths as well as Russian social structures and psychology all marked a new pinnacle in the development of world literature. When Tolstoy published the full novel in 1869, he renamed it *War and Peace*, after *La Guerre et la Paix* by the French anarchist Pierre-Joseph Proudhon. The masterpiece was met with an outpouring of critical and popular excitement previously unseen in Russia.

In the intervening years to 1869, Tanya, Ilya and Leo were born. With *War and Peace* now behind him, Tolstoy became restless, and battled with despair and depression. He started several writing projects but abandoned them, then bought a stud farm in Samara and again took on the role of benefactor, working alongside his serfs in the fields. He also returned to his early calling in education, creating a controversial series of primers to teach literacy.

In 1873, he began work on his next and perhaps greatest work, *Anna Karenina*. Serialised in the *Russian Messenger* between 1875 and 1877, the tragic story of aristocratic Anna's adulterous affair with Count Vronsky gripped the nation. The novel's intertwining plots, dealing with Anna, who is undone by her passions, and Levin, a stand-in for Tolstoy (Levin literally means 'of Lev', Leo's first name in Russian) who finds happiness in rustic toil and religious faith, reflected the strains in Tolstoy's own conflicts. Many of the themes in *Anna Karenina* came directly from the great transformations that were taking hold in his life.

The novel's opening line is often quoted: 'Happy families are all alike; every unhappy family is unhappy in its own way.' This is a clear reflection of the sadness and personal tragedy Tolstoy endured over this period. By 1873 Marya and Petya, his fifth and six children, had been born, but at the end of the year little Petya died suddenly of croup. The following year his beloved cousin Toinette passed away, and his seventh child, baby Nicolas, died before the age of one. Shortly afterwards, Sonya delivered their eighth child, a girl, who died soon after birth. These deaths weighed heavily on Tolstoy and slowed the course of his writing. In addition, he was coming to identify more with the peasants working his lands, feelings which he poured into the character of Levin. His full conversion came when he turned away from his aristocratic upbringing and renounced his position in Russian society.

Tolstoy now struggled to complete *Anna Karenina* because he felt the story of Anna's aristocracy was unworthy of the telling. He wrote to his friend N.N. Strakhov: 'My God, if only someone would finish *Anna Karenina* for me. Unbearably repulsive.' With the outbreak of the Serbian War in 1877, Tolstoy became disheartened by the war fever gripping the country. Perhaps more clearly than at any other time, he was consumed by a new sense of the evil of violence. He found solace in Christ's gospels and especially the pacifist teachings of the Sermon on the Mount, working these views into the final instalment of *Anna Karenina* by condemning the Serbian War. Levin says near the end:

> Oh, my theory's this: war is on one side such a beastly, cruel, and awful thing, that no one man, not to speak of a Christian, can individually take upon himself the responsibility of beginning wars; that can only be done by a government, which is called upon to do this, and is driven inevitably into war.

The editor of the *Russian Messenger* demanded changes because he found the ending unpatriotic. Tolstoy refused, and the final chapter was published only as an editorial summary, purged of any anti-war rhetoric. A year later, the novel was published in its entirety, Tolstoy's original ending intact.

With the completion of *Anna Karenina*, Tolstoy renounced all his earlier fiction. As he explained, 'I wrote everything into *Anna Karenina* and nothing was left.' In fact, quite the contrary was true—just as his spiritual conversion was transforming his life, he entered an immensely prolific period of writing on behalf of peace, faith and equality.

## THE KINGDOM OF GOD IS WITHIN YOU

Put off by the trappings of the Russian Orthodox Church and the coercive authority of the state, Tolstoy came to see himself more as a sage and a spiritual leader than a novelist, and during the 1880s wrote a great number of essays, articles and stories that outlined a new kind of theology, critical of both the government and the Church. He wrote first *A Criticism of Dogmatic Theology* and later, obsessed with ridding himself of the guilt he held from his early life of excess, *Confessions*. Both attacked the Church for what he saw as distortions of Christ's message. He wrote an interpretation of the New Testament gospels, reordering them and compiling them into a single narrative called *Union and Translation of the Four Gospels*. All of these works were heavily censored by the state, in conjunction with the Church, and were read only in their full form through an underground system that distributed and smuggled them out of the country.

In 1884 he completed *What I Believe*, an ambitious work that set out to explain his combination of Christian pacifism, non-resistance, anarchism and agrarian utopianism in one volume. He was, by this time, being watched closely by the secret police. The book was banned in Russia and copies were seized from the printer; but the manuscript was passed from hand to hand until it could be smuggled out of Russia and published in Western Europe. In the introduction, the translator Constantine Popoff summed up Tolstoy's state at the time:

> During this period he has withdrawn from the world and its vanities and has devoted himself to the study of the teachings of Christ. Having become profoundly impressed with the Saviour's words concerning the duty of living a life of unselfish toil for the benefit of others, he has been endeavouring in a practical way to carry out his Master's commands and has devoted himself to ministering to his fellows.

By this time Tolstoy wished to live as an ascetic, and in the same year made his first attempt to give up his estates and live as a poor peasant. He was supported in this desire by a new influence in his life, Vladimir Chertkov, a wealthy officer he had met the previous year. Chertkov was so moved by Tolstoy's writings that he became a driving force behind a Tolstoyan movement. Sonya, however, was not about to accede to this wish. Since the publication of *Anna Karenina*, she had given birth to four more children and buried another child, Alexis, only four years old. Family relations were strained; the more the world saw Tolstoy as virtuous, the more Sonya saw him as villainous, and she was not about to let him give away their fortune. Eventually they struck an unhappy compromise: Tolstoy handed over to Sonya the rights to all his works prior to 1881 and control of their properties. For the remainder of his life, they would be at odds over his estates and the fortune provided by his works. Sonya could never understand how Tolstoy would put the concerns of the peasants before those of his family.

## ADIN BALLOU AND HOPEDALE

Tolstoy and the American Unitarian minister Adin Ballou corresponded in 1890, over the last year of Ballou's life. A pacifist, abolitionist and advocate of non-violent opposition to authority, Ballou's theories made quite an impression on Tolstoy, who wrote in *The Kingdom of God is Within You* that, '[I] would have thought Ballou's work would have been well known, and the ideas expressed by him would have been either accepted or refuted; but such has not been the case.' In 1839, Ballou and a few ministerial colleagues composed 'The Standard of Practical Christianity' as a radical pacifist extension of their ministry. Believing that any organisation relying on force to keep order was unjust, he and his followers withdrew from the morally corrupt 'government of the world'. In 1841, the sect purchased a farm in Milford, Massachusetts which they called Hopedale, where they established a utopian community dedicated to their spiritual and moral principles.

In 1846 Ballou published *Christian Non-Resistance*, his main treatise on pacifism. In it, he stressed that the choice not to participate in government was in no way an endorsement of rebellion against authority by force. 'We cannot employ carnal weapons,' Ballou wrote, 'nor any physical violence whatsoever, not even for the preservation of our lives. We cannot render evil for evil ... nor do otherwise than "love our enemies".' The Hopedale community lasted only until 1856 when several key members withdrew their financial support. Eventually, the group was assimilated back into the mainstream Unitarian church.

Unlike most other Christian pacifist leaders, Ballou opposed the American Civil War and supported conscientious objectors. After the war, in 1866, he helped found the Universal Peace Union, an anti-war and disarmament organisation which condemned American imperialism and military conscription. Ballou remained an active Unitarian minister and peace advocate for the remainder of his life. Although Ballou was largely forgotten after his death, Tolstoy was instrumental in introducing his pacifist writings to Mohandas Gandhi and, much later, Martin Luther King Jr.

All his life, Tolstoy was uneasy about his aristocratic standing and his ownership of serfs. Through much of his youth, he grew increasingly aware of the conditions that made their lives so miserable. Since 1679, when Russia formally converted its agricultural slaves into serfs, they were bound to their landowners, making it a criminal offence to flee. Although slavery remained an institution until 1723 when Peter the Great finally converted the last of his estate slaves into serfs, landowners still maintained near autonomous control over them. The landowners could sell individual serfs while keeping ownership of their property and family. By the mid-1800s there were more than twenty-three million privately held serfs in Russia, more than one in three of the population. At the same time, the United States had about four million slaves, England and Brazil each had under a million. Tsar Alexander II freed all Russian serfs in 1861, fearing a peasant uprising, especially after his serf army sustained such heavy casualties in the Crimean War. While Alexander understood that reform was necessary, the terms of reform were harsh and the peasants' wellbeing remained wholly dependent on the landed aristocracy. To this end, Tolstoy attempted to empower his former serfs through education and his Christian anarchist views.

The foundation of this belief came from his strict interpretation of the gospels and especially the Sermon on the Mount, from which he took five moral obligations: the avoidance of anger; refusal to take oaths; abstinence from sex outside of marriage; renouncement of all violent resistance to evil; and the love of one's enemy. He further developed these precepts in *What Then Must We Do?* in 1886 and, most significantly, *The Kingdom of God is Within You* in 1894. The latter, his most influential book on passive resistance, was published in Germany after being banned in Russia. Drawing on personal observations, theology, anarchist theory and even the 'Practical Christianity' of American Adin Ballou, this small book suggests a means for societal organisation based on non-violent opposition and pacifist Christian beliefs (see 'Adin Ballou and Hopedale, page 93). The title comes from a passage in Luke's gospel:

Once, having been asked by the Pharisees when the kingdom of God would come, Jesus replied, 'The kingdom of God does not come with your careful observation, nor will people say, "Here it is", or "There it is", because the kingdom of God is within you' (Luke 17:20–21; King James version).

Tolstoy had come to believe fully that the admonitions of Christ offered the only hope for humanity. He now had the trust of his former serfs, and feared their latent hostility was driving Russia towards violent revolution. He prophetically explained in the book how this would fail to make things any better, a prophecy which proved true for most of Russia's disadvantaged following the revolutions of 1905 and 1917, civil war, and oppression under communist rule.

Tolstoy's blueprint for passive resistance had a great influence on another key twentieth century reformer. It was *The Kingdom of God is Within You* that first inspired Mohandas K. Gandhi to consider non-violent resistance. At the time, Gandhi was a young lawyer and activist living in South Africa and had not yet started his great work in India. Several years later, in 1908, Tolstoy wrote the short essay 'A Letter to a Hindu', which outlined how the Indian people might overthrow colonial British rule through passive resistance. When Gandhi read the essay, he wrote to Tolstoy asking for permission to translate it into his native language of Gujarati and publish it. The two corresponded throughout the final year of Tolstoy's life, largely about the practical and theological application of passive non-violence. The last letter Tolstoy wrote before his death was to Gandhi.

As Tolstoy's stature grew, his rejection of state and Church authority brought increasing pressure on him and his family. Fearing that sending him into exile might incite a peasant revolt, the tsarist authorities turned their attention to Tolstoy's followers. Many, including Chertkov, were persecuted and expelled from Russia. This was a particular blow to Tolstoy, as Chertkov had become much more than a follower: a confidant, close friend and trusted publisher. Over the next couple of years, Chertkov and other Tolstoyan acolytes in exile began distributing his pacifist writings through a publishing arm in London called the Free Age Press. Tolstoy, however, withdrew from active participation in any of this. He fully embraced non-resistance and a kind of peasant-like agrarian asceticism that precluded meat and alcohol and centred on a chaste and devout life.

He continued to write and publish both essays and fiction in abundance. With the publication in 1899 of his novel *Resurrection*, the Russian Orthodox Church turned completely against him. An intense and fevered condemnation of state oppression, the novel follows a Russian prince's personal 'resurrection' when he embraces the teachings of Christ and helps a prostitute who has borne him a son. The final straw for the Church was Tolstoy's decision to give all the proceeds of the book to a non-violent Christian sect called the Doukhobors, to whose cause he contributed heavily. Persecuted for their antagonism to the Church and for their refusal to bear arms on behalf of the tsar, the Doukhobors were eventually deported to Canada (see 'The Doukhobors', page 96). The Church excommunicated him and the ageing Tolstoy fell into a serious illness. On his recovery, he expected to join the Doukhobors as a member, and

# THE DOUKHOBORS

The Doukhobors were a dissident Christian sect dating back to the sixteenth century who lived mostly in the southern Caucasus region of Russia. Similar in some ways to the Quakers, they believed in the presence of God in every person and disputed the need for sacraments or clergy. They opposed secular government as well as all church rituals and icons. They also rejected the divinity of Jesus, and the Bible as divine revelation. Also like the Quakers, their name was originally meant as an insult. *Doukhobor* translates as 'spirit wrestler', and was coined around 1785 by the Archbishop of Yekaterinoslav, who mocked their heretical rejection of the sacraments.

At the end of the nineteenth century, during the pre-revolutionary ferment in Russia, the Doukhobors were widely persecuted. Their belief in non-violence as a direct precept of Christ brought them into conflict with the tsarist government. In 1894, when the authorities tried to conscript about 20,000 Doukhobors into the armed forces, they passively resisted. Brutal persecutions and atrocities followed, but the Doukhobors bore all the consequences of their actions rather than kill their fellow human beings. Tolstoy, seeing great similarities to his beliefs, took up their cause.

In 1895, the Doukhobors, en masse, ceremoniously burned all their weapons. 'The Burning of Weapons' became a definitive moment in their history and Russian forces responded with force, gaoling, killing and sending many into exile. Tolstoy, with the support of British and American Quakers, conceived a plan to resettle the Doukhobors in Canada. Tolstoy paid nearly half the emigration costs of 7500 people from his royalties, and the Quakers covered the rest. Today, the Doukhobors have mostly assimilated into mainstream Canada. With about 20,000 descendants, most in southeastern British Columbia, Alberta and Saskatchewan, they still honour Tolstoy's memory with statues of him in their settlements.

attempted to hand his estate over to Vladimir Chertkov. But Sonya and others in his family blocked his efforts.

Over the last decade of his life, Tolstoy grew increasingly saddened and weary by his country's empirical oppression, by the lack of progress for the peasant class, and by the endless conflicts within his family. He wrote in his journal in 1903: 'I am now suffering the torments of hell: I am calling to mind all the infamies of my former life—these reminiscences do not pass away and they poison my existence.' He grew bitter and isolated, but still he wrote. His later works include *On Life and Death*, *The Light Shines in Darkness*, *The Law of Love and the Law of Violence* and his last novel, *Hadji Murad*, which he didn't try to publish, knowing it would be censored. Outside Russia, Tolstoy was considered an international sage. But few among Russia's elite understood the man once considered 'the greatest genius in all Russia'. His friend, the composer Peter Tchaikovsky, said of him, 'Tolstoy is for me the dearest, the deepest, the greatest of all artists. But this concerns the Tolstoy of yesterday, who had nothing in common with the exasperating moralist and theoriser of today.'

The members of Tolstoy's family were the most perplexed and exasperated by his conversion. Tolstoy wished to cast off his material goods and, like other great sages before him, live the life of a wandering ascetic in his remaining years. Sonya battled constantly to maintain control of his considerable writings and to keep him from giving away all his lands and property. New skirmishes erupted when Tolstoy assigned the rights to his private diaries to Chertkov. All but his youngest daughter Alexandra turned against him. And finally, on a blustery night in October 1910, in a scene right out of King Lear, the 82-year-old Tolstoy stormed out of the house after an ugly fight with Sonya, Alexandra chasing after him. Railing against the limits of old age, he made it only as far as the Astapovo train station where he collapsed and was carried to the stationmaster's house. He died there days later of pneumonia, surrounded by his family, Sonya begging his forgiveness. His last words to her were: 'To seek. Always to seek.'

News of the death of the great Tolstoy brought Russia to a momentary standstill. Although the Russian Orthodox Church had banned all memorials, on the day he was buried over 6000 people descended on Yasnaya Polyana. Tolstoy had made his burial wishes clear in his will: 'There should be no ceremonies while burying my body; a wooden coffin, and let anyone, who will be willing to, carry it to the Stary Zakaz Wood, near the ravine, to the place of the magic green stick.' On 9 November 1910, his body was laid to rest near the spot where so many years before, his brother Nikolay had inspired his great life with a little story about the secret to peace.

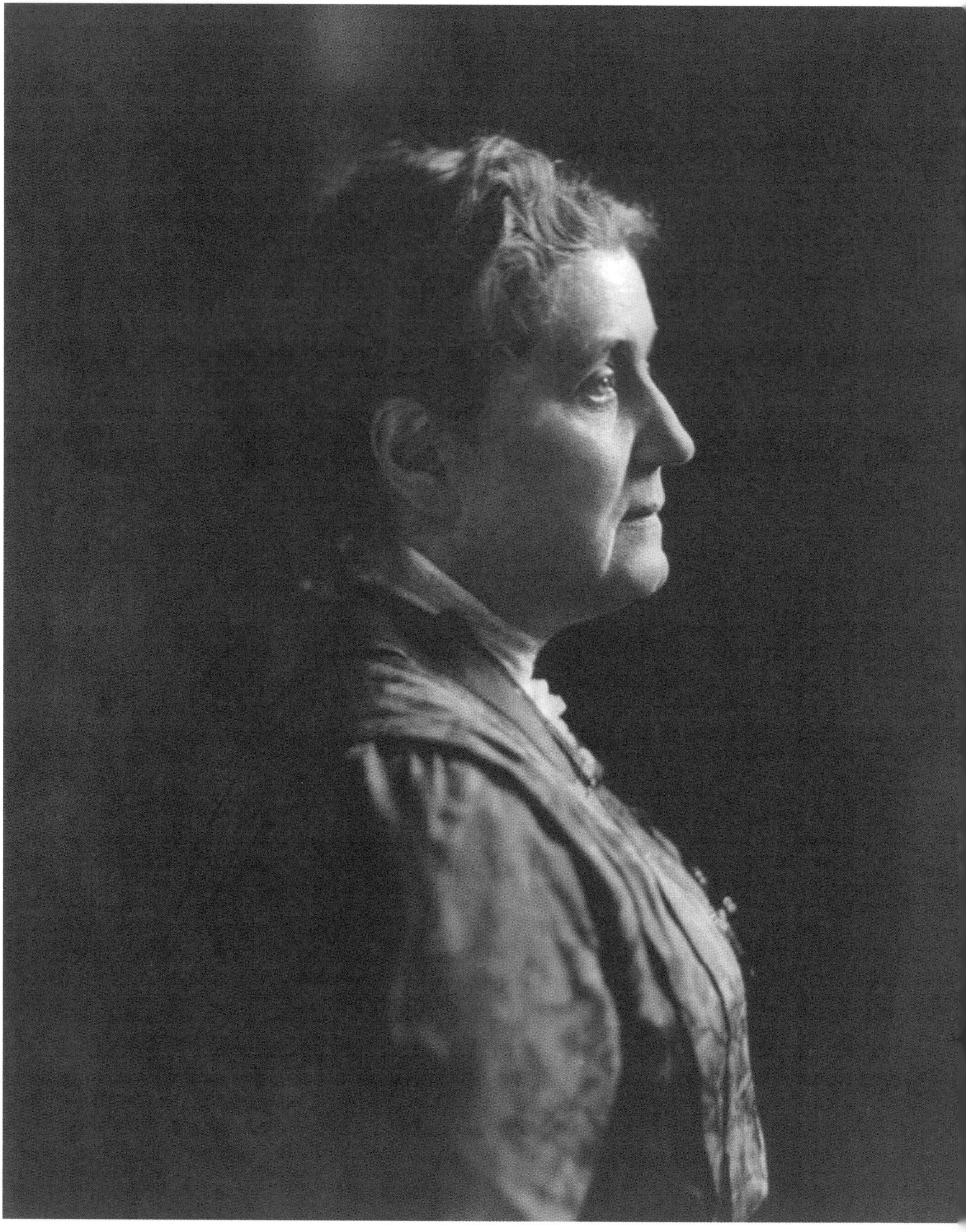

# JANE ADDAMS: IDEALS OF PEACE

JANE ADDAMS' LIFE SPANNED THE PERIOD FROM THE AMERICAN CIVIL War to Roosevelt's New Deal in the depths of the Great Depression. She was celebrated for her social reform work in founding Chicago's Hull House and she was vilified as an outspoken pacifist and resister to America's entry into World War I. A humanist, feminist and advocate of tolerance, she was the first American woman to receive the Nobel Peace Prize.

She was a champion of the poor and improved the lives of thousands through her establishment of the Hull House Settlement in Chicago. Her advocacy on behalf of the dispossessed was hailed by presidents and celebrated throughout the world. But her most courageous work was on behalf of peace—she risked everything as an outspoken critic of World War I. Her writings still stand as some of the most articulate on behalf of the oppressed and in support of non-violence.

—

## 'UGLY, PIGEON-TOED LITTLE GIRL'

LAURA JANE ADDAMS CONSIDERED HERSELF AN UGLY LITTLE GIRL. BORN on 6 September 1860, in the small Illinois hamlet of Cedarville, the youngest of six living children of John and Sarah Addams, she was afflicted with a curvature

Jane Addams in about 1914: a strong, thoughtful face radiating calmness and determination.

of the spine that caused her great pain throughout her life. Her father was a prosperous and well-regarded Quaker, banker, legislator and mill owner. From an early age, she feared that her appearance was an embarrassment to him. She recalled how once when she went to visit her father at work, 'I prayed all my heart that the ugly, pigeon-toed little girl, whose crooked back obliged her to walk with her head held very much upon one side, would never be pointed out … as the daughter of this fine man.' But instead, as she came up the steps to the Second National Bank where he was president, John Addams gallantly removed his hat and bowed deeply, introducing her to all his associates. She would never forget this grand gesture nor ever again allow her self-esteem to be diminished by her own doubts.

Addams had come to Cedarville from Pennsylvania, where his great-grandfather had settled. He supported the abolitionist movement both as an Illinois Republican legislator and as a link in the Underground Railroad, transporting slaves to freedom in the north. He was also a friend and supporter to another young Springfield legislator named Abraham Lincoln. He worked to get Lincoln elected president in 1860, just two months before Laura Jane's birth, and kept a small treasure trove of letters from him. He would occasionally take these letters out, each addressed to 'My Dear Double D'ed Addams', and show them to Jane, who grew to admire the man as much as her father admired him.

Jane hardly knew her mother Sarah, who died delivering a stillborn baby when Jane was only two years old. Lonely, shy and quiet, Jane hardly came out of her shell until her father married Anna Halderman six years later, in 1868. The widowed Anna came with two sons, 18-year-old Harry and George, just a few months younger than Jane. She took to her new stepmother immediately but it was her friendship with little George that truly brought the frail child out of her shell. She and George soon became inseparable.

About this time Laura Jane had a pivotal life experience. Accompanying her father on a rare trip away, they stopped to visit a dingy mill town. She later recalled how frightened she was by the rundown little houses stacked one on top of the other, thronged around the mill. When she asked her father why people had to live in these 'horrid little houses', he explained that it was all they could afford. Little Jane declared that when she grew up she would buy a big house in the middle of little houses like these. It would be a peaceful place for everyone to share, with a big yard so that all the children could come and play. She was already imagining her life's work.

# THE ROAD TO HULL HOUSE

JOHN ADDAMS INSISTED THAT HIS DAUGHTER GET A COLLEGE EDUCATION, a very progressive notion for the era. Jane attended Rockford Seminary, later Rockford College, and was one of the first two women to receive a degree there. The experience left her brimming with confidence and drive. On graduating in the autumn of 1881, Jane set her sights on becoming a doctor, a field only recently opened to women, but her father opposed the idea. Crushed, as she adored him and would never go against his wishes, she became despondent and began to suffer serious back problems. To make matters worse, a series of events followed that was to drag Jane into a deep depression that would last for years.

One of Jane's few close Cedarville friends, Flora Guiteau, was the daughter of her father's head cashier at the Second National Bank. The Guiteaus, including Flora's half-brother Charles, who suffered from a mental illness, were regular guests in the Addams household. In the summer of 1881, on 2 July, a delusional Charles Guiteau stole into the old Baltimore train station in Washington, DC and shot President James Garfield. For two and a half months Garfield lingered on in agony before dying of his wounds. The assassination enraged the country and the press descended on Cedarville, looking to dig up information on anyone connected to the Guiteaus. All of Flora's friends abandoned her, except Jane. She remained loyal throughout the ordeal, even accompanying Flora a year later when Charles was hanged for the murder.

In the midst of the chaos, however, John Addams decided to take Jane and her stepmother away from all the unwelcome attention. On the trip, while scouting mining property in northern Michigan, he was struck with severe stomach pains. The family immediately started back for home but made it only as far as Green Bay, Wisconsin where, on 17 August, John Addams died from a ruptured appendix. The tragedy left Jane devastated. Her father had been the most influential person in her life; she would later admit that his death left her emotionally and spiritually 'at sea'. Jane turned to her closest Rockford friend, Ellen Gates Starr, for support but warned her before she came to the funeral: 'The greatest sorrow that can ever come to me has passed. I will not write of myself or how purposeless and without ambition I am, only prepare so you won't be disappointed in me when you come.'

Jane tried to pull herself out of depression by rekindling her dream of 'being a doctor and living among the poor'. She used some of her considerable inheritance to enrol in the Women's Medical College of Philadelphia and moved in with her older sister Alice. Alice had married, after a tempestuous love affair and against her father's wishes, her stepbrother Harry Halderman, who was now a successful surgeon in Philadelphia. But Jane's studies didn't go well. Unabated grief, relentless back pain and the stress of her studies resulted in a complete nervous breakdown. Jane dropped out of medical school and was hospitalised for months, restricted to the fashionable 'rest cure' for women with nervous conditions. She came out of hospital in even worse shape.

Jane's stepmother Anna became convinced that the best way for Jane to get past her grief was to marry. Her son George had long loved Jane and she tried to convince Jane that they, like Alice and Harry, could find happiness together. But Jane had other ideas. She had learned of an experimental spinal surgery that could help relieve her pain and begged Harry to perform it. Harry was willing, but warned her that the procedure had risks. Jane was desperate, sure that she could not go on living with this condition. The surgery was a success but Jane's

## MARY ROZET SMITH: A ROMANTIC FRIENDSHIP

Recent biographies have attempted to 'out' Jane Addams as a lesbian by pointing to her long-standing relationship with Mary Rozet Smith. In all likelihood there was a romantic side to their friendship and certainly Mary was a devoted companion, tending to Jane's social correspondence, arranging her travel plans, and caring for her later in life. But it is unlikely that Jane would ever have called herself a lesbian or referred to her relationship with Mary in that way.

Mary Rozet Smith was as dedicated to Hull House and the peace effort as she was to Jane. Born in 1868, the daughter of one of the wealthiest businessmen in Chicago, Mary never attended college, probably because of her severe asthma. But she found her way to Hull House in the first year it opened. Beginning in 1890, she volunteered by teaching and leading children's clubs.

She became an essential benefactor and fundraiser, using her family connections to Chicago's elite to solicit donations. Her stately home on Walton Street was a regular retreat for Jane. Mary and Jane later bought a vacation home in Bar Harbor, Maine, which they shared until Mary's death in 1933.

After Mary's death, Jane destroyed most of their correspondence. She may have wanted to cover up a sexual relationship or simply to keep their personal affection private. But a couple of letters survived. In one, when Jane was travelling alone, she wrote: 'I miss you dreadfully and am yours 'til death.' Mary wrote back, 'You can never know what it is to me to have had you and to have you ... I feel quite a rush of emotion when I think of you.' They never sought to hide their affection, but the times may not have been right to fully reveal their love.

recovery was slow. After two months in bed, her back improved enough to be fitted with a steel and whalebone brace. But she was to receive another blow: Harry had discovered during the surgery that Jane could never bear children.

After her recovery, Jane took 'the grand tour' of Europe like many affluent young women of the time. But rather than sightseeing and shopping in the capitals, Jane found herself increasingly drawn to the poor and downtrodden sections of these cities. In London's East End slum she witnessed the desperate auction of rotten vegetables to the poor. She was heartbroken by the child beggars and street urchins and furious over their lack of the most basic necessities. She returned to London the following year with a specific goal in mind. With her friend Ellen Gates Starr in tow, she visited Toynbee Hall, a new 'settlement house' in the impoverished East End. Named for Arthur Toynbee, who had dedicated his life to London's underclass, Toynbee Hall provided adult training, children's classes, childcare, meals and even temporary shelter to the destitute. This grand social experiment, staffed by young Oxford men who 'settled' in the neighbourhood they hoped to affect, was making waves throughout England. Jane and Ellen knew at once that they had found their calling. But their American settlement house would have one essential difference; it would be run by women.

⏤

## A FELLOWSHIP OF WOMEN

In the winter of 1889 Jane and Ellen Starr set to work realising Jane's childhood dream of providing a 'large house amidst the horrid little houses' in the boom town of Chicago. With over a million people, Chicago had ballooned from its humble beginnings ninety years earlier, when Jean Baptiste Pointe du Sable, the black son of a French pirate and a Haitian slave girl, had first established his trading post on the shores of Lake Michigan. Second only to New York City in population, the city became a hub of commerce in 1848 with the completion of the Illinois and Michigan Canal, connecting Lake Michigan to the Mississippi River. By 1889 its rapid growth had brought all manner of urban problems and the disparity between rich and poor was in stark contrast. On one side were the stately mansions along the lakefront, on the other were some of the worst slums in the country.

Jane's sense of drive and purpose had returned and with it her eight-year depression finally lifted. As winter turned to spring, Jane and Ellen found a 'fine old house' in a hardscrabble neighbourhood of immigrant labourers.

The Nineteenth Ward was one of the poorest of Chicago's thirty-four wards. Rundown tenements and rickety shacks, nearly all without indoor toilets or running water, were stacked one on top of another. The streets were teeming with vendors, carthorses and the indigent. The stench of uncollected garbage was overwhelming. It was no wonder the ward had the city's highest death rate. And yet this is where Jane Addams decided to settle.

The house they found had been built forty years earlier by a wealthy real estate developer named Charles Hull. Meant as an urban residence but never lived in, it now was in disrepair, used only as storage space for a nearby factory. Hull had died several years earlier leaving the property and much of his fortune to a cousin, Helen Culver. Jane had a considerable sum from her own inheritance, but it was not nearly enough to purchase the house. By a stroke of good fortune, Helen Culver was so persuaded by Jane's enthusiasm that she soon gave them the use of the house for nothing and in fact would become a lifelong friend and benefactor. In tribute, they named their new settlement after Charles Hull and set to work readying the manor to open to their neighbourhood of Italian, Irish, Polish and Russian immigrants.

Hull House was not the first settlement house in the country—University Settlement House on New York's Lower East Side has that honour—but within a few years it was the best known. As soon as its doors were opened in 1889, Hull House was offering classes in everything from languages to civics to cooking. For children there were youth clubs, gymnastics, storytelling, debate clubs, citizenship classes, and all manner of organised activities meant to keep kids off the streets and help clean up the neighbourhood. Eventually, Jane and Ellen opened a day nursery for working mothers; they bought out the saloon next door and converted it into the Hull House Diet Kitchen providing low-cost meals; and they added a separate laundry and bathing facilities for local families who had no running water. There was a boarding house with subsidised rents for working women in a separate facility; they even offered emergency funds for those who were laid off.

At a time when there was basically no municipal support for the poor, Hull House became known throughout Chicago and the country as the model for charitable work in action. By the end of the century the settlement house had grown to thirteen buildings, including an art gallery and 750-seat auditorium. With forty full-time residents, upwards of 9000 people took part in activities at Hull House in any given week. Jane was tireless in her fundraising, organising, managing and advocacy.

In addition to Ellen Gates Starr and Helen Culver, Jane developed a loyal 'fellowship of women', many of whom went on to gain recognition in their own right. Soon after opening, Florence Kelley joined the residents at Hull House. The daughter of a tough Philadelphia politician named William 'Pig Iron' Kelley, she was the first woman to graduate from Cornell University and earned a law degree while at Hull House. She later received an economics degree from the University of Zurich. Florence started at Hull House organising job training programs for immigrant women and would, through the course of her life, become world famous for her efforts in reforming child and adult labour laws.

Other standouts included Julia Lathrop, who worked at Hull House for twenty years and later became the first Chief of the United States Children's Bureau. Frances Perkins was a resident who would become Secretary of Labor under presidents Franklin Roosevelt and Harry Truman; she was the first woman to be appointed to the US Cabinet. But of Jane's many loyal cohorts, Mary Rozet Smith would have the biggest impact on her, both professionally and personally. Tall and blonde, from one of the wealthiest families in Chicago, Mary found her way to Hull House at the age of twenty-one. She and Jane were lifelong companions, sharing in all the ups and downs as Jane's popularity soared because of her work with the poor and plummeted because of her ardent pacifism on the world stage (see 'Mary Rozet Smith: a romantic friendship', page 102).

## 'SAINT JANE'

DURING THE 1890s, JANE'S STATURE IN THE COMMUNITY AND FAME throughout the country only increased. She took on the corrupt Nineteenth Ward political boss Johnny 'De Pow' Powers and briefly became the ward's garbage inspector, shaming the city into following through on promises of rubbish removal. Along with Florence Kelley, she exposed the city's sweatshops and the despicable child labour practices, winning concessions from business owners and gaining legislative approval for an eight-hour workday. Many of these local gains would become national policy under the leadership of Florence Kelley and Frances Perkins.

Jane became a sought-after public speaker and prolific writer. In her lifetime, she authored over 500 articles and published eleven books. These included sociological works such as *Democracy and Social Ethics*, *The Long Road of Women's Memory*, *The Spirit of Youth and the City Streets*, which was her favourite, and

*The Excellent Becomes the Permanent*. She wrote several memoirs, among them *Twenty Years at Hull-House* and later *The Second Twenty Years at Hull-House*. Her second book, however, *Newer Ideals of Peace*, published in 1907, met with scathing critical reviews and outrage. A clear and frank argument against war, this work offered radical views about peace and disarmament that were ahead of the times. This negative response foreshadowed the extent to which Jane's later pacifist activities would antagonise the public.

But in the early 1900s, Jane's popularity was such that she was regularly dubbed 'Saint Jane' in the press. *Ladies' Home Journal* proclaimed her 'First American Woman' ahead of Helen Keller and she was frequently compared to her childhood hero Abraham Lincoln. There was even talk of drafting her for president, years before women had gained the right to vote in 1920. This was soon to change, for as the world teetered towards war and Jane found her second calling as an ardent pacifist, much of the nation would turn against her.

Jane Addams' meeting with Count Leo Tolstoy in 1896, at his country estate in Russia, may have opened her eyes to the necessity of pacifism, although by all accounts her brief visit with the great man was hardly historic. Tolstoy did not warm to her and even mocked her fashionable dress with its large, puffy sleeves, noting she wore enough material on one arm to make a child's dress. Jane, however, was greatly impressed. She read his works voraciously and later wrote in the introduction to *Newer Ideals of Peace*:

> Count Tolstoy drags us through the campaign of the common soldier in its sordidness and meanness … We see nothing of the glories we have associated with warfare, but learn of it as it appears to the untutored peasant who goes forth at the mandate of his superior to suffer hunger, cold, and death for issues which he does not understand.

It is more likely, however, that her pacifism was directly influenced by her father's Quakerism and extended naturally from the international community she had built around Hull House.

The catalyst for her staunchly pacifist views was the outbreak of the Great War in Europe and the question of whether America would be drawn into it. At the beginning of 1915, Jane lent her considerable prestige to the peace effort by joining 3000 representatives from various women's groups at a large gathering in Washington, DC. The conference organised the Women's Peace Party and elected Jane their president. She was the natural choice, for she had already done a great deal of political organising on a national scale. Twice she had stumped

# HENRY FORD'S PEACE SHIP

The father of the auto industry, by 1915 Henry Ford was a lion of US business. But he was also a man of vacillating contradictions, as became clear in his brief flirtation with pacifism at the outbreak of World War I. In the second year of the war and on the heels of the Women's Peace Party conference at The Hague, Jewish Hungarian peace activist Rosika Schwimmer convinced Ford to sponsor a peace conference in Stockholm, Sweden. Ford became excited by the idea of a 'peace ship' that could carry world dignitaries and peace leaders to the conference. He chartered a Scandinavian–American liner, the *Oscar II*, and set about convincing world leaders to, literally, come on board. Looking to gain maximum exposure and press, he hastily organised the venture for the beginning of December, grandly promising that all soldiers would be 'out of the trenches by Christmas'.

Ford met with President Wilson but could not get him to grant his support. Other A-list leaders and dignitaries politely refused; yet many others gallantly accepted, 170 in all. Jane Addams signed on reluctantly, worried that Ford's plan was too flamboyant. That was exactly what Ford liked about it. 'The chief effect I look for is psychological,' he explained. His primary goal was to grab attention by 'putting peace on the front page'. Unfortunately, at this point Jane became seriously ill and was hospitalised. Had she been able to take part, she may have provided a stabilising influence on the venture.

Almost immediately the project became the target of ridicule. The *Oscar II* was dubbed the 'ship of fools' for the carnival-like atmosphere that preceded its departure for Europe, and newspapers across the country skewered Ford's folly. Still, over 15,000 people crowded the Hoboken, New Jersey dock and cheered the ship's departure while a band played 'I Didn't Raise My Boy to be a Soldier'. On board, a sense of camaraderie and shared purpose soon gave way to bickering, fanned by a cynical press which continuously filed satirical reports. Many of the participants turned their ire on the aggressive Schwimmer. The press picked it up, adding anti-Semitic whispers and noting that she came from the belligerent country of Hungary. Blaming a cold, Ford retreated to his cabin for most of the voyage. By the time the *Oscar II* arrived in Stockholm, Ford was thoroughly disillusioned and he slipped off the ship, never to appear in public. The peace conference itself achieved little notice and produced no concrete recommendation.

Schwimmer, resentful and disappointed, organised the International Committee for Immediate Mediation the following year. Ford's pacifist leanings were short-lived and he went on to make huge profits as a munitions manufacturer after America entered the war in 1917. Ironically, by the outbreak of World War II, Ford was revealed as an anti-Semite and hero to Adolf Hitler, the only American mentioned in *Mein Kampf*. Hitler proudly displayed a life-sized portrait of Henry Ford in his office.

Jane Addams (centre) aboard the *Noordam* with a group from the Women's Peace Party, arriving at Rotterdam for the International Conference of Women at The Hague in 1915. The woman at the left is identified as Frieda Lawrence.

for Teddy Roosevelt, first on the Republican ticket and later as the Progressive Party candidate. Roosevelt had been a frequent visitor to Hull House and was a supporter of Jane's Chicago reforms. But the two parted company on the issue of war. Painfully, Roosevelt said of her: 'Jane Addams—don't talk to me of Jane Addams! I have always thought a lot of her … but she's all wrong about peace!'

At the end of 1915, President Woodrow Wilson was still maintaining his efforts to keep America neutral, but the anti-German clamour had grown. The Women's Peace Party grew to 40,000 and Jane, along with forty other women from the United States, travelled to the International Conference of Women in The Hague. The women—many said naïvely—voted to put their efforts behind drawing the belligerent and neutral countries back to mediation. Delegates were sent to each country in the hopes of convincing heads of states to take part in the conference. Many of the leaders scoffed at women trying to draw warring nations into negotiations; none had obviously read Aristophanes' play (see '*Lysistrata*: make love, not war', pages 18–31). But Jane was optimistic that they might at least help set the stage for negotiations.

On her return, Jane reported to President Wilson about the conference. Some of the conference recommendations may have eventually made their way into Wilson's famous 14 Points following the end of the war, but at the time any talk of peace was being shouted down, especially after German submarines sank the British ship *Lusitania*, killing 1195 people, twenty-eight of them Americans. Up to this point, Jane's vocal support for peace had been tolerated in light of the high regard in which she was held as a social reformer. Painful as it was that her former champion Teddy Roosevelt now said to her, 'Pacifists are cowards, and your scheme is both silly and base,' she still garnered grudging respect. But this was about to change.

## 'MISS ADDAMS KNOWS NOTHING OF THE JOY OF COMBAT'

ON 9 JULY 1915, JANE GAVE A SPEECH TO A CROWD OF OVER 3000 people at Carnegie Hall in New York City. She spoke mostly about her efforts at the conference in The Hague and her tour of war-torn Europe. She called it 'an old man's war' that was being forced on young soldiers. As she spoke about the fighting, she made a comment that would return to haunt her for much of her life. She recounted how many of the soldiers she had met had confessed to her the horrors of this 'modern war'. Then she described how many admitted to being primed with drugs and alcohol to muster the courage to make a bayonet charge. She touched a nerve by questioning the myth of the noble soldier—and even though she was quick to explain that this was not a symptom of cowardice but because of soldiers' 'general loathing of killing', the damage was done. For the first time in her life, Jane was heartily booed.

The press went to town on her the next day. Headlines screamed: 'Troops Drink-Crazed, says Miss Addams'. Articles and editorials were scathing. One editorial in the *New York Times* stated: 'Miss Addams evidently knows nothing of the joy of combat; whatever faults the soldiers have, they are not cowards.' Others tried to link her comments with the American suffragist movement, taking potshots at both; from the *Rochester Herald*:

> [Jane Addams] knows no more of the discipline and methods of modern warfare than she does of its meaning. If the woman conceded by her sisters to be the ablest of her sex, is so readily duped, so little informed, men wonder what degree of intelligence is to be secured by adding the female vote to the electorate.

Lost on the wider public was her main point, namely, that nations will fight for self-protection so long as neutral powers fail to provide the opportunity for peace and disarmament.

Hate mail poured into Hull House. Jane received death threats. Her speeches were boycotted or disrupted and former supporters abandoned her. Those who continued to champion her social reforms ridiculed her naïveté about war. To Jane, it seemed very strange that speaking out about peace and caring for one's fellow man could stir up such hatred, anger and threats of violence.

The furore did not slow Jane's efforts to keep America from entering the war. Against her better judgment she agreed to join auto manufacturer Henry Ford on his 'peace ship', a well-intended anti-war publicity stunt that was to become a celebrated target of ridicule (see 'Henry Ford's peace ship', page 107). So much negativity had an effect, for Jane's health suffered. She contracted pneumonia and pleurisy, forcing her to convalesce and drop out of Ford's peace mission.

In 1917, Wilson finally sought a declaration of war from Congress and America entered the conflict. With public opinion overwhelmingly favouring the war, peace efforts were largely shelved. Jane again became depressed, writing of this difficult period in *Peace and Bread in Time of War*:

> Indeed the pacifist in war time, with his precious cause in the keeping of those who control the sources of publicity and consider it a patriotic duty to make all types of peace propaganda obnoxious, constantly faces two dangers. Strangely enough he finds it possible to travel from the mire of self pity straight to the barren hills of self-righteousness and to hate himself equally in both places.

## 'THE MOST DANGEROUS WOMAN IN AMERICA'

For the duration of America's involvement in the war, Jane reined in her anti-war rhetoric and focused her attention on helping victims of the conflict, especially children. She raised awareness of food shortages in Europe and encouraged Americans to consume less and to grow more on under-used farmland. She returned to running Hull House, which she now used also to help retrain returning injured soldiers. In late 1918, just a month before an armistice would end hostilities, the tragedy of war hit Jane personally. Her oldest nephew John Linn, the son of her deceased sister Mary, whom she had helped raise, was killed at the Battle of the Argonne Forest in France. A captain and chaplain for a US artillery unit, Linn was

## WOMEN'S INTERNATIONAL LEAGUE FOR PEACE AND FREEDOM

The Women's International League for Peace and Freedom (WILPF) traces its roots to the Women's Peace Party (WPP), started in 1915 by Jane Addams and the well-known suffrage leader Carrie Chapman Catt. That same year, Addams, Catt and other representatives of the WPP travelled to The Hague to attend an international peace conference of neutral and belligerent countries organised by the German feminists Anita Augspurg and Lida Gustava Heymann, and the Dutch pacifist Aletta Jacobs. The goal of the conference was to present a unified protest against the war, suggest a plan for negotiating its immediate end, and lay the groundwork for lasting peace. To that end, they established the International Committee of Women for Permanent Peace and elected Jane Addams its president. This organisation would later become known as WILPF.

Today, as the oldest women's peace organisation in the world, WILPF is headquartered in Geneva, Switzerland and maintains a United Nations office in New York. The organisation's mission is 'to bring together women of different political views and philosophical and religious backgrounds determined to study and make known the causes of war and work for a permanent peace'. A non-profit and non-governmental organisation, WILPF has offices in thirty-seven countries and enjoys special consultative status to a host of UN organisations, including UNESCO and UNICEF. Two WILPF presidents have received the Nobel Peace Prize for their efforts on behalf of the organisation, Jane Addams in 1931 and the Quaker peace activist Emily Greene Balch in 1946.

killed by an artillery shell while doling out chocolate and prayers to the men in the foxholes. This blow, beyond everything else, drove home to Jane the futility and senselessness of war.

The end of the war left the world in a kind of global shell shock: nearly ten million soldiers had died, as had an equal number of civilians. Twenty-one million soldiers were wounded. Much of Europe was in ruins and millions more civilians were homeless or displaced. Jane renewed her efforts and set to work organising aid for war victims and laying the groundwork to prevent a war like this from ever happening again. As head of both the US Women's Peace Party (WPP) and the International Committee of Women for Permanent Peace, newly renamed the Women's International League for Peace and Freedom (WILPF), Jane called in her delegates and set a plan in motion (see 'Women's International League for Peace and Freedom', above).

Representatives of the victorious Allied nations met in Paris in 1919 to frame the peace treaty. Germany and other defeated nations were excluded from the talks, and would be forced to accept the terms. The WILPF decided to hold their second international conference in Zurich, Switzerland, concurrent with the Paris conference. Before the conference, Jane and other Hull House residents, including Mary Rozet Smith and Dr Alice Hamilton, the first woman appointed to the faculty at Harvard University, toured war-torn Europe with the Red Cross. Jane went to the Argonne to search for the grave of her nephew John and miraculously found his small grave marker near a bombed-out farmhouse in a row of about forty small crosses, sitting between the names of Italian and Slavic soldiers.

The six-day WILPF conference included representatives from victorious and defeated nations alike and focused mainly on ways to relieve hunger among all the war victims. The delegates supported President Wilson's call for a League of Nations but opposed most of the harsh terms being forced on the defeated countries. In a statement, they prophetically warned that the oppressive terms Germany was forced to accept would 'create animosities which can only lead to future wars'.

Following the conference, Jane went to Paris and reported to President Wilson on WILPF's recommendations. Wilson was hardly receptive, however, and the recommendations had little impact on post-war negotiations. Then Jane was approached by Herbert Hoover, then serving as US Food Administrator for President Wilson, about helping in a humanitarian venture. A Quaker relief organisation called the American Friends Service Committee had raised about $30,000 to feed Germany's starving citizens. With Hoover's assistance Jane, Mary Rozet Smith and Alice Hamilton purchased tonnes of goods and accompanied a group of English and American Quakers to distribute the food. Arriving in Berlin just nine days after the final Paris Peace Accord was signed, they spent two weeks visiting children's hospitals, nurseries and soup kitchens in many of Germany's destroyed cities. Jane wrote: 'What [they] are facing is the shipwreck of a nation and they realize that if help does not come quickly and abundantly this generation in Germany is largely doomed to early death.'

Jane was not ready for the anger she met with on her return to America. More than 350,000 US servicemen had been killed or wounded and Germany was universally blamed. Her calls for understanding and for help feeding starving German children were met with disdain. In addition, with Russia going through the convulsions of the communist revolution and emerging as the Union of Soviet Socialist Republics, Americans feared revolution would spread to their own country. Jane had previously allowed all types of groups, including communists, to use Hull House for meetings. Now she found herself reviled for being a pacifist, abused for trying to help the Germans, falsely accused of being a communist and called out as 'the most dangerous woman in America'. She'd come a long way from the 'Saint Jane' of the past.

⌁

## DISARMAMENT

Throughout the 1920s new peace groups and organisations came into being. With time, the war was given some context and pacifism took on a new, if short-lived acceptance. Jane turned her focus to disarmament, convinced that nations without militaries could not threaten one another. Again called naïve, this stance made her even less popular and she was forced to contend with critics challenging her patriotism. She was kicked out of the conservative organisation the Daughters of the American Revolution, and attacked regularly in the press. Now in her sixties, and still president of WILPF, she decided to seek out friendlier audiences and began extensive travels around the world. She focused the organisation's considerable reach on disarmament and spoke to world leaders, community groups and individual citizens. She visited many of the countries of Europe, as well as Burma, Korea, China and Japan.

Reports from around the globe of Jane's warm reception from world leaders combined with the fact that memories of the war were fading led to a revival of her popularity at home. When she returned this time she was met at Hull House with a hero's welcome. Now one of the world's best-known pacifists, she was again inundated with mail. She continued to write and publish. Her account of her efforts for peace and support of the war's victims was chronicled in *Peace and Bread in Time of War*. She continued her vigorous schedule, speaking in so many places that she wore down her critics. How could anyone not respect this gentle, grandmotherly woman who had dedicated her life to peace and the betterment of others? With the publication of *The Second Twenty Years at Hull-House* in 1930, she again stepped squarely into the nation's conscience as the champion of the disenfranchised.

But 1929 had seen the crash of the stock market. As the nation slid into the Great Depression, Jane's good works on behalf of Chicago's poor were now needed on a national scale. Her advice was sought by Franklin Roosevelt's Administration as the nation witnessed unemployment climb to 25 per cent.

She worked with former Hull House resident, now Secretary of Labor, Frances Perkins, and became a close friend of Eleanor Roosevelt, as she advised on many Depression-era social reforms that still stand today.

In 1931, while Jane was hospitalised for surgery on an ovarian tumour, the news came that she had been chosen for the Nobel Peace Prize, the first American woman to receive the award. Sharing the prize with Nicholas Murray Butler, President of Columbia University, she was front-page news once again, with congratulations pouring in from all corners of the globe. The citation acknowledged Jane primarily for her international peace efforts with the Women's International League for Peace and Freedom, and also recognised her for the contributions of Hull House. Unfortunately, having barely survived a bad reaction to the anaesthesia, Jane was too weak to attend the awards ceremony. It was to be months before she left her hospital room, and then only to be moved to Mary's house.

With her declining health and the crowning achievement of her Nobel Prize, many people assumed Jane Addams would slow down. But no—the Nobel Prize had widened her platform. It gave her the opportunity to spread her message as a popular lecturer and through radio and movie newsreels. But in 1933 Jane was again hospitalised after suffering a heart attack. She convalesced at Mary Rozet Smith's home in Chicago. Mary, who took care of her night and day, may have neglected her own health in caring for Jane, as she developed pneumonia and died days later, in the room next to Jane. So great was Jane's grief that she no longer wished to live. 'I could have willed my heart to stop beating, and I longed to do that,' she later wrote. 'But the thought of what [Mary] had been to me for so long kept me from being cowardly.' Still too ill to attend Mary's memorial, held downstairs, she listened from her bedroom to the many speeches by friends and family and to the Hull House choir as they filled the house with song.

Five months later, Jane was finally well enough to travel. A huge event was planned in New York, as both a twentieth anniversary celebration of WILPF and an occasion to honour Jane. Addressing an audience of dignitaries, including Eleanor Roosevelt, she took the opportunity to warn of the threats of war from Japan's invasion of Manchuria and the rise of Chancellor Hitler in Germany, saying to her rapt listeners:

We don't expect to change human nature, we people of peace. But we do hope to change human behaviour. We may be a long way from permanent peace, and we may have a long journey ahead of us in educating the community and public opinion … But it tests our endurance and our moral enterprise, and we must see that we keep on doing it.

The next morning, on 3 May 1935, Jane took part in the historic two-day 'Round-the-World Peace Broadcast' as the highlighted speaker among an international cast of peace activists. The broadcast was heard in every major city of the world, by millions of people. It was Jane's last time speaking in public. Suffering from inoperable cancer, she passed away two and a half weeks later. On 21 May, her big heart finally gave out.

The news of Jane Addams' death rang out in headlines throughout the world. Newspapers, radio and newsreels celebrated her life and work as letters poured into Hull House. Chicago's City Council, refusing to let any other tribute outshine their own, passed a resolution calling Jane 'the greatest woman who ever lived'. Her funeral at Hull House was mobbed. Everyone from the rich and famous to newly arrived immigrant neighbours filled the streets, streaming past her casket at a rate of 6000 an hour.

Today, Jane Addams is remembered mostly for her work with Hull House. With World War II looming at the time of her death, much of her pioneering effort for world peace was quietly forgotten. Although called a saint for her social reforms, she was labelled naïve for working so tirelessly to keep America out of war and for her advocacy of global disarmament. But she wove a stellar life from the two threads of social justice and world peace. A passage from *Bread and Peace in Time of War* best sums this up:

> My temperament and habit had always kept me rather in the middle of the road; in politics as well as in social reform I had been for 'the best possible'. But now I was pushed far toward the left on the subject of the war and I became gradually convinced that in order to make the position of the pacifist clear it was perhaps necessary that at least a small number of us should be forced into an unequivocal position.

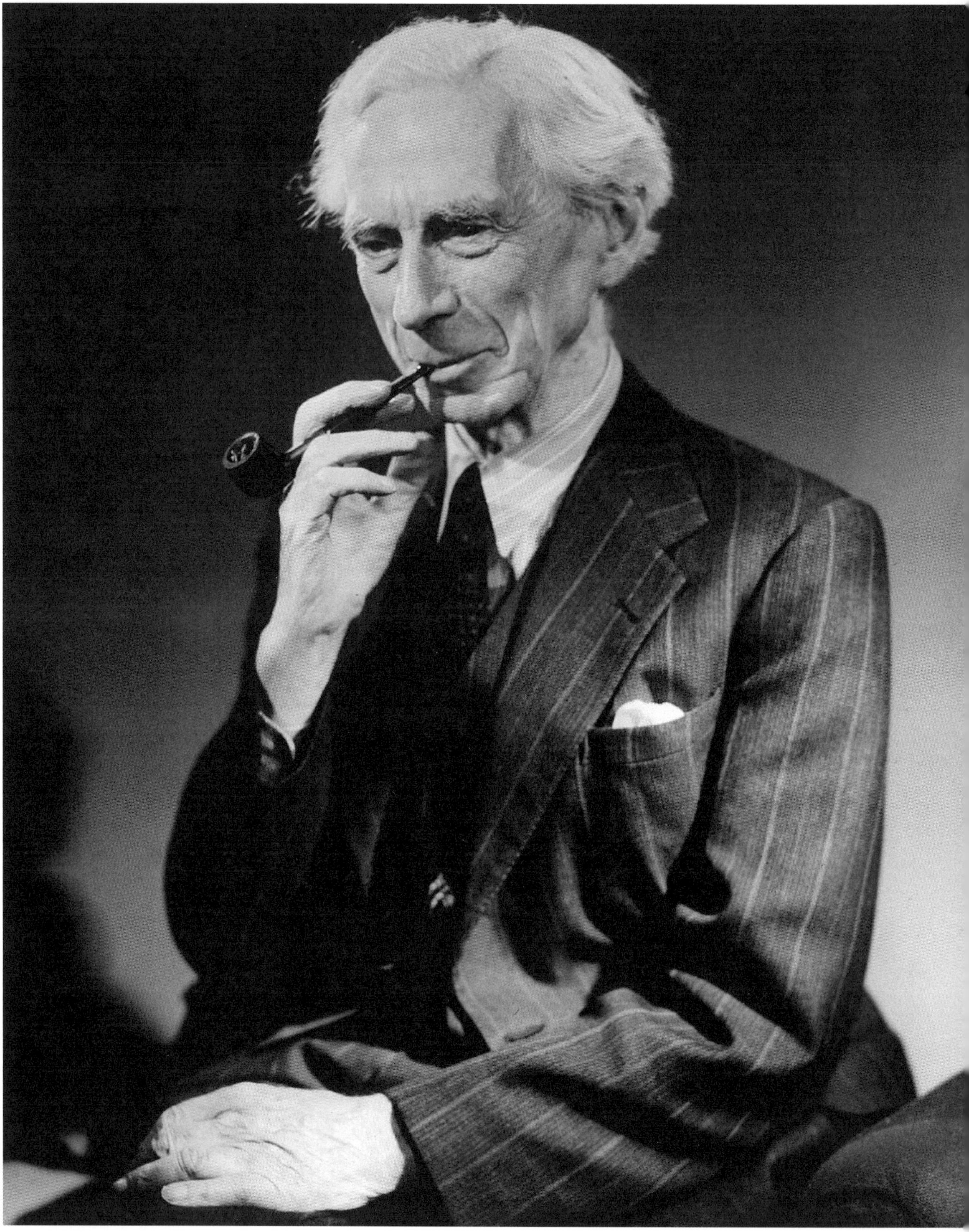

# BERTRAND RUSSELL:
# THE PARADOX OF PEACE

BERTRAND RUSSELL, THE 3RD EARL RUSSELL, HAD ONE OF THE GREATEST philosophical minds of the twentieth century; yet he held a paradoxical view of peace. A logician, mathematician, philosopher, political activist, social critic and pacifist, he spent his life debating a relativist view of peace. During World War I his anti-war activities cost him his professorship at Trinity College, Cambridge and landed him in gaol; fifty years later, in his nineties, his nuclear disarmament activism would do the same. Yet he also argued that war was just under certain conditions, such as against Hitler and Nazi Germany, and even went so far as to suggest the validity of a first strike against the USSR. Always the logical synthesiser, he called his stance 'relative political pacifism'.

In his long life, Russell authored over seventy books, hundreds of essays and nearly 30,000 personal letters. He received the Order of Merit from King George VI and a Nobel Prize in Literature in 1950. One of the foremost logicians since Aristotle, he was also a public intellectual and gifted writer who popularised a wide range of scientific, social and political topics. As a pacifist, his activism touched on nearly every social and political controversy of the twentieth century: he opposed World War I, nationalism, nuclear proliferation and the Vietnam War; he supported the suffrage movement, sexual freedom and reproductive rights, religious free thought, and peace. He was a wit, a

Bertrand Russell pictured in 1955 at the age of eighty-three. He was heavily involved in the nuclear disarmament movement at the time.

'well-known collector of mistresses', and a humanist who lived passionately by his motto: 'the good life is one inspired by love and guided by knowledge'.

— ⌐ —

## SAVED BY EUCLID

RUSSELL'S CHILDHOOD WAS INFLUENCED BY HIS TRADITIONAL LINEAGE and radical social non-conformity. His grandfather was Lord John Russell, the second son of the Duke of Bedford and twice prime minister under Queen Victoria in the 1840s and 1860s. His father, Viscount Amberley, was an atheist and social radical. He, like his wife, the Viscountess Katharine Louisa, supported women's right to vote and to birth control, a scandalous attitude, which cost him his seat in Parliament. Russell's father even consented to his wife's ongoing affair with their children's tutor, the eminent biologist Douglas Spalding.

Born in 1872 in Trellech, Monmouthshire, Russell was only two when his mother and older sister Rachel died of diphtheria. Suffering from severe depression, Russell's father died twenty months later. He had retained Spalding as Russell's older brother Frank's tutor and, wishing his boys to be raised agnostic, named Spalding their guardian in his will. However, the nature of Spalding's relationship with Bertrand's mother soon came to light. 'This discovery,' Russell later wrote of his grandparents, 'caused them the utmost Victorian horror.' Exercising their considerable influence, Lord John Russell and his second wife Countess Russell, secured custody of the boys and Spalding was dismissed.

Lord John passed away several years later and, ignoring her stepson's wishes, Lady Russell raised the boys Presbyterian. They moved to Pembroke Lodge in Richmond Park, amid the formality and repression expected from a lorded family with peerage back to the early Tudor dynasty. Russell grew into an awkward adolescent. 'After the age of fourteen,' he remembered, 'I found living at home only endurable at the cost of complete silence about anything that interested me.' The misery of the repressive atmosphere and, later, his rebuff by a pretty housemaid made him suicidal. What saved him was Euclid, the ancient Greek mathematician and 'Father of Geometry'. Older brother Frank introduced him to Euclid's axiomatic theories—he became so taken with mathematics that he cast away all thoughts of suicide. More importantly, for the first time he began to believe in his own intellect.

In 1890, Russell received a scholarship to read mathematics at Trinity College, Cambridge. He did so well on his entrance exams that his reputation preceded him. Suddenly, eager colleagues surrounded the awkward boy who had previously been too shy to make friends. He came under the wing of Alfred North Whitehead, with whom he co-authored one of his greatest works, and befriended the younger G.E. Moore, an early collaborator. He graduated with a BA in mathematics in 1893 and added a fellowship in philosophy two years later.

When he was seventeen, Russell had met Alys Pearsall Smith, an American Quaker. Her parents were well-known evangelicals who summered in England near Pembroke. Five years his senior, she was quite beautiful, intelligent, broadminded in many ways but also restrained by her Quaker upbringing, and a recent graduate of Bryn Mawr College near Philadelphia. Her family were friendly with Walt Whitman and the psychologist William James, brother of author Henry James. They seemed to enjoy showing off their association with 'Lord John's grandson', and Russell soon fell in love with Alys.

While still at Cambridge, Russell announced his intention to marry Alys. His grandmother opposed it, marching out alarmist doctors with horrific tales of madness in the Russell family who warned that should Russell and Alys have children, they would surely grow up insane. The young couple vowed never to have children, and against Lady Russell's wishes married in 1894.

In the early years of their marriage, 'Bertie' and Alys were quite happy together. Russell had come into his inheritance and was in control of his own finances. They travelled extensively and lived in Berlin, where Russell studied German Social Democracy. 'In those days Social Democrats were fiery revolutionaries,' he wrote in his autobiography. He soon published his first book on the subject. He continued to explore the intersection of mathematics, logic and philosophy and later recalled that, while walking in Berlin's Tiergarten one day, he realised how he might pursue a career as a writer:

> I thought that I would write one series of books on the philosophy of the sciences from pure mathematics to physiology, and another series of books on social questions. I hoped that the two series might ultimately meet in a synthesis at once scientific and practical … I have to some extent followed this in later years.

Returning to Trinity as a lecturer, Russell would follow this basic roadmap throughout his career. He spent his life as a 'synthesiser' of philosophy, logic, mathematics and social criticism through his groundbreaking theories, social activism, and as a populariser of science. His earliest works dealt with the crosscurrents of mathematics, philosophy and logic, and he was already finding interrelations between the fields. His critical analysis of the German mathematician Gottlob Frege's 'naïve set theory'—the criteria and logic behind mathematical sets simplified to common language—led to his discovery of certain irreconcilable contradictions that became known as Russell's Paradox. His *Principles of Mathematics* brought him wider recognition as he evolved the theories of Frege and others, including the nineteenth century logician Bernard Bolzano. Although a lesser influence than Frege, Bolzano was also a pacifist and social critic whose life had many parallels to that of Russell's (see 'Bernard Bolzano', below).

In 1905 Russell published his breakthrough essay on linguistic philosophy, 'On Denoting', which still stands today as a pivotal twentieth century philosophical paradigm. In 1910 he published *Principia Mathematica*, his three-volume opus on the foundations of mathematics, written with Alfred North Whitehead,

## BERNARD BOLZANO

Although Bertrand Russell's great scholarly work in mathematics, logic and philosophy only touched tangentially on similar theories of Bernard Bolzano from a century earlier, the two men shared a remarkably similar life of intellectual pursuit, social reform and pacifism. Bolzano was born in 1781 in Prague, Bohemia, which by that time had been absorbed into the Austrian empire of the Habsburgs. He was an ordained Catholic priest as well as a mathematician, philosopher, logician and anti-militarist, which put him at odds with the conservative and oppressive reign of Emperor Franz Joseph II.

In 1805 Bolzano became a professor of philosophy at Prague University. His work in mathematics and logic was an early precursor to that of Russell, and he stated in 1810 that 'a discussion of mathematical method is basically nothing but logic'. His major works were *Theory of Science*, published in 1837, and *Paradoxes of the Infinite* (which Russell cited several times in *Principles of Mathematics*), published

posthumously in 1851, in which the mathematical term 'set' was used for the first time. But it was Bolzano's beliefs in free thought, social justice, pacifism and equality that most closely paralleled Russell's interests.

Bolzano used both his university lectures and his fiery religious sermons to champion a moral philosophy of pacifism and human rights, arguing for the equality of all peoples. He made an impassioned case for a kind of demilitarised utopian socialism and was highly critical of discrimination, especially against the oppressed Czech-speaking Bohemians and the Jews of Prague. He pushed for reforms in the educational, social and economic systems, and urged peace over armed conflict. These views alienated other scholars and Church leaders and in 1819 cost him his university position. Bolzano was forced into house arrest and banned from publishing, although he devoted himself to writing for the remainder of his life. He died of respiratory ailments in Prague in 1848.

in which he and Whitehead illustrated how all mathematical truths could be derived from a set of axioms and symbolic logic. It has become the seminal work in mathematical logic and philosophy since Aristotle and made Russell an international star in his field. But with his fame came whispers of infidelity and added tensions in his marriage to Alys, which had become a mostly sexless, intellectual union, for Russell found himself put off by Alys's puritanical repression. Eventually he fell out with Alys's mother, whom he felt was cruel and controlling. By 1910 they were married in name only and spent very little time together. He began an affair with the married Lady Ottoline Morrell and when he revealed this to Alys she left him for good. They remained married until 1921, but did not see each other again until the 1950s.

At Trinity, he was a sought-after lecturer and mentor. One of his students was the poet T.S. Eliot, then married to the beautiful Vivien Haigh-Wood. Russell took the moody and despondent genius under his wing. He also, apparently, had an affair with Vivien, who soon left Eliot. Russell would also become the champion of another student, the philosophical genius Ludwig Wittgenstein, a young, brash Austrian whom he saw as his successor in logic. Over the next decade and throughout World War I, Russell exerted considerable energy encouraging Wittgenstein through his various phobias and bouts of despair to publish his master work, *Tractatus Logico-Philosophicus*.

Russell was, by 1913, at the zenith of his early career. He was a world-renowned philosopher and author, Fellow of the Royal Society, respected intellectual and sought-after lecturer. He was deeply appreciative of his position at Trinity and had recently gifted the university his considerable inheritance, believing that inherited wealth was immoral. He even tried his hand at politics, running unsuccessfully for Parliament on the Liberal ticket as the candidate for the Women's Suffragette Society. But with the advent of war in Europe, all this was about to change.

———

## WORLD WAR I

'I never had a moment's doubt as to what I must do,' Russell wrote years later in his autobiography. 'I have at times been paralysed by scepticism, at times I have been cynical, at other times indifferent, but when the War came I felt as if I had heard the voice of God. I knew it was my business to protest, however futile protest might be.' Because of this protest, Russell sacrificed nearly everything he had worked for. Initially he helped to organise

petitions urging Britain to remain neutral. After Britain entered the war, he became a vocal agitator for peace. During the first two years of the war, over three million men volunteered to serve in the British military. Then, due to heavy losses, the government introduced the *Military Service Act* in 1916, the first compulsory military conscription in British history. At forty-five, Russell was too old to be conscripted but he worked with conscientious objectors through the No-Conscription Fellowship, an organisation that vigorously opposed forced conscription and lobbied on behalf of imprisoned conscientious objectors.

Nearly 16,000 British men were prosecuted for refusing to fight in the war. Russell lobbied the government on their behalf and helped them prepare for their tribunals. He visited objectors in prison and aided in their defence. But mostly he wrote—letters to officials, essays, pamphlets, newspaper and magazine articles. 'No single one of the combatants is justified in the present war,' he cautioned in the essay 'The Ethics of War'. Still, ever the relativist, his pacifism was not absolute, and he refused to take the 'extreme Tolstoyan view that war is under all circumstances a crime'. He further agitated through several books, including *Justice in War-time* and *Political Ideals*.

All this led to his being ostracised by his Liberal Party friends. When Trinity College dismissed him he was nearly crushed. With no job, no income and no money, for he had given the university his inherited wealth, he had little to fall back on but his continued activism. Fortunately, Lady Ottoline Morrell supported him and his opposition to the war. Though their relationship was tempestuous and mostly clandestine, his involvement with her brought him into contact with the 'Bloomsbury Group', for which she was a celebrated hostess. The group included intellectual notables Virginia Woolf, E.M. Forster and Lytton Strachey, and many of its members were equally opposed to the war. Russell began a brief but steamy affair with Lady Constance Malleson, a beautiful young actress better known by her stage name, Collette O'Neil, who also worked with the No-Conscription Fellowship.

In 1918 Russell met Dora Black, who became his secretary. She was a slim, dark-eyed feminist with boundless energy who would become a champion of birth control rights. She would also, after the war, reluctantly become Russell's second wife. She wrote in her autobiography:

> My first impression of him was that he was exactly like the Mad Hatter. The thick and rather beautiful grey hair was lifting in the wind, the large sharp nose and odd tiny chin, the long upper lip were outlined against the sky; of middling height, lean and spare, he moved with impetuous energy, but jerkily, not with the grace of an athlete.

She joined in his anti-war efforts and they became lovers. But soon afterwards Russell was arrested and convicted under the *Defence of the Realm Act* for an article opposing America's entry into the war. He spent six months in gaol.

His time in prison gave him the opportunity to begin work on the *Introduction to Mathematical Philosophy*, which he published after the war in 1919. But the Great War hardened his view of human nature: 'I learned an understanding of instinctive processes which I had not possessed before,' he later wrote. One of the great watersheds of twentieth century history, the war led to the fall of the German, Russian, Austria–Hungarian and Ottoman dynasties. It helped usher in the Bolshevik revolution, left much of Europe in ruin and unleashed even greater regional nationalism that eventually led to a second world war. By the time the Great War was over, no one seemed even sure why it had been fought. Russell noted this irony when he wrote: 'Wars don't decide who's right. They only decide who's left.'

# A JUST WAR

AFTER THE WAR, RUSSELL JOINED A DELEGATION OF LABOUR PARTY officials to view the Bolshevik revolution first hand, and in 1920 he and Dora travelled to Moscow where he met both Vladimir Lenin and Leon Trotsky. Initially enthusiastic about the revolution, Russell's opinions quickly changed as he became disenchanted by what he saw, noting Lenin's 'impish cruelty'. Disenchantment grew into foreboding antagonism, and Russell threw himself into his highly critical *The Practice and Theory of Bolshevism*. He and Dora spent the remainder of the year in China, where he guest lectured at the University of Beijing.

When they returned to England in 1921, Dora was six months' pregnant. Russell had repeatedly asked Dora to marry him but she, calling marriage a restriction on women's liberty, had refused. But Russell wanted a legitimate heir, and she finally acquiesced. He arranged a hasty divorce from Alys and married Dora soon after the birth of their son John Conrad. John would become the 4th Earl Russell but, as his grandmother had forewarned, suffered from mental illness much of his life. A daughter, Katharine, was born in 1923.

The 1920s brought a new sense of liberalism. Russell and Dora threw themselves into education and founded the Beacon Hill School in West Sussex. Similar in ways to Tolstoy's efforts in Russia fifty years earlier, and modelled somewhat on the Summerhill School founded around the same time, Beacon Hill became a laboratory for Russell's theories of libertarian education. As headmaster, he allowed the students a great deal of personal autonomy, believing that the school should fit the child rather than the other way around. He published his ideas on education in 1929 in *On Education, Especially in Early Childhood*.

The school was to last longer than Russell's second marriage. Dora and Russell had agreed to an open marriage and both took lovers, but the strain became too great. Dora's ongoing affair with American journalist Griffin Barry resulted, ironically given her views on birth control, in two more children, and Russell left her in 1931. Barry returned to the United States and Dora stayed on at the school for another ten years. Russell married his third wife, an Oxford undergraduate thirty years his junior named Patricia Spence, in 1936. Their son Conrad Sebastian Robert, born in 1937, became a well-respected historian, leading Member of Parliament and the 5th Earl Russell on the death of his older half-brother in 1987.

In the midst of all this family turmoil, Russell produced some of his most progressive books. He explored his liberal views on sexuality and marriage,

# THE PUGWASH CONFERENCE

In 1955, when Bertrand Russell and Albert Einstein released their manifesto against the proliferation of nuclear arms, they called for a conference of scientists dedicated to ending nuclear weapons. The wealthy Canadian philanthropist Cyrus Eaton, who had known Russell since 1938, agreed to finance the conference at his estate in Pugwash, Nova Scotia. Joseph Rotblat joined Russell as a founder and the first Pugwash Conference on Science and World Affairs was held in 1957. Twenty-two eminent scientists attended from many of the major countries of the world, including the Soviet Union. Although Russell was unable to attend because of illness and Einstein was no longer living (he died in 1955), the conference adopted the Russell–Einstein Manifesto as its official charter.

In its first fifteen years, the Pugwash Conference dealt with the Berlin Crisis, the Cuban Missile Crisis, the Soviet invasion of Czechoslovakia and the Vietnam War. It played an active role in providing an unofficial means for opening international discussions, and offered support for the Partial Test Ban Treaty in 1963, the Non-Proliferation Treaty in 1968, the Anti-Ballistic Missile Treaty and the Biological Weapons Convention in 1972, and the Chemical Weapons Convention in 1993. Pugwash Conferences are now held annually all over the world; in the last fifty years, over 250 conferences have been held with scientists of all political persuasions.

Today, Pugwash's visibility has diminished but the organisation and its conferences still play an active role in many of today's arms-control issues, including conventional nuclear arms, chemical and biological weapons, space-based weaponry, and nuclear proliferation in the Third World. In 1995, forty years after the signing of the Russell–Einstein Manifesto, the Pugwash Conferences and Sir Joseph Rotblat were awarded the Nobel Peace Prize 'for their efforts to diminish the part played by nuclear arms in international politics and, in the longer run, to eliminate such arms'.

as well as his agnosticism, in *What I Believe* (co-written with E.M. Forster), published in 1925, and *Marriage and Morality*, published in 1929. With war again brewing in Europe, Russell published several books and a string of essays in response. In 1936 he published *Which Way to Peace?*, laying out a theory of non-resistance to Germany's increasing militarism. England, he argued, should not re-arm, as doing so would lead to a German invasion and the ultimate destruction of Europe. When war with Germany finally broke out, Russell renounced this book, taking the unusual step of declaring his views of passive resistance as extreme and flat-out wrong.

Russell had never considered himself a pacifist in the mould of his first wife Alys's Quaker family. He was not an absolutist in any field and it was his nature to be nearly always willing to review his opinions and modify them. World War II offered such an opportunity. Early in the lead-up to the outbreak of hostilities, he sided with Prime Minister Chamberlain and appeasement. But as Hitler's intentions in Europe became clear, he came to view Germany's defeat as essential. Even in the dark days before World War I, Russell had argued that certain wars were just; now he again made that case, with what he would come to call 'relative political pacifism'. In his opinion, a commitment to pacifism is relative to the nature of war, nearly always dictated by political institutions rather than individuals. 'Very few wars are worth fighting,' he later wrote in 'The Future of Pacifism' for *The American Scholar*, 'and … the evils of war are almost always greater than they seem to excited populations at the moment when war breaks out.' War was always a great evil but in some certain extreme cases, such as was the case with Hitler's designs on Europe, it was the lesser of two evils.

—

## THE BERTRAND RUSSELL CASE

ODDLY, RUSSELL SPENT THE DURATION OF THE WAR IN THE UNITED States. In 1939 he, Patricia and Conrad moved to Santa Barbara, California, where he lectured on philosophy at the University of California. In 1940 he was appointed Professor of Philosophy at the City College of New York. But shortly before he was to take his position, it was revoked. Because of his published views on marriage and sexual morality from the 1920s, and perhaps partly from the example he set, the mother of a student at the college brought a suit before New York's Supreme Court. The judge in the case found that Russell's 'libertine' views could undermine the morals of the students and, as he stated in his ruling, 'bring them, and in some cases their parents and guardians, in conflict with the Penal

Law'. Many intellectuals argued in Russell's defence and students staged sit-ins. Educator John Dewey and philosopher Horace Kallen collected a series of articles on his dismissal and published them as *The Bertrand Russell Case*.

Marooned in America by the war, Russell found that his sudden notoriety had scared away employers and publishers, and was unable to gain access to his finances in Great Britain due to currency restrictions. He was desperately in need of work when the millionaire industrialist and art collector Albert Barnes, eccentric and irascible, came to his rescue. He hired Russell through his foundation to present a set of lectures to a tightly selected student body. Within the year, however, he fell out of favour with his benefactor. Nonetheless, the lectures Russell gave at the Barnes Foundation formed the core of his most popular work, *The History of Western Philosophy*. Its publication and success ended his financial difficulties and was to help him regain favour with Trinity College. In 1944, Russell returned to England and again became a Fellow at Cambridge. World War I had ended his career at Trinity; World War II had revived it.

With the success of *The History of Western Philosophy*, Russell became much in demand as a lecturer all over the world. On one such trip in 1948, en route to a lecture in Trondheim, Norway, the seaplane he was flying in lost a pontoon on landing and crashed, flipping over and sinking within minutes. Of the forty-three passengers only twenty-four survived, the seventy-four-year-old Russell among them. All the survivors had been seated in the smoking compartment. A lifelong smoker, Russell quipped to a reporter after the crash that he'd secured a seat in smoking before the flight because 'if I cannot smoke, I shall die'.

During this period, Russell took another odd detour in his public activism. Ever since his trip to Russia in 1920, he had been increasingly anti-communist. This was only heightened after the Allied victory in World War II. He wrote to his old friend Collette O'Neil, 'Ever since the end of the war, I have been as anti-Russian as one can be without being thought mad.' Now with Stalin's atrocities all too clear, Berlin's partitioning and the Soviet 'iron curtain' closing around satellite countries, Russell became an outspoken critic of the USSR. Officials eager to capitalise on his leftist credentials were only too happy to support his transformation into a cold warrior.

Russell gave a speech in 1948 in which he warned of the USSR's continuing aggression towards countries of Eastern Europe. The Soviets did not yet possess an A-bomb and Russell stated that he felt it would be morally worse if the West went to war with the Soviets after they developed nuclear weapons. To many, this comment seemed to suggest his approval of a nuclear first strike. The outcry from intellectuals, pacifists and leftists was deafening; but the government was only too happy for his blessings. Russell attempted to clarify his remarks, arguing he was merely speaking of the usefulness of America's atomic arsenal for deterring Soviet aggression. The debate was soon rendered moot when the Soviet Union tested its first atomic bomb in 1949, launching a full-on nuclear arms race.

—

## NUCLEAR DISARMAMENT

BY THE EARLY 1950S, WITH A SERIES OF POPULAR LECTURES BROADCAST throughout the world by the BBC and having received both the Order of Merit from King George VI and the Nobel Prize for Literature, Russell was one of the most recognisable intellectuals in the world, second only to Albert Einstein. He became a vocal advocate of nuclear disarmament with the advent of the hydrogen bomb. Russell took on the very public role of nuclear alarmist, broadcasting his famous 'Man's Peril' lecture in 1954. And then, with the death of Stalin and the ascendancy of Nikita Khrushchev, Russell's dislike of the USSR cooled to such an extent that in 1957 he wrote to both President Eisenhower and Premier Khrushchev about the dangers of nuclear proliferation. To his and the world's surprise, Khrushchev wrote back and the two began a correspondence that would last for years.

In 1954, Russell joined with Albert Einstein and nine other pre-eminent scientists from Western and communist-controlled countries in issuing a statement in opposition to nuclear arms. The Russell-Einstein Manifesto, issued in 1955, was signed by Einstein only days before his death. It warned of the dangers of nuclear arms and concluded with a stern statement bluntly admonishing world governments that a future world war would threaten the existence of mankind. The statement urged the governments of the world to acknowledge publicly that because of the threat of nuclear weapons, their ends could not be furthered by war and that they must instead seek peaceful means for settling disputes. In addition, the Manifesto called for a conference which Cyrus Eaton, a wealthy Canadian industrialist, offered to sponsor. The Pugwash Conferences on Science and World Affairs took its name from Eaton's hometown of Pugwash, Nova Scotia where the first meeting took place in 1957 (see 'The Pugwash Conference', page 125).

Russell was now nearly eighty and had recently weathered an acrimonious divorce from Patricia and his son John's descent into schizophrenia. In 1952 he had married his fourth and last wife, Edith Finch, and together they devoted their efforts to concerns of disarmament and world peace. Out of the Pugwash

# ORIGINS OF THE PEACE SYMBOL

Gerald Holtom, a graphic designer and artist, was a British conscientious objector in World War II and active in the anarcho–pacifist organisation Direct Action Committee Against Nuclear War (DAC) in the 1950s. When DAC, along with the Campaign for Nuclear Disarmament, planned a massive demonstration and march from Trafalgar Square in London to the Atomic Weapons Research Establishment in Aldermaston in 1958, they approached Holtom to design their banners and a new symbol for the nuclear disarmament campaign. Holtom, a tall, soft-spoken Christian pacifist who'd spent the war years working on a farm in Norfolk, struggled over the task.

When he made his initial presentation, he explained that he was striving for a symbol that was not only informative but also summed up the essence of the disarmament message; in other words, a brand. What he came up with has become one of the most recognisable icons of the last century. Tasked with finding a shorthand way of saying 'unilateral nuclear disarmament', he turned to the British navy's semaphore flag language. The navy communicated ship to ship by using two hand-held flags to spell out messages. The 'N' was represented by holding two flags down at a 45-degree angle from the horizon, while the 'D' was made by holding one flag directly up and one down in a straight line. Simplified, superimposed and placed in a 'unilateral' circle, he not only encoded the letters signifying nuclear disarmament he also created a symbol that soon became associated with the entire peace movement and the 1960s counter-culture generation.

The new DAC logo was used for the Aldermaston march and was picked up by Bertrand Russell's Campaign for Nuclear Disarmament. Carried to the United States, the design soon caught on as a more general symbol for the anti-Vietnam War peace movement. From the beginning, certain factions of the American religious right have tried to argue that the peace symbol is actually an inverted cross and thus a symbol of the devil. Holtom, as a Christian, was leery of any satanic inferences and argued the design's origin throughout his life. At the initial presentation, one cynic warned that the design looked like chicken tracks and would never catch on. Today, the symbol is practically ubiquitous and serves as an international emblem of peace and a reminder of the 1960s counter-culture and anti-war movement. Holtom, who died in 1985, never copyrighted the design but always took great satisfaction in the part it played for peace.

Conference, Russell helped found the Campaign for Nuclear Disarmament (CND) to coordinate unilateral nuclear disarmament and support international arms regulations. It would expand to become Europe's largest peace campaign. Beginning in 1958, the CND organised an annual march from Trafalgar Square in London to the Atomic Weapons Establishment near Aldermaston. For the first of these marches, a young pacifist and designer named Gerald Holtom created a nuclear disarmament logo, which gained worldwide recognition during the 1960s as the peace symbol (see 'Origins of the peace symbol', page 128).

Russell very quickly became dissatisfied with the slow progress of the CND and resigned his presidency. In 1960, he founded with the Reverend Michael Scott the Committee of 100, a nuclear disarmament group with the goal of non-violent civil disobedience. Established with 100 public signatories, the Committee of 100 began an aggressive campaign of public demonstrations, sit-ins, strikes and rallies. In 1961, Russell and Edith were arrested at a huge ban-the-bomb demonstration at the Ministry of Defence. Once again, now at the age of eighty-eight, his anti-war activism landed him in the Brixton gaol. His six-month sentence was commuted to a week because of his age and state of health.

None of this slowed his activism or his active participation in world affairs. During the Cuban Missile Crisis in 1962, in which the United States and the Soviet Union came closer to nuclear war than at any other time, Russell played a small but pivotal role. Because of his friendly correspondence with Khrushchev, and through the influence of the Pugwash scientists, he was able to provide a backdoor communications channel between US President Kennedy and Khrushchev. In 1963 he turned his attention to America's policy towards Vietnam, warning of the latest in a series of 'proxy wars' fought between the West and the Communist East. He was equally a vocal critic of human rights abuses in the USSR and criticised the invasion of Czechoslovakia in 1968. He did point out, however, that in his view the Soviet treatment of the Czechs was far better than the US treatment of the Vietnamese.

In the final years of his life, Russell's boundless energy touched on nearly every important human rights issue. He maintained his fervent opposition to the Vietnam War through his associations with leading activists such as Thomas Merton and Thich Nhat Hanh. He was also one of the first to raise public inquiry into the official story of John F. Kennedy's assassination, in 1964, with his essay '16 Questions on the Assassination', still considered one of the best summaries of inconsistencies in the case. He tackled war abuses with writer Jean-Paul Sartre in his *War Crimes in Vietnam*, based on Nuremberg-like tribunals against US atrocities. He established the Bertrand

Russell Peace Foundation that continues his work for peace and social justice to this day.

In his last decade he also continued to publish at an amazing rate, including *Fact and Fiction* in 1961, *Essays in Skepticism* and *Unarmed Victory* in 1963, and *Russell's Peace Appeals* in 1967. At ninety-five he was frail, but his mind was clear and sharp. He completed his vast three-volume *Autobiography of Bertrand Russell* in 1969. Its opening lines read: 'Three passions, simple but overwhelmingly strong, have governed my life: the longing for love, the search for knowledge and unbearable pity for the suffering of mankind.' Its short handwritten dedication to Edith was in the form of a poem:

Through the long years
I sought peace.
I found ecstasy, I found anguish,
I found madness,
I found loneliness.
I found the solitary pain
That gnaws the heart,
But peace I did not find.

Now, old & near my end,
I have known you,
And, knowing you,
I have found both ecstasy & peace.
I know rest,
After so many lonely years,
I know what life & love may be.
Now, if I sleep,
I shall sleep fulfilled.

Bertrand Russell died on 2 February 1970 of influenza at his home in Wales. It's somehow fitting that the man who sought an end to war in such paradoxically opposing ways, who gave himself equally to the sciences and his passions, would ultimately find peace in the love of a woman.

'The essence of non-violence is love.
Out of love and the willingness to act selflessly,
strategies, tactics, and techniques for
a non-violent struggle arise naturally.'
**THICH NHAT HANH**

# PART III

## IN RESPONSE TO THE TWENTIETH CENTURY'S WARS

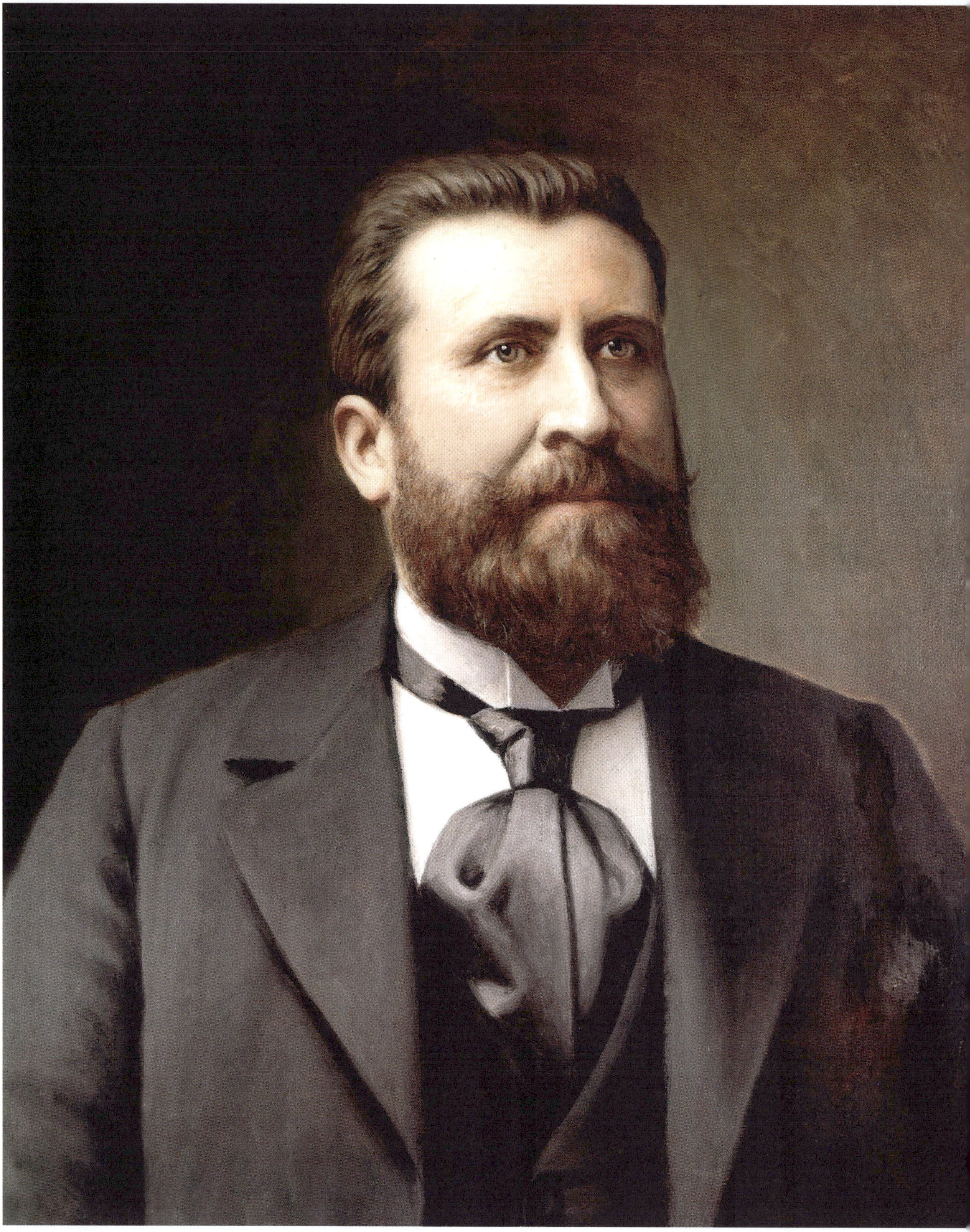

# JEAN JAURÈS:
# ANTI-MILITARY SOCIALIST

JEAN JAURÈS WAS ONE OF FRANCE'S EARLIEST AND MOST ADMIRED SOCIAL democrats and the nation's last, best hope for finding a peaceful way of avoiding World War I. At the end of July 1914, following a month of escalating European tensions and build-up to war, Jaurès was assassinated by a radical French nationalist. The head of the French Socialist Party and a committed pacifist, he had struggled against all odds to lead France and Germany to an end of hostilities through diplomacy. Warned that his actions would raise the ire of French nationalists who mistrusted the Germans and sought retribution for the country's loss of Alsace-Lorraine in the Franco–Prussian War, Jaurès persisted in trying to find solidarity between the organised workers of France and Germany. His efforts cost him his life, and two days later, the world descended into a war like none that had ever come before.

And it all might have been averted.

—

## A NEW ARMY

JEAN JAURÈS WAS A PACIFIST OF PRAGMATIC BENT. BORN IN 1859, HE WAS RAISED in a modest bourgeois family in Castres, a provincial town in southwest France that was transitioning from agriculture to trade and manufacturing.

Jean Jaurès, painted c. 1902–06 by Jean-François Batut (1828–1907). It is unlikely that Jaurès had the time to sit for the artist, who is thought to have worked from photographs.

His understanding of the working classes taught him that when wars were fought, it was the peasants and labourers who suffered the most. Bright, talented and a spirited speaker even as a young man, he graduated from the École Normale in 1881. Initially, he taught philosophy at a school in nearby Albi and eventually at the University of Toulouse. In 1885 he entered politics and was elected to the National Assembly as a delegate for the region of Tarn, including Castres and Albi. At twenty-six, he was the youngest member of Parliament.

Jaurès came to prominence in 1892 when he supported a strike by the miners of Carmaux, a parish in Tarn rich in coal deposits and glass manufactories. Striking over the dismissal of their charismatic leader Jean Baptiste Calvignac, the miners were pressing for an increase in wages and improvements in working conditions. Jaurès' efforts forced the government to intervene and Calvignac was reinstated. The following year, Jaurès was re-elected to Parliament and joined the Socialist Party.

Throughout his life, Jaurès strove to strike a balance between reform and revolution. He was a unifier, and believed in the need to break down the class structure of French society. Big and barrel-chested, with a full square beard, he was a warm and friendly man, a stark contrast to the often cold intellectuals who personified the Socialist Party. His oratorical skills were legendary. 'One had only to listen to the ringing voice of Jaurès,' wrote the young Russian revolutionary Leon Trotsky, 'to see his enlightened look, his imperious nose, his thick and unyoked neck, to say to himself: There is a Man!' By 1904, through sheer force of will, Jaurès had united the moderate and revolutionary factions of the French Socialist Party.

The Unified Socialist Party which he now led joined the mainstream of French politics and took as the key planks of its platform opposition to aggressive military internationalism, and support for the workers. Towards this end, Jaurès attempted to redefine the function of the military in a society that honoured peace equally with the labours of its workers. As early as 1907 he envisioned an *armée nouvelle* that would be voluntary, egalitarian and free of class patronage. He opposed a mandatory three-year draft and offered an alternative vision of a defensive military. He encouraged the influence of the European court of arbitration at The Hague, which was empowered to settle international disputes, guarantee national sovereignty and assure international justice. And, most controversially, he strove for understanding and solidarity with the workers of Germany. He wrote in *L'Humanité*, the socialist daily newspaper he co-founded as the mouthpiece for a more moderate socialism:

How can we best secure the chances of peace for France and for the uncertain world which surrounds her? And if in spite of her efforts and her wish for peace, she is attacked, how can we best secure the chances of safety, the means of victory? …

To ensure peace by a plain policy of wisdom, moderation and rectitude, by the definitive repudiation of all aggressive enterprises, by the loyal acceptance and practice of the new methods of international law which are capable of solving conflicts without violence; on the other hand, to ensure peace, courageously, by the establishment of a defensive organisation so formidable that every thought of aggression is put out of the mind of even the most insolent and rapacious.

This noble vision would be put to the test by the events that unfolded in July 1914.

⌐

## THE JULY CRISIS

ON 28 JUNE 1914, BOSNIAN–SERB NATIONALISTS ASSASSINATED ARCHDUKE Franz Ferdinand, heir to the throne of the Austro–Hungarian Empire. The event that would ultimately lead to world war might have remained a localised conflict between Austria and Serbia, but became the tipping point after two decades of escalating imperialism, distrust and rivalry between the two 'super-alliances' of Europe. Austria held Serbia accountable for the assassination and, sensing an opportunity to 'justify' war, made unreasonable demands for reparation. Russia, however, would not allow Austria to overrun Serbia for fear that it would threaten Russian security. And if Russia challenged Austria, Austria's ally Germany would be expected to respond. That would, in turn, draw in Russia's ally France. Great Britain, the world's pre-eminent power and also an ally of France, could not be expected to stay on the sidelines.

The French socialists had won their biggest electoral victory earlier in the year and Jaurès had been pushing hard for peace. But everything came unstuck after the assassination. In the first week of July, Austria demanded that Serbia accept responsibility for the plot and began preparing untenable terms under which reparations were to be made. At the same time Austria quietly prepared for war, and Kaiser Wilhelm of Germany promised a 'blank cheque' for whatever action they wished to take regarding retribution. In that same week Jaurès wrote a lengthy article (which did not appear in print until

## ROMAIN ROLLAND

The French writer and pacifist Romain Rolland was living in Switzerland when he received the Nobel Prize for Literature in 1915. As war raged in Europe, he was respected internationally but loathed in France for his anti-war sentiments, internationalism and support for the culture and artists of Germany. In his works he often intermingled political perspectives with narrative, and he fiercely attacked nationalism as a struggle against social and political justice.

When his collection of anti-war writings, *Above the Battle*, was published in 1913 in a Swiss newspaper, it led to protests in France and lifted Rolland to the position of one of the most prominent pacifist writers in Europe. He attempted to show the oneness of Western culture by highlighting the commonality between the people of France and Germany. But these opinions, along with his known adoration of certain German artists, got him labelled a traitor in France. He

moved to Switzerland permanently, joining a community of expatriate anti-war writers that included James Joyce. During World War I he wrote several pacifist essays condemning the conflict, which further outraged hardline militarists in France.

When war ended, Rolland was still *persona non grata* in France; he remained in Switzerland. He opposed the Treaty of Versailles for the harsh conditions imposed on Germany and warned that the terms would likely lead to war again. Finding himself drawn to Indian philosophy in the 1920s, Rolland wrote an early biography of Gandhi in 1924 and hosted Gandhi at his lakeside cottage. In 1932 he formed the International Congress Against War and Fascism, and later met Gorky and Stalin in the young Soviet Union. Although regularly called a communist, Rolland never aligned with any political party and came to oppose Stalinism. He died in 1939 after moving back to France, still agitating for peace as his prophecy of another world war was, unfortunately, coming true.

after his death) detailing a path to peace and arguing that, even given the many conflicts in the Balkans, war could be avoided if the capitalist countries of Europe would seek peaceful coexistence by sharing world markets and slowing their munitions manufacturing. Certainly an idealist, Jaurès argued that capitalist societies would never change their warring ways unless they felt the pressure of pan-European workers.

To this end, he called for workers in France and Germany to exert their influence on their governments and rein in Austria and Russia. Turning his attention to the annual National Socialist Congress on 14 July, he put his efforts into building support for general strikes in France and Germany. The issue was hotly debated. A general strike was 'one way of influencing and warning our rulers', Jaurès argued, to force them to seek arbitration from the World Court at The Hague. But many questioned whether the workers would rise up. Others feared that if France succeeded in unleashing an anarchist revolt against war, and Germany did not, the result would be a weakened and vulnerable France. 'If France were exposed to the aggressions of German imperialism,' Jaurès argued, 'Germany would be similarly threatened by Russia.' His argument carried the day, the congress narrowly agreeing to use every means it could to prevent a European war, including the general strike.

Now openly agitating for a general strike, Jaurès took a drubbing in the press. 'We must penetrate independent nations with the international spirit,' Jaurès wrote, 'and secure the evolution of social justice in universal peace, by the concerted effort of workmen in every country.' But by now his circle of pacifist supporters was shrinking. His Parliamentary colleague, the eminent Henri d'Estournelles de Constant, who had won the Nobel Peace Prize in 1909 for his advocacy of European peace and arbitration at The Hague, had fallen silent and would soon be actively supporting the war effort. Fellow socialist and early feminist Gabrielle Duchêne, who headed the French section of the Women's International League for Peace and Freedom, was ambivalent about the strikes. The famous writer Romain Rolland, whose pacifist novels had made him even less popular than Jaurès in France, was now in self-imposed exile in Switzerland (see 'Romain Rolland', opposite). Jaurès' main ally in the general strikes was Rosa Luxemburg, the Polish-German Marxist and revolutionary, who was attempting to lead the Social Democrats in Germany to support coordinated strikes.

On 15 July 1914, the president and the prime minister of France left for St Petersburg for 'secret talks' with Russian leaders. Jaurès had attempted to block funding for the trip in the National Assembly, but could not rally his party, which was splintering as the drumbeats of war grew and his calls for a socialist brotherhood across Europe were inflaming the nationalists. France's nationalist fringe had penetrated the mainstream, and now latched onto his views on international arbitration and his advocacy of a pan-European workers' union as traitorous. Increasingly, Jaurès was painted a villain as the nationalists fanned paranoia about what might happen if the socialists succeeded in coordinating Europe's workers. Support for a general strike soon dissipated.

Likewise in Germany, a crucial vote by the Social Democrats denounced Rosa Luxemburg's efforts and put the party's support behind the government's preparations for war. Luxemburg was crushed, and she would ultimately leave the Social Democratic Party to found the Spartacus League, a revolutionary organisation that became the Communist Party of Germany. Her agitation for revolution would also lead to her imprisonment during the war years and ultimately to her brutal murder by proto-fascist paramilitaries after the war.

On the heels of the French leaders' visit to Russia, and the announcement of an Austro–Hungarian ultimatum, the Russians warned that the least infringement on Serbia's autonomy would not be tolerated. The French president cautioned the Austrian ambassador that Russians and Serbs were warm friends, and reminded him that France was Russia's ally. But the influence of Germany's behind-the-scenes leadership resulted in Austria becoming even more dictatorial, its ultimatum of 23 July specifying ten points to which the Serbs would be forced to acquiesce and to publish verbatim. Austria demanded that the Kingdom of Serbia take responsibility for the plot to assassinate the archduke and purge anti-Austrian propagandists, societies and even military officers. Most threateningly, the ultimatum demanded that Serbia accept the 'collaboration' of Austro–Hungarian forces in suppressing subversive activities in the kingdom, an act sure to be seen as a de facto subjugation of Serbian authority. In fact, the German ambassador assured the Hungarian chancellor that the ultimatum would 'be so phrased that its acceptance will be practically impossible'. Serbia was given forty-eight hours to respond.

On 25 July, the Serbs capitulated on eight of the ten points. But the Austrian foreign minister had made clear that 'any conditional acceptance, or one accompanied by reservations, [would] be regarded as a refusal'; the Serbian response was therefore rejected, and the Austro–Hungarian Empire began mobilising for war. But so strong was the hope that peace might still be mediated that peace activists' plans for the Universal Peace Congress scheduled for Vienna in early September went ahead. The congress was to celebrate, ironically, the Austrian pacifist and Nobel Peace Prize winner Bertha von Suttner, who had died only a month earlier, on 21 June (see 'Bertha von Suttner and the Nobel Peace Prize', page 143). On 28 July, Austria–Hungary declared war on Serbia. Many of the Peace Congress delegates would shortly find themselves fleeing.

Jaurès still held out hopes that the war would remain local, that France and Russia would not become involved. On 29 July he spoke before the National Assembly, warning that a total European war would cause the workers to rise up and revolt. 'When typhus finishes the work begun by bullets,' he warned, 'disillusioned men will turn on their rulers, whether German, French, Russian or Italian, and demand their explanation for all those corpses!' But war fever was reaching fever pitch. As Austria bombarded the Serbian capital of Belgrade, the French press now openly called for the nation to rise up and seek revenge for defeat in the Franco–Prussian War and the loss of Alsace-Lorraine. With accelerating speed, negotiations across Europe were coming undone. Russia called for Germany and Austria to enter international arbitration at The Hague; Germany demanded that France state its intentions within twenty-four hours.

As 29 July drew to a close, Europe's armies were on the move: Austria–Hungary's forces were entering the Kingdom of Serbia; Russia was mobilising in Serbia's defence; Germany was mobilising against Russia; France was secretly moving forces even as they denied it; and Britain was threatening mobilisation if Belgium's neutrality was compromised. Throughout the next day, 30 July, Jaurès argued, lectured and pleaded with delegates, ambassadors and journalists for continued negotiations. But when evening arrived and the news came from Berlin that Russia's proposal for arbitration at The Hague had been rejected, Jaurès' hopes were dashed.

Feverish, exhausted beyond despair, Jaurès stormed out of the Assembly, declaring with the last of his energy, 'Tonight I will write a new *J'Accuse!* I will expose everyone responsible for this crisis!' He was referring to the historic work by Émile Zola, which twenty years earlier had exposed the false accusations of treason and the cover-ups that led to the imprisonment of a Jewish military officer named Alfred Dreyfus. The court case and its aftermath had laid bare the rift in France between the pro-military nationalists and the pro-worker socialists. What had become known as the Dreyfus Affair was a pivotal point in the history of the French Republic that provided a shift in popular support for the socialists (see 'The Dreyfus affair', page 146).

But Jaurès would never write his exposé. In a few short hours, war would be unleashed across Europe. And before that, Jaurès would be dead.

## A VILLAIN NAMED VILLAIN

Unaware, Jaurès had been stalked for several days by a pale young man with a scraggly beard. Half mad, his head filled with hate-inspired propaganda, he carried a revolver in the pocket of his loose overcoat. His name, appropriately enough, was Raoul Villain. A follower of the nationalist Charles Maurras, whose anti-Semitic Action Française political movement was an early influence on twentieth century fascists, Villain saw himself as a patriot. Maurras had for years decried Jaurès' socialist and pacifist views as traitorous to the Republic. Now Villain, who had lived an unexceptional life, formulated his delusional plan to kill Jaurès as a way to bring meaning to his life. The night of 30 July, he had followed Jaurès and his colleagues from the offices of *L'Humanité* to the bustling Le Café du Croissant nearby. But he had lost his nerve. He would not lose it the next time.

On 31 July, Jaurès once again spent the day in gruelling meetings and debates with members of the National Assembly. Germany had served Russia with an ultimatum and was awaiting France's promise of neutrality in the event of a Russo–German war. In his role as head of the Socialist Party, Jaurès tried, unsuccessfully, to meet with the premier. Failing that, he made his way to the Parliamentary chamber, where he took to the podium to argue for restraint. 'Are we going to unleash a world war?', he demanded. But the tide had turned and Jaurès could see that all his efforts in brokering negotiations, supporting arbitration and threatening a general strike had fallen on deaf ears. He alone seemed to have a full understanding of what total war would be like.

Late in the day he finally secured a meeting with Abel Ferry, Undersecretary of State for Foreign Affairs. Ferry respected Jaurès, but feared what he might do if France went to war. Sick and feverish from the threat of the escalating conflict, Jaurès hardly hesitated. 'We will clear our party of any guilt,' he answered. 'To the very end we will continue to struggle against war.' This was just as Ferry had feared. 'No, you won't be able to continue,' he replied sadly. 'You will be assassinated on the nearest street corner.' Little did anyone realise how immediately prophetic this prediction would turn out to be.

That evening, with news breaking that Germany had fully mobilised against Russia, Jaurès and his colleagues made their way once again to Le Café du Croissant. The Rue Montmartre was thronged with newspaper vendors and crowds snatching up late editions for any news of the impending war. The popular Croissant was a modest café with dirty, sawdust-covered floors, frayed chairs and marble-topped tables scattered about, and hand-written

# BERTHA VON SUTTNER AND THE NOBEL PEACE PRIZE

When writer and pacifist Bertha von Suttner accepted her Nobel Peace Prize in 1905, she complimented Jean Jaurès on his efforts to 'summon the socialists of all countries to a united resistance to war'. While she was the first woman to receive the award, von Suttner may well be the reason that industrialist Alfred Nobel decided to endow a peace prize in the first place.

Born a countess in Prague in 1845, Bertha von Suttner (née Bertha Kinsky von Wchinitz und Tettau) was the daughter of a field-marshal and raised in Austria's militaristic aristocracy. Her father died penniless and Bertha was forced, at the age of thirty, to take a position as governess with the von Suttner family in Vienna. Here she met her future husband, Baron Arthur von Suttner. Both families opposed the romance and they were forbidden to marry. Distraught, Bertha ran away to Paris where she answered an advertisement to become secretary and housekeeper to Alfred Nobel, the industrialist and inventor of dynamite. She remained in the position for only a week before returning to Vienna and secretly marrying Arthur. In that short time she had made such an impression on Nobel that the two corresponded for the rest of his life. When he sought to endow the Nobel Prizes, she made an impassioned argument for the inclusion of an annual peace award among them.

Bertha and Arthur exiled themselves to the Caucasus, where they eked out a living for eight years teaching music and writing. Bertha wrote several books during this time, establishing herself as a writer of some note. With her recognition growing and the von Suttners' opposition to their marriage cooling, the couple returned to Vienna in 1885. Here Bertha wrote most of her works, the most famous of them the novel *Die Waffen Nieder!* (*Lay Down Your Arms!*), which contained vivid descriptions of the horrors of war and strong indictments of militarism. With its publication in 1889 she became a leader in the peace movement and in 1891 founded the Austrian Peace Society. She edited the international pacifist journal *Die Waffen Nieder!*, named after the novel, and lectured, wrote and agitated for peace all over the world. In 1893 she learned, in a letter from Alfred Nobel, that following her recommendation he intended to endow a peace award after his death.

Along with her husband, Bertha worked for the creation of The Hague Peace Conference in 1899, which led to peace activists and legislators all over Europe rallying around the idea of a permanent court of arbitration. Following the death of her husband in 1902, she continued an arduous speaking schedule advocating for pacifism. In 1905, she became the fourth recipient of the Nobel Peace Prize and the first woman to be awarded it. For the rest of her life she continued to work for international cooperation and friendship between European nations and a reduction in military armaments. She died in 1914, only a month before her country declared war on the Kingdom of Serbia, setting off World War I.

chalkboard signs advertising house wines and special dishes. Close to many of the newspaper offices of Paris, it was always packed with politicians and journalists alike. Here Jaurès spoke briefly with a reporter from the pro-labour *Manchester Gazette*, expressing some hope that England's Foreign Secretary Sir Edward Grey might still induce Germany to negotiate. Peace might still be within reach if Europe's socialists were kept allied and a conference of some sort arranged to induce France and Germany to seek international arbitration. But, he was forced to admit, the hour might well have passed for such hopes.

Jaurès ordered dinner and sank wearily onto a leather settee near an open window. Around nine-thirty, as his party was finishing dinner, two shots rang out. At first the patrons thought the sounds had come from the street. But the screams from a woman nearby drew attention to Jaurès, slumped in his seat. Raoul Villain had finally steeled his nerve and seized the opportunity, stepping into the open window directly behind Jaurès and firing two shots point-blank into his head. Villain was seized and handed over to the gendarmes, who were forced to protect him from an unruly crowd. A doctor was hastily summoned but Jaurès died minutes later without regaining consciousness.

Within hours, news of the murder was eclipsing even the latest war headlines. The president quickly offered condolences and called for calm. Villain was taken to a police precinct where he was held, unwilling to say anything about his actions. But his ties to the nationalistic Action Française soon made his motives clear. The right-wing French press had long been denouncing Jaurès as an agent of Germany, and recently even more moderate patriotic journalists had bandied about the term 'traitor' for his attempts at organising a general strike. Still, the people of France knew Jean Jaurès as a man who deeply loved his country, a man free of vanity or ambition for power. As the outpouring of sympathy would show, even at the height of war fever, the country never doubted his honest wish to find a way to peace.

The following day Germany declared war on Russia, and France fully mobilised. By 3 August, Germany had declared war on France and invaded neutral Belgium, thus ensuring that Britain would enter the war. The socialists now abandoned any notions of peace and joined with the rest of France in supporting all-out war. Raoul Villain had achieved his objective—he had silenced the only man who might have kept the French left united for peace.

Villain would sit out the war in a prison cell in Paris. He was eventually tried in 1919 but by then outrage at Jaurès' murder had been replaced with euphoria at France's victory over Germany. That, no doubt, influenced the verdict. Many of the jurors thought of Villain as a patriot who had rid France of the anti-war

Sightseers, police and photographers crowd the street outside Le Café du Croissant following the assassination of Jaurès by Raoul Villain.

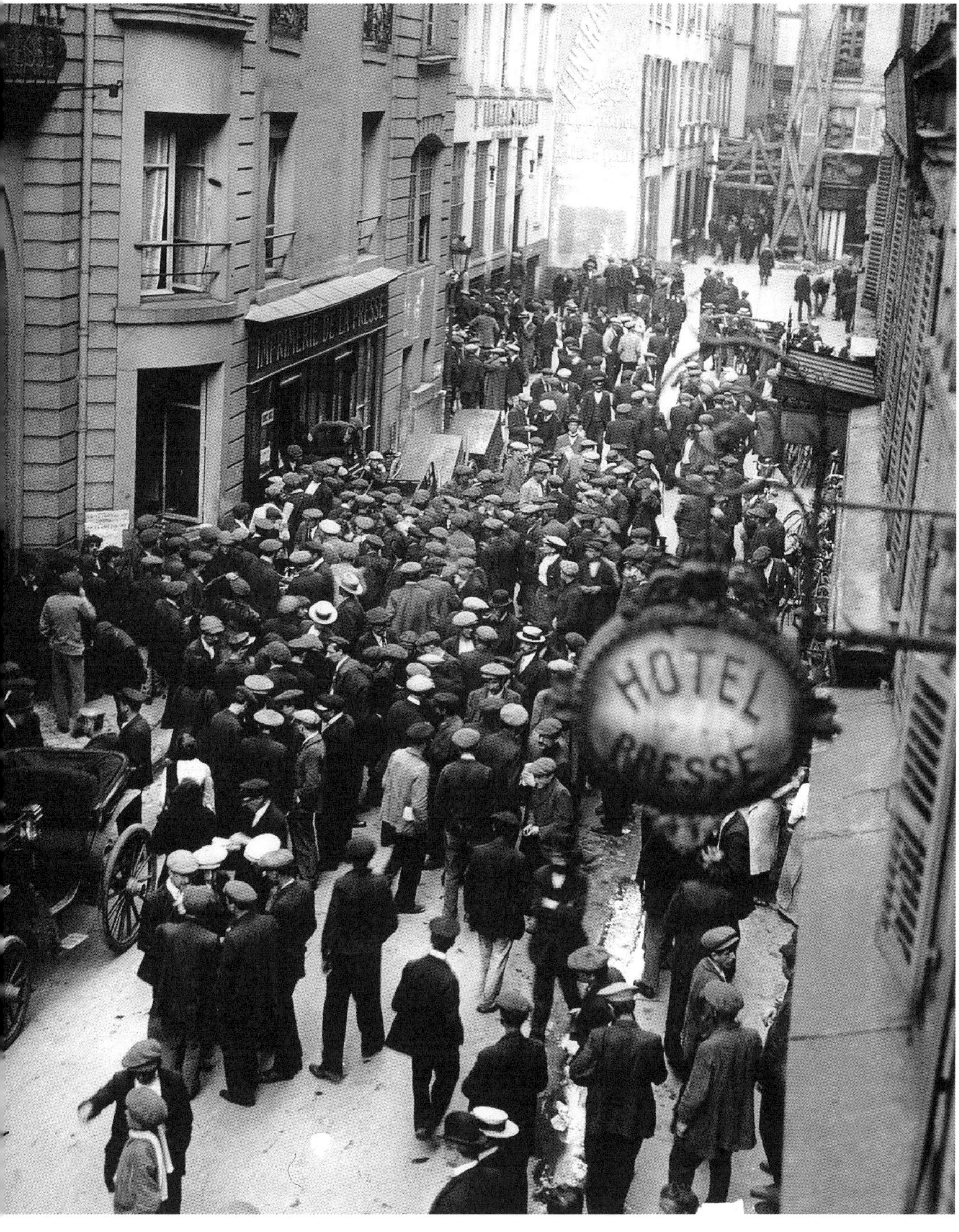
IMPRIMERIE DE LA PRESSE
HOTEL

An obscure Jewish army captain, Alfred Dreyfus was at the centre of a political scandal that shook the young French republic. In 1894, evidence came to light that a French officer was leaking secret information to the German government. Dreyfus became the key suspect. Suspicion only intensified when it became known that his Jewish family had emigrated from Alsace, fleeing to Paris following the region's annexation by the victorious Germany after the Franco–Prussian War. Despite highly questionable evidence and Dreyfus' pronouncements of innocence, he was found guilty by a secret military tribunal, publicly humiliated and given a life sentence on Devil's Island, the notorious penal colony in the Atlantic Ocean off French Guiana.

His story may well have ended there, except that support was to come from several unusual sources. First, Colonel Georges Picquart, an unabashed anti-Semite, was appointed chief of army intelligence two years later. His review of the case surprisingly concluded that the evidence didn't support a guilty verdict and that a major named Walsin Esterhazy was the likely culprit. However, the affair had become politicised with the involvement of many of France's institutions, including monarchist and republican parties, the Church and the military. Picquart's findings were officially suppressed and he was transferred; Esterhazy was found innocent. But with new evidence coming to light, the French left took up the cause.

In 1898, Émile Zola, the radical novelist, published *J'Accuse!*, his famous denunciation of the cover-up. Zola was subjected to persecution for his writings about the case, found guilty of libelling the army and sentenced to prison; he fled to Britain and didn't return until granted amnesty years later. His revelations nevertheless stirred public opinion and led to outright political warfare between the pro- and anti-Dreyfus camps. Jean Jaurès was an outspoken supporter of Dreyfus, calling in the National Assembly for a full accounting against racism and bigotry in the army. While the right tried to paint the Dreyfus case as a Jewish conspiracy set on destroying the prestige of the military, Jaurès defined it as a call for the defence of human and democratic rights.

Under pressure, in 1899 the army conducted another trial, again finding Dreyfus guilty. In response to overwhelming public pressure, however, the president issued a pardon. Dreyfus was returned to Paris, where he and his supporters continued to fight to clear his name. In 1906, twelve years after he was originally charged, he was exonerated and returned to the military, promoted to the rank of major. He served in World War I, and rose to the rank of lieutenant colonel before his death in 1935. The Dreyfus Affair did much to unite the French left in strengthening the Republic. In 1905 the Radical Party succeeded in passing legislation separating Church and state, based largely on the fact that the Catholic Church had meddled in French politics in its efforts to defame Dreyfus.

Jaurès at a time when solidarity was required. Amazingly, he was acquitted. Outrage ensued, and the socialists organised massive demonstrations. Villain was secreted out of the country to the island of Ibiza in the Balearics off Spain. He lived there until 1936 when, at the outbreak of the Spanish Civil War, he was assassinated by pro-communist Republicans.

Jean Jaurès was buried on 4 August 1914 in a ceremony both heavy with grief for the slain pacifist and rife with the excitement of war. Conservative President Raymond Poincaré said, 'Jaurès was often my adversary. But I admired his talent and his character. [Even] at an hour when national unity is more necessary than ever, I must convey to you the respect I had for him.' Would Jaurès, had he lived, been able to block France's entry into the war? Most likely not. But his would have been a voice of reason in a war that was desperately without any. A year after his death, Leon Trotsky visited Paris and wrote a tribute to the fallen pacifist. He closed by saying:

> Jaurès as the athlete of the idea died in the ring while fighting against the greatest disaster which has ever befallen mankind and humanity—*l'humanité*— while fighting against the war. And he will remain in the memory of mankind as a foreteller and a precursor of that more elevated human type which shall be born of the sufferings and defeats and out of hopes and struggle.

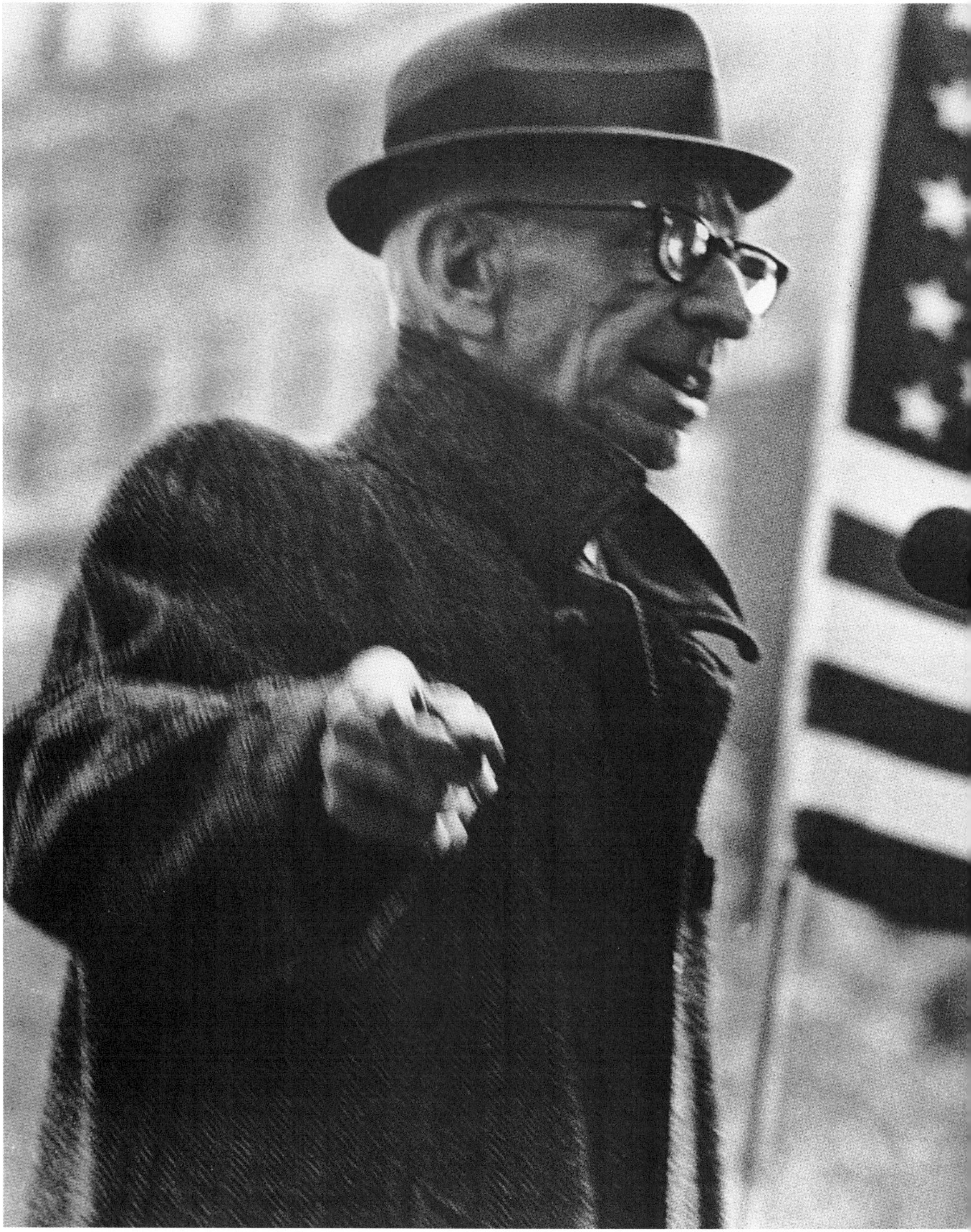

# A.J. MUSTE:
# PACIFIST REVOLUTIONARY

ABRAHAM JOHANNES MUSTE WAS ONE OF THE MOST RESPECTED PEACE advocates of the twentieth century. A radical, a revolutionary, even a prophet, A.J. (as he was universally known) often incensed his detractors and alienated his supporters by his dogged determination. A defrocked Calvinist minister, he became a Quaker; a socialist labour organiser turned revolutionary Marxist, he ultimately found his calling as a Christian pacifist.

His life was one of uncompromising belief in the fundamental dignity of all people, whether he was protesting against war or agitating for labour rights. Although his convictions were grounded in his religious beliefs, he is remembered more for the effect he had on others rather than for any theological or theoretical body of work. Over his long life, he either founded or had an impact on nearly all of the most influential peace and labour organisations of the twentieth century.

## FROM THE DUTCH REFORMED CHURCH
## COMES A SOCIAL REFORMER

A.J. MUSTE WAS BORN IN THE NETHERLANDS IN 1885 AND EMIGRATED to America with his family at the age of six to settle in Grand Rapids, Michigan. He was raised in the strict Calvinist tradition of the Dutch Reformed Church,

A.J. Muste speaking at a demonstration against the draft and the Vietnam War in New York in November 1965.

his pious parents maintaining a household 'soaked in the Bible and the language of the Bible', as he later described it. In 1905 he graduated from nearby Hope College. Several years later, after attending the theological seminary of the Dutch Reformed Church (now the New Brunswick Theological Seminary) in New Jersey, he was ordained a minister. In 1909 he became the first minister of the Fourth Avenue Washington Collegiate Church in New York City, and married his college sweetheart Anna Huizenga, who was soon pregnant with the first of their three children. Had he been a man less progressively curious, he might have settled into the simple life of a dutiful minister. But the world was unfolding in ways that would radically change A.J.'s perspective.

Enrolling first at New York University, then at Columbia, in 1913 A.J. graduated *summa cum laude* from the prestigious Union Theological Seminary with a doctorate of divinity. At that time, and throughout the twentieth century, Union Theological Seminary was a centre for some of the most liberal Christian teaching in the country. A.J. began to consider the inner-city plight of the less fortunate around him and soon found himself increasingly critical of the disparity between rich and poor in the United States. In 1912 he supported the socialist presidential candidate Eugene V. Debs and found himself growing steadily more uncomfortable with the conservative views of the Dutch Reformed Church.

The following year he moved his young family to Massachusetts where he became a pastor of the more liberal Central Congregational Church. A.J. had also been introduced to the Religious Society of Friends and admired their Christian pacifist beliefs. When war broke out in Europe and the United States began a national debate about entering the conflict, A.J. used his pulpit to call for peace and to remind his congregation about the pacifist teachings of Jesus. Tall, thin as a rail, with a chiselled angular face and booming voice, he cut such a figure that one congregant recalled, 'I imagine it was what the prophets must have sounded like.'

In 1915, Muste joined with sixty-eight other American pacifists, including Jane Addams, activist and pacifist Unitarian minister John Haynes Holmes and the Episcopal Bishop Paul Jones, in founding the US Fellowship of Reconciliation (FOR). Only recently formed in England, the FOR had arisen out of a pact between British Quaker Henry Hodgson and German Lutheran minister Friedrich Siegmund-Schultze who together declared: 'We are one in Christ and can never be at war.' Although the FOR was founded as a Christian peace organisation, in the United States the organisers broadened its reach to include all faiths. Created largely in response to the war in Europe, the FOR is to this day focused primarily on supporting non-violent alternatives to war and aiding war objectors and the rights of conscience.

After America entered the war in 1917, A.J. was unable to contain his radicalised pacifist views. 'I had to face,' he explained in his autobiography, 'not academically but existentially, as it were—the question of whether I could reconcile what I had been preaching out of the Gospel … with participation in war.' Already influenced by the beliefs of the Society of Friends, A.J.'s changing viewpoint drew him to the writings of its founders George Fox and William Penn and contemporary Quaker scholar Rufus Jones. Putting into action his writings on how religion, social concern and mystical experiences had led to great reforms in human history, Jones had recently helped found the American Friends Service Committee (AFSC), an organisation focused on promoting peace and aiding war victims (see 'Rufus Jones and the AFSC', page 156).

In March 1918, the news that the son of one his church members had been killed in the war led A.J. to preach an Easter Sunday sermon that offered up a blistering condemnation of the war's futility. Immediately after the service the congregation called a meeting and unanimously agreed to terminate his ministry, demanding that he and his family move out of the parsonage that afternoon. Stunned by this sudden action, A.J. turned to Rufus Jones, who helped the family relocate to Rhode Island and move into a Quaker household. A short while later, A.J. converted and became a minister with the Friends.

Deepening his ties with the FOR, A.J. began counselling conscientious objectors at nearby Fort Devens in Massachusetts. FOR's legal defence group, then called the Emergency Committee for Civil Liberties, help support war resisters arrested for failing to comply with sedition laws and provided legal advice for men wishing to establish a claim as a conscientious objector. Muste worked closely with the Unitarian minister John Haynes Holmes, and the program soon grew large enough to branch off. Muste saw in Holmes a model for the type of radicalised faith in action he wished to pursue and the new fledgling organisation merged with the National Civil Liberties Bureau, the remnants of the now-shuttered American Union Against Militarism. This new organisation would become known as the American Civil Liberties Union (ACLU) (see 'John Haynes Holmes', page 153).

In addition to his efforts in aid of war resisters, A.J. began to agitate for the creation of city and farm cooperatives. He travelled throughout the New England states speaking at churches and meetings, making the connection between the disparity in economic justice and his anti-military sentiments. Just as he had moved away from the conservative views of the Dutch Reformed Church, A.J. was about to make an even further leftward turn. Lawrence, Massachusetts, the seat of New England's textile manufacturing industry, was a hotbed of explosive labour disputes and strikes. Abuses and violence against striking workers led the labour unions to cry for help from the religious community. Muste responded.

⸻

## 'AND … WE WOULD SMILE AS WE PASSED THE MACHINE GUNS'

LAWRENCE HAD BEEN A CENTRE OF THE TEXTILE INDUSTRY SINCE THE early 1800s, and over the years had attracted wave after wave of low-wage immigrant workers. In 1919, when mill owners pushed through a reduction in wages, 30,000 mostly immigrant workers went on strike. As the bosses tried to break the strike, they called on the governor of Massachusetts to unleash the militia. A.J. and other religious leaders joined with the workers. He first raised money to support striking families but then, concerned about the escalating violence, joined the strikers and put himself at the front of the picket lines where he was beaten unconscious and arrested. On his release and recovery he found himself thrust into a position of leadership when he was unanimously voted in as executive secretary of the strike committee.

The strike continued for weeks. The police attempted to provoke violence by sending spies to infiltrate the picketers and encourage them to storm the police lines. Facing the machine-gun wielding police, A.J. recalled telling the strikers:

> I told them in line with the strike committee's decision, that to permit ourselves to be provoked into violence would mean defeating ourselves; that our real power was in our solidarity and our capacity to endure suffering rather than to give up the fight for the right to organise; that no one could 'weave wool with machine guns'; that cheerfulness was better for morale than bitterness and that therefore we would smile as we passed the machine guns and the police on the way from the hall to the picket lines around the mills.

After four months, A.J. and other leaders were able to negotiate a settlement to the strike. The workers had won the right to unionise, although they failed to win guarantees of wage increases and the rehiring of all striking workers; but for the time being, everyone could get back to work.

At the end of the strike, Muste found himself leading the newly organised Amalgamated Textile Workers of America (ATWA) as general secretary. He now carried considerable credibility with two different constituencies—by keeping the strike mostly peaceful he had maintained his base of radical Christian pacifists,

## JOHN HAYNES HOLMES

John Haynes Holmes, born in 1879, influenced several of the most important pacifist and social activist organisations in America. A prominent Unitarian minister in Massachusetts and a socialist, in 1908 he founded, along with other young radicals, the United Fellowship for Social Justice as a marriage of religious values and socialist activism. He was an organiser of the National Association for the Advancement of Colored People (NAACP) in 1909 and a founder and chair of the American Civil Liberties Union (ACLU). As a result of America's involvement in World War I, Holmes became a Christian pacifist. He was one of the founders of the American branch of the Fellowship of Reconciliation and the War Resistance League.

In 1917, he declared in 'A Statement to My People on the Eve of War' that warfare was an 'open and utter violation of Christianity'. He argued: 'If war is right, then Christianity is wrong, false, a lie. If Christianity is right, then war is wrong, false, a lie.' The very next day,

President Woodrow Wilson sought a declaration of war against Germany.

Holmes' fiery oratory eventually led to accusations of treason by the American Unitarian Association (AUA). He resigned his ministry from the AUA and watched as attendance at his independent church dwindled. Slowly, however, his promotion of pacifism attracted a new congregation, which grew substantially as the horrors of the first worldwide modern war became evident. By 1936, the Unitarian General Assembly reversed its 1918 repudiation of ministers who did not support the war and Holmes aligned his now sizeable congregation with the AUA. During World War II the AUA supported conscientious objectors and refused to suppress the views of pacifists who dissented from the AUA president's endorsement of the war.

Holmes died in 1964, in the early years of another war, in Vietnam, which he also vigorously opposed. A year before his death, he received the newly established Gandhi Peace Award from the American Friends Service Committee.

while at the same time his determination and negotiating skills had won the trust of the industrial unions. For the next three years Muste worked tirelessly as the head of the ATWA—nearly every week there was a new strike somewhere along the eastern seaboard. But Muste wanted to broaden his labour tactics.

While still working with the FOR as well as the American Federation of Labor (AFL), he became the founding chairman and head of faculty of the Brookwood Labor College in New York state. Through teaching theory and practice, the college sought to emphasise how the 'emancipation of the working class' would ultimately replace capitalism with socialism. The AFL initially sponsored Brookwood but by 1928 pulled its support because of the college's radical perspective. After a secret investigation, the president of the AFL broke off ties, claiming Brookwood was 'communistic, atheistic and anti-A. F. of L.'. Muste had, in a few years, gone from conservative minister to one of the most controversial figures in the trade union movement.

❦

## MARXIST

THROUGH THE 1920s, MUSTE BECAME INCREASINGLY OBSESSED WITH the disparity between rich and poor. He became disenchanted with both socialism and the labour movement, and increasingly embraced Marxist views. As America slumped into depression following the crash of 1929, Muste joined the Communist Party and used Brookwood to advocate his Marxist labour philosophy. But Brookwood's solvency was largely due to the generosity of its individual benefactors who now began to question the college's direction. Soon a major rift developed in the faculty and the board voted to reject revolutionary Marxism as the official doctrine of the college. Marginalised, Muste left the college in 1933. With the Great Depression deepening and enrolment dwindling, Brookwood closed for good in 1937.

Muste's frustration with the AFL's capitulation to business led him to revolutionise the organisation by creating the Conference for Progressive Labor Action (CPLA). Fundamentally revolutionary, the CPLA was essential to the establishment of the American Workers Party in 1933, which sought, through democratic means, to establish a revolutionary Marxist–Leninist tradition in America. With Muste at the helm, the CPLA kept close to labour issues and led the first sit-in strike in Ohio against the Electric Auto-Lite Company. This successful strike led directly to the formation of the United Auto Workers Union, still one of the strongest and most influential unions in America.

Muste, by this time, had all but abandoned his Christian pacifist leanings. Increasingly, he aligned with the US Communist Party and the Trotskyite American Workers Party and advocated open revolution in the United States. He became a target of suspicion and investigation by the US government. As he witnessed the Great Depression strip away worker dignity, Muste drifted steadily towards the most ardent revolutionary end of politics. But another transformation was looming. A.J. personally called it both an identity crisis and a prophetic revelation, but he found himself quite suddenly doubting the Marxist direction his life had taken.

Fully aware of how the Spanish Civil War was pitting Fascism against communism, and conscious of the rise of the Nazi Party in Germany, A.J. was troubled by the efforts of his own Workers Party in America. In 1936 he travelled to Norway to meet with Leon Trotsky, already in exile from the USSR. Although there is no record of their meeting, something happened in Norway that led Muste to begin turning against Marxism. He had never fully embraced the notion of armed revolution, and he was disillusioned by the way in which the Marxists had relied on armed insurrection, civil war and terrorism to achieve their goals. No doubt he argued with Trotsky that violent revolution was fundamentally reactionary: rather than destroying the exploitive capitalistic system, violence would only prove to perpetuate more violence. Trotsky would himself become a victim of this cycle; four years later he was assassinated by one of Stalin's agents.

Muste left Norway for Paris, where his personal transformation came to a head. When he stepped into a Catholic Church, he was overwhelmed by the feeling of having neglected his religious life. It suddenly became clear to him that he no longer belonged with the secular revolutionaries with whom he'd worked for so long. His life had started as a series of mystical explorations and now he felt called again: only through peace, he reasoned, through a return to the love promised by God and Jesus, would there be any hope of creating a new social order. He'd come to Europe an avowed communist but he returned to the United States a renewed Christian pacifist.

⁓

## AN ACT OF CONSCRIPTION

AT THE END OF THE 1930s, WHILE MUSTE CONTINUED TO WORK WITH labour organisations such as the Presbyterian Labor Temple in New York, he returned more aggressively to the Fellowship of Reconciliation. This would prove to be his most crucial effort on behalf of peace. From his travels in

# RUFUS JONES AND THE AFSC

Rufus Matthew Jones was one of the most influential Quaker pacifist scholars of the twentieth century. An activist, theologian and philosopher, he published nearly twenty books and innumerable articles over his lifetime. A popular professor at Haverford College near Philadelphia, he established the Haverford Emergency Unit in 1915 to oppose America's entry into World War I and support those who objected to serving. Two years later, the Emergency Unit was regrouped into the American Friends Service Committee (AFSC).

Jones was born in 1885 into a historic Quaker family from Maine. He received degrees from Haverford and Harvard and was editor of the *Friends Review*, a Quaker publication of faith and policy, for over twenty years. He returned to Haverford as a professor of philosophy and psychology, and was a member of the faculty for forty years until his retirement. A prolific writer and lecturer, Jones centred his Quaker teachings on the mystical quality of the Society of Friends. He encouraged an understanding of the direct connection to God that he called 'affirming mysticism'.

As the founder and first director of the AFSC, Jones initially focused the organisation on supporting conscientious objectors in World War I. Eventually, the AFSC grew into a global relief organisation offering humanitarian aid, and support for social justice, peace, human rights and the abolition of the death penalty. Between the wars, the AFSC worked in European reconstruction and in aiding victims of the Great War, especially children in Germany. In 1927, Jones toured Asia to address missionaries in China and to visit Japan, India and the Holy Lands. In India he met Mahatma Gandhi and was taken to the birthplace of the Buddha; he returned home committed to formulating a new vision of missionary work, one that gave humanitarian aid while respecting other religions without the previous emphasis on conversion.

In 1938, Jones, along with the new director of the AFSC, Clarence Pickett, led a delegation of peace activist clergy to Berlin in an effort to aid in the emigration of German Jews. He attempted to deliver a message to Hitler offering a way towards peace. After the war, the AFSC again returned to aid in European reconstruction and in 1947 the organisation was honoured with the Nobel Peace Prize. Jones accepted the award on behalf of all American and European Quakers.

Europe, A.J. felt sure that the world was again headed to war. It was, as always, his mission to advocate for peace but he also saw the need to pave the way for those who opposed military service to have options. Through his writings and his speeches he warned against American involvement in another war in Europe, and also against any US preparations. With the publication in 1940 of his book *Non-Violence in an Aggressive World*, he was clearly established, as *Time* magazine heralded him, as 'the Number One US Pacifist'.

When France fell to Germany in June 1940, it became clear that the Roosevelt Administration would call for a military conscription act. Muste directed his renewed pacifist clout against this latest development in America's quiet preparations for war. A plan for future conscription had been mapped out between the two world wars and A.J. now led the FOR, along with the War Resisters League and the ACLU, to push for provisions for conscientious objectors. When Congress passed the *Selective Training and Service Act* of 1940, the first peacetime conscription act in US history, it required all men of draft age to register—but the legislation also included provisions for objectors of conscience. Section 5(g) stated:

> Nothing contained in this Act shall be constructed to require any person to be subject to combatant training and service in the land and naval forces of the United States who, by reason of religious training and belief, is conscientiously opposed to participation in war in any form.
>
> Any such person claiming such exemption from combatant training and service because of such conscientious objections whose claim is sustained by the local draft board shall, if he is inducted into the land or naval forces under this Act, be assigned to noncombatant service as defined by the President, or shall if he is found to be conscientiously opposed to participation in such noncombatant service, in lieu of such induction, be assigned to work of national importance.

The act limited its provisions for objectors to members of religious groups having as part of their doctrine an objection to war. This included, even in its most liberal reading, only the historic peace churches—the Quakers, the Brethren and the Mennonites. The act was far from what the peace groups had agitated for. Besides limiting objectors to qualified members of the historic peace churches, there was no provision for those absolutist objectors who refused combatant, non-combatant and alternative service altogether.

But Muste was also pragmatic. He had put the considerable weight of the FOR and the ACLU behind advocating for the rights of religious conscientious objectors under civilian direction. The government had not made any initial effort to define 'work of national importance', however, and the Muste-led organisations stepped in to fill the void. As the first draft resisters faced punishment and imprisonment, the combined elements of the FOR, the ACLU, the Selective Service Administration, the historic peace churches and even President Roosevelt himself, hashed out a plan for the creation of an entity to handle them. The result was the Civilian Public Service (CPS) administration, created as an alternative to military conscription. As a government-authorised alternative service under civilian direction, the CPS would prove a true test of the nation's democratic principles.

CPS camps opened all over the country, working together in joint civilian and military administration. Many from both the left and the right opposed the camps, however, and any involvement with them. Because conscientious objectors were not paid for their work, were subjected to limits of freedom and assembly, were often treated harshly and even subjected to medical experimentation, many on the left likened the CPS camps to Nazi concentration camps. Others on the right saw them providing a free pass for men too cowardly to serve their country in wartime. Obviously neither extreme was accurate, but few were satisfied with the outcome. All in all, nearly 12,000 men passed through the CPS camps from 1941 to 1947, greatly influencing the pacifist movement in the second half of the century (see 'Civilian Public Service camps', page 160).

❦

## 'HOLY DISOBEDIENCE'

A.J. MUSTE REMAINED THE EXECUTIVE DIRECTOR OF THE FOR UNTIL 1953. He spent much of that time encouraging a sadly diminished pacifist movement, many of its supporters shocked into silence by the enormity of World War II. His direct experience with the highest levels of the Roosevelt Administration, advocating for the rights of conscientious objectors to do work of national importance in lieu of military service, was a fundamental breakthrough in the acceptance of an American peace stance. His influence would stretch to the efforts of objectors to the Korean and Vietnam wars, and to the nuclear disarmament campaigns and the Civil Rights Movement.

Muste 'retired' from the FOR in 1953 at the age of sixty-eight. But he never lost his fire, and for twenty more years he stirred the pot of social unrest. Ever the social radical, he wrote in his 1952 essay 'Of Holy Disobedience':

In trademark horn-rimmed glasses, hat and muffler, A.J. Muste is pictured at yet another protest rally in the 1960s.

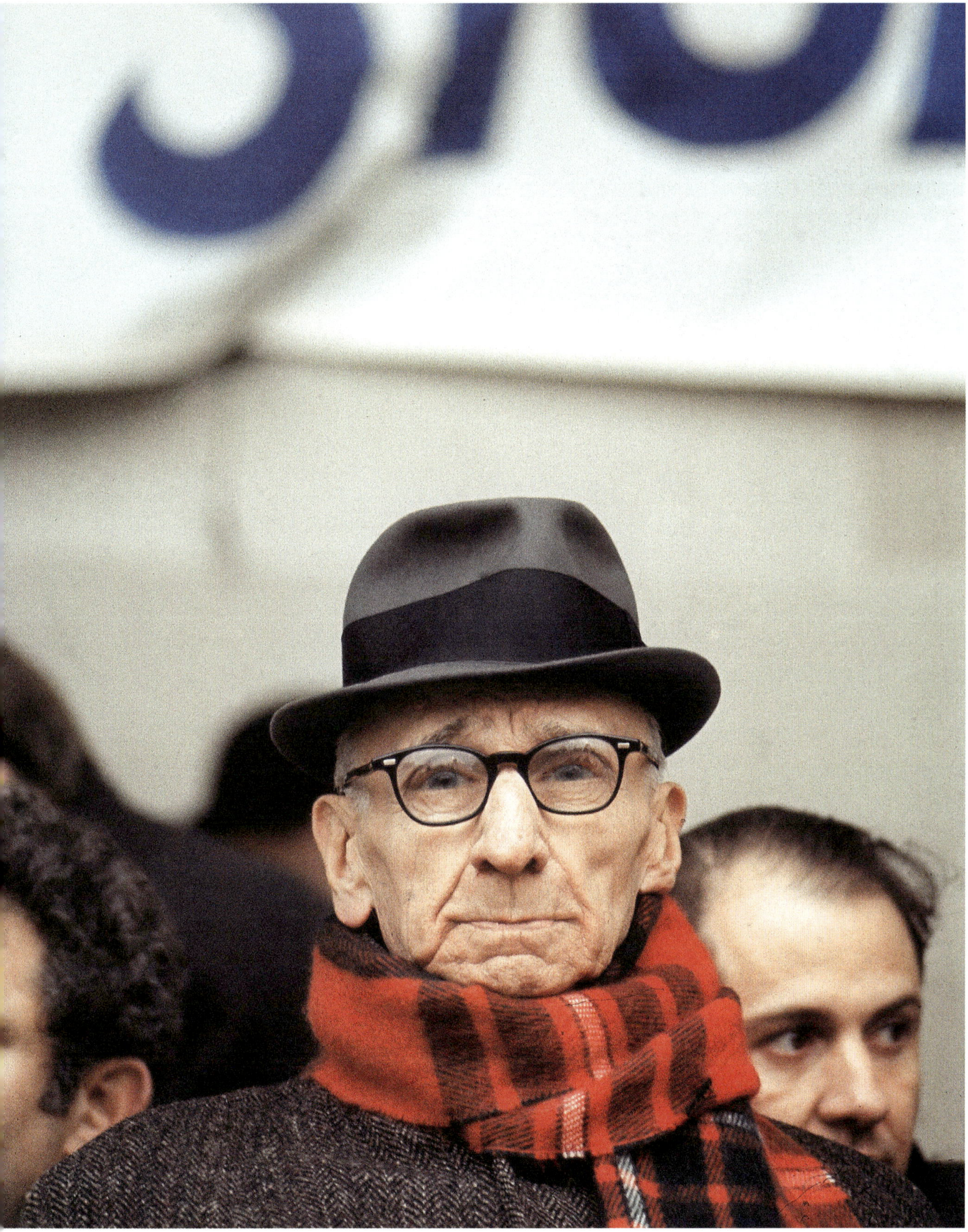

# CIVILIAN PUBLIC SERVICE CAMPS

The first Civilian Public Service (CPS) camp opened on 15 May 1941 near Baltimore, Maryland, shortly after President Roosevelt signed an executive order making the program official. The last camp closed in 1947, more than eighteen months after the War in the Pacific had ended; all in all, nearly 12,000 draftees were incarcerated in 152 CPS camps. Men were drafted into the CPS system because they were unwilling to do any type of military service, and were assigned to 'alternative service' in the areas of forestry, fire-fighting, soil conservation, social services, mental health and medical research.

The camps were administered by the newly created National Service Board for Religious Objectors. Some people wished for the administration of the camps to fall under the military, while the War Resisters League advocated for a separate camp system that was wholly secular. Optimistic supporters saw the camps as a means for building a community of pacifists, while cynics saw them as a means of marginalising the anti-war voice and punishing those who didn't support the war effort. Conscientious objectors who were not affiliated with the historic peace churches—the Quakers, Mennonites and Brethren—often found living under the CPS system difficult.

As the war dragged on, the rift between sectarian and secular conscientious objectors widened, weakening the pacifist movement and alienating some of its leaders. Eventually a compromise was hashed out, establishing a few new camps within the CPS system that were not affiliated with Church administration but run by the Selective Service System. These camps were frequently unruly, for they became the dumping ground for the most ardent anarcho–pacifists, many of whom goaded the government administrators and worked at disrupting the system. They became, in essence, the penal colonies of the CPS system.

One of the most notorious aspects of the CPS system was its use of conscientious objectors for medical research. A large number of men were subjected to infection with hepatitis, dysentery and malaria to test controversial treatments. Most volunteers were unaware of the health risks and several died from the experimentation. Others were put on starvation diets as a means for tracking the extremes to which their bodies could adapt. Some participants who fully understood the risks still opted to take part, willing to sacrifice alongside others during the war by doing vital alternative service. A lasting legacy of the CPS camps was the improvement in mental health services across America, a direct result of the work conducted by camp volunteers and the exposure to the plight of the mentally ill that their involvement engendered.

Non-conformity, Holy Disobedience, becomes a virtue and indeed a necessary and indispensable measure of spiritual preservation, in a day when the impulse to conform, to acquiesce, to go along, is the instrument which is used to subject men to totalitarian rule and involve them in permanent war. To create the impression at least of outward unanimity, the impression that there is no 'real' opposition, is something for which all dictators and military leaders strive assiduously.

He put his belief in 'holy disobedience' into action for the remainder of his life. From 1948 onward, he refused to pay income taxes as long as any of the funds would be allocated to the military. During the McCarthy-era 'red scare', Muste spoke up courageously on behalf of all accused communists, even though he had long broken off his ties to communism. He agitated for the end to hostilities in Korea and worked to focus the efforts of the United Nations on endeavours for peace rather than acting as an agent of war. And he took on, as many peace advocates would, the direct action of confronting the issue of nuclear proliferation.

In 1955 Muste joined with Dorothy Day, Ammon Hennacy and others in protesting the Cold War-inspired civil defence drills in New York City. The following year he joined with the American Friends Service Committee, the Catholic Worker Movement, the Women's International League for Peace and Freedom and the War Resisters League to coordinate the Walk for Peace, in which participants walked from San Francisco to Moscow, handing out more than 80,000 leaflets in the Soviet Union alone. The group spoke to hundreds of listeners every night along the walk and, through Muste's considerable influence, won the rare right to demonstrate on Red Square upon their arrival. In 1957 he became the leader of the Committee for Non-Violent Action, an organisation formed to focus world attention on the proliferation of nuclear arms by sailing ships into nuclear test sites in the Pacific Ocean. The Committee also protested on nuclear installations and rallied to block the launch of nuclear submarines.

In the early 1960s Muste travelled to Beirut, Lebanon to lead an international team in establishing the experimental World Peace Brigade as a global non-violent front. They set up a training centre dedicated to peaceful action in Dar es Salaam, Tanzania later that year in the hope of realising Mahatma Gandhi's vision of *Shanti Sena*, a worldwide 'peace army'. The next year the World Peace Brigade, along with other organisations, sponsored the voyage of *Everyman III* to Leningrad to protest the Soviet Union's nuclear testing.

A.J. had been a supporter of racial tolerance from the earliest stages of the Civil Rights Movement and was a member of the community that gave birth to the National Association for the Advancement of Colored People (NAACP). As the Civil Rights Movement gained momentum in the late 1950s and early 1960s, Muste mentored a young Baptist pastor from Montgomery, Alabama named Martin Luther King Jr. As King became the primary spokesman for non-violent civil rights protest, Muste provided him with advice and guidance, introducing him to the teachings of Gandhi and, in conjunction with the American Friends Service Committee, arranging for him to visit the Gandhi family in India in 1959. He also encouraged King to read the writings of Henry David Thoreau, Rufus Jones and Quaker pacifist and abolitionist John Woolman. Seeing the correlation between US expansionism in Southeast Asia and racial injustice at home, Muste encouraged King, along with the Buddhist monk Thich Nhat Hanh, to speak out in resistance to the war in Vietnam. Until the end of his life, A.J. remained one of Martin Luther King and Corretta Scott King's most trusted advisers.

Now in his late seventies, with the outbreak of the Vietnam War, A.J. again found himself called upon to help organise the opposition. Because of his work with socialists, the unions, the Civil Rights Movement and a wide spectrum of peace groups, he was one of the few American activists trusted by all anti-war radical groups. Much of the organised effort to end the war in Vietnam coalesced around him and he mustered a broad-ranging coalition of peace groups in a widespread series of protests. In 1965 he led over 50,000 people in an anti-war march down Fifth Avenue in New York. The following year he led an interfaith group of pacifists to Saigon in South Vietnam, where he met with Quaker, Catholic and Buddhist leaders to protest the war before the group was arrested and deported.

A.J. returned to Vietnam in 1967, this time to Hanoi, against the advice of his doctors. Even in failing health, he was unstoppable. He met North Vietnam's Premier Ho Chi Minh as part of a delegation of other peace-minded clergy. He returned home with an invitation to President Lyndon Johnson from Ho Chi Minh to attend direct talks in Hanoi to end the war. Too ill to hand-deliver the invitation, it was sent through intermediaries and dutifully ignored by the Johnson Administration. This would prove to be Muste's last witness for peace. He died a few weeks later.

Letters of condolence poured in from every corner of the world and every section of society, from voices as diverse as Ho Chi Minh, Robert Kennedy and Martin Luther King Jr. Speakers at his memorial service ranged from Church and religious leaders of all denominations, to trade union representatives and members of both the communist and socialist parties. It was Muste's broad history and inclusive nature that brought together a group representing so many backgrounds in remembrance of the man who famously said, 'There is no way to peace. Peace *is* the way.' He had actively opposed all the wars of the twentieth century, been one of the major radical leaders during the Great Depression, greatly influenced the labour movement and helped give rise to the American Civil Liberties Union and the Civil Rights Movement. Yet at his death he was hardly known by most of America.

This may very well have been what he wanted. A humble man who could move others to action with his ability to connect, A.J. Muste served in the background as a quiet revolutionary. His life is perhaps best summed up in his act of defiance at the height of the Vietnam War. Each night he stood before the gates of the White House, holding a single candle in solitary protest against the war. When a reporter asked, rather cynically, what he hoped to change in America by this, A.J. replied, 'Oh, you've got it all wrong. I'm not doing this to change the country. I do it so the country won't change me.'

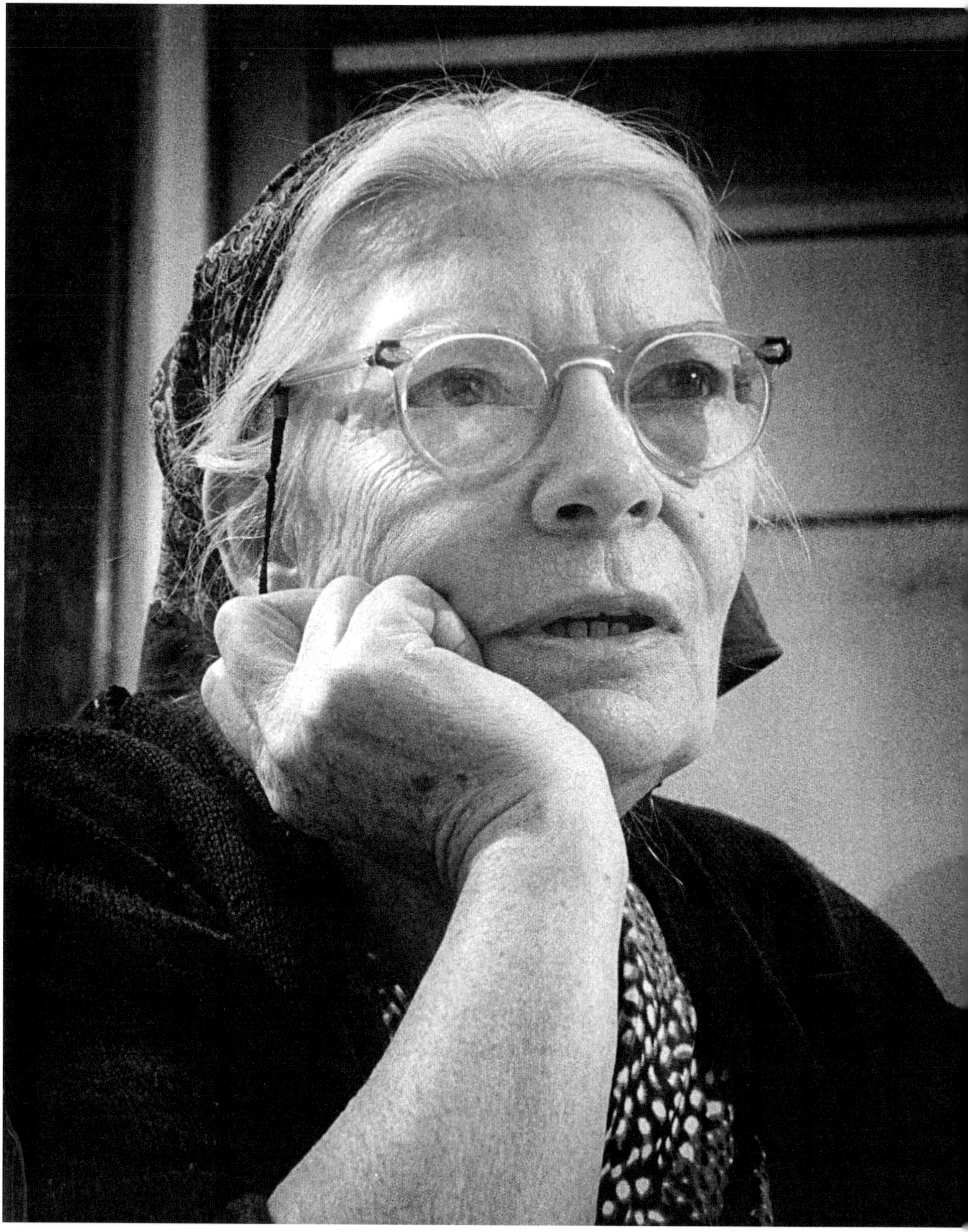

# DOROTHY DAY: CATHOLIC WORKER

DOROTHY DAY CLAIMED HER LIFE WAS SEPARATED INTO TWO PARTS: the first twenty-five years of floundering and the rest of her life, after she had found God and become a Catholic. But Dorothy Day was a Catholic unlike most before her. A Greenwich Village bohemian, she had lived in two common-law marriages, had an abortion and raised a daughter as a single mother. She was also a socialist, an anti-war activist, and a humanitarian who would become a symbol of revitalised Catholic charity, a globally respected advocate for peace, and a candidate for sainthood.

Day's greatest achievement was founding, along with her 'spiritual mentor' Peter Maurin, the *Catholic Worker*. What began as a simple broadside newsletter published from Day's Brooklyn kitchen grew into an international publication and a movement with thousands of volunteers, affecting the lives of millions. The *Catholic Worker* newspaper provided hope to the downtrodden during the Great Depression, a new view of Catholic action, and promoted a seemingly contradictory message of pacifism as the world clambered towards world war. And though Day was on the margin of mainstream Catholicism most of her life, she was eventually embraced by the Church for her pacifism and her humanism.

Dorothy Day, socialist, communist and Catholic, fought most of her life on behalf of her fellow workers and the poor and downtrodden.

# GREENWICH VILLAGE BOHEMIA

ONE OF DOROTHY DAY'S EARLIEST MEMORIES WAS OF THE TERRIBLE earthquake that destroyed San Francisco in 1906. She was born in 1897 in Brooklyn, New York, but her family had moved west when she was five. Dorothy's home in the Oakland hills across the bay from San Francisco was partially destroyed by the terrible tremors and she witnessed the fires across the Bay Bridge. 'The house [was] cracked from roof to ground,' she remembered. 'But there was no fire in Oakland. The flames and the cloud bank could be seen across the bay and all the next day the refugees poured over by ferry and boat.' Her parents gave aid to quake victims and helped shelter many who'd lost their homes. But with the city mostly destroyed, her father, a sports writer who covered the racetracks, was out of a job. The family, which included Dorothy's two older brothers and younger sister, headed east again.

They made it as far as Chicago, where they settled in a tenement building. As her father looked for work, Dorothy's middle-class life was turned on end by the tough inner-city turmoil of Chicago. When her father landed a job as a sports editor, they moved to the suburbs. But Dorothy's eyes were opened.

In 1914, Dorothy won a scholarship to the University of Illinois at Champaign-Urbana, which she attended for nearly two years. Her time there was devoted primarily to radical social causes rather than her studies and she avoided most social life. She insisted on supporting herself with odd jobs rather than taking money from her father and soon became disillusioned with college life. When her parents moved to New York, she followed and settled in Greenwich Village. Tall, beautiful and willowy, Day was soon a fixture in the bohemian village.

Like her father, she pursued journalism, but with a wholly different bent, almost immediately landing work with several socialist newspapers. As a reporter for *The Call*, New York's only socialist daily, she covered demonstrations and rallies, and profiled labour organisers and revolutionaries. She soon moved to *The Masses*, a socialist magazine that opposed America's entry into the war in Europe. In 1917, the US Post Office stripped the magazine of its mailing permit and the authorities seized its publications and subscriber lists. Most of the editors were charged with sedition. Increasingly radicalised, Dorothy took part in several anti-war demonstrations organised by socialists; at one rally she was clubbed by police and left bloodied, but narrowly avoided arrest.

That was not the case when she and forty other women staged a demonstration in front of the White House protesting women's exclusion from the vote. They were arrested and, refusing bail, sent to prison at the Occoquan workhouse in New

York. 'I was thrown to the floor,' remembered Dorothy of the unusually rough treatment by the guards. 'When another prisoner tried to come to my rescue, we found ourselves in the midst of a milling crowd of guards being pummelled and pushed and kicked and dragged, so that we were scarcely conscious.' Another prisoner was handcuffed to the bars of her cell throughout the night. As the abuses continued, the suffragettes decided to wage a hunger strike. Weeks passed and their plight became known in the highest halls of power. Eventually, all the women were freed when they were pardoned by presidential order.

The experience fully radicalised Day. Returning to New York, she became part of a radical literary circle which met at the notorious Greenwich Village bar, the Hell Hole, and included the playwright Eugene O'Neill and poet Hart Crane. The group took on all the radical social causes of the time, including the suffrage movement, socialism and birth control. At twenty-two she became pregnant from a brief but failed affair. She had a dangerous and illegal abortion, and afterwards was convinced the procedure had left her barren. She felt her life was spinning out of control but channelled her anxiety into an autobiographical novel called *The Eleventh Virgin*, chronicling what she considered the greatest tragedy of her life. The book was met with critical acclaim.

'For a long time I had thought I could not bear a child,' she wrote many years later in her autobiography *The Long Loneliness*, 'and the longing in my heart for a baby had been growing. My home, I felt, was not a home without one.' In 1924, flush from the sale of the movie rights to *The Eleventh Virgin*, Dorothy bought a beach cottage on Staten Island and settled into a common-law marriage with a young botanist and atheist named Forster Batterham. Dorothy became pregnant to Batterham and saw it as nothing less than a miracle. Batterham didn't share her enthusiasm. Opposed to marriage and religion and feeling it was unfair to bring another child into such a cruel and violent world, Batterham was a reluctant father. Tamar Theresa Day was born in 1927. Dorothy, who had for years been going through a slow spiritual awakening, declared she wanted to raise their child as a Catholic. Batterham was having none of that; after Tamar's baptism, he left for good.

On her own with a small child, Dorothy returned to freelance journalism and deepened her commitment to Catholicism. She felt such gratitude for the miracle of her child's birth that she decided to convert and be baptised. She had been drawn to the Catholic Church, 'the church of the immigrants, the church of the poor', as she described it, all her life, but struggled with how to merge its conservative faith with her radical social values. Again, she turned to her writing. She began publishing in the newly founded *Commonweal* magazine, which provided a slightly more liberal take on Catholic views of politics, culture and opinion.

When the stock market crashed in 1929 and the country began its descent into the Great Depression, Dorothy grew impatient with the Church's tepid response. By 1932, one out of every four people in New York was unemployed; the great metropolis was teeming with the indigent, the out of work and the homeless. In December of that year, national communist organisations staged a massive Hunger March on Washington, DC. Dorothy was conflicted. She yearned to serve as a delegate at the rally, but her pacifist and Catholic beliefs warned her to avoid the militant and anti-religion communists.

She resolved instead to take part as an observer, and covered the event for both *Commonweal* and *America* magazines. The march was thronged with ordinary Americans carrying signs calling for jobs, health care, affordable housing, unemployment insurance and relief for mothers with children. As with earlier marches, the military and police suppressed it violently. Dorothy was overwhelmed, and sought refuge in the unfinished Basilica of the Immaculate Conception. 'I offered up a special prayer,' she later wrote, 'a prayer which came with tears and anguish, that some way would open up for me to use what talents I possessed for my fellow workers, for the poor.'

Her prayer was answered the next day.

———

## THE *CATHOLIC WORKER*

WHEN DOROTHY RETURNED TO NEW YORK, SHE FOUND WAITING FOR HER an older man, shabby and determined, who was about to change her life. 'When I walked into my apartment,' she later recalled, 'I found waiting for me a short, stocky man in his mid-fifties, as ragged and rugged as any of the marchers I had left. I like people to look their part, and if they are workers, to look like workers … I like to see the shape of a man's hands, the strength of his neck and shoulders.'

His name was Peter Maurin and he had sought out Dorothy because of her writings. A born teacher and wandering ascetic, he had embraced the Franciscan attitudes of peace, poverty and celibacy. Born Aristode Pierre Maurin in 1877, he had left France because of his opposition to military conscription, and eventually made his way via Canada to upstate New York. There he lived humbly as a handyman at a Catholic boys' camp in exchange for meals, a place to sleep and the use of their library. Peter made his introduction and

# DAVID DELLINGER AND THE UNION EIGHT

When the Roosevelt Administration passed the *Selective Training and Service Act* of 1940 (the conscription Act), eight students at the Union Theological Seminary in New York refused to register with Selective Service. Although they came under intense pressure from the school as well as the heads of many of the leading pacifist organisations to change their minds, the eight men—David Dellinger, William Lovell, Richard Wichlei, Meredith Dallas, Joseph Bevilacqua, George Houser, Donald Benedict and Howard Spragg—persisted in their opposition. They became known as the Union Eight. At the same time on the West Coast, the first two pacifists to challenge the conscription law were Quaker professor Edwin Sanders and defrocked Methodist minister Paul Ackermann. Both were found guilty of failing to register under the conscription Act and were sent to the federal prison at DuPont, Washington. Sanders was later paroled into Civilian Public Service and after the war spent much of the rest of his life in Quaker peace activism with the American Friends Service Committee. Ackermann eventually registered but never returned to the Methodist Church.

In New York the Union Eight, led by David Dellinger, received much more notoriety and public scrutiny for their actions. All eight were tried, found guilty and sent to federal prison. Their absolutist and anarchist position, not supported by the seminary, was as much a political condemnation of what they considered the US government's move towards totalitarianism as it was an outcome of their moral and religious convictions. They released a group statement at their sentencing which read, in part: 'We believe ... that by opposing the Selective Service law, we will be striking at the heart of totalitarianism as well as war.'

Following the war, most of the Union Eight continued to work for peace in various ways. Dellinger joined with pacifist radical A.J. Muste in founding *Liberation* magazine in the 1950s as a voice for the non-Marxist left. He gained widespread notoriety in the 1960s as part of the Chicago Seven, a group of radicals who were gaoled for inciting riots at the 1968 Democratic National Convention in opposition to the Vietnam War. He worked with and maintained friendships with a diverse range of individuals including Eleanor Roosevelt, Martin Luther King Jr, A.J. Muste, Abbie Hoffman and members of the radical black power group, the Black Panthers. Dellinger died in 2004.

told Dorothy how he'd been given her address by George Shuster, the editor of *Commonweal* magazine. 'Also,' he said, 'a red-headed Irish Communist in Union Square told me to see you. He says we think alike.'

Dorothy and Peter did think alike. Almost immediately they saw in each other the means for helping the starving workers of the Depression. They fell into a 'teacher and disciple' relationship, with Peter tutoring Dorothy in Catholic doctrine and its charitable tradition. He convinced her that she should start a newspaper that promoted social teachings and that embraced, no less, the steps towards a peaceful transformation of society. Peter was expressing what was in her heart and she stood in awe that a second miracle had come into her life. He told her it was right to question why there were so many poor in the midst of the nation's great wealth. If the government would not solve the problems of poverty, a new social order must step in. They were laying the groundwork for what would become known as the Catholic Worker Movement.

Inspired by Maurin's workman-like demeanour, Dorothy began planning a new Catholic paper called the *Catholic Worker*. It would promote Catholic social teaching and reflect a new pacifist Catholic vision. Turning her kitchen table into an editorial desk, she negotiated a nominal fee with the Paulist Press to print 2500 copies of an eight-page tabloid. She and Maurin decided to sell the paper for a penny a copy, making it cheap enough for anyone to afford. The first copies were handed out by a few trusted volunteers on 1 May, in Union Square. Unlike any radical paper before it, the *Catholic Worker* was an immediate success. Within six months, Dorothy was selling over 100,000 copies a month. Not just another radical tabloid, the *Catholic Worker* was grounded in the Catholic faith, expressing dissatisfaction with the current social order but also challenging readers to make personal responses. It took the side of labour unions and questioned the country's urban and industrial direction. Soon it was reaching beyond the United States with subscribers throughout Europe. Dorothy recalled: 'A seminarian said that he had sent out his shoes to be half-soled in Rome and they came back to him wrapped in a copy of the *Catholic Worker*.'

Maurin pushed to do more. As winter approached, the homeless began arriving at Dorothy's door, drawn by Maurin's essays on the Christian responsibility for hospitality. Following the words of Jesus, Maurin said: 'I was a stranger and you took me in.' Soon an apartment was rented on the Lower East Side with enough space to house ten women. A similar house for men was opened in Greenwich Village. By 1936, the community moved into two buildings in New York's Chinatown. But no amount of space could house all the needy. Dorothy was overwhelmed by the numbers who found their way to her. They were 'the color of lifeless trees and bushes and winter soil', she wrote, 'who had in them as yet none of the green hope, the rising sap of faith'.

Soon 'hospitality house' collectives were opening in the country's farmlands, experimenting with farming collectives, first on Staten Island, soon afterward in Easton, Pennsylvania and eventually in New York up the Hudson in Newburgh, Tivoli and Marlborough. Dorothy and Maurin continued to see the efforts more as rural houses of hospitality than agricultural models and thus they became small radical pastoral centres. By 1936, there were thirty-three independent Catholic Worker communities throughout the country, and nearly thirty more had been established in Canada and the United Kingdom by 1941. The worldwide global depression had left many people in need of the movement.

As war again began to brew in Europe, Dorothy continued her radical social actions on behalf of peace. She wrote, picketed, prayed, fasted, protested and landed in gaol. Her use of the *Catholic Worker* as an instrument of non-violence was initially well received and tolerated by the Catholic Church. But the Church's attitude changed with the outbreak of civil war in Spain in 1936. The radical left supported the Republican side, a coalition of communists, socialists and anarchists. But because Franco and the Fascists presented themselves as saviours of the Catholic faith, nearly every bishop and Catholic publication rallied behind them. Dorothy warned that Catholics need only look to Nazi Germany and Mussolini in Italy, which both supported Franco, for what was to come. She was one of the first to voice anxiety about the Jews in Germany, and later founded the Committee of Catholics to Fight Anti-Semitism.

But Dorothy equally feared the Republicans in Spain, who were known to kill Catholic priests and nuns. So the *Catholic Worker* staked out neutral ground, refusing to support either side. 'We were not, of course, pro-Franco, but pacifists, followers of Gandhi in our struggle to build a spirit of non-violence,' she explained later. 'But in those days we got it from both sides; it was a holy war to most Catholics, just as world revolution is holy war to Communists.'

—

## CONSCIENTIOUS OBJECTION

For most of the Catholic Church's history it has made accommodations for warfare and for militaristic states. For a short while in the thirteenth century, St Francis of Assisi had returned the Church to the pacifist teachings of Jesus, but by the twentieth century it was practically unknown for Catholicism to be associated with pacifism. Church leaders, popes and bishops

# AMMON HENNACY

Ammon Hennacy, a radical pacifist and Christian anarchist, was a close collaborator with Dorothy Day in the Catholic Worker Movement. Born in 1893 in Ohio, to Quaker parents, he became a radical socialist in 1913, bent on the violent overthrow of the US capitalist government. Imprisoned for two years during World War I for opposing conscription, he experienced a religious conversion. He led a hunger strike that landed him in solitary confinement for eight months. During this time he solidified his anarcho–pacifist beliefs by deciding that Christianity required him to be a pacifist and, since governments used violence to inflict their will, he was an anarchist.

Hennacy worked as a migrant farm labourer for most of the 1940s and slowly made his way into the Catholic Worker Movement. In 1952 an anarchist priest baptised him a Catholic and Dorothy Day stood as his godmother. Moving to New York City in 1953, he became associate editor of the *Catholic Worker* and began working closely with Dorothy and others in anti-nuclear rallies and protests. In 1961 he moved to Salt Lake City, Utah, where he established the Joe Hill House of Hospitality, a Catholic Worker community. Named for the famous labour activist who was falsely convicted of murder and executed, the Joe Hill House provided shelter for the homeless and served as a centre for Christian pacifism.

Hennacy married in 1965 and left the Catholic Church, deciding that the Church's response to the Vietnam War was just another example of how St Paul had 'spoiled the message of Christ' by pushing Christianity away from its pacifist roots. He published a collection of essays called *The Book of Ammon* in 1968 and in 1970 and another collection, *The One-Man Revolution*. Following years of continued protests and speaking out on behalf of peace activism and against the war in Vietnam, Hennacy died of a heart attack in 1970.

had blessed armies and wars of religion, conquest and retribution. This was to change dramatically with the efforts of Dorothy Day.

As war erupted in Europe and the United States was once again marking time on the sidelines, the *Catholic Worker* continued to advocate for peace. This led to a widening gap between the mainstream Catholic establishment and the Catholic Worker Movement. As the historic peace churches of the Quakers, Mennonites and Brethren supported the establishment of rights for religious conscientious objectors, both government and Catholic leaders grew wary of anything that might siphon off support for war. When Roosevelt signed the *Selective Training and Service Act* into law in 1940, establishing a mandatory military draft, Dorothy came out in opposition. She supported those who opposed the Act, including a group of objectors from New York's Union Theological Seminary known as the Union Eight who were among the first to be arrested and imprisoned for violating the Act (see 'David Dellinger and the Union Eight', page 169). Dorothy's support deepened the rift with mainstream Catholics. Houses of hospitality were forced to close, and parishes across the country cancelled their subscriptions to the *Catholic Worker*.

With the Japanese attack on Pearl Harbor and America's declaration of war, Dorothy knew the outcry at her peace stance would grow louder. She wrote a letter to all the farm collectives and houses of hospitality and published it in the paper. 'We are still pacifists,' she wrote. 'Our manifesto is the Sermon on the Mount, which means that we will try to be peacemakers. Speaking for many of our conscientious objectors, we will not participate in armed warfare or in making munitions, or in buying government bonds to prosecute the war, or in urging others to these efforts.' Many in the movement opposed this position; they could not understand Dorothy's absolutism and, refusing to follow her authority, rebelled by closing more houses of hospitality. But Dorothy held fast. Each issue of the *Catholic Worker* reaffirmed her position on Christian pacifism and those who remained in the movement joined the ranks of conscientious objectors, either entering alternative service or landing in prison.

Peter Maurin's attitude towards the war was more tempered than Dorothy's. He could understand the argument justifying war, although he still considered himself a Franciscan and was opposed to violence. He supported Dorothy, but suggested that she might tone down her pacifism, telling her, 'Men are not ready to listen.' But Dorothy was not able to quiet her opinion. As one who had endured beatings and prison time for her beliefs, she never considered pacifism a weak position. And she was distressed whenever it was considered a sentimental yearning in the face of war. In a *Catholic Worker* editorial she wrote:

Another Catholic newspaper says it sympathizes with our sentimentality. This is a charge always leveled against pacifists. We are supposed to be afraid of the suffering, the hardships of war … Perhaps we are called sentimental because we speak of love. We say that we love our President, our country. We say that we love our enemies too.

Dorothy opposed conscription and supported conscientious objectors but she also did not favour the 'official' avenues for objectors established in the *Selective Training and Service Act*. To her, the state-sanctioned Civilian Public Service (CPS) and its camps were still part of the military system. As an alternative, she encouraged the Association of Catholic Conscientious Objectors (ACCO), which had branched out of the Catholic Worker Movement. The ACCO sponsored its own camp for Catholic objectors, and soon withdrew from CPS.

Dorothy was spied on by the FBI and watched for subversive activity. J. Edgar Hoover, the intractable head of the FBI, took personal interest in the movement, certain that it was a front for communists and a safe haven for draft evaders and objectors. Hoover even placed Day on his 'Custodial Detention List', which would allow him to imprison her without charge in the event of emergency. The Catholic Church helped with the investigation, claiming Day had neither asked nor received permission to use the term 'Catholic Worker'. But ultimately the Church reported that Dorothy was honest and sincere in her efforts and that her communist activities were long in the past.

Day's opposition to World War II came close to killing the movement. Monthly subscriptions to the *Catholic Worker* dwindled to a low of 27,500 from a high of 150,000, and by 1945 only ten houses of hospitality remained open. The war ended the idyllic social reform and unity of the early movement. Dorothy eventually followed Peter Maurin's advice and tempered her tone, focusing more on matters of spirituality. Maurin suffered a stroke in 1944 and slowly lost his memory, spending his last years on the Catholic Worker farm in Newburgh, New York. He died in 1949. But with the end of the war, Dorothy and the *Catholic Worker* would find new relevance in the dawning of the nuclear age.

## MOTHER OF PEACE

IN 1955, THE NEW YORK CHAPTER OF THE CATHOLIC WORKER MOVEMENT decided to boycott the annual civil defence drills, under which the city shut down in rehearsal for a nuclear attack. Arguing that such preparations for an attack condoned the whole charade that a nuclear war was survivable, Day joined with other pacifist leaders, including A.J. Muste, Bertrand Russell and the Christian anarchist Ammon Hennacy, protesting in front of City Hall when the sirens sounded (see 'Ammon Hennacy', page 172). Leaflets distributed by the group read in part: 'We will not obey this order to pretend, to evacuate, to hide. We will not be drilled into fear.' The protesters were reprimanded and released. But the protest became an annual event. The next year, Dorothy and her followers were arrested and gaoled for five days. By 1960, hundreds of protesters joined in a noisy and boisterous demonstration and many were arrested. In 1961, the participants swelled to over 2000. The following year the city discontinued the civil defence drills for good.

Dorothy also picked up the fight for civil rights. In 1957 she visited Koinonia, a Christian farm community in Georgia modelled on the Catholic Worker agricultural communities. She wanted to showcase the fact that black and white workers were living peacefully together. When she arrived, however, the compound was under attack by the Ku Klux Klan. The area had been strafed by machine-gun fire and crosses had been burned on community land. Dorothy, now in her early sixties, insisted on taking her turn as sentry at the entrance to the grounds. A truck approached slowly and someone suddenly opened fire; Dorothy ducked for cover as bullets struck just above her head.

Throughout the 1960s, Dorothy used the full force of the *Catholic Worker* to denounce the conflict in Vietnam. As America intensified its bombardment of large regions of Vietnam, killing thousands of civilians, widespread protests took place across the country. The military draft was reinstated and many young men in the Catholic Worker Movement were sent to prison for challenging conscription. Others did alternative service. And nearly all who had joined Catholic Worker communities engaged in protests and acts of civil disobedience. A number of the paper's editors across the country were gaoled for protesting. Dorothy herself was arrested several times during this period, the last in 1973 at the age of seventy-five.

Dorothy was deeply concerned by the Catholic Church's lack of response to the Vietnam War, so she went to Rome in 1963 at the time of the Second Vatican Council. Wishing to express her gratitude for Pope John XXIII's encyclical *Pacem in Terris* (*Peace on Earth*), which he stated was meant to restore 'the simple and pure lines that the face of the Church of Jesus had at its birth', she and fifty other 'Mothers of Peace' sought an audience with the Pope. Near death, Pope John was too ill to meet privately with them, but at one of his last public appearances he blessed the women and encouraged their continuing efforts. Dorothy returned

## FIVE STEPS TO SAINTHOOD

**STEP 1** A local Catholic bishop must first investigate and nominate a candidate for sainthood. Candidates must show evidence of heroic virtue through direct experience in their life or writings. The results of the investigation are sent to the Vatican.

**STEP 2** A panel of theologians and cardinals of the Congregation for the Causes of Saints evaluates the candidate's evidence. They submit their recommendation to the Pope.

**STEP 3** If the Congregation has given its approval, the Pope proclaims that the candidate is venerable and may be considered for beatification.

**STEP 4** A candidate must be proved to have been responsible for a posthumous miracle in order to be beatified. Martyrs—those who died for their religious cause—can be beatified without evidence of a miracle.

**STEP 5** The candidate may be considered a saint when there is proof of a second posthumous miracle. The Vatican must then verify these alleged miracles. If so blessed by the Pope, the candidate is canonised.

to the Vatican in 1965 with others to carry out a private fast in support of the Church's denunciation of war and military destruction.

Her efforts were rewarded later in the year when the Council of Bishops, meeting in Rome, approved the Constitution on the Church in the Modern World. The Council declared that any act of war 'directed to the indiscriminate destruction of whole cities or vast areas with their inhabitants [is] a crime against God and humanity'. The Council also called for legal provision for conscientious objectors and efforts to make it 'criminal' for military personnel to follow orders that led to the injury or death of innocent or defenceless non-combatants.

⟡

## A SAINT

IN THE FINAL DECADE OF HER LIFE, DOROTHY DAY FINALLY ACHIEVED THE recognition within the Catholic Church that many felt she had long deserved. She had travelled a long road from young communist to Vatican-respected protector of the poor and world-renowned pacifist. By the 1970s, when she was no longer well enough to travel, many visitors made the pilgrimage to her humble New York apartment, where she lived among the needy and the poor. One of those who made the trip was Mother Teresa of Calcutta. Sitting with Dorothy, speaking of their very different paths to the same reverence for faith in action, Mother Teresa pinned on Dorothy's dress the cross worn only by a fully avowed Missionary Sister of Charity.

Around this time, the Claretians, a Catholic community of active charity and missionary workers, began to advocate for the Church to recognise Dorothy as a saint. She hardly fitted the usual mould. She could be irascible and aggressive, stubborn and argumentative. She would not suffer any argument for a just war, and called warfare 'simply murder wrapped in flags'. She had little patience for those who sentimentalised her efforts or for any of the stereotypes of women. Once asked by a journalist to provide the soup recipe at one of her kitchens for the poor, she answered sarcastically: 'Chop vegetables until your fingers bleed.' And when the topic of sainthood came up, she dismissed it brusquely. 'Don't call me a saint,' she famously said. 'I don't want to be dismissed so easily.'

Dorothy Day lived her life in the midst of poverty, doing the work of charity day after day, from her youth into her eighties. She never gave up on peace, even during the most popular of wars and after being gaoled repetitively. She never lost her faith or her belief in the untapped faith in others. At the end of her life Dorothy was reunited with Forster Batterham, her common-law husband and father of her daughter Tamar. The three of them spent much of her last days together. Such was her influence that Batterham, a lifelong atheist, took the Eucharist at her funeral Mass. She died on 29 November 1980 in her small apartment and is buried on Staten Island, close to the little cottage by the sea that she bought so many years before.

After a lengthy review, Cardinal John O'Connor announced in 2000 that the Holy See for the Archdiocese of New York had given its approval to open the Cause for the Beatification and Canonisation of Day. The Vatican approved the first step, anointing Day a 'Servant of God' and beginning the investigative process that may lead to sainthood (see 'Five steps to sainthood', opposite). But the effort has been controversial. Traditionalists are critical of Dorothy's political beliefs, her early transgressions, and her radical advocacy of the Church laity. Liberals are equally concerned that her acceptance by the mainstream Church will trivialise her lay leadership and the power of her political views.

Undoubtedly, something that would have been more important to Dorothy than talk of sainthood was the action of the Catholic Church shortly after her death. In 1983, the Catholic bishops of the United States put forth a peace pastoral, *The Challenge of Peace*, crediting Dorothy with its inspiration. The pastoral affirmed pacifism and conscientious objection as a legitimate expression of the Catholic faith. Dorothy's legacy was the revitalisation of the Catholic faith as a church of peace rededicated to the original pacifist teachings of Jesus.

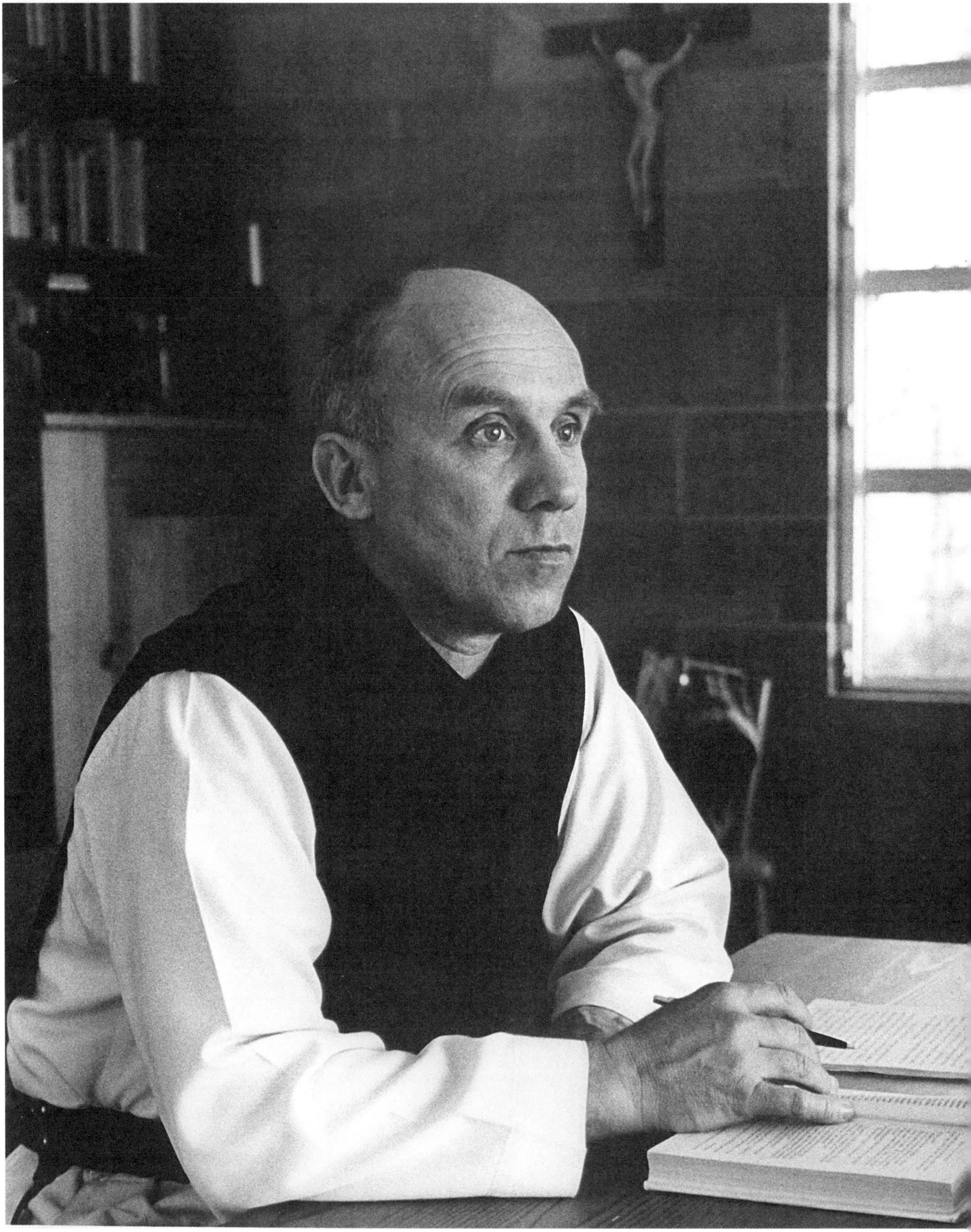

# THOMAS MERTON
# AND THICH NHAT HANH:
# PACIFIST MONKS

THE TRAPPIST MONK THOMAS MERTON AND THE BUDDHIST MONK Thich Nhat Hanh met only once. It was 1966 at the height of the Vietnam War, a period of social unrest in both the United States and in France where each lived, respectively. But the two pacifists' paths had been on course to meet for decades. Their encounter, in the rolling, remote hills of Kentucky at the Abbey of Our Lady of Gethsemani, where Merton was cloistered, formed a spiritual bond between the two men that is still the subject of study today.

When they met, Merton was a well-known writer, Catholic mystic and acclaimed author of *The Seven Storey Mountain*, a spiritual memoir already heralded as one of the most important religious works of the twentieth century. Handsome and charismatic, Merton was a reluctant influence on 1960s 'Catholic action' that roused a generation to non-violent protest against the war. Nhat Hanh was living in exile from his native Vietnam, banned for his pacifist efforts to end the war and aid its victims. A monk since the age of sixteen, he was the founder of a movement he called 'Engaged Buddhism', which brought the religion's meditative practices to pacifist civil disobedience. The two men together changed the dynamics of the anti-war movement and are still today heralded as non-violent spiritual leaders.

'The least of the work of learning is done in the classroom.' Poet, social activist and author, Thomas Merton worked hard to promote interfaith understanding, particularly with Asian spiritual leaders.

—

# BECOMING A MONK

THOMAS MERTON'S FATHER WAS A STRUGGLING NEW ZEALAND PAINTER; his mother was an American Quaker. Merton was born in Prades, France in early 1915, and baptised in the Church of England. The family was forced to move back to America with the outbreak of World War I and settled with relatives in New York's Queens, where Thomas's younger brother John Paul was born in 1918. Merton's father, restless to make a name for himself in the art world, returned to Europe and soon afterward Thomas's mother was diagnosed with stomach cancer; she died in 1921.

During almost the whole of his school years, Thomas was bounced around between boarding schools in France and England. He struggled to find his way, feeling deserted by his father and lonely for his family back in America. In 1931 his father died suddenly, leaving a former classmate named Tom Bennett as his sons' guardian. The following year, at seventeen, Thomas passed his entrance exams for Clare College, Cambridge. Bennett was a successful doctor and offered to pay for both his schooling and—somewhat reluctantly—a trip through Europe. For the first time, Merton remembered feeling cared for.

That summer, while visiting Rome, Merton became enthralled by the basilicas and religious frescoes. It was his first religious experience and would eventually change his life. On a whim, he purchased a Vulgate, the Latin Bible, and read the entire New Testament in one night. He wrote later in *The Seven Storey Mountain* that through the night he felt as if his father was in the room with him. The next day he visited a Trappist monastery, where the chapel gave him a sense of calm he had never experienced before, an experience that lingered for years.

When Merton arrived at Cambridge, his behaviour changed radically. He began drinking heavily, running up debts, and ignoring his studies. Handsome and mysterious, he found himself in a number of sexual adventures and apparently fathered a child with a local. Bennett, forced to handle the situation with the girl's parents, quietly dealt with the legal action taken against Merton and cut off the young man's allowance. The two came to an understanding: Bennett would keep quiet about the mess Thomas had made at Cambridge and Thomas would return to America at the end of the school year. After his exams, Thomas returned to Queens and enrolled at Columbia University.

Over the next three years, Merton applied himself and completed a degree in English literature. He spent his summers with his younger brother John Paul and slowly found his way to Catholicism. Two works influenced his spiritual transformation—*The Spirit of Medieval Philosophy* by Etienne Gilson, and *Ends*

*and Means* by Aldous Huxley. The former gave him an example of God that he found resonating and practical; the latter introduced him to mysticism, Eastern religions and the idea of pacifism (see 'The *Ends and Means* of Aldous Huxley', page 182).

Searching for a spiritual mentor, Merton became involved with the Catholic Worker Movement and began a friendship with Dorothy Day that would last his lifetime. They corresponded regularly for the next twenty-five years and Merton often contributed articles to the *Catholic Worker*. Years later, he would write the forward to *Loaves and Fishes*, Day's history of the Catholic Worker Movement. Dorothy encouraged him to volunteer at Friendship House in Harlem, the inter-racial Catholic mission run by the charismatic Catherine de Hueck Doherty. Within weeks he was offered a permanent position but turned it down. Quietly, Merton had decided he wanted to become a monk.

Ever since his experience in Rome, Merton had been drawn to the Trappists. The Order of Cistercians of the Strict Observance takes the name 'Trappist' from La Trappe Abbey in Normandy, France. The Trappist order was begun during the reform movement in France in 1664 as a response to the easing of practices in many of the Cistercian monasteries. Trappists are guided by the

16 March 2007: Thich Nhat Hanh taking part in a three-day requiem in Ho Chi Minh for those killed on both sides of the Vietnam War. 'Reconciliation is to understand both sides ...'

# THE *ENDS AND MEANS* OF ALDOUS HUXLEY

The English writer Aldous Huxley was a humanist and a pacifist, best known for his dystopian novels. Born in 1894, he lived through many of the twentieth century's wars, residing in both Europe and the United States. In 1911 he suffered from an eye disease that rendered him practically blind. After two years he had regained enough sight to resume his studies at Oxford, where he became close to Bertrand Russell and the writer D.H. Lawrence. His poor vision made him unfit for military service and after graduation in 1916 he spent the remainder of the World War I years as a farm labourer. Even though Huxley wrote some of the most thought-provoking novels of his generation, including *Animal Farm*, *Brave N ew World* and the pacifist-themed *Eyeless in Gaza*, he always considered himself a better essayist than novelist.

Huxley wrote numerous essays, on topics ranging from spirituality to mysticism to the taking of psychedelic drugs. His most influential collection of essays was *Ends and Means: An Enquiry Into the N ature of Ideals and Into the Methods Employed for Their Realization*, published in 1937, containing revealing tracts on war, religion, nationalism and ethics. As the title suggests, the collection focused primarily on why a society is unable to achieve a world of 'liberty, peace, justice, and brotherly love', even though so many have striven for it. He also wrote at length about meditation, vegetarianism and the concept of *ahimsa*.

Huxley became close friends with the Indian mystic Krishnamurti, whose teachings were highly influential on his intellectual and creative life. He moved to California between the wars and became an active proponent of Eastern philosophies, mysticism and hallucinogenic drugs. Way ahead of his time, he took mescaline in the 1930s and LSD in the 1950s as ways of searching for enlightenment. He wrote a series of essays on his experiences with drugs, published as the collection *The Doors of Perception*, which would become popular cult reading for hippies a decade later. In fact the 1960s rock group The Doors took their name from this collection. In 1963, on his deathbed from cancer, he convinced his wife Laura Archera to inject him with a powerful dose of LSD.

Rule of St Benedict, whose dictates on monastic life date back to the sixth century. The order is distinguished by its strict observance of the three vows from St Benedict: stability, fidelity to monastic life and obedience.

In 1941 Merton visited the Abbey of Our Lady of Gethsemani in north-central Kentucky for a Holy Week retreat. He felt called to the monastery and within the year was accepted as a novice monk. The following year his brother set to ship off to war, visited Thomas at Gethsemani. John Paul wished to convert to Catholicism and Thomas arranged his baptism the day before he left. That was the last time they saw each other. John Paul was killed the following year when his transport plane went down in the English Channel.

—

## A RELUCTANT LEADER

MERTON TOOK THE NEWS OF HIS BROTHER'S DEATH HARD. HE HAD ALWAYS kept a regular journal but with John Paul's death his writing took on a deeper significance. His journal had been personal to him, a way to hold a dialogue with his soul and quiet his doubts. But over the next several years, he began to write to the world. By 1946 he had published his first book, *A Man in the Divided Sea*, as well as a collection of poems, to some small acclaim. In the same year *The Seven Storey Mountain* was accepted for publication. The book tells his tale of restlessness and passion and how his quest for faith and peace led him at the age of twenty-six to become a monk in one of the most demanding of Catholic orders. When it came out in 1948, the story resonated with a post–World War II world in a way few religious works have. A sort of contemporary *Confessions of St Augustine*, the book was a critical and popular success and over the intervening years has become one of the most influential religious confessionals of the twentieth century.

Merton remained cloistered at Gethsemani for the next twenty years, in 'the four walls of my new freedom', as he described it. He wrote prolifically, producing over seventy books on spirituality, social concerns and monastic life, as well as novels and poetry. Some of the better known works are *Seeds of Contemplation* (1948), which has also become a classic in Christian writing, *The Waters of Siloe* (1949), *The Sign of Jonas* (1953), *The Silent Life* (1957), *Seeds of Destruction* (1964), *Gandhi on Non-Violence* (1965) and *Faith and Violence* (1968), to name but a few. Merton soon became recognised as a leading voice on liturgical renewal and increasingly, as the 1960s became engulfed in the Vietnam War, on issues of peace.

He viewed opposition to war and violence as one of the primary goals of a Christian and, indeed, of anyone living a religious life. He had no misgivings about the difficulties of personal pacifism. 'Peace demands the most heroic labour and the most difficult sacrifice,' he wrote in the *Catholic Worker* in 1961. 'It demands greater heroism than war. It demands greater fidelity to the truth and much more purity of conscience. The Christian fight for peace is not to be confused with defeatism.' He fostered a relationship with the Fellowship of Reconciliation, and his writing inspired others on the left who took a more extreme tack. He gave encouragement to Dr Martin Luther King Jr throughout their correspondence and inspired the radical Berrigan brothers, whose acts of civil disobedience became notorious during the Vietnam War years (see 'The Berrigan brothers: holy outlaws', page 186).

Merton's pacifism was one of deep personal commitment, but as he seldom left the monastery he was ambivalent about ever calling himself a pacifist leader. His pacifism was one of conscience more than action; he was a reluctant contributor to Vietnam protests, and wished to have no place in the violent race riots and cultural confrontations of the 1960s. In a letter to the renowned writer Czeslaw Milosz in 1962, he said:

> I certainly do not consider myself permanently dedicated to a crusade for peace, and I am beginning to see the uselessness and absurdity of getting too involved in a 'peace movement'. The chief reason why I have spoken out was that I felt I owed it to my conscience to do so. There are certain things that have to be clearly stated. I had in mind particularly the danger arising from the fact that some of the most belligerent people in this country are Christians, on the one hand fundamentalist Protestants and on the other certain Catholics. They both tend to appeal to the bomb to do a 'holy' work of destruction in the name of Christ and Christian truth. This is completely intolerable and the truth has to be stated. I cannot in conscience remain indifferent.

His influence would only continue to grow.

---

## ENGAGED BUDDHISM

BORN IN CENTRAL VIETNAM IN 1926, NHAT HANH ENTERED THE TU HIEU Temple at the age of sixteen. He went on to receive Zen training and became a monk (signified by the title Thich) in 1949. A well-regarded writer, he was soon the editor-in-chief of the peace-oriented periodical *Vietnamese Buddhism*, the journal of the Unified Vietnam Buddhist Association. By 1956 he had founded the Van Hanh Buddhist University and a wide-reaching Buddhist press. He moved to the United States in 1960 to study comparative religion for a year at Princeton University. Fluent in French, Chinese, Sanskrit, Pali, Japanese and English, Thich Nhat Hanh remained for another year as a lecturer in Buddhism at Columbia University. But with unrest tearing at his country, he returned to Vietnam in 1963 to join with other monks in their efforts to bring peace and help those already afflicted by war. He resumed teaching at Van Hanh and led students in a Call for Peace, declaring: 'It is time for North and South Vietnam to find a way to stop the war and help all Vietnamese people live peacefully and with mutual respect.'

Vietnam had been torn by war since the French invaded the country in 1946, after World War II, and entered into a guerrilla war with the Viet Minh. The French were eventually ousted in 1954 and the country was partitioned. North Vietnam coalesced around the Viet Minh and won recognition by Communist China and the USSR under the leadership of Ho Chi Minh. In 1956, fearing a win by communists in South Vietnam's national elections, the government rigged the outcome and initiated harsh anti-communist repression. In response, the communists in South Vietnam began a campaign of terror, killing hundreds of government and civil officials. War escalated between communist North Vietnam and South Vietnam, which was supported by the United States and member nations of the South-East Asia Treaty Organisation (SEATO).

Nhat Hanh had founded Van Hanh Buddhist University on his philosophy of Engaged Buddhism, which sought to merge elements of Zen meditative practice with active social civil disobedience. As the Vietnamese conflict widened throughout the 1960s, Nhat Hanh worked endlessly to reconcile the attitudes of North and South. He founded the School of Youth for Social Service (SYSS), a sort of Peace Corps for young Vietnamese domestic relief workers to help rebuild villages afflicted by the conflict. His efforts were met with disdain and both governments saw him as an irritant and a threat. Nhat Hanh decided to return to the United States, leaving his trusted second, the Buddhist nun Sister Chan Khong, in charge of the SYSS. But on his departure, the university's chancellor quickly broke off ties with Khong and the SYSS, accusing her of being a communist. She came under great pressure as members of the order, monks and peace workers were assaulted, imprisoned and killed for their efforts at helping the disadvantaged and supporting reconciliation (see 'Sister Chan Khong', page 190).

## THE BERRIGAN BROTHERS: HOLY OUTLAWS

For a time in the 1960s, American brothers Daniel and Philip Berrigan—anti-war activists, Christian anarchists and Catholic priests—were both on the FBI's Ten Most Wanted Fugitives list. Daniel was a Jesuit priest, poet and activist in the US peace movement. Philip became disillusioned by war after his experience as a lieutenant in World War II; after being ordained a Josephite priest, he became an activist and champion of civil rights in the 1950s and 1960s. They joined with Thomas Merton in founding an interfaith coalition against the Vietnam War in the mid-1960s.

In 1967, Philip took part in an act of civil disobedience by raiding the Customs House in Baltimore, Maryland. He and other activists stole Selective Service draft records and doused them with blood in a symbolic act against the war. Philip was arrested and sentenced to six years in gaol. After his release on bail in 1968, he was joined by Daniel in repeating the act in nearby Catonsville, Maryland, this time using homemade napalm to burn Selective Service records. Both were arrested and sentenced to three years's imprisonment. Released on appeal, they went on the run from authorities. A national manhunt turned up letters written by Philip that alleged a conspiracy by the brothers to kidnap Secretary of State Henry Kissinger and blow up city steam tunnels. Daniel went into exile in France, where he sought asylum with Vietnamese monk and anti-war activist Thich Nhat Hanh.

While on the run, Daniel was interviewed for a documentary called *The Holy Outlaw* that raised national sympathy for the brothers' cause. The Berrigans were eventually captured and sent to prison. Released in 1972, they again went on trial on the conspiracy charges. With the war in Vietnam at an end, the trial became a sensation and their controversial acquittal made them instant folk heroes among the anti-war movement. Throughout the 1970s and 1980s, they continued to carry out acts of civil disobedience; they also started the Plowshare Movement, which carried out demonstrations against the nuclear arms industry. Still an ordained priest, Philip married and had three children, for which he was excommunicated from the Catholic Church. He died of cancer in 1982. Daniel is still active with Plowshare and teaches and publishes in New York City.

In America, Nhat Hanh sought solidarity with Martin Luther King Jr, a man he felt could match his own struggle for non-violence. In 1965 he wrote a letter to King entitled 'In Search of the Enemy of Man', in which he said:

> Now in the confrontation of the big powers occurring in our country ... thousands of Vietnamese peasants and children lose their lives every day, and our land is unmercifully and tragically torn by a war which is already twenty years old. I am sure that since you have been engaged in one of the hardest struggles for equality and human rights, you are among those who understand fully, and who share with all their hearts, the indescribable suffering of the Vietnamese people.

The letter had a strong effect on King, especially as it opened his eyes to the treatment of anti-war monks in Vietnam. The government's violent clampdown on protesting monks of Nhat Hanh's order in 1963 led many of them to ritually immolate themselves. Images of the monks in flames had outraged the world and it was hard for Westerners to understand how they could kill themselves as a protest to the war. Nhat Hanh explained in the letter:

> The self-burning of Vietnamese Buddhist monks in 1963 is somehow difficult for the Western Christian conscience to understand. The Press spoke then of suicide, but in the essence, it is not. It is not even a protest. What the monks said in the letters they left before burning themselves aimed only at alarming, at moving the hearts of the oppressors and at calling the attention of the world to the suffering endured then by the Vietnamese.

Nhat Hanh met with Martin Luther King in 1966 and convinced him to vocally oppose the war. Since 1963, South Vietnam had steadily lost ground to the North and US involvement had escalated into open engagement, first with bombardments and eventually with the commitment of American ground forces in 1965. The initial contingent of 3500 Marines would grow to 200,000 by year's end. In 1967 King gave his famous speech at Riverside Church in New York City in which, for the first time, he publicly denounced his country's involvement in Vietnam. Having received the Nobel Peace Prize two years earlier, King now openly nominated Nhat Hanh for the prize. 'I do not personally know of anyone more worthy than this gentle monk from Vietnam,' King said. 'His ideas for peace, if applied, would build a monument to ecumenism, to world brotherhood, to humanity.' It is likely that the committee would have chosen Nhat Hanh for the prize that year, but because King revealed his name along with a public request for consideration, the committee decided that tradition and protocol were compromised. No peace prize was awarded that year.

Exiled by the governments of both North and South, Nhat Hanh could not return to Vietnam. He gained asylum in France in 1968, and the following year attended the Paris Peace Talks as a member of a Buddhist Peace Delegation. Although there was some progress towards a resolution, the talks eventually broke down and the war continued for another four years. By 1972, however, US forces had suffered several costly defeats and troop withdrawals began. With the fall of Saigon, the remaining troops were evacuated as North Vietnam's forces overran the South. The Paris Peace Accord of 1973 officially ended US involvement in the war, but by then the conflict had exacted a huge human toll: three to four million Vietnamese, on both sides, were killed; approximately two million Laotians and Cambodians died, many from indiscriminate US 'carpet bombing'; and 58,000 US soldiers were killed. Nhat Hanh remained in exile in France.

~

## A HISTORIC MEETING

THE MEETING ORGANISED BY THE FELLOWSHIP OF RECONCILIATION BETWEEN Thomas Merton and Thich Nhat Hanh in 1966 was brief, but fostered a friendship that would set a tone of peaceful understanding for the remainder of the war. They met at the Abbey of Our Lady of Gethsemani in Kentucky. Nhat Hanh was on a speaking tour of the United States, gaining a small following for his quiet but determined assertiveness for peace. He provided a very different perspective on the war, new to Merton and to most others who heard him speak, a perspective that proffered neither the communist position nor the popular American view, but reflected the desire of the majority of Vietnamese for a quick end to the conflict. Merton had yet to speak out publicly on the war, although through his writing he was known for his pacifist stance.

The two men clicked. Merton wrote afterwards that Nhat Hanh 'was a true monk; very quiet, gentle, modest, humble'. Nhat Hanh was moved by Merton's 'capacity for dialogue'. Each listened to the other and a new understanding was born. Merton would soon speak out against the war and in praise of interfaith dialogue. 'One of the most important aspects of the interfaith dialogue,' he later wrote, 'has also so far been one of the least discussed: it is the special contribution that the contemplative life can bring to the dialogue, not only among Christians, but also among Christians and the ancient religions of the East.'

Nhat Hanh revealed to Merton his enthusiasm for a kind of Buddhism that went beyond passive meditation, filled instead with the energy of action. He later explained:

When I was a novice in Vietnam, we young monks witnessed the suffering caused by the war. So we were very eager to practice Buddhism in such a way that we could bring it into society. That was not easy because the tradition does not directly offer Engaged Buddhism. So we had to do it by ourselves. That was the birth of Engaged Buddhism.

He saw that the teachings of the Buddha were essential to help defuse the hatred and violence that was overrunning the country.

Merton heard Nhat Hanh's words as a call to action. He began to speak out on behalf of Catholic opposition to the war. He reflected on the Sermon on the Mount, of course, but he also looked to the writings of Henry David Thoreau and Gandhi. He wrote increasingly in the *Catholic Worker* of the need for action, of the power of prayer. He joined with Nhat Hanh in convincing Martin Luther King Jr to speak out. But it was his support of interfaith dialogue that put him at the forefront of the pacifist ecumenical movement.

For the last two years of his life, Merton's message of peace carried an interfaith component. From the earliest days of his spiritual quest, he had been interested in Eastern religions. He had studied Zen Buddhism, Hinduism, Jainism and Taoism, written a book on Gandhi and met with the Dalai Lama in India. But it was his meeting with Nhat Hanh that led Merton to write an essay tying together his belief in peace and his connection to Buddhism. In 'Thich Nhat Hanh is My Brother' he wrote the most succinct declaration of solidarity possible, a reflection that in matters of peace, religious doctrine is unified: '[Thich Nhat Hanh] is more my brother than many who are nearer to me in race and nationality, because he and I see things exactly the same way.'

Merton's interest in Eastern philosophy deepened when he toured Asia in 1968. Visiting the ancient city of Polonnaruwa in Ceylon (present-day Sri Lanka), where he viewed the enormous Buddha statues, he had a mystical experience. At the end of the year, while attending a conference of monks in Bangkok, Thailand, he was killed suddenly, electrocuted in a tragic accident. Still wet from bathing, Merton touched a defectively wired fan when he either fell against it or was trying to move it. He died instantly, hit with 220 volts without any time to prepare himself.

## SISTER CHAN KHONG

Chan Khong was born in Vietnam in 1938 and became an expatriate Buddhist nun, peace activist, and a follower and collaborator of Thich Nhat Hanh. At the University of Saigon in 1958 she became the university's student leader, taking part in political action and helping care for the poor in the city's slums. In 1959 she joined Thich Nhat Hanh as a nun in his order. Following additional schooling in France, she helped Nhat Hanh in 1963 to found Van Hanh Buddhist University and the School of Youth for Social Service (SYSS). She focused her considerable talents in organising medical, educational and agricultural facilities in rural areas of Vietnam. At one point, she led over 10,000 peace workers in rebuilding villages that had been destroyed by the war. When Nhat Hanh left for the United States, he put Khong in charge of the SYSS, but she soon found herself persecuted, falsely accused of being a North Vietnam communist sympathiser, and was forced to flee Vietnam.

Khong joined Nhat Hanh in Paris in organising the 1969 Buddhist Peace Delegation, campaigning tirelessly for an end to the war in Vietnam. For over fifty years she has worked side by side with Thich Nhat Hanh in establishing the Plum Village Zen Monastery in France and other Buddhist communities in America. She continues to organise relief work for poor children in Vietnam and travels regularly with Nhat Hanh, including his celebrated return to Vietnam first in 2005 and again in 2007. In 1993 her autobiography *Learning True Love: How I Learned & Practiced Social Change in Vietnam* was published to great acclaim.

His sudden and untimely end at the age of fifty-two left many of his admirers in dismay. After his body was returned to Gethsemani and buried, much speculation arose as to how this great spiritual thinker could have been silenced in his prime. Some questioned whether his death might have been brought on by some deep moral conflict he was experiencing. His fame in the world was in stark contrast to his monastic solitude; his deepening empathy with Eastern philosophy was putting his Catholic faith to the test; and he could have been questioning his monastic vows, having recently fallen in love with a young nurse who cared for him following surgery. Although the relationship was never consummated and he broke it off well before his death, journal entries and poems he wrote about her reveal the turmoil this love aroused in him. No one knows what direction his path might have taken in his later years, but he could have been looking beyond his monastic life and even questioning his faith.

# 'PEACE HAS TO BEGIN WITH ONESELF'

THE INFLUENCE OF BOTH THOMAS MERTON AND THICH NHAT HANH has increased over the years. Following Merton's death, the publications of his writings secured his reputation as one of the twentieth century's most important Catholic thinkers. At his request, some of his more radical writings on social issues, including those related to civil rights and the abolition of nuclear arms, were withheld from publication for twenty-five years after his death. The royalties from his books have furthered the efforts of the Trappists and his papers have been collected at the Thomas Merton Center at Bellarmine University in Louisville, Kentucky. The Thomas Merton Center for Peace and Social Justice, later established in Pittsburgh, Pennsylvania, sponsors an annual peace award.

Thich Nhat Hanh has written over 100 books on spirituality, peace, meditation and monastic life, and he has become recognised as one of the leading figures in peace awareness. His better known works include *Love in Action, Peace Is Every Step: The Path of Mindfulness in Everyday Life, The Miracle of Mindfulness, No Death, No Fear* and *Interbeing: Fourteen Guidelines for Engaged Buddhism*. Nhat Hanh's influence as a Zen Buddhist teacher is perhaps second only to that of the Dalai Lama. He is recognised now as a Dharmacharya and the spiritual leader of the Tu Hieu Temple in Vietnam, where he began his monastic life. Thousands trek to his Plum Village Zen Monastery in France every year or attend retreats at his Zen centres throughout the United States.

In 2005 Nhat Hanh returned to Vietnam for the first time since his exile. Although the Unified Buddhist Church of Vietnam, which he organised in 1966, is still officially banned, Nhat Hanh was allowed to travel the country. After lengthy negotiations, he was permitted to teach and publish certain books in Vietnamese and ultimately return to the Tu Hieu Temple. A second visit in 2007 allowed him to support new monastic members and to conduct 'Great Chanting Ceremonies' to help heal the wounds remaining from the war. But his wish to chant for soldiers of both the South Vietnamese and American armies was met with opposition. Still, he spoke with thousands throughout the country, from politicians to intellectuals to street vendors and taxi drivers. Joined by his lifelong follower, assistant and partner, Sister Chan Khong, they conducted mindfulness practices and led chanting and celebrations.

'Non-violence and compassion are the foundations of a peace movement,' he told his followers. 'If you don't have enough peace and understanding and loving-kindness ... your actions will not truly be for peace. Everyone knows that peace has to begin with oneself, but not many people know how to do it.'

*'Peace can only last where human rights are respected,
where the people are fed, and where individuals and nations are free.'*
**TENZIN GYATSO, 14TH DALAI LAMA**

# PART IV

# SET MY PEOPLE FREE

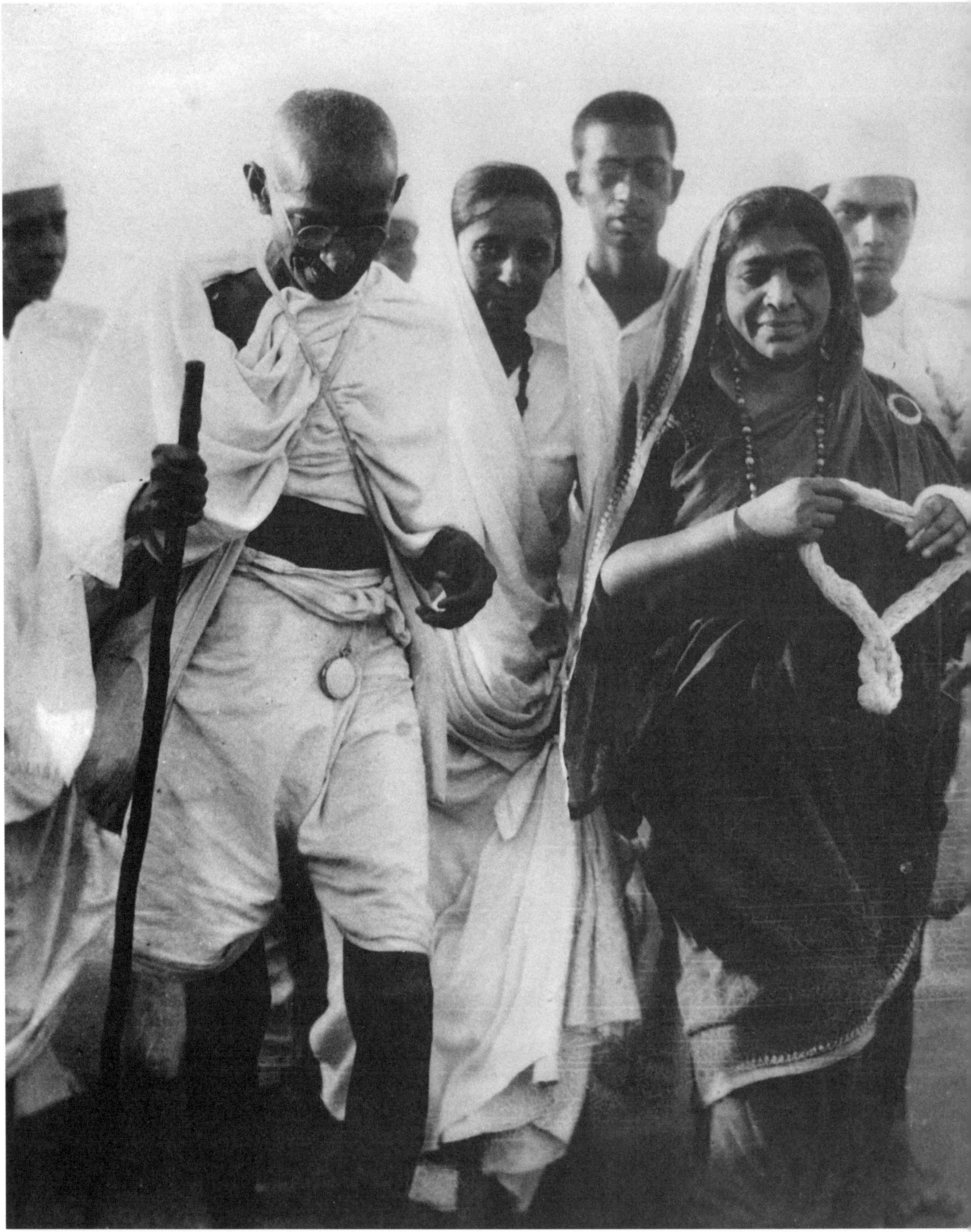

# MOHANDAS K. GANDHI: NON-VIOLENCE FREES A NATION

SUCH IS THE LEGACY OF MOHANDAS KARAMCHAND GANDHI THAT THE mere mention of his name or the calling to mind of the diminutive Indian's gentle smile, bald pate and round glasses conjures an instant image of non-violent resistance. For many, he is the personification of pacifism. Romain Roland, the French anti-war writer, said in his early biography of Gandhi: '[He] began the greatest moral and ethical movement in the politics of the last two thousand years.' Gandhi not only led a nation to independence, he cemented a philosophy of non-violent activism that changed the world and has affected practically every struggle for peace and freedom since.

Gandhi's views on peaceful civil disobedience grew directly from his Hindu beliefs and its tenet of *ahimsa*, the opposition to violence. Also influenced by Jesus' Sermon on the Mount and the writings of Leo Tolstoy and American Henry David Thoreau, Gandhi brought these threads together into a convergence of *ahimsa* and civil disobedience that he called *Satyagraha*, the active engagement of passive resistance. From his earliest days as a lawyer in South Africa agitating for the civil rights of Indian workers, to his ultimate calling as the spiritual leader and deliverer of independence in India, Gandhi demanded that violence play no part in these struggles. His is *the* story of how non-violence changed the world.

Gandhi, here accompanied by fellow activist Sarojini Naidu, began the Salt March on 12 March 1930; it ended at Dandi on the coast of the Arabian Sea on 6 April, with Gandhi contravening the Salt Act by gathering salt from the shore.

# AN INDIAN BARRISTER

PORBANDAR, THE BUSY PORT OF THE PRINCELY PROVINCE OF THE SAME name in British India, in what is now Gujarat state, had been a hub of commerce for over 3000 years by the time of Gandhi's birth in 1869. Situated on the west coast of India, jutting into the northern end of the Arabian Sea, Porbander was the seat of the Hindu Modh community. Gandhi's father, Karamchand Gandhi, was *diwan*, or prime minister of the province. His mother Putlibai, his father's fourth wife, came from the Pranami Vaishnava community, which was steeped in the Jain traditions of the region. Gandhi was raised in a conservatively religious family, a Hindu greatly influenced by the Jain practices of vegetarianism, self-purification, religious tolerance, and by the concept of *ahimsa*, belief in the non-violent sanctity of all life.

At thirteen, young Mohandas married Kasturba Makhanji in an arranged child marriage, as was the custom. He affectionately called her 'Ba' throughout their long life together; they had four sons. When Gandhi was fifteen, his father died, and pressure was exerted on him to finish his schooling and become a barrister so that he might help support the family. At eighteen he left for London, having been accepted into the law school at University College. He vowed to his mother—in front of a Jain monk—that he would abstain from meat, alcohol and promiscuity while in the imperial capital.

London of the 1890s was a difficult place for an Indian, especially one who wouldn't eat meat, but Gandhi had taken his promise to heart and for the first time in his life embraced vegetarianism as an intellectual and spiritual matter. After nearly starving on the voyage, in London he sought out the Vegetarian Society and found that many of its members were also involved with the Theosophical Society, an organisation that since 1875 had been dedicated to nurturing a 'Universal Brotherhood' of all religions and beliefs. With a particular interest in India and Hinduism, many of these people would become centrally involved in India's Home Rule movement, the precursor to Gandhi's independence efforts. Gandhi later credited his election to the Vegetarian Society's executive committee with giving him valuable experience at organising.

Three years later, Gandhi completed his training and passed the bar examinations. He returned that year to Porbandar and took a position with a small law practice in Rajkot, the nearby state capital, making a modest living helping litigants with their petitions until the practice was forced to close over a business dispute with a British officer. Out of work and still shouldering the pressure of supporting his family, his older brother helped arrange work on a trade dispute involving two rival Indian merchants in South Africa. Reluctantly, Gandhi agreed to the one-year appointment and again left his family.

Immediately on entering South Africa he felt the oppressive effects of their racial intolerance of Indians. He was forced off a train when he refused to move to a third-class compartment although he had purchased a first-class ticket. Continuing by stagecoach, he was humiliated and beaten by the driver when he refused to ride outside the coach when a European demanded his seat. He was barred from certain hotels and ordered to remove his turban, which he refused to do. All these actions awakened in him an acute awareness of the institutionalised racism that was simply a more radical form of what he experienced in India. For the first time, he began to question his status within the broader imperial structure of Great Britain and what the future held for his people.

At the end of his one-year contract, he was asked to remain in Durban to help litigate against a Bill limiting the rights of Indians to vote in South Africa. He wrote and circulated petitions to the Natal Legislative Assembly and to the British magistrates in opposition to the Bill and rallied popular support among the more prominent Indian citizens. Although the Bill failed to pass, the young barrister's campaign helped air Indian grievances—and brought him a considerable amount of negative attention. He decided to continue fighting for voter rights, and in 1897 moved his wife and children to Durban.

Shortly after his family joined him, he was set upon by an angry white mob that beat him. 'The crowd began to abuse me and shower upon me stones and whatever else they could lay their hands on,' he recalled. 'They threw down my turban. Meanwhile a burly fellow came up to me, slapped me in the face and then kicked me. I was about to fall down unconscious when I held on to the railings of a house near by … I had almost given up the hope of reaching home alive.' A sympathetic police inspector came to his rescue and, by disguising him as a constable, was able to sneak Gandhi away. The inspector encouraged Gandhi to press charges against the men but, in a sign of what was to be a lifelong principle, he refused to use the courts to redress personal wrongs.

❧

## SATYAGRAHA

Mohandas Gandhi's twenty years in South Africa strongly shaped his philosophy of non-violent civil disobedience. In the face of the humiliation he had suffered at the hands of white South Africans, Gandhi began to develop and articulate his view on non-violent non-cooperation. Several

Nelson Rolihlahla Mandela's rise to the presidency of South Africa after twenty-seven years in prison began with the pacifist teachings of Mohandas Gandhi. In 1944 Mandela joined the anti-apartheid African National Congress (ANC). In the early 1950s he led the ANC's Defiance Campaign of non-cooperation with racist apartheid policies. At the time he was committed to non-violent resistance, following in the footsteps of Gandhi, assassinated only a few years earlier. In 1952 Mandela, with Oliver Tambo, opened the first black legal firm in South Africa and became deputy leader of the ANC. By 1956 he and 150 other ANC members had been charged with treason. Following years of trials, all the defendants were acquitted.

In 1960, over 5000 peaceful demonstrators marched against oppressive 'pass laws', which limited the travel of the non-white majority, in the township of Sharpeville, in Gauteng province. White South African police opened fire on the protesters, killing nearly 100 people, including women and children. The outcry was overwhelming. More radical elements challenged the ANC leadership, disrupting activities and calling for armed rebellion against white rule, and Mandela, seeing the lack of progress achieved by his non-violent action and fearing loss of control of the ANC, turned to armed struggle. In 1961, he founded Umkhonto We Sizwe (Spear of the Nation), the ANC's military wing, and began a bombing and sabotage campaign against military and governmental institutions. Always claiming that the turn to violence was a last resort, Mandela also raised money abroad for paramilitary training and began a guerrilla campaign.

After months on the run, Mandela was arrested in 1962 and tried for sabotage and treason. He pleaded guilty and was sentenced to life in prison on South Africa's notorious Robben Island. His reputation grew, but the ANC's armed struggle turned increasingly violent through the 1980s, resulting in substantial civilian casualties. Eventually the ANC was outlawed and labelled a 'terrorist organisation'. Mandela was released in 1990 by order of South Africa's president F.W. de Klerk, and recommitted the newly legalised ANC, and himself as its deputy leader, to peaceful negotiations for an end to apartheid. He realised his dream in 1994 when he was elected President of South Africa with over 62 per cent of the vote, the first multiracial election in the country's history. He and F.W. de Klerk were honoured with the Nobel Peace Prize in 1993.

important influences helped him to crystallise his thinking. Primary to the process were the writings of Leo Tolstoy, particularly *The Kingdom of God is Within You*, which argues that non-violent resistance to oppression is well within a literal interpretation of Jesus Christ's teachings; important also was Gandhi's later correspondence with the Russian pacifist. But it was a letter that Tolstoy wrote to the Bengali Indian revolutionary Tarak Nath Das that most influenced Gandhi. 'A Letter to a Hindu', as it was later published in the Indian newspaper *Free Hindustan*, inspired Mohandas to write to the great Tolstoy and ask if he might translate the letter into his native Gujarati and publish it in his own South African paper, *Indian Opinion*, in 1909.

Tolstoy's *Letter* argued against the violent overthrow of the British, asserting instead that only through love could the Indians free themselves. Tolstoy suggested peaceful strikes, protests and 'non-resistance' as the best means for ending British rule. Most in the India Home Rule movement found these ideas ludicrous. But they struck a chord with the young Gandhi. 'One of the accepted and "time-honoured" methods to attain [independence] is that of violence,' he wrote in the published letter's introduction. '[But] Tolstoy's life has been devoted to replacing the method of violence for removing tyranny or securing reform by the method of non-resistance to evil. He would meet hatred expressed in violence by love expressed in self-suffering.' Specifically, Tolstoy had written: 'Do not resist the evil-doer and take no part in doing so, either in the violent deeds of the administration, in the law courts, the collection of taxes, or above all in soldiering, and no one in the world will be able to enslave you.'

This was in line with other influences that Gandhi would later cite. He had studied Christian writings and found the Sermon on the Mount wholly enlightening, but a more contemporary example of the type of civil action he wished to foster came in the writings of the American transcendentalist and naturalist Henry David Thoreau. Gandhi had read Thoreau's treatise 'Civil Disobedience', published in 1866, which encouraged citizens to question and oppose authority that went against individual morality. It also laid out ways to disrupt society through peaceful non-cooperation, in Thoreau's case the opposition to a poll tax foisted on all American citizens to pay for the Mexican–American war. When Thoreau was imprisoned for his refusal, he noted, 'under a government which imprisons any unjustly, the true place for a just man is also a prison'. These, too, were words that greatly affected Gandhi.

'Satyagraha', Gandhi's term for 'civil disobedience', was coined through the influence of Thoreau and Tolstoy, but is not an exact translation. *Satyagraha* is derived from the Sanskrit words *sat*, 'truth', and *graha*, 'firmness' or 'force'.

# ANNIE BESANT: THEOSOPHIST

Born in 1847 to parents of Irish descent, Annie Woods grew up in London. When her father died, she was taken in by a wealthy family friend who ensured she got a good education and instilled in her a sense of independence, rare for a woman of that era. At nineteen she married Anglican clergyman Frank Besant and had a son and daughter. Their marriage quickly fell apart when Annie embraced many progressive causes and began to question her religious beliefs. She left her husband and the Church and supported her children by writing for the *National Reformer*, the newspaper of the National Secular Society. She took up the cause for women's rights to birth control and in 1877, along with Charles Bradlaugh, published the American birth-control advocate Charles Knowlton's inflammatory *The Fruits of Philosophy*. Their arrest and notoriety turned the book into a bestseller; they were found not guilty on a technicality. The trial and scandal allowed Frank Besant to win sole custody of their children.

Annie became a socialist and supporter of Irish Home Rule. Through her relationship with George Bernard Shaw she joined the Fabian Society, supporting Britain's 'de-colonisation'. Later she fell in love with Edward Aveling, who translated Marx's writings into English. She was crushed when he left her for Eleanor, Marx's daughter. She threw herself into politics and in 1888 was the first woman elected to the London School Board. Upon her victory, she declared, 'Ten years ago, under a cruel law, Christian bigotry robbed me of my little child. Now the care of the 763,680 children of London is placed partly in my hands.'

Besant long believed she was clairvoyant and found herself drawn to the Theosophical Society after meeting its founder, Helena Blavatsky, in 1889. Within ten years she was its president and moved to India, refocusing the organisation on the study of Hinduism. She founded the Central Hindu College for boys in Varanasi and through devoted study of Hindu texts came to believe that the next great World Teacher would soon arrive on Earth. She believed she had found that person in a mystical young boy named Jiddu Krishnamurti, who lived with his father on the grounds of the Theosophical Society. In a twist on the loss of her own children, Annie took Krishnamurti and his younger brother away and raised them herself. Their father sued in court for their return but lost, and Krishnamurti remained with Annie until he broke off relations with the Theosophists in 1929. He opposed the notion that he was the incarnate World Teacher they predicted, but became one of the most renowned Indian philosophers, writers and mystics of his generation.

At the same time, Annie became deeply involved in India's Home Rule movement. She joined the Indian National Congress and at the onset of World War I. She helped launch the Home Rule League following the war and in 1917 was arrested. Her defiance briefly united the Indian National Congress and the Muslim League, and the threat of nationwide protests led to her release and to vague promises that Britain would move towards Indian self-government. She then became president of the Indian National Congress. When a new leader emerged in Mohandas Gandhi, Annie initially opposed his tactics, favouring negotiation with the British. Although she was overshadowed by Gandhi's rise, she remained an avid supporter of Indian self-rule until her death in 1933.

Gandhi imbued the literal meaning, 'the force of truth', with a sense of non-violent action. Although he valued 'Civil Disobedience' as a 'masterly treatise', he did not think it went far enough. He was also aware that Thoreau was not an outright advocate of non-violence; in fact, Thoreau's support of radical abolitionists justified open violent revolt. Gandhi's idea of *Satyagraha* was of active non-violent resistance as opposed to what he saw as 'passive resistance', a term he disliked. He made the distinction clear:

> If we continue to believe ourselves and let others believe that we are weak and therefore offer passive resistance, our resistance will never make us strong, and at the earliest opportunity we will give up passive resistance as a weapon of the weak. On the other hand … *Satyagraha* postulates the conquest of the adversary by suffering in one's own person.

Gandhi called *Satyagraha* a 'soul force' that could give an individual moral power over physical power. He was adamant that the ends and the means of a struggle were inseparable. In other words, it was an inherent contradiction to take violent action to achieve a peaceful end; a just outcome would never excuse unjust actions.

South Africa's Jan Christiaan Smuts was an abrasive, militaristic Afrikaner field marshal, lawyer and statesman who wholly subscribed to racial segregation. He was the first to use the word *apartheid* to describe the policy of state-sponsored racism that South Africa endured for the bulk of the twentieth century. Yet he was also a student of poetry, a philosopher and educator, and a prudent negotiator, who later in life would advocate for the League of Nations and write the preamble to the United Nations Charter as an agency of international peaceful arbitration. He would also force the first major test of Gandhi's *Satyagraha* movement. In 1906 Smuts was appointed Colonial Secretary of the newly autonomous Transvaal region within South Africa. Already suffering under an oppressive poll tax that kept indentured labourers in debt, the Indian population was further oppressed when the government demanded that they register their nationality in order to enforce a ban on their right to vote. At a mass protest in Johannesburg, Gandhi organised his first protest using his still-evolving *Satyagraha* method. He called on Indians to join together and resist peacefully any compliance with the registration laws, suffering whatever punishment should come.

For seven years the struggle continued. Gandhi and thousands of other Indians were imprisoned for refusing to register, burning their registration cards, and joining in non-violent protests, work stoppages and resistance. The crackdown was brutal and many protesters were beaten and killed. Although the protests did not win a retraction of the registration act, they were highly successful in winning popular sympathy to the Indian cause. When in 1912 the South African Supreme Court declared that only Christian marriages would be considered valid—essentially classifying all Indian wives as mistresses and all Indian children as illegitimate—Gandhi intensified his struggle. From his homestead, which he had named the Tolstoy Village in recognition of the great Russian's influence, the resistance eventually spread to over 50,000 indentured Indian workers, called 'coolies' by the South Africans. Thousands more educated 'free' Indians like Gandhi were imprisoned. Eventually, the public outcry was such that Smuts was forced to seek a compromise, admitting, 'we can't imprison 30,000 Indians'.

Smuts was impressed by Gandhi's courage before his overwhelming might. He was tough and respectful in negotiations, as was Gandhi. Ultimately, Gandhi won key concessions including the legalisation of Indian marriages, an end to a poll tax on 'coolies', a scheduled end to the practice of indentured servitude, and some freedoms of travel for Indians within South Africa. Of course, the ultimate goal of equality for South Africa's non-white majority would take another eighty years to realise. Nelson Mandela and the African National Congress, initially using many Gandhian Satyagraha techniques before turning to armed struggle, would eventually dismantle apartheid and win the presidency in 1994 (see 'Nelson Mandela', page 198).

Gandhi spent much of the seven years of struggle in prison, trusting that his example of suffering would create the public outcry needed to foster change. While in prison, Gandhi and Smuts corresponded, building a certain level of personal friendship. The Afrikaner sent Gandhi books, and Gandhi sent him a pair of handmade sandals. In 1939, Smuts returned the sandals as a gift for Gandhi's seventieth birthday. 'I have worn these sandals for many a summer since then,' he wrote, 'even though I may feel that I am not worthy to stand in the shoes of so great a man.'

## IN INDIA

BY THE END OF WORLD WAR I, AN ALLIANCE OF PROMINENT INDIAN CITIZENS and other leaders had begun to demand self-government within British rule. The Home Rule League, centred in Delhi, Bombay (present-day Mumbai) and Calcutta (Kolkata), attracted members from the Indian National Congress and the All India Muslim League. The League voted as its head Englishwoman Annie Besant, once leader of the Theosophical Society in London and now its leader in India, where she'd lived for nearly twenty years. Besant unified the moderate and radical factions of the League, an amazing accomplishment in itself. Members of the League gave impassioned speeches, gathered thousands of signatures and petitioned the government often. When the British authorities arrested Besant, the Indian populace was enraged and the movement spread to include the Punjab, Gujarat and Madras. The pressure became so intense that the British backed down and released Besant, who was welcomed out of gaol as an Indian hero (see 'Annie Besant: theosophist', page 200).

Such was the reputation that Gandhi had acquired from his efforts in South Africa that when he returned home in 1915 to take up the struggle for Indian independence, he became quickly known quite simply as Mahatma, or 'great soul', and even more affectionately as Bapu, 'father'. Many in the Home Rule League, however, including Annie Besant, opposed his tactics, thinking they were simplistic and ineffective; others favoured direct negotiations with the British. But such was Gandhi's popularity that the League was forced to acknowledge his leadership and he was elected its president in 1920. Within the year, he was able to merge the League with the Indian National Congress to form a united front in pursuit of independence.

Gandhi first focused the attention of the unified membership on surveying the conditions in villages, cataloguing atrocities and suffering, directing funds to build hospitals, and encouraging village leaders to work to ease the rampant alcoholism and social malaise wrought by years of oppressive rule. But with his reputation preceding him, Gandhi was a target of the oppressive *Rowlatt Acts*, named for British judge Sir Sidney Rowlatt, which authorised the government to imprison anyone suspected of revolutionary activity or terrorism without trial. Gandhi's reaction was to focus his *Satyagraha* efforts on Kheda, in the state of Gujarat, where he had established an ashram. When he was ordered out of the region, hundreds of thousands came out to protest his expulsion; the British were forced to back down and grant him permission to stay.

This victory encouraged large-scale demonstrations throughout the country, but when two popular Indian National Congress leaders were arrested and taken to a hidden location, some of the protests turned violent. British troops called into Amritsar to disperse the crowd fired on the unarmed picketers; several demonstrators were killed. The populace rose up, setting fire to municipal buildings and cutting telegraph wires; a number of Europeans were killed in the violence. After a brief respite from the mayhem, over 5000 men, women and children gathered at the Jallianwala Bagh gardens near the Golden Temple, where they were confronted by a testy military. The troops opened fire on the unarmed citizens, massacring nearly 400 and leaving over 1500 casualties.

Condemning the British actions and the retaliatory violence, Gandhi declared that *Satyagraha* must remain a non-violent movement and that all who followed him must follow the principles of *ahimsa*. The death of so many made Gandhi determined to pursue outright *Swaraj*, the complete political, economic and spiritual independence for India. Initially reluctant, the Indian National Congress eventually voted its full support, and by 1921 Gandhi was handed complete authority over the Congress. He organised a new constitution for the Congress and made *Swaraj* the cornerstone of all its future efforts.

Calling for a return to simple economic freedoms for villagers, Gandhi also made broad efforts to bring women into the movement, a controversial attitude at the time. The Congress set up small cottage industries that encouraged villagers to become self-sufficient. This included the manufacturing of *khadi*, a homespun cloth. Soon, the wearing of *khadi* was seen as a patriotic act opposed to purchasing, at inflated prices, British-manufactured cloth and clothing. Gandhi's prestige as the symbol of a free India grew. He became increasingly ascetic in his outlook, rejecting material goods, promoting vegetarianism and advocating simplicity in all things.

*Satyagraha* spread throughout the country, attracting people from all castes and levels of society. But the risk was always present that at some time a group would deviate from Gandhi's way of peace. This happened in 1922 when a violent clash erupted in Uttar Pradesh, leaving dead on both sides. The tension rose to crisis point and Gandhi, fearing his followers were about to embrace armed resistance, abruptly called for a halt to *Satyagraha*, fundamentally ending all civil disobedience and demonstrations. Gandhi took full responsibility for the deaths and made no argument against accusations of sedition. He was sentenced to six years in prison, and vowed to abstain from politics and the movement until it was once again united behind peaceful resistance.

## NIGHTS AT THE ROUND TABLE

WITHOUT GANDHI'S PRESENCE TO UNITE THE MEMBERSHIP, THE INDIAN National Congress began to crack along factional lines. Hindus and Muslims had, throughout the peaceful protests, cooperated in their singular goal. Now they began to pull apart, even though Badshah Khan, the Muslim pacifist and devotee of Gandhi, struggled to keep the two factions unified. His organisation, the Khudai Khidmatgar (Servants of God) worked side by side with the Congress, of which he was also a senior and respected member (see 'Badshah Khan: king of chiefs', page 210). The Congress further split on whether or not to participate in the British-controlled legislature. In prison Gandhi wearied of the infighting and went on a three-week fast, one of many over his life, to draw attention to the rift. But still, the Congress remained divided.

Two years into his sentence, Gandhi was released from prison to allow critical surgery for appendicitis. After his recovery he decided to stay out of politics, instead increasing his efforts to elevate awareness and treat his people's domestic woes. He continued to organise initiatives directed at poverty, alcoholism, opium addiction and, most significantly, India's unique issue of untouchability. But by the end of the decade he was drawn back into politics, primarily at the request of the young activist and follower Jawaharlal Nehru. In December 1928, at the meeting of the Indian National Congress held in Calcutta, Gandhi called for a resolution demanding that Great Britain grant India dominion status or face renewed resistance with the ultimate goal of total independence. The British refused to respond. Gandhi had promised a one-year waiting period for an answer; when there was no response he began a new *Satyagraha*.

In 1930, Gandhi launched renewed action against a hated tax all Indians were forced to pay on salt. The British owned a monopoly on distilling sea salt in India, which they sold at a huge profit. Declaring that salt was a given right of all Indians, Gandhi organised a march from Ahmedabad to Dandi on the Indian Ocean, a distance of 400 kilometres (250 miles); there they would make their own salt. At first the members of Congress could not see what this had to do with gaining independence. But Gandhi had an innate understanding of the psyches of both his people and the British.

The Salt March attracted hundreds of thousands of Indians along the way and ultimately led to the imprisonment of over 60,000 people. With incredible discipline, all the *Satyagrahists* refused to be intimidated, and endured beatings, arrest and persecution. But the march garnered international attention for India's cause. Viceroy of India, Lord Irwin, ultimately signed an agreement with Gandhi, known as the Gandhi–Irwin Pact, which set all the political prisoners free in exchange for an end to the civil disobedience. The pact also cancelled the salt tax, made a vague promise of dominion status in the future and gave Gandhi a seat, as the sole representative of the Indian

National Congress, at the second Round Table Conference in London in 1931 to establish a new Indian constitution.

Members of the Indian National Congress, many of whom were in prison for civil disobedience, had boycotted the first Round Table Conference. The second conference would also prove to be a major disappointment to Gandhi and the Indian nationalists, as Britain sought to build alliances with princes and minority representatives rather than discuss a transfer of power. Returning home, Gandhi led further civil disobedience campaigns and was again arrested, this time isolated from his followers. This tactic backfired, leading more Indians to follow his path. Freed, Gandhi attended the third Round Table Conference in 1932, continuing to call for complete self-rule against growing consensus on the British side for granting dominion status. As the meetings dragged on, many lasting late into the night, no clear interpretation of what dominion status meant could be agreed upon. Gandhi again left disheartened.

When a new constitution was ratified by the 1932 conference, India's untouchables, the lowest caste in their ancient hierarchical system, were allocated a separate electorate. Gandhi refused to accept this. The removal of the untouchables, whom Gandhi renamed the Harijans, the 'children of God', from the general electorate created, in essence, the exact system that Gandhi had fought so hard against in South Africa. The Congress fell into a stalemate and again Gandhi used the one tool he knew he could count on: his own suffering. He began a three-week fast that successfully forced the British to adopt a more equitable arrangement for the Harijans. Gandhi also called on all Indians to end their ancient caste system. As time would show, this would prove as difficult a task as bringing together the Hindu and Muslim populations.

❧

## QUIT INDIA

Britain's entry into World War II signalled a step-up in independence efforts, for the declaration of war unilaterally included India, without consultation. All elected Indian officials resigned en masse and Gandhi declared that the country would not be drawn into a war fought for democratic principles if India were denied those very same freedoms. Support for the war effort would come only with independence—the rallying cry became 'Quit India'. As the war progressed, Gandhi's movement intensified its efforts by resisting cooperation. The British retaliated brutally. Thousands were killed and injured in military actions, hundreds of thousands were arrested.

By 1942, the entire leadership of the Indian National Congress was in gaol, Gandhi himself under detention for two years in Pune. In 1944, personal tragedy struck when Ba, his beloved wife of nearly sixty years, died in prison. Only weeks later Gandhi, suffering from malaria, was released by the British for fear that he too might die in captivity, setting off new waves of revolt at a crucial time in the war. That same year, having recognised the strength of the Quit India movement, the British finally acquiesced: power would be turned over to India. With that, Gandhi called an end to the struggle and the British released nearly 100,000 political prisoners, including the leaders of the National Congress.

One stipulation by Britain would nearly cripple the independence effort: Muslim and Hindu parties would be required to come to agreement on power sharing. As details of independence took shape, violence between Hindus and Muslims exploded. By 1948, more than 5000 people had been killed in violent clashes between religious factions. Gandhi was absolutely opposed to partitioning India into two countries, but an overwhelming majority favoured it. The Muslim League had vast support in the West Punjab and the North-West Frontier provinces. Fearful that an all-out civil war between Hindus and Muslims was increasingly likely, the Congress approved the partition plan, although they knew it could never achieve popular support unless Gandhi gave his stamp of approval. Gandhi's strongest supporters and closest friends, including Jawaharlal Nehru, who had ascended to Congress leadership and was touted as the key candidate for prime minister, encouraged him to support Partition as the only way to avoid civil war. Eventually, nearly heartbroken by the decision, Gandhi gave his approval.

When independence was declared, Gandhi chose to avoid any of the official events and went to Calcutta, the scene of some of the most intense Hindu–Muslim violence. Fasting for peace, he declared he would fast until death if rioting and ethnic violence did not cease. Fearful of losing their great leader, the Hindus backed down and the Muslims soon followed. Within days, violence in the region ceased, the opposing sides brought together in sympathy for their Mahatma. This came to be known as the Calcutta Miracle and would be repeated in towns large and small across India.

However, a new crisis quickly unfolded. Following Partition, India had promised to pay the newly created Muslim state of Pakistan reparations for disputed territories that had been given up. But fearful that Pakistan would use the money to wage war against India, the new government, with Jawaharlal Nehru as its prime minister, decided not to honour the promise. Gandhi was adamant that the payments must be made. Again he fasted, calling for India to make the

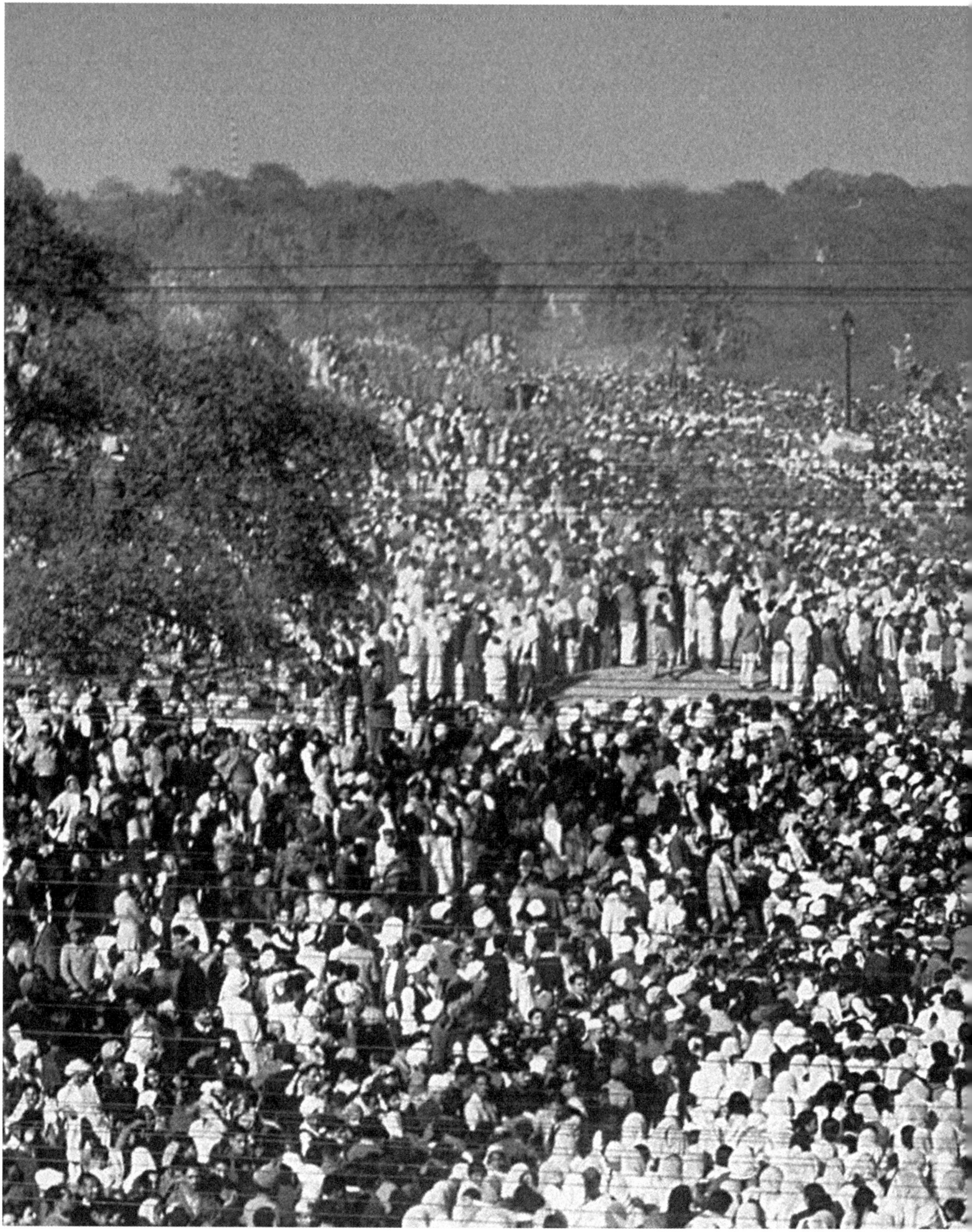

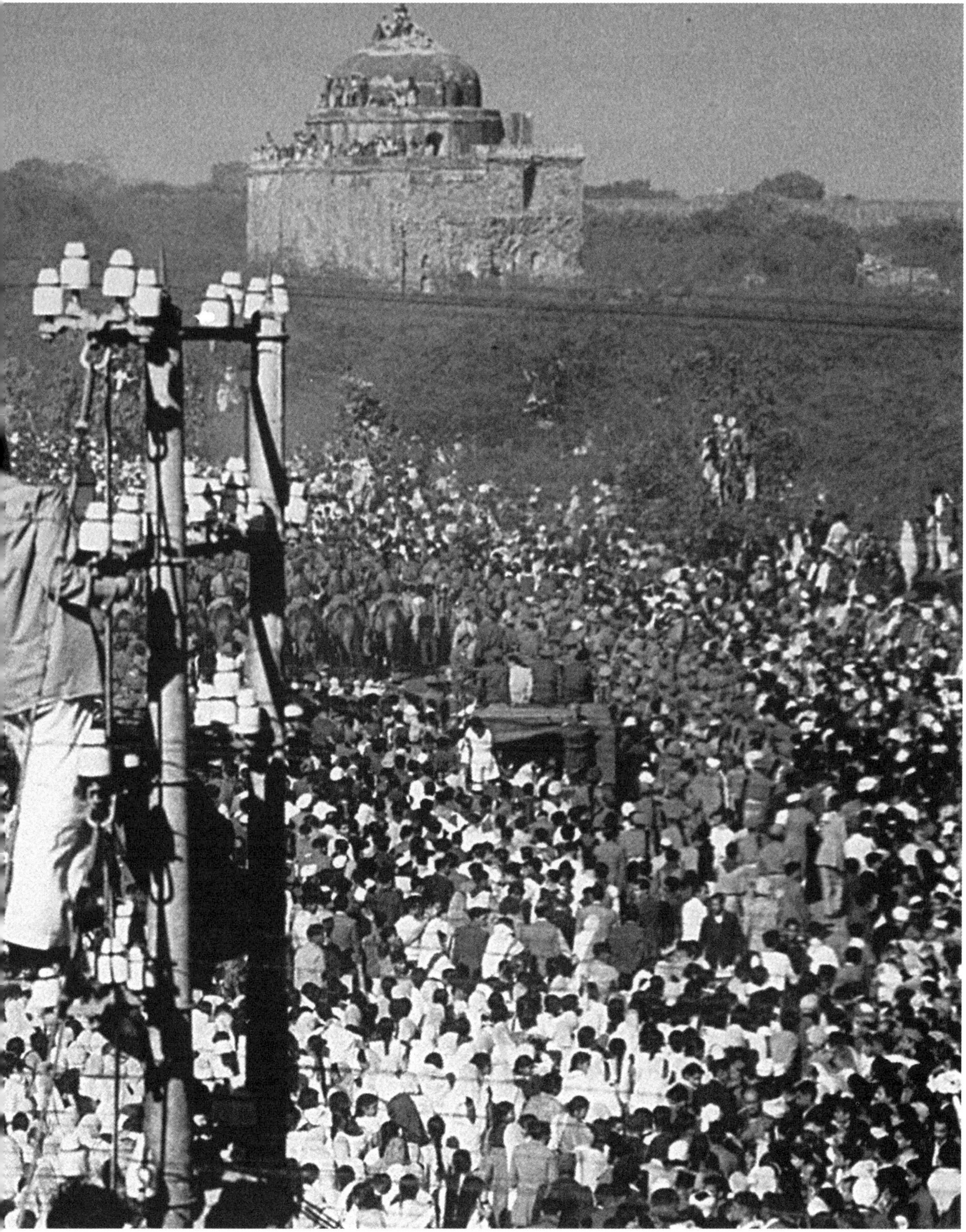

Khan Abdul Ghaffar Khan was born in 1890 in the Islamic Pashtun region of Charsadda in British India, in what is now part of Pakistan's northwest frontier along the Afghanistan border. His father was a wealthy landowner and farmer and Khan was educated by the British. When his mother barred him from further education in London, he turned his considerable energy to opening schools throughout the North-West Frontier Province. Although he faced considerable objections, he worked tirelessly, visiting all 500 settled districts. The feat won him considerable praise from Frontier locals, who named him Badshah Khan, 'King of Chiefs'.

Following World War I, Kahn joined in the efforts for an independent India. He founded the Khudai Khidmatgar, 'Servants of God', as the Pashtun arm of the independence movement, basing the organisation on Gandhi's concept of *Satyagraha*. He and Gandhi forged a lifelong spiritual bond and close personal friendship. Khan carefully coordinated the efforts of the Khudai Khidmatgar with those of the Indian National Congress and continuously threw his support behind Gandhi.

He joined with Gandhi in the famous Salt March, being arrested along with thousands of others. In 1930 some 250 protesters from the Khudai Khidmatgar were massacred in Peshawar when British soldiers fired on the unarmed protesters.

Badshah Khan also championed women's rights, and argued throughout his life that Islam was compatible with non-violence. As India moved towards independence, Khan remained staunchly opposed to Partition, and felt betrayed by the Indian National Congress when they ultimately sanctioned an independent Pakistan. His attitude towards India aroused suspicion in the newly independent Pakistan, and despite having fought and suffered for independence, he spent most of the years between 1948 and 1964 imprisoned by his own government. Released because of illness, he was eventually exiled to Kabul in Afghanistan. He died in Peshawar in 1988, again under house arrest. Badshah Khan spent fifty-three years of his life either in prison or in exile for his pacifist views and his compassionate belief in a unified Hindu–Muslim India.

payments and for Pakistan's leaders to assure peace and renounce violence. Only when Gandhi was near death did the parties acquiesce; Gandhi ended his fast. Even so, war soon broke out between India and Pakistan in the disputed kingdom of Kashmir.

Further ethnic rioting ensued, and Gandhi went to New Delhi in January 1948 to once more call for an end to the violence. On 30 January, as Gandhi took his nightly walk in the grounds of the beautiful Birla Bhavan, he was gunned down by a radical Hindu named Nathuram Godse, a member of the extremist Hindu Mahasabha, the organisation that held Gandhi responsible for sacrificing Indian strength by making the payments to Pakistan. As he lay dying, Gandhi's last words were 'Oh God'. So stunned was the country by the assassination of their beloved Bapu that racial violence almost immediately waned. His death was seen as an event of such historic significance that it could only be measured against the greatest events in history. A period of mourning was declared by the United Nations General Assembly. Nathuram Godse was tried, convicted and executed the following year.

Condolences came in from every corner of the world. Spontaneous memorials took place in nearly every major city. Gandhi's teachings soon began to influence a new generation of activists and leaders, from the smallest to the greatest nations on Earth. In the United States, a young civil rights leader named Martin Luther King Jr was just beginning to study the teachings and actions of Gandhi. So was a young anti-apartheid leader in South Africa named Nelson Mandela, and an even younger High Lama from the country of Tibet. Gandhi's legacy lives on today in every act of non-violent resistance that strives to free a repressed people or end an oppressive rule. 'When I despair,' Gandhi famously said, 'I remember that all through history the way of truth and love has always won. There have been tyrants and murderers and for a time they seem invincible but in the end, they always fall—think of it, *always*!'

Previous pages: Despairing mourners climbed telegraph poles for a better view of Gandhi's funeral procession in New Delhi in February 1948. His ashes were divided among a number of urns that were sent across India for memorial services.

# DR MARTIN LUTHER KING JR: CIVIL DISOBEDIENT

Martin Luther King Jr and fellow members of the Montgomery Improvement Association, formed to boycott the city's segregated transport system, riding a Montgomery bus in company with Rev. Glenn Smiley of the Fellowship of Reconciliation on 21 December 1956.

AMERICA'S GREATEST NON-VIOLENT LEADER WAS A SPIRITUAL DESCENDANT of Gandhi. Martin Luther King Jr came of age in a time of great moral upheaval, when social and political norms were being challenged by the post-war world order. With peoples and nations seeking independence, American blacks became acutely aware of the limitations of segregation. Martin Luther King Jr didn't initiate the Civil Rights Movement, nor was its work anywhere near complete when he was assassinated in 1968. But because of his non-violent leadership, his charisma, strength and sacrifice, the Civil Rights Movement won the most significant gains for blacks since the end of slavery a hundred years earlier.

King was no saint, nor would he have wanted to be portrayed that way. As more radical black power advocates came to the fore during the later 1960s, his pacifist tactics were increasingly challenged. But he never wavered in his call for black Americans to challenge the core of entrenched racial intolerance and reach for civil, political and labour equality through non-violent means. Much has been made of his legacy but perhaps his greatest achievement was holding together a movement that fundamentally remained non-violent in an era when violence abounded. He left an America far more racially just.

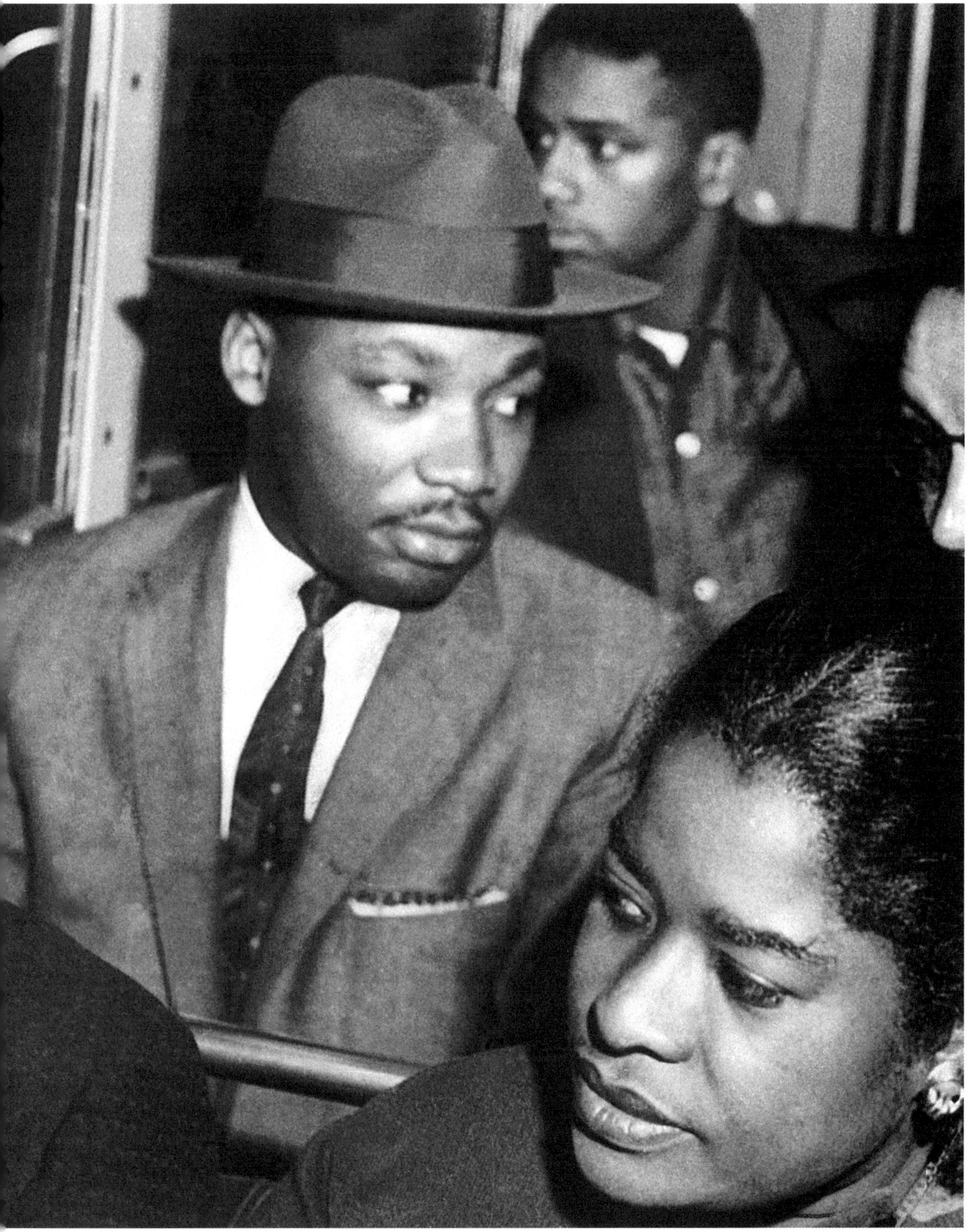

# THE BACK OF THE BUS

'Sweet' Auburn Avenue in Atlanta, Georgia was known as the 'black Wall Street' for its congregation of profitable black-owned businesses and prosperous churches. Martin Luther King Jr grew up on the avenue, the son and grandson of Baptist ministers. His father was pastor of the prestigious Ebenezer Baptist Church, as was his father-in-law before him. Steeped in this Southern black ministry, young Martin gained a solid middle-class education in a stable and loving family. Born Michael King Jr in 1929, both father and son would change their names after the family visited Germany in 1934. Michael King Sr was so impressed by the teachings of the German Protestant leader, Martin Luther, that he legally changed both his and his son's names upon their return.

At the age of only fifteen, Martin began study at Morehouse College in Atlanta, having skipped both the ninth and twelfth grades. In the summer before he started college, he worked on a tobacco farm in Connecticut, where he witnessed for the first time blacks and whites working side by side in harmony. It stirred in him a deeper dislike for the racial segregation and intolerance he experienced at home. By 1948 he had graduated from Morehouse and enrolled in Crozer Theological Seminary in Pennsylvania and, later, Boston University where, in 1955, he received his doctorate in systematic theology. His dissertation on the comparative conceptions of God was well regarded, although years later, after his death, it was revealed that he had plagiarised some sections. While in Boston he met Coretta Scott, a beautiful young music student at the New England Conservatory, and they married in 1953. Settling first in Montgomery, Alabama, where King became the pastor of the central Dexter Avenue Baptist Church when he was only twenty-five, they soon had two sons and two daughters.

King's concern for the plight of Southern blacks had been brewing throughout his childhood, but several early influences helped to channel his thinking. Howard Thurman, a classmate of King's father at Morehouse, wrote a famous theological study called 'Jesus and the Disinherited', which had a profound affect on him. While studying in Boston he had visited the noted ethicist and early civil rights champion; the older man took him in, mentored him and became a lifelong spiritual adviser. Thurman was also an adviser to the radical Christian pacifist A.J. Muste, who in turn helped lead King to both the pacifist writings of Leo Tolstoy and the non-violent civil disobedience of Mohandas K. Gandhi.

Another, and far more controversial, influence in King's life was the young non-violent activist Bayard Rustin. He too had studied Gandhi's teachings and served as one of King's main advisers and an essential organiser throughout his early acts of civil disobedience. Rustin's homosexuality and links to the Communist Party would later cause concern among conservative black civil rights leaders, who advised King to cut him loose. At first King refused to turn his back on a trusted friend, but as revelations about Rustin's personal life lost him a vaunted position with the Fellowship of Reconciliation and he openly advocated for gay and lesbian rights, King eventually distanced himself (see 'Bayard Rustin', page 222).

When Rosa Parks famously refused to move to the back of the bus in Montgomery, Alabama on 1 December 1955, her action provided the final impetus to a coalition of civil rights groups that had been waiting to spring into action. Rosa Parks was not, however, the first to challenge segregated buses. Nine months earlier a fifteen-year-old high school student named Claudette Colvin had refused to give up her seat to a white man and had been dragged from the bus in handcuffs. But she was hardly the best test case for a legal challenge. Colvin was said to have yelled obscenities at both the driver and the police, her father mowed lawns for a living and the family came from one of the poorest areas of Montgomery. A short while after her arrest, news came that Colvin was pregnant to an older, married man, whom she claimed had raped her. Black leaders were worried that the courts and the press would manipulate her story, and that this could lose them the support of the religious black community and sympathetic whites. The decision was made to wait for another case.

Months later Rosa Parks, a forth-two-year-old seamstress and secretary with the National Association for the Advancement of Colored People (NAACP) refused to give up her seat. The strict segregation laws dictated that buses were to be filled by blacks from the back to the front, and by whites from the front to the back. When there were no more open seats for whites, an entire row of people sitting in the 'black' seats had to move back to make room for a white person. If there were no more seats, the blacks had to stand. This was the case with Rosa Parks, who refused to give up an entire row so one white person could sit. She was arrested and taken off the bus by the police.

Her actions kicked off the Montgomery Bus Boycott, led by local activist Edgar Nixon and supported by King. Edgar Nixon, head of the Montgomery chapter of the NAACP, and Ralph Abernathy, senior pastor of the First Baptist Church, the largest congregation in Montgomery, put pressure on other Montgomery clergy to support the challenge to segregation laws. Fearing the other clergy might buckle under the pressure, however, Nixon and Abernathy nominated King to lead the strike, who, as a fairly new face in town and pastor of one of the city's most prominent churches, would likely be acceptable to a wide coalition. Under the banner of the Montgomery Improvement Administration, the committee of ministers and volunteers began planning Rosa Park's defence. The next day, flyers went out and news spread announcing a boycott of Montgomery's public bus system. So few black riders used the buses the next day that it was decided to continue the boycott. Black people began car-pooling and using every other means of travel possible, from bicycles to carts to mules. Black cab drivers joined in, providing rides for the same cost as the bus. Montgomery authorities attempted to fine the cab drivers for this action, and began arresting those boycotters, including King, who picketed bus stops. With nearly two-thirds of the ridership down, the economic impact took hold.

Tensions grew as other segregation laws, called 'Jim Crow' laws, were challenged. The term Jim Crow, referring to a derogatory song-and-dance routine about blacks, was commonly used to describe a large set of laws enacted between 1876 and 1965 mandating separate public facilities for whites and blacks. Although the laws were supposed to support 'separate but equal' facilities, they institutionalised inferior conditions for blacks. These included segregated public schools and transportation as well as public restrooms, open spaces, restaurants, hotels and even drinking fountains.

The Montgomery boycotters were attacked and beaten; King and Abernathy's homes, along with four black Baptist churches, were firebombed, but the boycott was maintained for 381 days. The arrests of King and 150 others drew national attention to the boycott. Finally, in December 1956, after Alabama's federal district court had ruled that the segregation laws were unconstitutional, the ruling was upheld by the Supreme Court. Martin Luther King Jr had stepped onto the national stage as a leader in the civil rights struggle.

## 'NON-VIOLENT RESISTANCE IS THE MOST POTENT WEAPON AVAILABLE'

WITH THE SUCCESS OF THE MONTGOMERY BUS BOYCOTT, KING, RALPH Abernathy, Bayard Rustin and other Southern ministers and civil rights activists, recognising the need to seize the momentum, began laying the groundwork for a larger movement. In 1957, sixty members of the clergy and civil rights leaders met in Atlanta, Georgia at the Ebenezer Baptist

Church to form an organisation that would coordinate non-violent actions against Jim Crow laws across the South. King was nominated president and the organisation, first called 'The Negro Leaders Conference on Non-violent Integration' soon became known as the Southern Christian Leadership Conference (SCLC). A small office was established on Auburn Avenue, and from these humble beginnings King would establish a base from which to operate a national organisation.

King began writing and lecturing all over the country, meeting with groups large and small to discuss race relations and actions on behalf of civil rights. He published *Stride Toward Freedom*, which recounted his efforts with the Montgomery Improvement Association in organising the bus boycott. In 1958, while signing copies of the book at a department store in Harlem, New York, a deranged black woman named Izola Curry stepped forward and stabbed King in the chest with a letter opener. He was rushed to hospital, where doctors found that the razor-sharp tip was resting against his aorta. Had the tip pierced the aorta, he would surely have bled to death. As soon as King was well, he issued a statement confirming what he called 'the redemptive power of non-violence' and saying, 'I felt no ill will toward Mrs Izola Currey [sic] and know that thoughtful people will do all in their power to see that she gets the help she apparently needs.' She was found incompetent to stand trial and spent the rest of her life in a psychiatric facility.

On his recovery, King resumed his lecturing and travels. In 1959, just a decade after independence and Gandhi's assassination, he visited India on a trip arranged by A.J. Muste and sponsored by the Quaker relief organisation, the American Friends Service Committee. During the visit he held discussions with India's Prime Minister Jawaharlal Nehru. Meeting members of Gandhi's family and immersing himself in the concept of peaceful non-compliance—*Satyagraha*—that Gandhi had championed, King became convinced that non-violent resistance was the most effective way to free oppressed people. On his last evening in India he gave a radio address that was broadcast across the country. He told his audience:

> Since being in India, I am more convinced than ever before that the method of non-violent resistance is the most potent weapon available to oppressed people in their struggle for justice and human dignity. In a real sense, Mahatma Gandhi embodied in his life certain universal principles that are inherent in the moral structure of the universe, and these principles are as inescapable as the law of gravitation.

King moved permanently back to Atlanta in 1960 where he took over as co-pastor with his father of the Ebenezer Baptist Church. With his growing national reputation and serving as head of the SCLC, King felt sure the time was right for further challenges to Jim Crow. The opportunity presented itself almost immediately. Black college kids from local schools began testing the segregation laws by staging sit-ins at all-white lunch counters. King joined them and was arrested along with thirty-three others at an Atlanta department store lunch counter. He was sentenced to a term at the state prison farm for 'breaking his parole' because of a minor traffic violation earlier, and the case immediately erupted onto the national stage as outraged protesters decried Georgia's harsh treatment. Because of fears for King's safety, appeals were made to President Dwight D. Eisenhower for his release, but Eisenhower refused to intervene. King was finally released when John F. Kennedy, then a Democratic presidential candidate, brought attention to his plight. Many historians have credited Kennedy's win a year later in part to this action.

## 'THE DREAM'

ONE OF THE BIGGEST TESTS OF KING'S NON-VIOLENT ACTION CAME IN Birmingham, Alabama, in the early 1960s. In one of the most racially divided cities in America, where the disparity between the rights and opportunities for blacks and whites was stark, any action taken by blacks to better their lot was met with harsh retribution. King brought the SCLC into the city in 1963 and began boycotting businesses that denied employment opportunities to blacks, then focused on desegregating public spaces, facilities, stores and restaurants. Local businesses resisted the boycotts and King upped the stakes, coordinating a number of marches, protests and occupations specifically designed to provoke arrests. The Birmingham police complied en masse. The SCLC quickly ran low on adult protesters and began recruiting young adults and children, a highly controversial move. The 'Children's Crusade' was criticised for putting minors in harm's way, especially when the police force, led by the brutal Eugene 'Bull' Connor, released police dogs and turned high-pressure fire hoses on child protesters and innocent bystanders. Media coverage exploited the issue across the nation. An image in *Life* magazine of youngsters being blasted by water cannon became known as an 'era defining photo' and led to stark comparisons between the police actions in Birmingham and the apartheid system in South Africa.

While in the Birmingham prison, King sent a letter to eight white clergymen in Birmingham who had been calling for him to end the boycott and civil disobedience. They claimed to sympathise with the unjust practices in the city but argued in a statement entitled 'A Call For Unity' that change should be made in the courts, not on the streets. King's response, excerpts from which were published almost immediately without his consent, stated passionately that without non-violent action, true civil rights would never be achieved. 'One has not only a legal but a moral responsibility to obey just laws,' he wrote. 'Conversely, one has a moral responsibility to disobey unjust laws. I would agree with St Augustine that "an unjust law is no law at all".' Protesters and sympathisers rallied around his statements while those opposed called the letter a staged event that obviously had to be part of a 'black anarchic plot'.

The crisis reached boiling point in May 1963, when thousands of gaoled protesters clogged the prisons and black protesters brought Birmingham's downtown commerce to collapse. King called for sympathy protests in hundreds of cities and the nightly news was dedicated solely to the story. Finally, white business owners met with King and other protest leaders to work out a compromise. While business leaders were willing to meet the protesters' demands, promising to desegregate businesses and hire black workers, they claimed to have no control over politics. King continued to pressure political leaders, who held fast, refusing to desegregate public spaces or release the arrested.

On 10 May, King announced that a settlement had been reached. The city would desegregate lunch counters, restaurants, hotels, public restrooms, drinking fountains and fitting rooms within ninety days. Jobs would be offered to blacks as salespeople, clerks and other 'white collar' roles. But the terms were vague, the protesters were not released, and rollout was hampered by additional violence. The Gaston Motel, where King had been staying only hours earlier (and singer Joan Baez had stayed the night before, having performed a free concert for protesters), was bombed and destroyed. King's brother's house was bombed, and new clashes erupted with brick-throwing black youths. President Kennedy helped coordinate support from the United Auto Workers Union, the AFL and other unions to raise bail for all protesters held in custody. Days later, federal troops were deployed to Birmingham to restore order.

The summer saw more bombings of black targets and the city was again thrust into international news when members of the Ku Klux Klan, the white supremacist group, bombed the Sixteenth Street Baptist Church on a Sunday morning, killing four young black girls. At the end of the summer, Alabama's irascible governor George Wallace refused to acknowledge the desegregation of

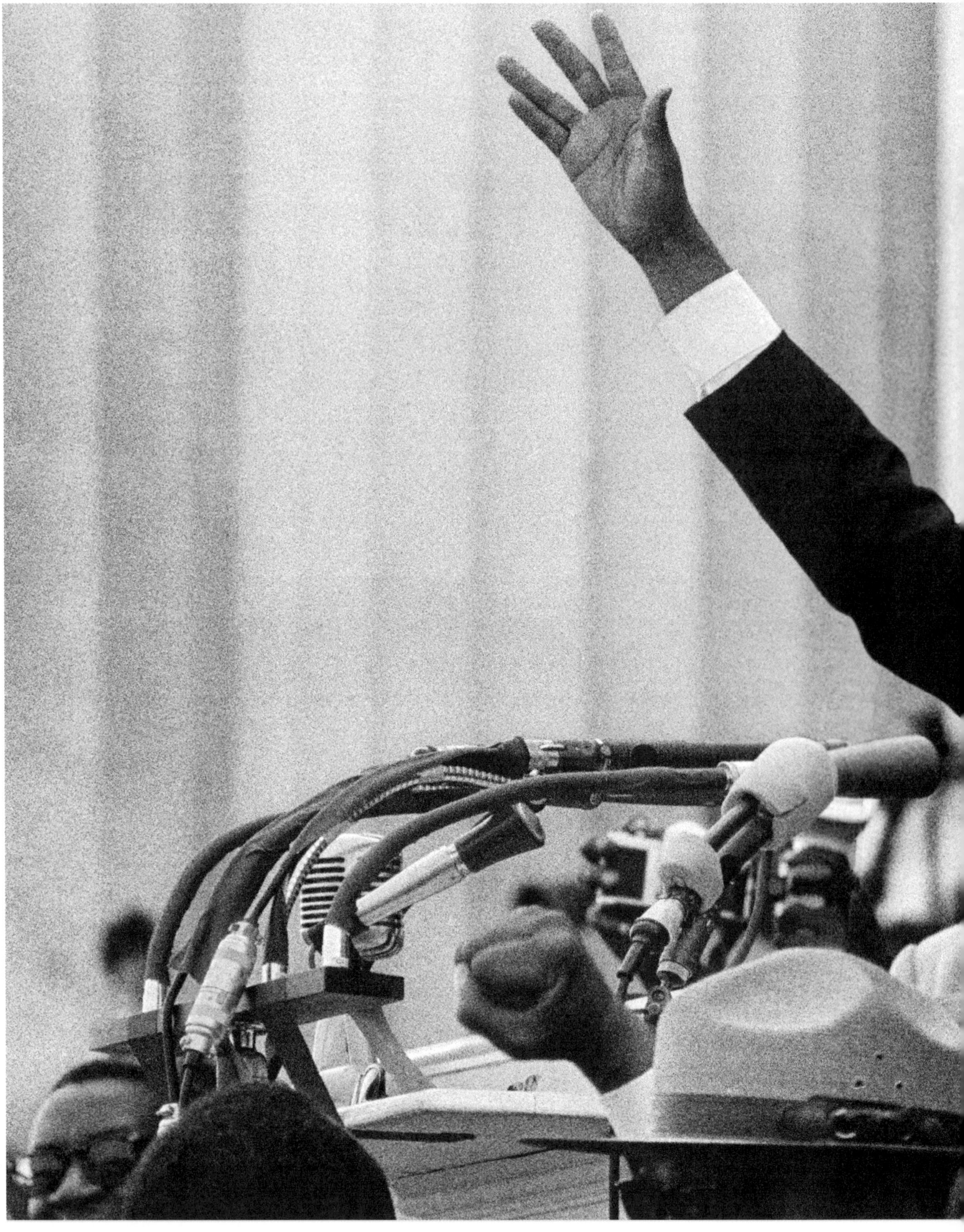

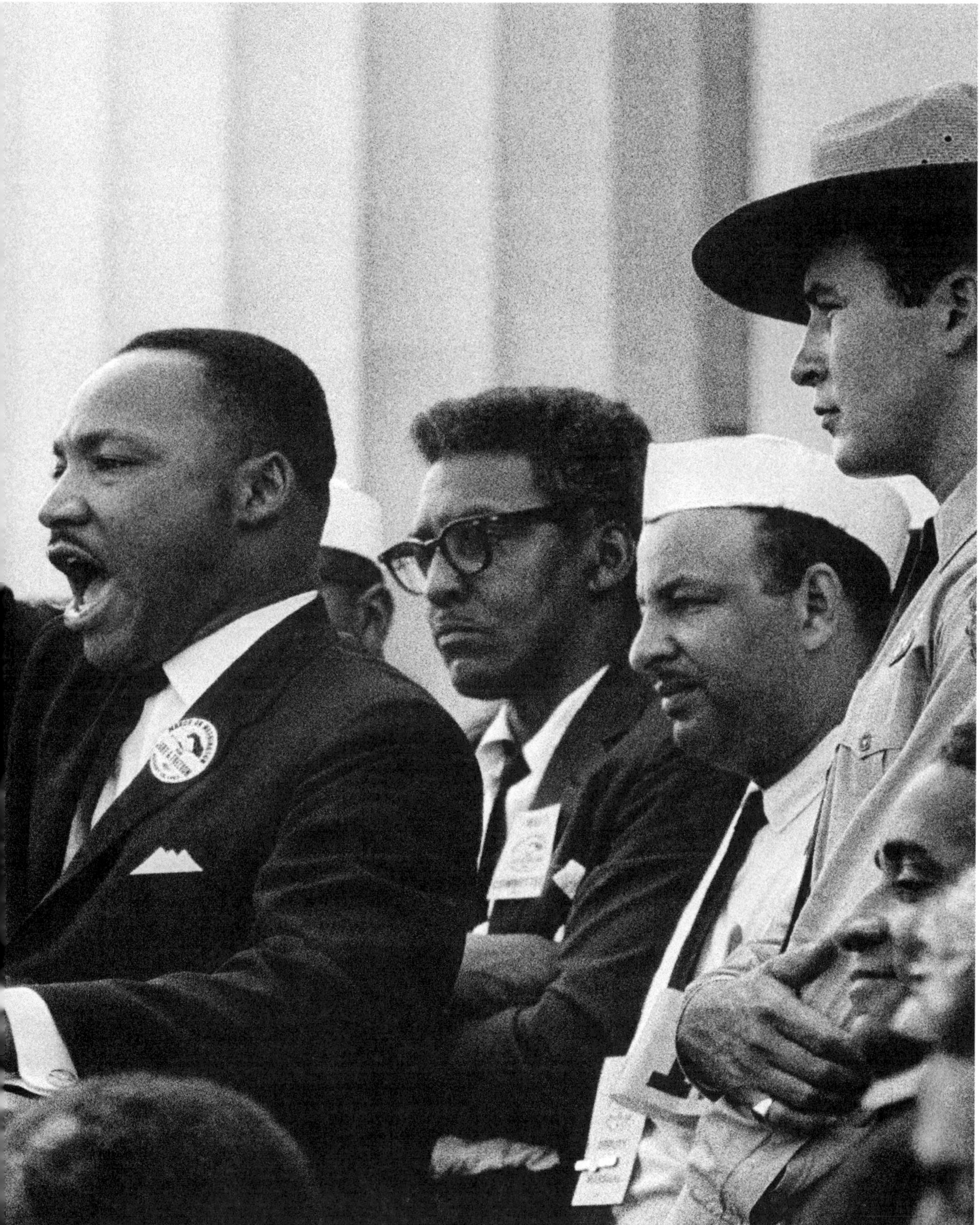

Bayard Rustin was born in 1912 and raised by his grandparents in Pennsylvania. His grandmother, a Quaker and a member of the NAACP, often hosted NAACP leader W.E.B. DuBois in her home. In 1937, after completing college and a non-violent activist training program with the American Friends Service Committee, Rustin joined the Young Communist League, moved to Harlem, and began attending Quaker Meetings. He immediately threw himself into the young Civil Rights Movement, championing the cause of the Scottsboro Boys, nine young black boys who were falsely convicted of raping two white women.

Rustin became disillusioned with the Communist Party after it broke off its support of civil rights in favour of America's entry into World War II. In 1941 he joined with A. Philip Randolph and A.J. Muste in organising a march on Washington for equal work opportunities for blacks, which was called off when President Roosevelt signed an executive order meeting their demands. He went to California early in the war to help protect the property of Japanese-Americans who were imprisoned in internment camps. He joined Muste in the Fellowship of Reconciliation (FOR) and served as a founder of the Congress of Racial Equality (CORE), dedicated to Gandhian non-violent action against US segregation. His violation of the *Conscription Act* of 1940 landed him in prison for two years. Once out of prison, he went to India and South Africa to join non-violent protests, but was arrested and deported from both countries. In 1948 he returned to India to learn non-violent techniques at a conference that had been organised by Gandhi himself shortly before his assassination.

Rustin was arrested in California in 1953 on charges of 'sexual perversion', which for the first time brought his homosexuality into the open. He was fired from the FOR and shortly afterwards became executive secretary of the War Resisters League. In 1956, when King was organising the Montgomery Bus Boycott, Rustin advised him on Gandhi's teachings and tactics. The two became close and began organising the Southern Christian Leadership Conference, although other black leaders advised King to break off ties because of Rustin's avowed homosexuality. Several years later, when King, Rustin and Randolph organised the 1963 March on Washington, Senator Strom Thurman damned Rustin as that 'Communist, draft-dodging homosexual!' and produced an FBI photograph of King and Rustin while King was bathing, alleging an affair between them. Although untrue, the accusation forced King to distance himself and join with the NAACP in denying Rustin any public role in the march.

Despite this, Rustin continued to work on behalf of human rights throughout the 1970s and 1980s. Increasingly he took up the fight for gays and lesbians. In 1987 he gave a speech on behalf of gay rights entitled 'The New Niggers Are Gays'. In part he said:

> **Today, blacks are no longer the litmus paper or the barometer of social change. Blacks are in every segment of society and there are laws that help to protect them from racial discrimination. The new 'niggers' are gays ... The question of social change should be framed with the most vulnerable group in mind: gay people.**

Birmingham's public schools and sent National Guard troops to keep returning black children out. President Kennedy reversed Wallace's order, commanding the troops to stand down. Tensions remained, but the tide had turned. King set his sights on the next national effort, a massive march on Washington, DC.

The March on Washington for Jobs and Freedom was the brainchild of civil rights leader A. Philip Randolph, who was president of the Negro American Labor Council and the Brotherhood of Sleeping Car Porters, and vice-president of the AFL-CIO. Along with A.J. Muste and Bayard Rustin, Randolph had proposed a similar march over twenty years earlier, in 1941, protesting racial discrimination in the war industry. Then President Franklin Roosevelt had been fearful of the impact the march might have on the military build-up, and had signed Executive Order 8802, the *Fair Employment Act*, banning discrimination within the munitions industries. The march was cancelled, but many in the Civil Rights Movement's infancy felt betrayed because Roosevelt's order did nothing to desegregate the military. Randolph had long dreamed of again organising such a march, and now the time was right.

Many of the organisers differed in what they hoped to achieve. Roy Wilkins, president of the NAACP, and Whitney Young, president of the Urban League, pushed for the march to throw support behind President Kennedy's civil rights legislation. James Farmer, president of the Congress of Racial Equality, and John Lewis, president of the Student Non-violent Coordinating Committee (SNCC), wanted to use it to condemn Kennedy's lack of progress on civil rights. King, Randolph and Rustin adopted the middle ground, supporting the Kennedy Bill but pushing to bring national attention to racial and economic issues beyond those addressed in the Bill. In the end, nearly all speakers lined up behind the position held by King, Randolph and Rustin. The only controversy centred around the fiery Lewis, whose speech was critical of Kennedy's slow progress on civil rights (see 'The Student Non-violent Coordinating Committee', page 228).

It is estimated that on 28 August 1963 a quarter of a million peaceful protesters marched from the Washington Monument to the Lincoln Memorial, rallying around speakers, performers, politicians and celebrities. The march is best known for Martin Luther King's famous and inspirational 'I Have a Dream' speech, which has come to be viewed as one of America's, if not all of history's, greatest speeches. He spoke movingly of his desire for a future where blacks and whites would live together as equals. As King famously said, he foresaw a nation of equal opportunity: 'I have a dream that my four little children will one day live in a nation where they will not be judged

Previous pages: Martin Luther King Jr in an impassioned moment during the delivery of his famous 'I Have a Dream' speech at the Lincoln Memorial, Washington, DC, on 28 August 1963.

by the color of their skin, but by the content of their character.' Years later, US Representative John Lewis would say of the speech:

> … the speech by Martin Luther King, Jr. was so inspiring, is so uplifting. When I listen to the speech and remember that day, Dr. King had the power, the ability and the capacity to transform those steps on the Lincoln Memorial into a modern day pulpit. By speaking the way he did, he educated, he inspired, he informed the people there, but people throughout America and unborn generations.

Following the speech, King was named Man of the Year for 1963 by *Time* magazine and was awarded the Nobel Peace Prize the following year. He was, and remains, the youngest person ever awarded the prize. But perhaps most importantly, his speech and the entire March on Washington are credited with tipping the balance in favour of the passage of the *Civil Rights Act* of 1964 and a year later, the *National Voting Rights Act*. The *Civil Rights Act* was a landmark piece of legislation, championed by President Kennedy, that outlawed nationally all practices of racial segregation and prohibited discrimination in all public facilities, schools, government and economics. It did away with, once and for all, the South's Jim Crow laws. Tragically, Kennedy was assassinated in 1963 and never saw the Bill's passage into law. The *National Voting Rights Act* of 1965 brought to an end widespread voting discrimination that had long disenfranchised black voters in the South. But racial discrimination in America still had a long way to go, and King was about to take another stand, one that would lead to considerable controversy even within the movement.

—

## THE VIETNAM WAR

EVEN AT THE HEIGHT OF KING'S INFLUENCE AND PRESTIGE, HE WAS UNDER intense pressure from inside and outside the Civil Rights Movement. He had long been under round-the-clock FBI surveillance and was a primary target of J. Edgar Hoover, the FBI's dictatorial director, who was convinced that communists had infiltrated the movement. King also faced opposition within the movement from militant factions, some of whom advocated armed revolt to bring about radical change and accelerate the pace to achieve social equality. Remarkably, King maintained the Gandhian essence of non-violent resistance in the face of deepening social unrest, violent agitation and political upheaval. The first open opposition to his leadership came in Selma, Alabama in 1965.

King organised a march from Selma to the State Capitol in Montgomery to protest against voter discrimination. At the time it was common practice in many Southern counties to suppress all black voter registration and inflate the white voter rolls. King didn't take part in the march, which was led by John Lewis of the SNCC. The day became known as 'Bloody Sunday' because of the brutality of the police. With film and camera crews rolling, the police went after demonstrators with full force, and horrifying images of bloodied marchers, many hospitalised with severe injuries, topped the news and made international headlines. King decided to lead a second march. Under great pressure from Washington to cancel the march, he was also under pressure from radical black leaders roused by the images, who wanted another confrontation.

Leading approximately 1500 marchers across the Edmund Pettus Bridge, King came up against a cordon of troopers blocking the far end. On reaching the barricade, instead of forcing a confrontation he knelt in prayer, then surprisingly, turned around and marched the protesters back again. Many black radicals were furious, suspecting that he had brokered a deal with authorities. However, a week later, King led 25,000 people to the State Capitol in a protest that President Lyndon Johnson credited with helping to secure national voting legislation favourable to blacks.

Many of the inner-city poor were impatient for change, and the nation's black slums were ready to explode. King's middle-class, religious pacifism was increasingly seen as out of touch with urban black militancy. Riots in the ghettos of Watts, in Los Angeles, Newark, Chicago and Detroit risked alienating moderate support. King and the SCLC instituted a drive to tackle the economic and political disparity in urban areas, but many of their initiatives against poverty and unemployment failed to catch hold. Rage and frustration turned many black youths away from the calm, older-looking King and increasingly towards incendiary leaders like Malcolm X of the Nation of Islam, and Stokely Carmichael of the SNCC.

In the face of mounting criticism, King took what many considered his most courageous stand. He came out against the war in Vietnam. He had long weighed his response to the increasingly unpopular war. While many in the peace movement called for him to speak out against it, drawing parallels between the ambiguous goals in Vietnam and the oppression of blacks at home, most in the Civil Rights Movement saw America's first war with a desegregated military—even an unpopular war—as an arena for racial gains. And the Washington establishment, which had only just come around to supporting civil and voter rights, was not going to tolerate any mainstream opposition. In King's first public statement against the war he called for an end to the bombing of North Vietnam.

Spiritual mentors in King's life—such as A.J. Muste, Thomas Merton and, most importantly, Buddhist monk Thich Nhat Hanh—had long been calling for him to speak out publicly, but he had mostly given his support behind the scenes, leaving his wife Coretta Scott King to speak out on behalf of an end to the war. But a change had come to him. King described his decision:

> I said to myself, 'Never again will I be silent on an issue that is destroying the soul of our nation and destroying thousands and thousands of little children in Vietnam.' I came to the conclusion that there is an existential moment in your life when you must decide to speak for yourself; nobody else can speak for you.

King took that opportunity in 1967 when he gave his first public speech opposing the war at Riverside Church in New York City. He committed himself irreversibly to opposing US involvement in Vietnam. He spoke of the tragic consequences of the war, of the moral outrage of its execution and, most immediately, of its effects on race and poverty in America:

> There is a very obvious and almost facile connection between the war in Vietnam and the struggle I and others have been waging in America. A few years ago there was a shining moment in that struggle. It seemed as if there was a real promise of hope for the poor—both black and white—through the poverty program … Then came … Vietnam, and I watched this program broken and eviscerated as if it were some idle political plaything of a society gone mad on war.

His speech was almost uniformly condemned in the media, and in no uncertain terms he was told by members of the Civil Rights Movement that he was 'overreaching'. But King became convinced that the peace movement and the civil rights struggle were indelibly linked, saying at a massive anti-war rally in New York shortly after the Riverside Church speech:

> I would like to see the fervour of the civil-rights movement imbued into the peace movement to instil it with greater strength … I believe everyone has a duty to be in both … movements. But for those who presently choose but one, I would hope they will finally come to see the moral roots common to both.

# THE DREAM DEFERRED

KING'S SPEECH AT RIVERSIDE CHURCH WAS MADE ONE YEAR TO THE DAY before he was assassinated in Memphis, Tennessee. During those twelve months he spoke out often against the war and rededicated himself to the urban and rural poor. He and the SCLC organised the 'Poor People's Campaign', which culminated in another march on Washington, promising civil disobedience until Congress passed a Bill of rights for America's poor. But the Civil Rights Movement was fraying as various goals and tactics pulled in different directions. King continued to make the point that civil rights meant rights for all the poor and disadvantaged, and chastised the government for unending spending on the war while ignoring poverty. Others in the movement felt this tactic watered down the movement and some, like Stokely Carmichael, advocated separatist black power, finding the idea of racial integration offensive.

At the end of March 1967, King went to Memphis to support striking sanitation workers. His flight had been delayed by a bomb threat. On 3 April, addressing a large rally at the Mason Temple, he gave his famous 'I've Been to the Mountaintop' speech. Addressing the bomb threat, he said:

> We've got some difficult days ahead. But it doesn't matter with me now. Because I've been to the mountaintop. And I don't mind. Like anybody, I would like to live a long life. Longevity has its place. But I'm not concerned about that now. I just want to do God's will. And He's allowed me to go up to the mountain. And I've looked over. And I've seen the promised land. I may not get there with you. But I want you to know tonight, that we, as a people, will get to the promised land. And I'm happy, tonight. I'm not worried about anything. I'm not fearing any man. Mine eyes have seen the glory of the coming of the Lord.

The speech was eerily prescient. The next evening, standing on the balcony of the Lorraine Motel outside the suite where he'd often stayed, King was shot once through the head by a high-calibre rifle. He died an hour later without regaining consciousness. According to civil rights leader Jesse Jackson, King's last words were addressed to the musician Ben Branch, who was to play that night at the rally: 'Ben, make sure you play "Take My Hand, Precious Lord" in the meeting tonight. Play it real pretty.' It was his favourite song.

King's assassination set off riots in cities across the nation. Presidential nominee Robert Kennedy, the younger brother of assassinated president John F. Kennedy, when informed of King's death, gave an impassioned speech

# THE STUDENT NON-VIOLENT COORDINATING COMMITTEE

In 1960, the Southern Christian Leadership Conference (SCLC) provided an $800 grant to a group of students at Shaw University in Raleigh, North Carolina led by a young activist named Ella Baker. Calling themselves the Student Non-violent Coordinating Committee (SNCC), the group had been organising sit-ins and demonstrations at segregated public spaces in and around Raleigh and now looked to grow their base. From these humble beginnings grew one of the most active civil rights organisations of the 1960s, one that started with a dedication to non-violent tactics but would eventually grow to embrace its own brand of black revolution.

Among the SNCC's original members were Baker, Julian Bond, Stokely Carmichael, John Lewis and Marion Barry (later the scandal-plagued mayor of Washington, DC). Rather than become the youth division of the SCLC, the SNCC positioned itself as the civil disobedient 'shock troopers' of the movement. Through the increasingly violent demonstrations, protests, sit-ins and integrated Freedom Rides across the South, members of the SNCC were at the forefront, often in the midst of the most dangerous conflagrations. They became a ready target for the Ku Klux Klan.

Becoming frustrated with the movement's slow progress, some SNCC members' belief in non-violence began to wane. The organisation played a key role in the 1963 March on Washington, but director John Lewis spoke out against the Kennedy Administration's lack of support and protection for Southern black civil rights workers. After the marches in Selma, Alabama, where many questioned Martin Luther King Jr's willingness to confront the brutal tactics of the police, the organisation began to split. Some wished to remain true to the Gandhian techniques espoused at its inception, but others, like Stokely Carmichael, advocated a turn to more revolutionary, non-integrationist black power ideologies. Nevertheless, in 1965 the SNCC still had the largest staff of all the civil rights organisations and was active in direct action and voter-registration drives in thirteen Southern states.

In 1966 Carmichael replaced John Lewis as the head of the SNCC. Arguing that it was 'criminal' for blacks not to defend themselves when attacked, he began agitating for violent revolution to overthrow white oppression, rejecting the recently hard-won civil rights legislation as merely a patina of real social change. Carmichael left the SNCC in 1967 to join the revolutionary Black Panther Party, and was replaced by the equally fiery H. Rap Brown. Dropping any pretence of non-violent tactics, Brown changed the organisation's name to the Student National Coordinating Committee and openly advocated violence against whites. That year the Department of Defense advised: 'SNCC can no longer be considered a civil rights group. It has become a racist organisation with black supremacy ideals and an expressed hatred for whites. It employs violent and militant measures which may be defined as extreme.' With dwindling membership and its leadership fragmented, the organisation faded away in the 1970s.

calling for calm and a return to non-violent protest. A year later he too would be assassinated. President Lyndon Johnson declared a day of mourning, and millions across the country stopped to pay tribute to the slain pacifist leader. Two month later James Earl Ray, an escaped convict, was arrested at London's Heathrow Airport and charged with King's murder. Extradited to Tennessee, he confessed to the crime and pleaded guilty, but a short while later recanted his confession. He was sentenced to ninety-nine years in prison and spent the rest of his life professing his innocence, claiming he was set up and attempting, unsuccessfully, to win a new trial. Before his death in 1998, the King family met with Ray in prison and issued a statement supporting his call for a retrial.

Like the assassination of President Kennedy, conspiracy theories abound about who truly murdered Martin Luther King. Many inconsistencies remain in the evidence implicating Ray. Loyd Jowers, the owner of a restaurant across the street from the Lorraine Motel, claimed to have received $100,000 to arrange King's assassination and that it was a conspiracy by the government and the Mafia. Although the King family won a wrongful death lawsuit against Jowers and other 'unknown co-conspirators', the US Department of Justice found no evidence to support his claim. Jowers died less than a year later in 2000. Many have pointed to the FBI director J. Edgar Hoover's hatred of King; Hoover always insisted that King was in league with communists, and said of him that he was 'the most dangerous and effective Negro leader in the country'. King was under nearby surveillance by the FBI at the moment he was assassinated and questions remain as to why the agents didn't respond quickly when the shot was fired.

The Lorraine Motel has been converted into the National Civil Rights Museum. In recognition of King's contribution to the fight for equal rights for all Americans, a federal holiday was created and reluctantly signed into law by President Ronald Reagan in 1983. Although Reagan had vowed to veto the Bill for a Martin Luther King Jr federal holiday, it passed in Congress with a veto-proof majority. States in the South were slow to accept the holiday, but today every state in the union celebrates the third Monday of January as a tribute to the non-violent leadership of Dr Martin Luther King Jr.

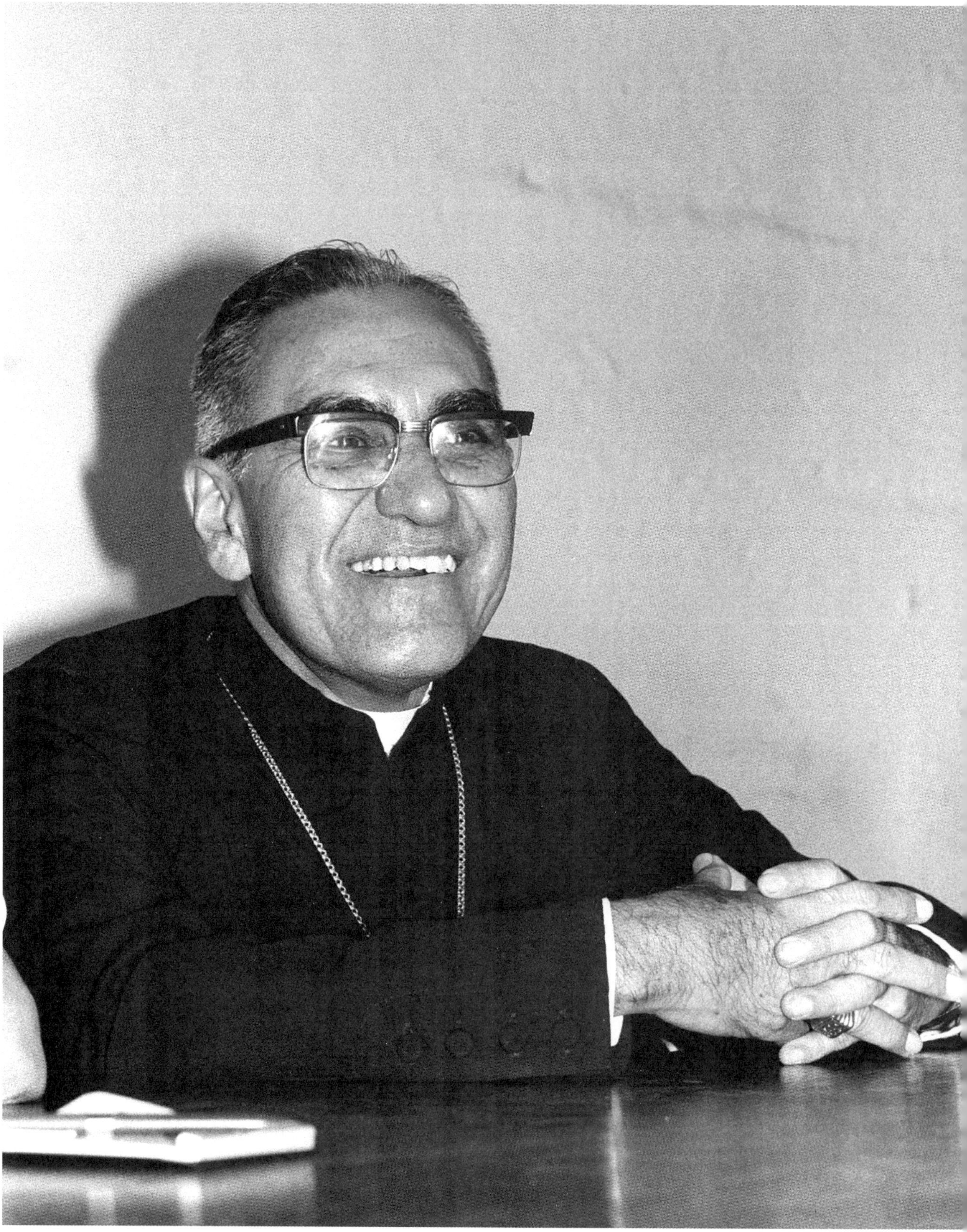

# ARCHBISHOP ÓSCAR ROMERO: MARTYR FOR PEACE

WHEN ÓSCAR ROMERO BECAME ARCHBISHOP OF SAN SALVADOR IN February 1977, his country was on the brink of civil war. El Salvador's military-led right-wing dictatorship celebrated his appointment, certain that the new archbishop, who was known for his conservative views, would restrain clergy who advocated a revolutionary brand of Liberation Theology. On the left, hopes were dashed that the outgoing Monseñor Chávez y Gonzalez, who had called for more funds for the poor when he famously said, 'we must stop building cathedrals and start building the Church', would be replaced by an archbishop who was at least equally progressive. Both sides were about to be very surprised.

Less than a month after his appointment, his dear friend Father Rutilio had been gunned down by a death squad, one of many secret groups empowered by the government to assassinate priests and peasants (*campesinos*) who opposed the government. The two priests had been close associates, although Father Rutilio had chosen to work among the poor while Romero turned to more scholarly pursuits that had led him to study in Rome. But now the shy bishop was facing his own crisis. He would undergo a conversion that would radically change—and end—his life and forever alter the course of Salvadoran history.

Archbishop Óscar Romero at his home in San Salvador, just weeks before his death. 'I do not believe in death without resurrection. If they kill me I will rise again in the people of El Salvador' (interview, March 1980).

# THE MAKING OF A BISHOP

Ciudad Barrios rests high in the Salvadoran mountains near the border with Honduras. In 1917, when Óscar Arnulfo Romero y Goldámez was born there, Ciudad Barrios was accessible only by foot or on horseback. Romero's father was a telegraph operator and although the family was better off than most of their neighbours, their small house had no electricity or running water and the seven children, of whom Romero was the second, had to sleep on the floor. Public school was offered only up to the third grade, so Romero was privately tutored until he was twelve. But his father could not afford to continue his education, and so at thirteen he was apprenticed to a nearby carpenter. He took to his craft and showed promise. But Romero, who spent much of his free time at one of the village's two churches, had already decided he wished to become a priest and follow the teachings of Jesus. Although his father wished for him to continue with a trade, he relented when Romero was accepted into the minor seminary in San Miguel. Romero would later say he traded an apprenticeship with one carpenter for another.

Promoted to the national seminary in the capital city, San Salvador, in 1938 Romero travelled to Rome to continue his studies at the Gregorian University. He received his Licentiate in Theology and was ordained in 1942 at the age of twenty-five. Wartime travel restrictions kept his family from attending his ordination, so he planned to stay at the Vatican and pursue a doctorate in theology, until a shortage of priests in El Salvador called him home. The return trip was delayed by a stop first in Spain, still reeling from a bloody civil war. There his orthodox allegiance would presumably have called on him to support Franco's forces, seen as the protectors of a persecuted Catholic Church, but his non-violent nature might have drawn him to the humanitarian pacifists, such as José Brocca, who were aligned with the Republicans (see 'José Brocca: Spain's forgotten pacifist', page 238). From Spain Romero travelled to Cuba, where he was arrested and held in an internment camp, suspected for his ties to the Fascists in Italy and Spain. He was released after several months to escort a sick priest back to Latin America, sailing first to Mexico City and eventually home to the lush mountains of Ciudad Barrios.

He began the life of a quiet parish priest in tiny Anamorós in the hilly east of El Salvador. He was soon transferred to the larger city of San Miguel, where for twenty years he dedicated his energies to his parish, encouraging devotion to the Virgin of the Peace and supporting the construction of a new cathedral. He was later appointed rector of the inter-diocese seminary.

Shy, contemplative, and admittedly unsure of his 'people skills', he was surprised when he was appointed to the very public role of Secretary of the Episcopal Conference for El Salvador. He felt better suited to administrative tasks, such as editing the archdiocesan newspaper *Orientación*, which became more conservative under his directorship by focusing on promoting the teaching authority of the Church. This positioned him among the most conservative of El Salvador's Catholic clergy, and he was regarded with considerable suspicion by those progressive priests who put the *campesinos* of their Church ahead of the sacraments.

These suspicions became clearly evident when, in 1970, Romero was appointed Auxiliary Bishop to the popular and progressive Archbishop of San Salvador, Luis Chávez. Deeply influenced by the Second Vatican Council, the elderly Monseñor Chávez was implementing pastoral reforms in support of lay leadership throughout the archdiocese. Many of these progressive reforms were troubling to Romero, who submitted unquestioningly to the hierarchical structure of the Church. Although he carried out his assignments dutifully, he was never accepted by the progressive priesthood. In 1974, it was to everyone's relief that he was appointed Bishop of Santiago de Maria, and left the capital to return to the area of his birth.

—

## LIBERATION THEOLOGY

FATHER RUTILIO GRANDE WAS FROM THE SMALL VILLAGE OF EL PAISNAL, north of San Salvador by some 40 kilometres (25 miles). A Jesuit, and fairly orthodox in his theological training, he had over the years come to question the Church's efforts towards the poor in his country. He was outspoken and demonstrative, two qualities that cost him his position at the seminary where he had become friends with Óscar Romero. He asked to be assigned to a parish church in Aguilares, a town near his birthplace. There, in the fertile Aguilares Valley, near industrial San Salvador, he would come to understand the teeming contradictions that were driving the country towards class conflict. The four sugar mills in Aguilares were in constant need of low-wage workers in the sugarcane plantations that surrounded the town and fed the mills. The *campesinos* rented whatever leftover land they could get, mostly rocky and barren, where they tried to grow corn or wheat, but were unable to subsist on their arid plots. They thus were forced to work on the plantations—for less than US$2 a day.

Father Rutilio had been inspired by a gathering of bishops in Medellin, Columbia in 1968 that addressed the need for an active clergy engaged with the needs of the poor. At the outcome of the conference, their statement read:

> [A Christian] believes in the value of peace for the achievement of justice, he also believes that justice is a necessary condition for peace. And he is not unaware that in many places in Latin America there is a situation of injustice that must be recognised as institutionalised violence, because the existing structures violate people's basic rights: a situation which calls for far-reaching, daring, urgent and profoundly innovative change.

The Medellin Conference had crystallised several strains of new socially active Catholic thought that had been taking hold over the previous ten years. Over the years of the Second Vatican Council, the Latin American Episcopal Conference had pressed for a more socially conscious Church. Many in the Church, like Dom Hélder Câmara, the Archbishop of Olinda and Recife in Brazil, had been calling for a theology that was not merely spiritual but active towards empowering the oppressed. Câmara's short tract *The Spiral of Violence* saw the Vietnam War as demonstrating how violence begets violence, and held up the war as a cautionary tale for Latin America (see 'Dom Hélder Câmara and the spiral of violence', page 242). The Peruvian priest Father Gustavo Gutiérrez and the Brazilian theologian Rubem Alves were among the first to call this movement Liberation Theology. Highly controversial at the time of its inception, Liberation Theology brought together Marxist class struggle and socio-Catholic teachings, influenced by the Catholic Worker Movement in America, to form an action-oriented theology of direct engagement in bettering the lives of the poor and the oppressed.

Father Rutilio Grande embraced this new Liberation Theology even though it was not sanctioned by the Church and was violently opposed by the right-wing government of El Salvador. He understood that at the core of this new philosophy was an understanding that the Church must go beyond good deeds of charity to the deeper causes that continue the cycles of poverty and oppression. He saw it as his mission to instil self-worth in the *campesinos*, and teach them that God's love makes them equal to anyone else, which began to instil a new courage for protest among the downtrodden. As the theology took hold, it outraged the minority landowners and the right-wing government, who accused 'meddling priests' of being influenced by outside communist forces bent on the destruction of Salvadoran society.

Since El Salvador gained independence from Spain in 1823 it has been buffeted by several revolutions, each usually followed by a period of consolidated oppression of the rural areas. From the mid-1800s, coffee was the staple of the economy. Eventually, the majority of land became owned by a handful of powerful families. In 1931, following a military coup, the suppression of peasants' rights turned brutal; a peasant uprising in 1932, which became known as La Matanza (the massacre) was violently put down. Over 30,000 *campesinos*, indigenous people and political opponents were killed, imprisoned or exiled. The landed oligarchy then aligned with the military to run the country, calling sporadic presidential elections that were seldom free or fair. By 1980 all but one of El Salvador's presidents had been a military officer.

During the 1970s, resentment of the subhuman conditions in which the vast majority of El Salvador's rural poor existed rose to boiling point. The government increasingly scapegoated priests and blamed 'outside Communist agitators' for peasant unrest. In Aguilares, Father Rutilio grew more vocal and defiant in his call for reforms. While his close friend Óscar Romero, and the established Catholic Church, pleaded with him to tone down his efforts and his rhetoric, other leftist priests were emboldened by his actions. 'Mouths are full of the word "democracy",' said Father Rutilio in a famous sermon, 'but let us not fool ourselves. There is no democracy when the power of the people is the power of a wealthy minority.' By 1976, the oligarchs were calling for the elimination of these 'Communist priests', singling out Father Rutilio in Aguilares in particular. But the government of Colonel Arturo Molina feared too harsh a crackdown would spread anarchy throughout the countryside. Molina proposed a modest plan for 'agrarian transformation' (refusing to use the words 'agrarian reform' because of their Marxist connotations) by providing a small bit of land, bought at full market value, for redistribution among the peasants.

The response from the landed oligarchy was severe. They attacked Molina in the press as the 'Communist Colonel' and began a campaign of terror in the countryside. The first of the notorious 'death squads', teams of paramilitary assassins, were dispatched. Leftist leaders, priests, nuns and common *campesinos* were murdered. Any outright demonstrations were suppressed with tear gas and machine guns. Most horrifying, many people simply disappeared, vanishing in the torrent of terror. Fearing the threat of another coup, Colonel Molina quietly axed his plan and stepped into line, turning a blind eye to the atrocities while waiting out the rest of his presidential term.

# ROMERO Y ROMERO

IN 1977, ÓSCAR ROMERO'S APPOINTMENT BY THE VATICAN AS ARCHBISHOP of San Salvador was met with great relief by the ruling elite. Gone was that old troublemaker Archbishop Luis Chávez, who had openly supported the 'Communist' clergy. On the left, news of the appointment caused dismay and outright consternation. El Salvador was in the midst of a tense presidential campaign to elect Molina's successor, and the left viewed the timing of Romero's appointment as suspect. The oligarchy and military-backed establishment supported another Romero, Colonel Carlos Humberto Romero, no relation to the new archbishop; the united progressive parties ran the left-leaning Colonel Ernesto Claramount, a former officer. Five years earlier, the popular progressive candidate José Napoleón Duarte had lost to Molina in an overtly corrupt election and had been forced to flee to Venezuela, where he remained in exile. Violence against the *campesinos* was on the rise and tensions were high.

Just weeks after the new archbishop was quietly sworn in, Colonel Romero was elected president with a majority that made a mockery of the election. Intimidation, stuffed ballot boxes and outright murder had suppressed the progressive vote and maintained the right-wing status quo. The landed oligarchy wanted to drive home the message, and upped their attacks on progressive priests in and around Aguilares. Several of the more outspoken were arrested and tortured; the brother of another priest was murdered. Then, on 12 March, Father Rutilio was returning to his home village of El Paisnal, where he was going to lead evening Mass. On a dusty back road, a truck pulled in behind his beat-up Land Rover as he slowed for construction work ahead. It was a trap. The road workers were paramilitaries, who opened fire on Father Rutilio's vehicle as it passed. He was struck in the throat. Machine-gun fire erupted from the truck behind, the spray of bullets instantly killing an old man and a young boy who were passengers in the vehicle and cutting Father Rutilio nearly in half.

News spread quickly of Father Rutilio's death. Archbishop Romero came directly to the scene and, late on the night of his murder, stood alone in the room of his dear friend. He fingered the few earthly possessions of the slain priest and spent the night in solemn prayer and contemplation. He met with and listened to testimony from Aguilares' sugarcane workers of all the good that Father Rutilio had brought to their lives. He was very moved when they spoke of the faith he had instilled and their belief that Jesus would send them a new champion. The shy, scholarly man of peace emerged from this meeting spiritually awakened. He believed that God had sent him his true calling.

On his return to the capital, the ruling elite and the president-elect, expecting the new, previously compliant archbishop to turn a blind eye to the mayhem in the countryside, would immediately feel the impact of his spiritual transformation. President Molina had declared a state of siege following the contested election, but the new archbishop called for demonstrations to mourn his slain friend and his innocent companions. He closed all Catholic schools for three days, sending the children home with study guides and information about how the Church was being persecuted. He demanded that President Molina investigate the killings, and announced that he would not take part in any official functions until the murders were solved. On the second Sunday after Father Rutilio's murder he presided over the one and only Mass in the archdiocese. One hundred thousand people gathered in and around the San Salvador cathedral that Sunday as Archbishop Romero celebrated Mass and called for peace and an end to the killings in the countryside.

Colonel Romero and the ruling elite were initially stunned and then outraged by the archbishop's turnaround; the landed oligarchy cried foul. They ratcheted up the violence and now the death squads went after clergy and peasants alike, killing, torturing and raping, prompting retribution from the left. Officials were killed or kidnapped and ransomed for the release of political prisoners. The government tried to blame everything on the Church, openly declaring that the priests were being supported by Cuba or the Soviet Union—ironically two of the more atheistic countries in the world. Archbishop Romero put himself at the forefront of the opposition, calling for peace on both sides in his weekly sermons, which were broadcast live over Catholic radio throughout the country. Each sermon contained a message of hope, of a promise for a return to dignity for every Salvadoran, and a plea for an end to violence.

To support his words, he established a permanent office to investigate reports of human rights abuses. He met directly with progressive priests to better understand the issues in the field and to direct peaceful action. He did not embrace entirely the Liberation Theology that many followed, because it advocated the right to violent opposition in the name of God, but he did support the Church's responsibility to protect its flock and to seek peace alongside the rights of the oppressed. Still the editor of *Orientación*, he turned the publication into the voice of the newly active Church and personally wrote a column each week. Soon his sermons became the most popular weekly broadcast in the country, and the transistor radio became a beacon of hope in the farthest corners of El Salvador. Such was Romero's influence that he became known everywhere simply as 'Monseñor'.

When President Carlos Romero took office, he found himself in an increasingly tight spot. On one side, the oligarchs pressed for total repression of the left. On the other, the left had gained international support and the United States was withholding urgently needed financial aid until the state of siege was lifted. The new president had to address, in some manner, reforms in the countryside before the country collapsed into total civil war. He struck a conciliatory tone, calling for dialogue and inviting exiled leaders to return. He lifted the state of siege and for the first time acknowledged the plight of political prisoners as an issue. But the right-wing interests were openly discussing the need to put down the priest-led *campesino* unrest, as had been done in 1932—on their part, the only question

## JOSÉ BROCCA: SPAIN'S FORGOTTEN PACIFIST

José Brocca was born in Andalusia in 1891 of Italian and Spanish descent. He was a professor in Madrid at the outbreak of the Spanish Civil War in 1936 when a group of conservative army generals, supported by the fascistic Falange, attempted a coup against the Second Spanish Republic. Although Brocca aligned with the Republicans, he was first and foremost a pacifist and a humanitarian, spurred into action in part by the fact that two of his sons fought on opposing sides in the civil war. He resigned his position at the university and dedicated himself, as head of the Spanish War Resister League (WRL), to helping the disadvantaged in the ensuing war. Supported by War Resisters' International, headquartered in London and organised by pacifist British MP George Lansbury, and the Fellowship of Reconciliation, Brocca organised agricultural workers to maintain food supplies and coordinated humanitarian efforts with war refugees. He is said to have once saved the life of a local Catholic priest (priests were targeted by the Republican military for their close ties to Franco's forces), by loaning him his car as a means of escape.

During World War II, Brocca helped war refugees escape into France through the treacherous mountain passes of the Pyrenees. He took up the cause of war orphans and helped many escape from the Nazis and relocate in southern France and Mexico. Brocca himself was captured and taken to a concentration camp in occupied France where he would have surely died but for a daring rescue by the French Resistance. He escaped to Mexico, where he was separated from his wife and children for many years. Finally, through the efforts of the Fellowship of Reconciliation, he was reunited with his family. A forgotten figure in Spain's civil war, José Brocca died suddenly in Mexico City in 1950, having never returned to his native Spain.

was whether twenty, thirty or 100,000 would have to die to bring 'peace' to El Salvador.

The violence escalated. Between the disappearances and killings by state-sanctioned death squads, and the orders to the National Guard, police and paramilitary units to shoot demonstrators on sight, the countryside was become a killing field. President Romero was losing his grip on power; by the end of the year he would be forced out, the victim of a military coup that would further complicate El Salvador's political situation and bring it one step closer to open civil war.

———

## MADNESS IN THE COUNTRYSIDE

ARCHBISHOP ROMERO'S SPIRITUAL TRANSFORMATION WAS NOT AS SUDDEN as many saw it. Always a theological conservative, his roots among the poor of El Salvador had allowed him to understand their plight from the very beginnings of his religious service. His original belief that the Church should stay above a country's socio-political controversies had been eroded by the escalating abuse by the country's aristocratic 'fourteen families'. His ministry was growing rapidly, swelling with the farm workers, the labourers and the unemployed who turned to the Church's social teachings. Many joined small Christian communities where they were taught how the gospel provided guidance for social reform, often in an attempt to defuse those who saw violent revolution as the only means for societal change. The military government and the elite dubbed any such efforts Marxist. The killings intensified; paramilitary death squads across the country killed, tortured and raped priests, nuns and anyone assumed to be politically opposed to the ruling party; they collected a cash bounty for each person they victimised.

As Bishop of Santiago de Maria, Romero had travelled throughout his mountainous diocese, much of it on horseback, visiting *campesino* families, seeking how best to serve them. He heard horrifying stories of abuse, of denied pay, beatings and killings; of how many people were starving and dying from the lack of the most basic health care. He used the finances of the diocese and, when that money ran out, his own meagre funds to do what he could. Though his actions were still well under the government's radar, and he adhered to a strictly conservative stance on the Catholic rites, he realised that simple charity was not enough; he arrived at a more radicalised understanding that the Church must foster the environment for peaceful social change.

239

'The world of the poor teaches us that liberation will arrive only when the poor are not simply on the receiving end of handouts from government or from churches,' he wrote in his journal in 1976, 'but when they themselves are the masters and protagonists of their own struggle for liberation.'

With the murder of Father Rutilio Grande, followed soon afterward by the assassination of another archdiocesan priest, Father Alfonso Navarro, Romero came to understand that his orthodox reluctance to publicly address political issues was, in essence, a tacit endorsement of the repression. And so began his public testimony against right-wing-sponsored violence in the countryside. But he elevated his opposition, calling on the United States and the administration of President Jimmy Carter to end its support of the military dictatorship. He became internationally acclaimed for his witness to El Salvador's horrors. He travelled to Europe and spoke on the need for peace in his country. He met the pope and brought him detailed reports of the institutionalised murder, torture, kidnapping and disappearances throughout the country.

El Salvador's political instability was soon matched by economic flight. As the economy turned from bad to worse, a younger generation of military officers led a coup against the presidency of Colonel Romero. This new junta consisted of two officers and three civilians, with varying degrees of left and right political leanings. But together, their ambition initially was to bring economic stability to the country, address some of the social concerns of the peasants and quash any communist revolutionary movements. But this more liberal government apparatus had very limited influence on the far more conservative military forces—violence against opposition groups, among which the Church was most often included, increased dramatically. The escalating violence led to the dissolution of the junta and its replacement by a second. Fresh from exile in Venezuela, José Napoleón Duarte became part of the new junta, eventually consolidating enough power to become its leader.

Although Duarte wished to implement leftist reforms, the junta under his leadership could not stem the political killings and disappearances, and the leftist coalition of revolutionary factions refused any form of cooperation. A kind of madness gripped the countryside, with tit-for-tat assassinations, the slaughter and violent repression of the masses. Archbishop Romero could eventually do little to prevent the violence beyond bearing witness and remaining the international voice of peace and reason. His sermons, still broadcast nationwide, were both messages of hope in a frightening time and a source of news on the progress of the left. Efforts by the military apparatus to intimidate the archbishop failed—priests were killed, or tortured and harassed; the Catholic radio station was bombed; the offices of *Orientación* were attacked; and threats on his own life steadily increased in number.

Romero knew his country was teetering on the brink of all-out civil war and should that happen, the poor and the disenfranchised would suffer the most. To this end, he hoped and prayed that social change could come from peaceful means. He also knew his sermons, his involvement with the highest levels of the Vatican in the plight of El Salvador's Church and his admonitions against the United States for supporting a government bent on such violent repression were likely to lead to his death.

'I am bound, as a pastor, by divine command to give my life for those whom I love,' he said in a newspaper article just two weeks before his death, 'and that is all Salvadorans, even those who are going to kill me.' On 23 March 1980, just days after the Catholic radio station returned to service after being bombed, Romero took his message directly to the soldiers and killers in the field. In his speech, live before a cheering crowd and broadcast throughout El Salvador, Costa Rica, Venezuela, Brazil and beyond, he said:

> Brothers, each one of you is one of us. We are the same people. The campesinos you kill are your own brothers and sisters. When you hear the words of a man telling you to kill, remember, instead the words of God, 'Thou shalt not kill.' God's law must prevail. No soldier is obliged to obey an order contrary to the law of God. It is time that you come to your senses and obey your conscience rather than follow a sinful command … In the name of God, in the name of our tormented people who have suffered so much and whose laments cry out to heaven, I beseech you, I beg you, I *order* you: in the name of God, stop the repression!

The next evening, the archbishop gave a funeral Mass in a small chapel in the hospital known as La Divina Providencia. He began with the parable of the wheat. 'Those who surrender to the service of the poor through love of Christ, will live like the grain of wheat that dies,' he told those in attendance. 'It only apparently dies. If it were not to die, it would remain a solitary grain. The harvest comes because of the grain that dies.' Moments later, while he held the Eucharist, two bullets crashed through his head and chest, killing him instantly. He collapsed on the floor, his blood spattering the altar. The congregation was stunned into silence. There had been no explosion of gunfire because the hired assassin had used a silencer. Only slowly did they all realise that El Salvador's beloved Monseñor was dead.

# DOM HÉLDER CÂMARA AND THE SPIRAL OF VIOLENCE

In Latin America, an iconic 1960s revolutionary poster quoted Dom Hélder Câmara: 'When I give food to the poor, they call me a saint. When I ask why the poor have no food, they call me a Communist.' As Archbishop of Olinda and Recife in Brazil's underdeveloped north, Câmara was an advocate for the impoverished and a firm believer in peaceful social change. A highly influential thinker and practitioner, his activist interpretation of the gospel provided the impetus for a number of social reforms throughout Brazil. It also led to his being labelled a communist and being in constant danger of assassination throughout the 1970s and 1980s.

Câmara's short tract *The Spiral of Violence*, published in 1971, became his means for addressing both the violence of poverty and the violence of revolt. By focusing on the Vietnam War, he addressed what he saw as the world's two central problems: poverty, which keeps nearly two-thirds of the world's people repressed; and the violent oppression of peaceful revolt, which allows the demands of the poor to be crushed by the powerful. Citing examples such as Gandhi's pacifist actions to free India and Thich Nhat Hanh's efforts to end the war in Vietnam, Câmara pointed out how violence only begets further violence and peace comes only from the establishment of justice. He wrote:

> As for peace, it is well known that there can be instances of false peace, with the same deceptive beauty as stagnant marshes in moonlight. The peace which speaks to us, which moves us, for which we are prepared to give our lives, presupposes that the rights of all are fully respected: the rights of God and the rights of men. Not just the rights of some men, a privileged few, to the detriment of many others: the rights of each man and of all men.

Dom Hélder Câmara was nominated for the Nobel Peace Prize in 1973 by the American Friends Service Committee. He lived to see many of the reforms he installed in Brazil rolled back by his conservative successor, Archbishop José Cardoso Sobrinho. He died in 1999.

Romero had refused the government's offer of protection, claiming that it was the people of El Salvador who required protection. The junta called for three days of mourning and promised to track down the killers. But the judge put in charge of the investigations was soon the target of another assassination attempt and fled the country. A quarter of a million people attended the funeral on 30 March, thronging the centre of San Salvador in the largest gathering in Salvadoran history. Fifty thousand alone crammed into the cathedral square. It was a massive outpouring of grief and shock which soon turned to terror. Car bombs exploded in the corners of the square, trapping the mourners. Snipers appeared on the roofs above them and began firing into the crowd. Panic ensued and people were trampled as the crowd rushed to the still-unfinished cathedral. Five thousand people packed inside, crushing more. When it was over, nearly fifty people were dead and hundreds more were wounded.

Romero had been the last hope for bringing peaceful change to El Salvador. His murder cut the last string holding the country back from civil war. Now the opposition forces coalesced into the Farabundo Martí National Liberation Front (FMLN) in active support of armed revolution. The spiral of violence deepened. As the leftist insurgents gained power, the military-led government won further financial support from America's new president, Ronald Reagan. Even the backlash vote in 1984, which brought an end to the junta and elected the left-leaning José Napoleón Duarte as president, could not end the violence and the chaos. For twelve more years, the country was awash with terror. Over 3000 *campesinos* died each month; in all nearly 80,000 Salvadorans would be officially noted as killed and 300,000 more would disappear, never to be heard from again. Over a million more people were displaced, fleeing to other countries. All this in a nation of only five and a half million people.

Romero's assassin was never found. Investigations years later uncovered evidence that a former army major named Roberto D'Aubuisson had planned and ordered the assassination. Long known for his brutality and described by former US ambassador Robert White as a 'pathological killer', D'Aubuisson was called 'Blowtorch Bob' by political prisoners in reference to his favoured means of torture. As a leader of the death squads, he openly called for the extermination of 300,000 *campesinos* to supposedly return peace to El Salvador. He founded the Nationalist Republican Alliance (ARENA) party, which he led to power in 1982, following Romero's assassination, but lost in general elections to José Napoleón Duarte in 1984. He died of cancer at the age of forty-seven in 1992, near the end of the civil war, and was never tried for his crimes.

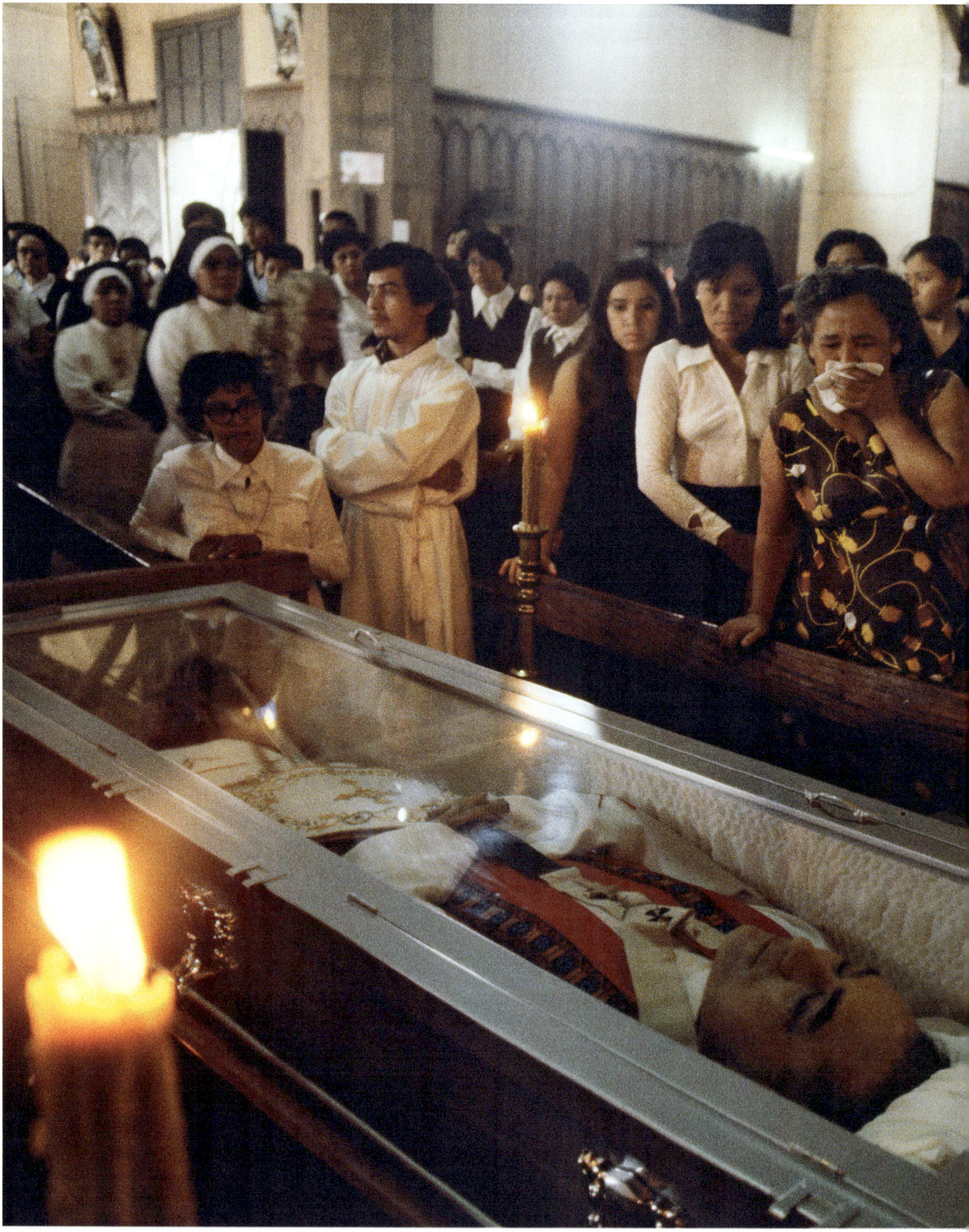

Through the efforts of the Latin American leaders, most notably pacifist President Oscar Arias of Costa Rica, El Salvador's warring adversaries were coaxed to the negotiating table in 1984. With the signing of the Chapultepec Peace Accords in Mexico that year, a new constitution was created. It regulated the armed forces, established a civilian police force, converted the FMLN guerrilla army into a political party, and transferred land to eligible beneficiaries from both the guerrilla and national armies. An amnesty law was promoted in 1993 and a United Nations Truth Commission was established to sort out the deaths of so many and investigate the disappearances over the many years of unrest. Although the rural violence has subsided greatly, ARENA and the ruling aristocracy have continued to hold power in El Salvador. In 2009, however, for the first time the leftist FMLN party gained power with the election of their candidate Mauricio Funes to the presidency.

On the tenth anniversary of Óscar Romero's assassination, Monseñor Arturo Rivera, the sitting Archbishop of San Salvador, submitted the documentation for Romero's cause of beatification and canonisation. In 1997 the documents were accepted by Pope John Paul II and the Congregation for the Causes of Saints; Romero received the title of 'Servant of God'. Although his canonisation seemed all but certain, the process has stalled in the intervening years. The official reason from the Vatican has been new liturgical changes implemented by Pope Benedict XVI, but many of the left-leaning clergy of Latin America believe that the delays are because Romero became closely aligned with—although not directly involved with—the controversial Liberation Theology. Regardless of whether he ever gains the Catholic Church's seal of martyrdom, Óscar Romero remains to this day the peaceful saint of the people of El Salvador.

The funeral of Archbishop Óscar Romero, 30 March 1980: 'Peace is not the product of terror or fear. Peace is not the silence of cemeteries. Peace is not the silent result of violent repression. Peace is the generous, tranquil contribution of all to the good of all. Peace is dynamism. Peace is generosity. It is right and it is duty' (Óscar Romero).

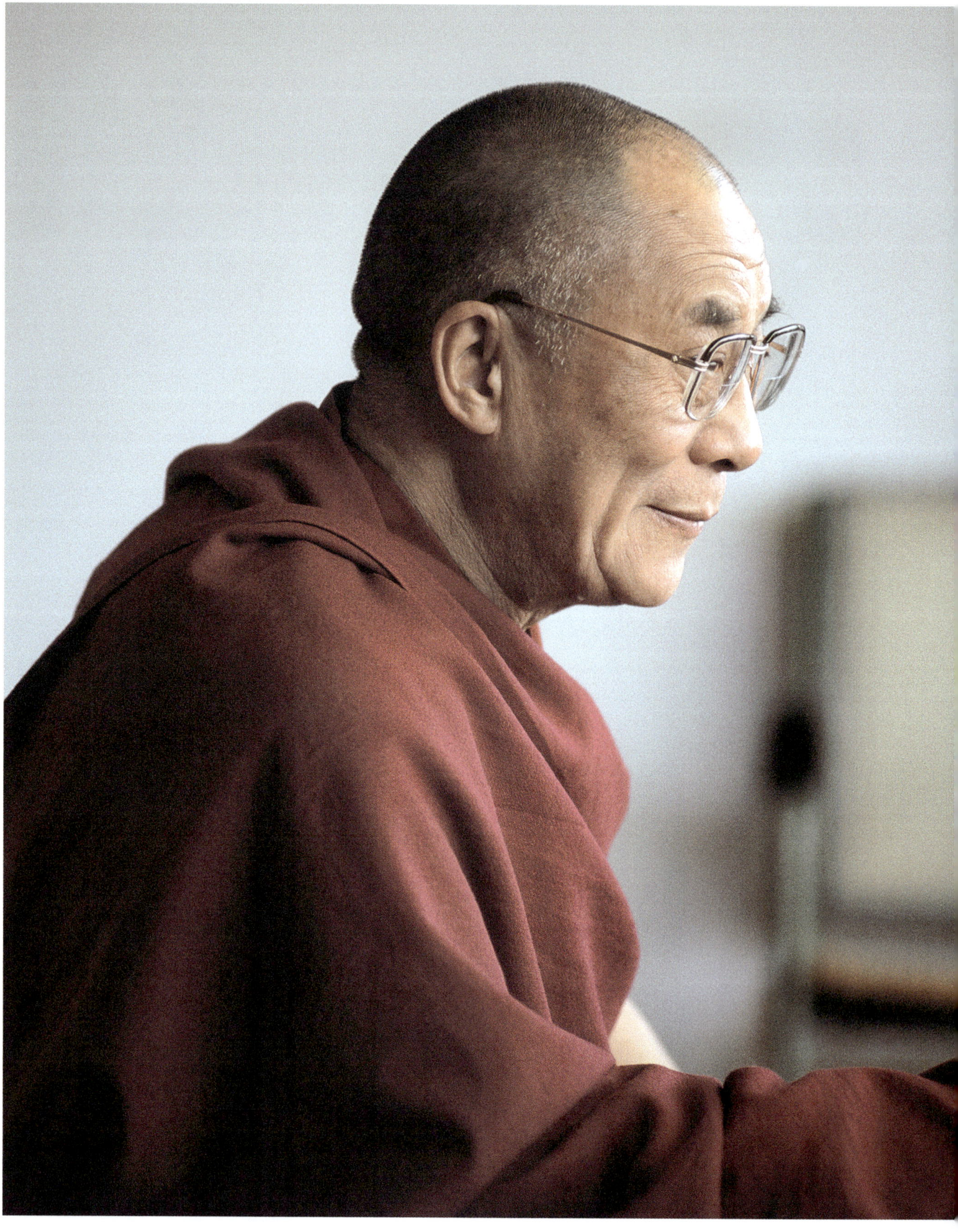

# THE DALAI LAMA: GENTLE EXILE

To many, Tenzin Gyatso, the 14th Dalai Lama of Tibet, is the living embodiment of non-violence in practice. In exile from his native country since 1959, he has led the people of Tibet against Chinese repression and ruled in absentia as the head of the government-in-exile. He has become an international symbol of stoic non-violent opposition, of patient compassion and of an engaged Buddhist philosophy of active resistance. Probably the best-known Buddhist leader and philosopher alive today, he is a beacon of hope for his countrymen and an example of the power of non-violent spirituality.

The Dalai Lama's passive opposition to Chinese rule over Tibet has not been without controversy, however. Some in his country have opposed his willingness to compromise with the Chinese in light of their ongoing strategies of repression and assimilation. Others have grown impatient with his pacifist teachings and have demanded forceful action. His quiet assurances that all may be as they should be, that the suffering caused by the Chinese may, in pure Buddhist teachings, be a gift of understanding, compassion and insight into the intransigence of life, has angered even long-term supporters. But none has doubted his wisdom or the suffering he has endured as the exiled leader of a country rapidly losing its cultural identity.

Awarded the Nobel Peace Prize in 1989, His Holiness the Dalai Lama advocates for individual and universal responsibility.

# THE LITTLE LAMA

In 1935, at the age of two, Lhamo Döndrub was discovered to be the tulku, the reincarnation of the 13th Dalai Lama of Tibet. The search had begun four years earlier. As has been the case for Tibetan Buddhism since the fifteenth century, tradition dictates that the eternal emanations of the bodhisattva Avalokitesvara, the reincarnated 'mindstream' of each predecessor, will be found through signs and omens. Because the Dalai Lama will serve as both the spiritual and head of state, it is the responsibility of both the high lamas of the Gelugpa, or Yellow Hat, sect and the Tibetan government to find the reincarnation. The first sign occurred when the body of the 13th Dalai Lama was said to have mysteriously turned from facing southeast to northeast, indicating the direction in which the new lama would be found.

The Regent of the High Lamas, after consulting with the Nechung Oracle, journeyed to the sacred Lake Lhamo La-tso, high up in the Tibetan central plain. Legend has it that Palden Lhamo, the female guardian spirit of the lake, promised the very first Dalai Lama, Gendun Drup, that she would protect the reincarnation lineage. The second Dalai Lama, Gendun Gyatso, established the protocol for the regent and other monks to journey to the lake to seek a vision to the new Dalai Lama's whereabouts.

The majestic peaks of the Himalayas surround the still, azure waters of Lake Lhamo La-tso. At this elevation, the sky literally touches the lake's waters, and the ring of grey mountains creates rapidly changing weather that reflects in ever-shifting patterns on the pool's glassy surface. The monks pray and meditate, and when in the right frame of mind wait for visions to appear in the pool's reflections. This was how the 14th Dalai Lama was found. The regent was said to have had a vision that indicated their new Dalai Lama was residing in the eastern Amdo region of Tibet. They were to look for a single-storeyed house, displaying unique red rain gutters and decorated with a fanciful pattern of tiles.

After an extensive search, the little house with the bright tiles was found. And so was little two-year-old Lhamo Döndrub, the fifth child of sixteen in a family of poor farmers in the remote village of Taktser, high in the mountains near the border with China. To verify that the child was indeed the continuation of the lineage, he had to be tested. Questioned and eventually presented with various relics and toys, a few of which had belonged to the 13th Dalai Lama, the child was said to have exclaimed 'That's mine!' to each of the items that had belonged to his predecessor. The boy was declared to be the fourteenth incarnation of the Dalai Lama and renamed Jetsun Jamphel Ngawang

Lobsang Yeshe Tenzin Gyatso, which translates as 'Holy Lord, Gentle Glory, Compassionate, Defender of the Faith, Ocean Teacher'. In Mongolian, *dalai* means 'ocean' and is translated from the Tibetan name 'Gyatso'. In Tibetan *lama* is the same as the Sanskrit word 'guru'; together the honorific translates as 'Ocean Teacher', or one who is as spiritually deep as the ocean.

Taken to Lhasa, Tibet's capital and holy city, young Tenzin Gyatso began his monastic education at the age of six under two learned Buddhist monks. When he was eleven he spotted a strange sight in the garden below. A yellow-haired Westerner, one of only six in all of Lhasa, had been brought to the garden to treat a sick peacock. The man knelt down and spoke reassuringly to the injured bird in both the Lhasa dialect and the honorific Tibetan. The young Dalai Lama was amazed. He would discover that this strapping Austrian mountain climber named Heinrich Harrer had escaped from a British internment camp in India and traversed the Himalayas on foot to reach Tibet. They soon became friends, the young Tenzin Gyatso affectionately calling Harrer *Gopse*, meaning 'yellow hair'. For three years Harrer served as the young Dalai Lama's unofficial tutor, teaching him about geography and English and, most importantly, about the world outside Tibet. They remained close friends for sixty years, until Harrer's death in 2006 (see 'Heinrich Harrer's seven years in Tibet', page 253).

Much of the remainder of the Dalai Lama's childhood was spent in religious studies under the strict protocol of life in the winter Potala Palace and the summer residence of Norbulingka. He was unaware that political tensions were on the rise with the Chinese government of General Chiang Kai-shek. In 1949, the Tibetan Parliament decided to expel all Chinese connected with the newly established Kuomintang government. By the end of July that year, the Chinese were gone, but the tensions had only increased.

The following year, with the Kuomintang routed in China, conflict with the new People's Republic of China broke into the open. The Chinese invaded in October 1950, and the People's Liberation Army (PLA) easily broke Tibet's defences. Having been a basically peace-loving country for generations, Tibet had but a modest armed force with few modern weapons. China insisted their invasion was a 'peaceful liberation' and pulled up on the outskirts of Lhasa. The Tibetan Parliament called for the enthronement of fifteen-year-old Tenzin Gyatso two years earlier than expected. The country needed a leader to face the forces of the Chinese and the young boy who had lived most of his life in spiritual seclusion was to be that leader. His rule would prove to be short.

OVER 5000 BRAVE BUT OUTMATCHED TIBETAN SOLDIERS DIED AS THE swift-moving PLA forces swept towards the capital. Situated at 3360 metres (11,024 feet) on the central Tibetan Plateau, Lhasa is surrounded by some of the world's most majestic mountains. Its scenic beauty is legendary—the name translates as 'seat of the gods'—but it provided scant defences against the Chinese. The remaining Tibetan soldiers quickly surrendered and the PLA halted its advance. After confiscating the surrendered soldiers' weapons, lecturing them on communism and sending them home, the PLA demanded of the new young leader that he surrender the country to China's 'peaceful liberation'.

Initially, the Chinese sought to win over the Tibetans. 'The Chinese were very disciplined,' remembered the Dalai Lama, 'even better than the British, because they distributed some money. So they carefully planned.' They released some prisoners, built roads and paid for their food and housing. The newly enthroned Dalai Lama immediately sent emissaries to India, Nepal, Britain and the United States seeking support against the Chinese; all were turned down. Even the United Nations would not support Tibet; the only country to do so was tiny, war-torn El Salvador in Latin America. In 1951 the Tibetan delegation to Peking returned to Lhasa, and to the young Dalai Lama's horror he was informed that he had not only agreed to but also 'signed' a Seventeen Point Agreement for the Peaceful Liberation of Tibet.

The 'agreement' gave the People's Republic of China sovereignty over Tibet and dictated a step-by-step program for its assimilation into 'the motherland'. The Dalai Lama would retain status as the head of the Tibetan government but would now maintain 'friendly' relations with his Chinese 'brothers'. With the arrival of the signed agreement, later revealed to have been forged under duress by the Peking delegation, troops arrived en masse in Lhasa. The sudden influx of nearly 60,000 troops nearly doubled the size of the city, and food and other resources became scarce.

Over the next several years, an uneasy truce held in Lhasa. The Dalai Lama continued with his religious studies while also, with the assistance of his two foreign secretaries, increasingly handling the affairs of state and negotiations with the occupying Chinese generals. However, in Kham and Amdo, the territories furthest east and closest to China, tension turned to violence as China refused to restore self-rule. By 1956 armed conflict had erupted between Tibetan resistance fighters and Chinese troops. Guerrilla skirmishes resulted in increasingly brutal reprisals, including torture, beatings, rape and the starvation of prisoners. Stories of the sexual abuse of monks, nuns and children swelled the guerrilla forces until they numbered in the tens of thousands, using the network of monasteries to hide fighters. Even as the Dalai Lama tried to broker peace, resistance spread throughout Tibet.

The conflict reached Lhasa in March 1959. The rebels had been brutally put down in the outlying areas but Lhasa had attempted to follow the statutes of the Seventeen Point Agreement. Now, rumours abounded that the Dalai Lama would be abducted or possibly assassinated. Then, in a not-so-subtle ploy, the Dalai Lama was extended a strange invitation to attend a performance at the Chinese military headquarters on the outskirts of Lhasa—and told not to bring his traditional armed escort. Tibetan government officials smelled a rat and spread the word among the locals. On the day of the performance, 10 March, 300,000 Tibetans surrounded the Potala Palace, refusing to let the Dalai Lama leave or to allow the Chinese to come and get him. The day is celebrated as Tibetan Uprising Day throughout the country.

Soon protesters were in the streets calling for independence. The Chinese military moved into fortified positions around the city while the Kashag (Tibetan Parliament) prepared a petition in support of the armed rebels outside the city and appealed to the Indian consul for assistance and safe harbour for their leader. Over the next several days, the vastly outnumbered Tibetan army attempted to fortify its positions and secure an escape route for the Dalai Lama. After Chinese forces moved artillery into range of the winter palace and fired off several rounds, the escape plan was set in motion. As the Dalai Lama's troops fortified the route to India, the Chinese turned their wrath on the remaining 30,000 Tibetans who surrounded the Potala Palace, shelling the palace grounds for two days. But when they entered the palace, the Dalai Lama and his retinue were gone. The daring escape garnered headlines across the globe, and the young Dalai Lama was introduced to the world on the cover of *Time* magazine with the headline, 'The Escape that Rocked the Reds'.

So began a reign of terror that by 1962 had resulted in the destruction of all but seventy of the original 2500 monasteries in the country. The Chinese forced into exile a vast majority of the country's monks, many of whom followed the Dalai Lama through the escape route to India secured by rebel fighters. The United Nations and human rights groups have estimated that 1.2 million Tibetans died through military action, famine, execution, torture or imprisonment.

In India, the Dalai Lama was welcomed by Prime Minister Jawaharlal Nehru, who had worked side by side with Mohandas Gandhi in India's fight for independence. Nehru had his own difficulties with the Chinese, constantly smoothing over skirmishes in the disputed Kashmir border areas. He had initially encouraged the young Tibetan leader to work with the Chinese to improve conditions under the Seventeen Point Agreement. But when the rebellion broke out, Nehru facilitated the Dalai Lama's government-in-exile in Dharamshala and provided for a steady stream of refugees to the area.

The Tibetan rebel fighters focused their guerrilla activities on protecting the escape route into India. Over 80,000 Tibetans made the trek across the mountains into Dharamshala's rugged refugee camps. The Dalai Lama set his sights immediately on establishing the area as the centre for the exiled Tibetan community, in what has become known as 'Little Lhasa'. Here he established his government-in-exile, with a freely elected Parliament made up of Tibetan refugees gathered from around the world. The heads of government were elected from this Parliamentary body. By 1963, the government-in-exile had established a new constitution based on the UN's Universal Declaration of Human Rights, and called for Tibetan self-rule. The Dalai Lama appealed directly to the United Nations for the right of return to Tibet, and the international body passed resolutions in 1959, 1961 and 1963 condemning the Chinese, calling on them to respect human rights and the Tibetans' right to self-rule.

The Dalai Lama and the new Tibetan government set up agricultural settlements in the Dharamshala region, and quickly established an educational system to provide the children of Tibet with an understanding of their language, culture, religion and history. For further education, the Dalai Lama founded the Central Institute of Higher Tibetan Studies, which became the main Tibetan university in India. The Tibetan Institute of Performing Arts and later, in the 1970s, the Library of Tibetan Works and Archives were established to carry on traditional Tibetan arts and writings, the latter eventually holding some 80,000 original books and manuscripts. It is considered the ultimate treasure trove of resources on Tibetan history, politics and culture. In addition, the Dalai Lama set out to re-establish many of the monastic orders destroyed by the Chinese invasion. In all, nearly 200 monasteries and nunneries have been re-founded to preserve the Tibetan Buddhist heritage.

❧

## A ZONE OF *AHIMSA*

The Dalai Lama became an internationally known figure, not just as the titular head of Tibet and champion of his country's human and political rights, but also as a Buddhist teacher and spiritual master. He

# HEINRICH HARRER'S SEVEN YEARS IN TIBET

Born in the Austrian village of Hüttenberg, Heinrich Harrer was an Olympic-calibre skier, a mountaineer and geographer. He was also a sergeant in the Nazi Party's notorious SS, though he always claimed he joined only because he wanted to take part in a German mountaineering expedition. Harrer described his brief exposure to the Nazi Party as a youthful mistake and insisted that his true beliefs were formed in Tibet and through the unique friendship he fostered with the young Dalai Lama.

In 1939, Harrer joined an expedition to climb Nanga Parbat in the Himalayas, the ninth highest mountain in the world. While the expedition team crossed British-controlled India, World War II broke out in Europe. Harrer was captured and incarcerated with over 1000 other enemy aliens and prisoners of war in the Dehradun internment camp. Over the next five years he made multiple escape attempts. In May 1944 he escaped for good, along with fellow countryman Peter Aufschnaiter. He and Aufschnaiter traversed the Himalayas and eventually crossed the 5800 metre (19,030 feet) Tsang Chok-la Pass into Tibet. They roamed southwestern Tibet for many months before making it to Lhasa in February 1946.

The two Austrians talked their way into the holy city, essentially doubling Lhasa's non-Tibetan population. Harrer found work as a palace gardener while Aufschnaiter, who was trained as an engineer, was soon leading civil engineering projects for the Tibetan government. The eleven-year-old Dalai Lama had often spotted the strapping, blond-haired Harrer on the streets with his telescope. Summoned to the palace, he and the young Dalai Lama struck up a friendship that would last sixty years. Harrer became the Dalai Lama's unofficial tutor, teaching him English, mathematics, geography and, most importantly, much about the world outside Tibet.

With the Chinese Communist invasion in 1950, Harrer travelled with the Dalai Lama out of Lhasa and eventually fled the country. Returning to Austria, he wrote about his experience in the bestselling books *Seven Years in Tibet* and *Lost Lhasa*. He spent much of the 1950s and 1960s leading ethnographic and mountaineering expeditions in the Amazon, Alaska, Peru and New Guinea, and wrote more than twenty books about his adventures. He also made over forty documentaries and later in life became an international golf champion. He helped found the Tibet Museum in Austria, which included many of his own photographs and is still considered one of the best archives of traditional Tibetan culture.

In 2002, the Dalai Lama presented Harrer with the International Campaign for Tibet's Light of Truth Award, celebrating all he had done to bring Tibet's plight to the attention of the world. 'Wherever I live, I shall feel homesick for Tibet,' Harrer wrote in *Seven Years in Tibet*. 'My heartfelt wish is that my story may create some understanding for a people whose will to live in peace and freedom has won so little sympathy from an indifferent world.' He died in 2006 at the age of ninety-three.

continued his studies, published widely and circled the globe meeting with world leaders on behalf of his displaced people while also lecturing and leading workshops on the Tibetan Buddhist practice of Dzogchen. The 'Great Perfection,' Dzogchen is a meditative form of Buddhism that is considered by practitioners to be the most direct route to enlightenment. Fostering a kind of primordial, open and peaceful condition, a follower who is able to maintain the Dzogchen state continually purges any sense of *dukkha*, or feelings of discontent, tension and anxiety about everyday life. The Dalai Lama has often cited this ability as giving him the patience to endure exile from his beloved Tibet for the last fifty years.

Contrary to the Dalai Lama's wishes, armed rebellion continued in the Tibetan outlands. Throughout the 1960s these flare-ups tracked to China's shifting political currents and its harsh repression and small reforms. The Cultural Revolution of the 1960s and early 1970s was a particularly brutal period for Tibet, witnessing the destruction of a vast majority of the remaining temples and causing widespread famine and starvation. In 1972, when the administration of President Richard Nixon, wishing to foster closer US relations with China, withdrew support of Tibet's freedom fighters, the rebellion was crushed. China also sought to deepen its political hold on Tibet through the

## NEPAL'S ZONE OF PEACE

Nepal's King Birendra once called his country a soft yam between the two large stones of India and China. In 1973 he declared: 'Nepal, situated between two of the most populous countries of the world, wishes her frontiers to be declared a zone of peace.' Throughout the 1970s, as US–Soviet detente changed the world's political environment, as China emerged from its Cultural Revolution and Pakistan and India continuously rattled sabres, the political and geographical landscape of the region was in constant flux. King Birendra formally requested that countries endorse his idea of a Nepali peace zone and it has been a centrepiece of Katmandu's foreign policy ever since, fostering neutrality and free trade between China and India through the country.

In the intervening years, over 110 countries, including China and the United States, have endorsed Nepal as a 'zone of peace'; unfortunately neither India nor Russia has done so. With the start of Nepal's ten-year civil war in 1996, much of the rationale for a peaceful Nepal came into question. But since the conflict's settlement, renewed calls for the country's neutrality in the volatile region have been met with growing support.

manipulation of the country's political succession. In the mid-1970s, Tenzin Gyatso openly suggested the possibility that he might never reincarnate, thus ending the Dalai Lama lineage. This outraged exiled Tibetans, who declared that he had no say in the matter, that it was an issue for the people and the government.

China jumped on this question, declaring that it had the sole right to approve the reincarnations of Tibet's High Lamas. Although the People's Republic of China (the PRC) is officially a secular state, it maintains this right is based on the precedent set by the Qianlong Emperor during the Qing Dynasty (1644–1911). The emperor had, for a brief period, instituted a lottery system for selecting the Dalai Lama and his second in command, the Panchen Lama. This came to a head when, following the death of Tenzin Gyatso's Panchen Lama, the PRC named their own reincarnate, Gyancain Norbu. The Dalai Lama and exiled Tibetans do not recognise him as the legitimate Panchen Lama and have called international attention to the fact, fearing that China is attempting to establish a precedent for choosing the successor when the current Dalai Lama passes away.

From 1987 to 1993, unrest returned as frustrations grew over the status of Tibetans and the destruction of their customs through the influx of Chinese Han peoples. A generation of Tibetans had now grown up either as angry exiles or as a disenfranchised minority under Chinese rule. As brothels, bars and shopping centres sprang up in the shadow of Tibet's most holy shrines, and as Tibetans feared the 'cultural genocide' taking place in their country, tensions rose. Led by monks and students, protests in Lhasa and outlying areas were brutally suppressed. Demonstrations turned into riots and the riots led to several massacres by Chinese troops. By 1989 China had declared a state of emergency, giving the authorities additional powers to suppress revolt and bolster the gains of the immigrant Chinese. In response, the Dalai Lama prepared a new appeal to the United Nations and the rest of the world.

In 1987 the Dalai Lama travelled to Washington, DC to address the Congressional Human Rights Caucus. He announced a Five Point Peace Plan before presenting it to the United Nations as a roadmap to peaceful relations in Tibet. The plan called first and foremost for Tibet to be declared a 'zone of *ahimsa*', that is, a country based on non-violence, akin to what the country of Nepal had declared and China had accepted (see 'Nepal's zone of peace', opposite). The plan required the withdrawal of Chinese troops and military outposts as well as an end to China's use of Tibet for nuclear arms manufacturing, testing and disposal. The remaining four points called for an end to China's 'transfer policy' of the Han Chinese; respect for Tibet's human rights and political autonomy; the restoration and protection of Tibet's environment and natural resources; and a return to negotiations 'in good faith' of Tibet's future.

Applauded, lauded and encouraged by most world nations, the Five Point Peace Plan was summarily rejected by the PRC. However, the Dalai Lama's renewed efforts at broaching a peaceful settlement in Tibet and fostering better relations with China, along with his years of teaching non-violent opposition in line with the spirit of Mohandas Gandhi, won him the Nobel Peace Prize in 1989. In accepting the award, he said:

> I feel honoured, humbled and deeply moved that you should give this important prize to a simple monk from Tibet. I am no one special. But I believe the prize is a recognition of the true value of altruism, love, compassion and non-violence which I try to practice, in accordance with the teachings of the Buddha and the great sages of India and Tibet. I accept the prize with profound gratitude on behalf of the oppressed everywhere and for all those who struggle for freedom and work for world peace.

## 'VIOLENT OPPRESSORS ARE ALSO WORTHY OF COMPASSION'

MANY RELIGIOUS LEADERS AND ORGANISATIONS, FROM POPE JOHN PAUL II and the Archbishop of Canterbury to Hindu, Muslim and Buddhist scholars, including such advocates of non-violence as Thich Nhat Hanh of Vietnam and Aung San Suu Kyi of Burma, have offered support and sought the counsel of the Dalai Lama. But he has come under criticism as well. Some leaders have come to question his passive attitude, wondering quietly if he has grown too accustomed to his life outside Tibet. Japan's Daisaku Ikeda, a Nichiren Shoshu Buddhist and controversial president of the lay organisation Soka Gakkai International, has kept his distance from the Dalai Lama, instead fostering better relations with China in hopes of broadening his organisation's base in that country (see 'Daisaku Ikeda and the SGI', opposite).

Others in the movement for a free Tibet have grown frustrated with the slow or non-existent progress towards some form of acceptable political autonomy. Those Tibetan rebels who have pushed for total independence find great suspicion in the Dalai Lama's apparent embrace of a brotherhood between

# DAISAKU IKEDA AND THE SGI

The thirteenth century Japanese monk Nichiren Daishonen taught that devotion to the Lotus Sutra and the chanting of *Namu-myoho-renge-kyo* was the sole means for reaching enlightenment. In 1930, Nichiren Buddhist disciple, educator and pacifist Tsunesaburo Makiguchi, along with his colleague Josei Toda, founded Soka Gakkai—'Value-Creation Society'—as a Nichiren lay organisation dedicated to reforming Japan's militaristic educational system. Prior to World War II, as Japan's totalitarian government clamped down on dissent and religious freedoms, Makiguchi and Toda were both arrested and imprisoned for their Nichiren Shoshu beliefs and opposition to war. Makiguchi died in prison, a victim of the harsh conditions.

Toda was released after the war and with the return of religious freedom he rededicated himself to realising Makiguchi's dream. Under Toda's leadership and through the mouthpiece of his small publishing empire, Soka Gakkai experienced tremendous growth in the post-war years. After Toda's death in 1958, his disciple Daisaku Ikeda ascended to the presidency of the organisation and immediately set out on an aggressive campaign to spread the Nichiren Shoshu Buddhist practice throughout the world. By 1975, when he reorganised the society into Soka Gakkai International (SGI), it had taken root across the globe. Ikeda has grown SGI into a Japanese powerhouse, with one in ten Japanese belonging to the organisation, and nearly twelve million members worldwide. Ikeda has become an internationally recognised figure, dedicated to spreading SGI's message of personal transformation and the value of peace, culture and education for creating a new society.

Although Ikeda is greatly admired in many circles, he remains dogged by controversy. In 1992 he was excommunicated from the Nichiren Shoshu sect for doctrinal disputes, especially for statements he made implying he superseded Nichiren as the True Buddha. SGI and Nichiren Shoshu Buddhism are now separate entities. This has led to many published accounts challenging that the organisation is a cult of personality based around its charismatic leader. Ikeda's emphasis on *shakubuku*, the evangelising practice that requires new members to renounce past religious beliefs, has been called intolerant. Further, as Ikeda has amassed a personal fortune from his publications and business dealings, and quietly used his influence to help found and finance the right-centrist New Komeito political party in Japan, many have questioned his motives. The party made considerable gains in Japan's last election and now holds significant sway over national policy, especially in light of Ikeda's desire to expand SGI's reach into China and Russia.

Regardless of the criticism, Ikeda and SGI have made huge strides in raising humanitarian issues throughout the world and building a global network of peace advocacy. Whatever his motives, he stands as a major twenty-first century figure dedicated to fostering personal growth and a new spiritual 'human revolution'.

THE DALAI LAMA

257

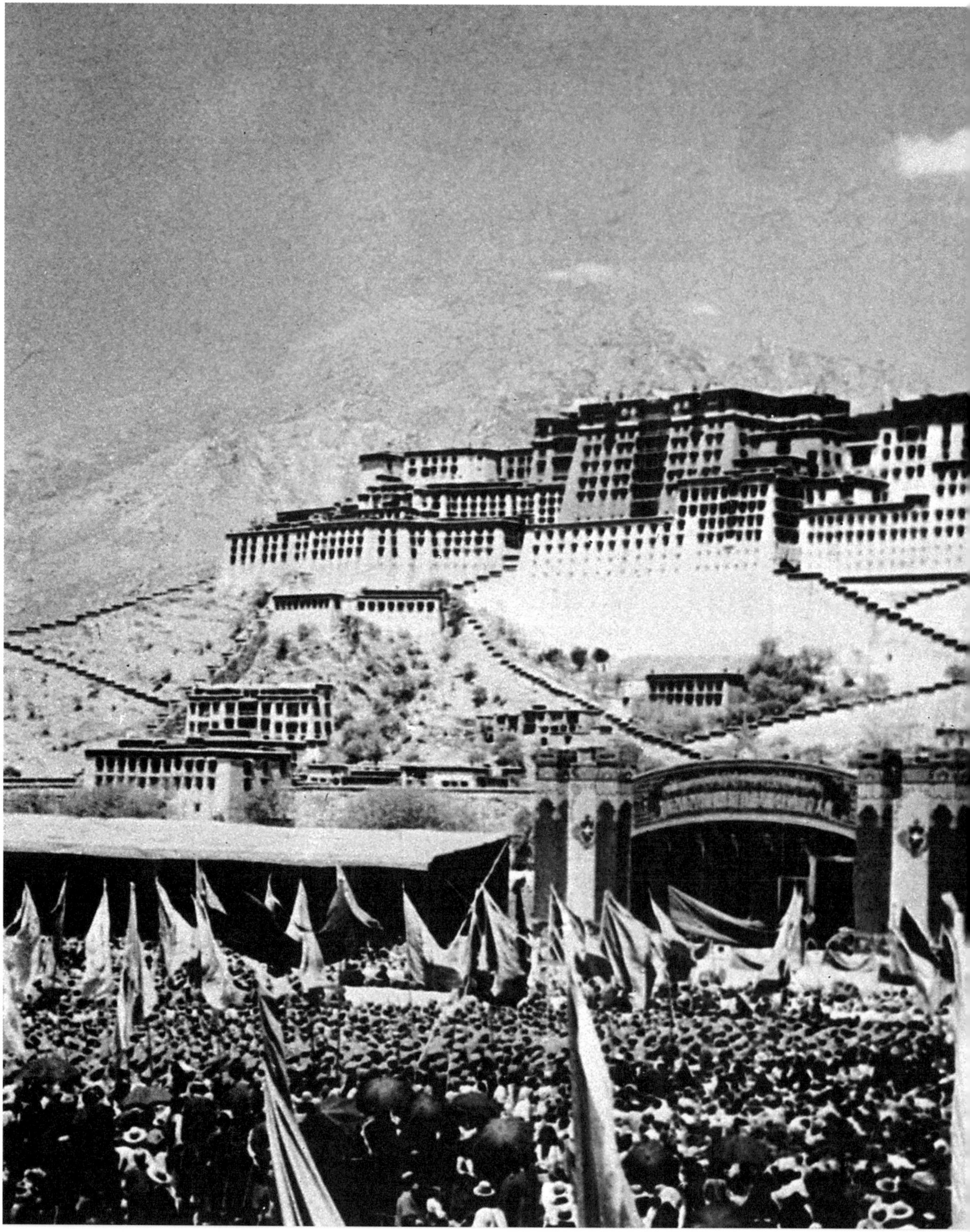

the Chinese and Tibetan people, especially the increasingly conciliatory tone he strikes towards the interlopers. His own views have fanned these concerns. He has spoken at length about taking the long view of political and spiritual evolution, and has even suggested that the suffering of the Tibetan people has much to offer in the way of teaching them about humility, compassion and impermanence. He has even wondered aloud whether Tibetans have benefited from their oppression at the hands of the Chinese because of the depth of compassion it has engendered. As he has said, even 'violent oppressors are also worthy of compassion'.

Strangely, his calls for renewed understanding between the Chinese and Tibetan people have been met with considerable suspicion in China. As unrest returned to Tibet in the lead-up to the 2008 Olympic Games in Beijing, riots led by monks in Lhasa and elsewhere were violently put down by Chinese forces. And while the Dalai Lama sought to defuse these outbursts and has consistently called for Tibetan autonomous rule rather than independence, he has still been labelled as the instigator of this unrest. He has denied it, going so far as to warn violent protesters that should they continue, they may well lose their most important weapon in the struggle, that of moral superiority. But he treads a fine line, holding support for Tibetan self-rule while advocating friendlier relations with the oppressing country. He seems to understand that fostering a modern Tibet may very well rely upon a union with a modern China. In a 2008 interview with *Time* magazine, the Dalai Lama said:

> As long as I am alive, I am fully committed to amity between Tibetans and Chinese. Otherwise there's no use. More importantly, the Tibetan Buddhist cultural heritage can eventually help bring some deeper values to the millions of Chinese youth who are lost in a [moral] vacuum. After all, China is traditionally a Buddhist country ... I truly believe that a new reality has emerged. The times are different. Today different ethnic groups and different nations come together due to common sense. Look at the European Union ... really great. What is the use of small, small nations fighting each other? Today it's much better for Tibetans to join [China]. That is my firm belief.

Having reached his venerable seventies, the clock is ticking. Who can say whether the Dalai Lama will ever realise his vision of an autonomous Tibet in peaceful union with its Chinese neighbour to the east.

On 10 March 1959, in front of the Potala Palace, traditional winter home of the Dalai Lama, thousands of armed Tibetans gathered in a failed uprising against Chinese rule.

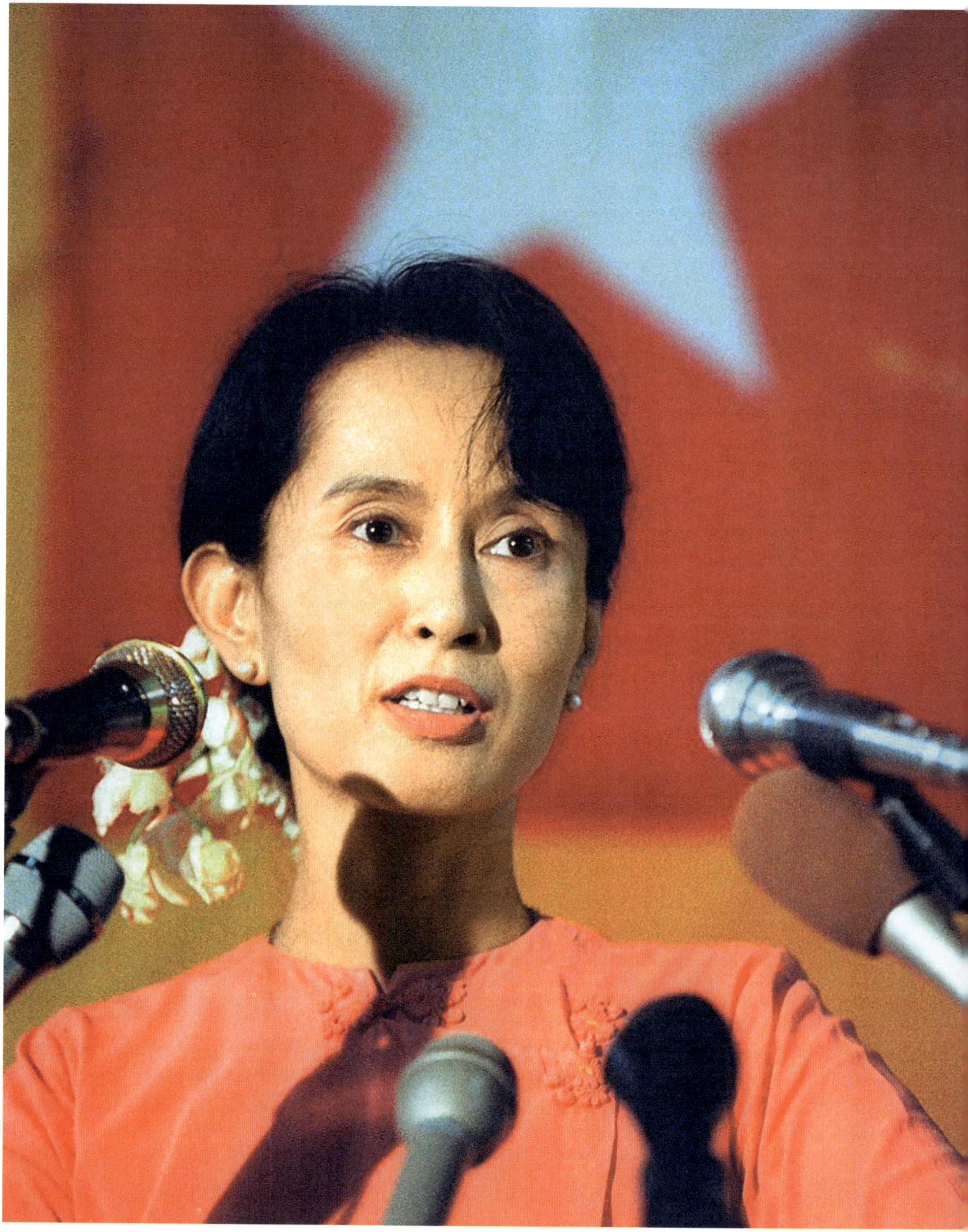

# AUNG SAN SUU KYI:
# PRISONER OF CONSCIENCE

IN 1990, THE SOUTHEAST ASIAN NATION OF BURMA, KNOWN AS MYANMAR by its military junta, seemed poised to finally end thirty years of repressive dictatorship. Aung San Suu Kyi, the daughter of Burma's great liberator General Aung San, led the National League for Democracy to a landslide majority in national elections. But it proved a hollow victory. Already under house arrest, Suu Kyi began a peaceful vigil against the illegitimate junta. As swiftly as the poll results were announced, democracy was stifled under a fog of trumped-up excuses for the military government's failure to relinquish power. In the ensuing crackdown, the military violently repressed the urban pro-democracy supporters in Rangoon (Yangon).

Denied her elected right to assume the role of Burma's new prime minister, Suu Kyi began a life as a prisoner of conscience that has lasted up to the present day. A follower of Gandhian principles of non-violent passive resistance, she led a disciplined, peaceful revolt against Burma's corrupt and repressive government. For nearly twenty years she has remained under detention, held hostage away from her people, her husband and her children. Choosing to share in the hardships and fate of her repressed countrymen, Suu Kyi's story is unfinished, as she awaits the day she will again be free to lead her people in democracy.

Backed by the flag of the National League of Democracy, Aung San Suu Kyi addresses a press conference in Rangoon on 23 May 1996, in the period between her release from six years of house arrest in July 1995 and her being placed under almost continuous house arrest in September 2000.

# THE FATHER OF BURMESE INDEPENDENCE

BURMA IS THE LARGEST COUNTRY IN SOUTHEAST ASIA, SITTING AT the strategic crossroads of trade between China and India. China borders the country to the northeast, Laos to the east, Thailand to the southeast, Bangladesh to the west and India to the northwest. A third of the country's border lies along the coast of the Bay of Bengal, to the southwest. Colonised in the 1880s by Great Britain, Burma first came under the administration of British India and eventually, in 1937, became a self-governing colony. The British brought in large Indian and Chinese populations, intending to stimulate trade, and eventually these immigrant communities outnumbered Burmese in the urban areas. Predominantly followers of Theravada Buddhism, one of the oldest and most conservative of the Buddhist sects, the Burmese have built some of the most majestic temples anywhere in Southeast Asia, including the 98 metre (322 foot) gilded Shwedagon Pagoda in Rangoon.

During World War II, Burma was the scene of some of the most horrific fighting in Asia, as the British were forced to abandon the country ahead of a successful Japanese invasion. Over 300,000 refugees streamed across the jungle into India, tens of thousand dying on the trek. Most of the remaining Burmese threw their lot in with the Japanese and the newly created Burmese Independence Army. Many of the ethnic minority groups in the outlaying areas joined with the British Indian Army in a counter-offensive. Under the command of General Aung San, the Burmese Independence Army fought with the Japanese from 1942 to 1944, but switched allegiance as the tides of war shifted in 1945.

Aung San had been a revolutionary and a leader of the independence movement in Burma since the 1930s. At the outbreak of war with Japan he had attempted to travel to China to seek assistance but was intercepted by the Japanese. In Japan he was promised aid and Burma's independence in exchange for allegiance to Emperor Hirohito. After receiving army training and reorganising the Burmese military, he began to doubt this promise and became worried about Japan's ability to win the war. In 1945 he met secretly with the British in India to plan the overthrow of Japanese forces and help the Allies retake Burma. At war's end Aung San, as head of the Executive Council of Burma, established to write the new constitution in advance of complete independence, was for all intents and purposes Prime Minister of Burma. In 1947 he signed an agreement in London with British Prime Minister Clement Attlee guaranteeing independence. A few years earlier

General Aung San had met and married Khin Kyi and together they had three children. The youngest, born in 1945, was Aung San Suu Kyi.

Shortly after General Aung San's return to Burma, while meeting with the Executive Council prior to general elections, armed paramilitaries stormed the Secretariat Building in downtown Rangoon and machine-gunned the entire cabinet. Aung San and six cabinet members were killed. The country was thrown into turmoil as a rival politician named U Saw was convicted and hanged for ordering the assassinations. Aung San, a national hero, affectionately known as 'Bogyoke' (General), was universally recognised as the Father of Burmese Independence. He is remembered annually on 'Martyr's Day' with pilgrimages to his mausoleum at the foot of the Shwedagon Pagoda.

## A DIPLOMAT'S DAUGHTER

Only two years old when her father was assassinated, Aung San Suu Kyi grew up in Rangoon with her mother Daw Khin Kyi and older brothers Aung San Lin and Aung San Oo. Tragedy was to strike again, however, when her favourite brother Aung San Lin died in a drowning accident when she was only eight. Her mother held up General Aung San's legacy by becoming a prominent political figure in the democratic Union of Burma government. Following Aung San's assassination, U Nu was elected Burma's first prime minister leading a bicameral parliament, made up of a Chamber of Deputies and a Chamber of Nationalities. In 1960 Daw Khin Kyi was appointed Ambassador to India and Nepal, and Suu Kyi went with her mother to live in New Delhi.

Suu Kyi spent her teenage years in India, attending a Catholic school. She socialised with Rajiv and Sanjay Gandhi, the sons of Indira Gandhi and grandsons of Prime Minister Jawaharlal Nehru. Since her father had met Nehru several times to consult on independence prior to his death, Nehru treated Khin Kyi and Suu Kyi with great warmth, providing them with a luxurious home while Khin Kyi was stationed at the embassy (see 'Jawaharlal Nehru: architect of modern India', page 267). When Suu Kyi finished high school, Prime Minister Nehru arranged her enrolment at Lady Shri Ram College, which was associated with Delhi University and considered India's foremost school of higher learning for women. Here she learned about the politics and philosophy of Gandhi, about his advocacy of non-violent civil disobedience and about *Satyagraha*. Although the introduction was in an academic setting, Gandhi's model for confronting an authoritarian government would greatly influence Suu Kyi's decisions later in life.

Another key influence in young Suu Kyi's life was the friendship of Lord and Lady Gore-Booth, who had for a long while been close to her mother. They were 'dearly-beloved friends who taught me much about kindness and caring', she later remembered. Paul Gore-Booth was then the British High Commissioner in Delhi but had previously served as the British Ambassador to Burma from 1953 to 1956, when he had befriended Daw Khin Kyi out of his respect for her deceased husband. He and Lady Patricia Gore-Booth were preparing to return to England, where Sir Paul was to become Permanent Under-Secretary at London's Foreign Office, the pinnacle of his distinguished diplomatic career. Witty, erudite and a lover of poetry and Sherlock Holmes, Gore-Booth ran in an eclectic circle of intellectuals, artists and politicians. The Gore-Booths would become Suu Kyi's 'British guardians', opening their home to her when she won a place at Oxford to study politics, philosophy and economics in 1964.

Although Daw Khin Kyi was reluctant to let her only daughter study abroad, she was reassured by the Gore-Booths' oversight. Had she known that she was paving the way for Suu Kyi to meet, fall in love with and marry an Englishman, she would certainly have thought otherwise. England was leaning left at the time, both politically and socially, from the victories of the Labour Party to Beatlemania sweeping the nation. Suu Kyi, however, well aware of the rare opportunity she had been granted—made abundantly clear by the warnings of her mother—was a serious and determined student. But as one of only a handful of students from the East, and strikingly beautiful, graceful and always fastidiously dressed in her long Burmese *hta-main*, it was difficult to go unnoticed.

The Gore-Booths' twin sons David and Christopher were Suu Kyi's age. David was also at Oxford; Christopher was studying at Durham University in the southeast of England. He had become close friends with another set of twins, Michael and Anthony Aris, and introduced Michael to Suu Kyi in 1967. Although both were in the midst of studying for their finals, Michael quickly became infatuated with the exotic Burmese student. The grandson of a South Pacific explorer and son of a career diplomat, at twenty Michael was already clear on his direction, choosing to study Tibetan Buddhism and focus his attention on the Himalayan kingdoms of Bhutan and Nepal, both sanctuaries for many of the displaced monks and lamas escaping the Chinese invasion of Tibet. Tall, good-looking in a tousled way, and intellectually curious, Michael was born in Cuba and had lived in Peru before returning to England. Suu Kyi soon found herself smitten as well.

Their love affair was to move slowly however, as Burmese cultural mores made it nearly taboo for women to consort with 'foreigners'—and they would soon find themselves at opposite ends of the globe. Michael had landed a dream job, perfectly suited to his interest and adventurous spirit: he was about to leave for the tiny kingdom of Bhutan, the Himalayan 'little Tibet', to become a tutor and instructor of English to the Bhutanese royal family. Suu Kyi had been accepted for postgraduate work at New York University in the United States, where she would be hosted by Ma Than E, another close family friend who like Suu Kyi's mother had found herself in a diplomatic role, eventually landing at the UN headquarters in New York. Ma Than E, a famous beauty and chanteuse of Burmese love songs in the 1930s, had escaped to India ahead of the invading Japanese. She became a regular on Voice of America during the war and later a hostess in London during General Aung San's famous negotiations for independence. Now she would again host, this time opening her fashionable New York apartment to Suu Kyi.

⟊

## BURMA UNRAVELS

In 1967, Suu Kyi's mother decided to retire early from her post in India and return to Burma. After six years she no longer wished to represent the repressive regime of General Ne Win, who had come to power in a coup d'état in 1962, displacing the elected but ineffectual Prime Minister U Nu. Daw Khin Kyi personally disliked Ne Win, whom her husband had attempted to have shot for deserting his post in 1941. As the story goes, a lieutenant named Bo Ta Yar was unable to bring himself to carry out the order to execute Ne Win and arranged his escape instead. He would later lament about how many Burmese lives might have been saved if he had been able to carry out the order.

Daw Khin Kyi returned to a Burma in economic freefall, stifled under a totalitarian government that left millions starving in poverty and relied upon the fear of its brutal Tatmadaw (armed forces) and the slave labour of ethnic minority groups to stay afloat. Opposition parties were outlawed, the nation was increasingly isolationist and a cloud of paranoia pervaded a government that suppressed even the smallest protest with brutal force. Ne Win took power at a time of increasing ethnic unrest in Burma's rural areas. Prime Minister U Nu had been re-elected by a wide margin in 1961, but his passive and indecisive leadership style chafed with the military elite, even as he turned a blind eye to the atrocities Ne Win's forces carried out on ethnic insurgents. Ne Win had quietly secured a circle of loyal generals, weeding out those who opposed his view. When, at midnight on 1 March 1961, Ne Win gave the order, the military rolled into Rangoon, seizing key positions and taking U Nu and other cabinet ministers into custody.

At first the new military dictator seemed to offer a plan, though draconian, for Burmese renewal. But his 'Burmese Way to Socialism' soon revealed itself as markedly totalitarian, employing the most repressive tactics used in the Eastern bloc communist states. Ne Win installed himself as dictator, immediately disposed of the country's constitution and established a Revolutionary Council with total authority. With the creation of the Burma Socialist Programme Party (BSPP), Burma was transformed within two years from a democratic republic to one of the most repressive socialist states in the world. Nearly all industry and agriculture was nationalised, schools and universities were put under state control, privately owned newspapers were shut down and the courts were taken over by the military. Corruption and total control by the clique of loyal military generals began a downward spiral for the country that quickly led to severe food shortages and inflation that wiped out regular Burmese life savings.

Offering a taste of what was to come, when students at Rangoon University staged a protest over a shortage of rice in 1962 the military moved in and immediately opened fire, killing at least 100 protesters and injuring hundreds more. Treatment of ethnic groups was far worse, and an exodus took place. Rangoon was soon emptied of nearly its entire robust Indian and Chinese business class, taking with them their entrepreneurial skills and financing. Although Daw Khin Kyi had returned to Rangoon, she severed all ties to the dictator. Ne Win had counted on her support to align himself as the natural heir to the beloved Bogyoke, and he took his revenge by taxing all the income the former diplomat received while in service in India. He also tried to curry favour with young Suu Kyi, inviting her to his lavish English estate while she attended Oxford in 1967. She coldly refused, further angering the despot.

In New York, sharing an apartment with Ma Than E, nearly forty years her senior, Suu Kyi wrote letters every day to Michael Aris in Bhutan. Tiring of

# JAWAHARLAL NEHRU:
## ARCHITECT OF MODERN INDIA

Born in 1889 to a wealthy Brahmin family, Jawaharlal Nehru became a leading figure in the movement for an independent India and one of Mohandas Gandhi's closest friends and followers. After completing his law degree in Cambridge, Nehru returned to India in 1912 to practise law. Radicalised by the British massacre at Amritsar in 1919, he joined the Home Rule movement and later, rising quickly in the Indian National Congress, became Gandhi's trusted second. An avid follower of Gandhi's *Satyagraha* philosophy, Nehru was gaoled seven times over the next thirty years of struggle for independence.

A prolific writer and electrifying speaker, he was the natural choice to become an independent India's first prime minister. Along with Gandhi, he was staunchly opposed to the partition of India in 1947 but was unable to overcome the opposition of Muhammad Ali Jinnah and the Muslim League and reluctantly gave his approval. Following the devastating assassination of Gandhi, all of India turned to him for comfort and guidance. He famously said, 'Friends and comrades, the light has gone out of our lives, and there is darkness everywhere.' The same words were repeated on his death years later.

Nehru is the longest-serving Prime Minister India has had, winning general elections in 1952, 1957 and 1962. An internationalist, he sought peaceful relations with China, courted both the United States and the Soviet Union by remaining neutral in the Cold War, and eventually facilitated the birth of the Non-Aligned Movement of Third World countries. He spent much of his life endeavouring to build a modern infrastructure in his country, from schools to industry to relief from overwhelming poverty. As a pacifist, he was criticised for neglecting India's military defences; in 1962 his efforts at maintaining peace with China came undone when border clashes near Kashmir turned into open war and a humbling defeat for the Indian army. Stung by this failure, his health began to suffer and he died from a heart attack in 1964. Two years later, his daughter Indira Gandhi was elected prime minister; later, his grandson Rajiv Gandhi would also lead India.

the academic life, Suu Kyi jumped at the chance to work at the United Nations when Ma Than E arranged a relatively low-level position in the budgetary office. It also helped that the Secretary-General at the time was U Thant, one of the most widely respected UN heads since its inception and Burma's most recognised citizen throughout the world. After being screened and vetted, Suu Kyi took her position in the Advisory Committee on Administration and Budgetary Questions, getting first-hand knowledge into the management and financial processes for the World Health Organization and UN Development Programme. U Thant took her under his wing, inviting her to lazy Sunday brunches at his estate in Riverdale, New York. He had, of course, known General Aung San and kept in touch with Daw Khin Kyi and so it was only natural that he took a paternal liking to Suu Kyi (see 'UN Secretary-General U Thant', page 271).

After years of corresponding, Michael and Suu Kyi became engaged in 1970 when Michael stopped in New York on his way home to London. His three-year adventure in Bhutan had been far more successful than he'd ever imagined. Beyond serving as the tutor to princes and princesses, the children of King Jigme Dorje, he had become a trusted adviser and interpreter, relied upon to translate sensitive government documents for delivery to India and beyond. Michael had also become a devoted Buddhist, following the teachings of Dilgo Khyentse, who had been one of the 14th Dalai Lama's teachers in Lhasa before escaping the Chinese. Suu Kyi understood Michael's love of Bhutan and wished to share the experience with him. They were married a year later on New Year's Day, 1972, in a simple Buddhist ceremony in the Gore-Booths' living room in London. Daw Khin Kyi, who could not yet reconcile herself to Suu Kyi's marrying a non-Burmese, refused to attend; her estranged brother Aung San Oo, now an American citizen and close to the Burmese junta, also failed to show.

Her romance and engagement was a period of great moral turmoil for Suu Kyi. In the seven months leading up to their wedding, she wrote nearly 200 letters to Michael as she wrestled with the weight of the responsibilities she felt to him and to her heritage. All her life she had felt she was training to continue the efforts of her parents on behalf of the Burmese people. 'I only ask one thing,' she wrote to him, 'that should my people need me, you would help me to do my duty by them.' Michael understood. She was her father's daughter, and though he could not know what was to come, Michael understood that should Suu Kyi be called upon to lead, he must be willing to let her go.

## FROM BHUTAN BACK TO BURMA

For the next ten years, Suu Kyi refashioned herself as a dedicated wife and later as the mother of two sons. After their wedding the couple moved to Bhutan, where Michael resumed his duties and they structured a simple life in the capital of Thimphu. It wasn't an easy time for Suu Kyi and when, in late 1972, she became pregnant with their first child, they began planning for life after Bhutan. Much to Suu Kyi's relief, they returned to England where Alexander was born the following year. Michael set about organising his copious notes on his Bhutan experience for publication and as a means for launching his academic career.

Their second son, Kim, was born in 1977. Michael completed his doctoral degree and secured a position at Oxford. Suu Kyi followed him into academia, pursuing a PhD in Burmese literature in 1985. That year she was invited to join the Center for Southeast Asian Studies in Japan and Michael received a two-year appointment to teach at the university in Simla, India, in the Himalayan foothills. The family scattered: Michael to India, Alexander to boarding school in England and Suu Kyi and eight-year-old Kim to Kyoto. While she was in Japan, Suu Kyi used the chance to investigate the independence movement in Burma. There, for the first time, she came to understand the truly multi-ethnic makeup of the Burmese population, which included the indigenous Karens, Kachins, Chins and Arakanese, all of whom were being brutally suppressed while fighting a seemingly hopeless war of insurgency in the jungles. These were her people just as much as the urban students of Rangoon and the military elite of her father.

In 1987 the family reunited in England, with the prospects of the academic couple being a Southeast Asian dynamic duo: Michael the pre-eminent Tibetologist and Aung San Suu Kyi the authority on all things politically and literarily Burmese. But fate had other plans in store. Michael remembered:

> It was a quiet evening in Oxford like many others. The last day of March 1988. Our sons were already in bed and we were reading when the telephone rang. Suu picked up the phone to learn that her mother had suffered a severe stroke. She put the phone down and at once started to pack. I had a premonition that our lives would change forever.

On her arrival in Rangoon, Suu Kyi learned that her mother's condition was critical, that she was growing weaker each day. The same could be said for the state of Burma. After twenty-six years of Ne Win and the BSPP, Burma had gone from a promising independent republic to one of the world's poorest countries, a corrupt and internationally admonished pariah. Hated by Suu Kyi and her mother, feared by the populace, and propped up by the sadistic Tatmadaw, Ne Win was now in his seventies and had degenerated into a paranoid, superstitious strongman who relied increasingly on his personal numerologists and soothsayers for advice and comfort. In the outlying areas, especially bordering Thailand and Laos, communist armies, ethnic insurgents and warlord militias were engaged in endless bouts of territorial conflict. Ne Win's strategy was to pit one against the next in an ever-changing round of deals and double-crossings. Narcotics trafficking had become the primary source of funding for these conflagrations, and opium fields covered the foothills surrounding the Burmese plain. By the late 1980s, Burma had become the world's second leading source of heroin production after Afghanistan. Clearly, Ne Win's military protected and benefited from this sinister industry.

Suu Kyi practically moved into the hospital room where her mother lay incapacitated. Flowers filled the suite from well-wishers, a peaceful sanctuary for the honourable wife of the great Bogyoke. But outside, the streets of Rangoon were anything but peaceful. Fed up with a system stacked against them, disillusioned by a university education that was watered down and by an economy that couldn't promise any jobs after graduation anyway, students returned to the streets, as they had many times over the years. Riots, protests and demonstrations over food shortages, poorly paying jobs and a lack of political freedom had broken out throughout the 1970s: the Tatmadaw had violently crushed anti-government protests at the funeral of former UN Secretary-General U Thant in 1974 and again in 1975, 1976 and 1977. Thousands had died in clashes with the military or were languishing in gaols.

By the mid-1980s, the many thousands of refugees seeking sanctuary had flooded Thailand and Bangladesh. The economy was out of control. Finally, in 1987, Ne Win's government 'solved' the economic crisis in a style so devastatingly incompetent that it boggled the mind. With a single sweeping edict, Ne Win demonetarised all banknotes except the 45 and 90 *kyat* notes, rendering them no longer legal tender. Apparently having consulted regularly with a numerologist, Ne Win chose to keep the only two notes divisible by nine, his lucky number. The result was devastating, wiping out the cash savings of a huge number of struggling Burmese and invalidating 75 per cent of all the banknotes in circulation.

# UN SECRETARY-GENERAL U THANT

In 1961 the UN Secretary-General, Swedish diplomat Dag Hammarskjöld, one of the most respected statesmen in the world, was killed in a plane crash in Rhodesia (present-day Zimbabwe). He would have been a hard act to follow for anyone, but when the UN General Assembly unanimously voted an unknown, bookish Burmese named U Thant his successor, many outsiders questioned the appointment. That U Thant could match and even out-do his predecessor during his ten years leading the United Nations would silence all doubters.

U Thant was born in Lower Burma, educated at Rangoon's University College and was a close friend of U Nu, first prime minister of the newly independent Burma in 1948. U Nu asked U Thant to join his administration as Director of Broadcasting and later as Minister of Information during the 1950s. U Thant served as U Nu's most trusted adviser and confidant, arranging his travel plans, writing his speeches and meeting with foreign dignitaries. In 1955, U Thant represented Burma at the first Asian–African Summit, called by India's Jawaharlal Nehru, and actively supported the Non-Aligned Movement of Third World countries born from the conference.

U Thant was appointed to the United Nations at the end of the decade and began serving as Acting Secretary-General upon Hammarskjöld's death. The following year, on the Security Council's recommendation, he was unanimously appointed to fill Hammarskjöld's unexpired term. Almost immediately he was drawn into a world crisis when the Soviet Union and the United States came to the brink of nuclear war over revelations that the USSR was establishing missile bases in Cuba. He was widely seen as a major force in defusing the Cuban Missile Crisis. Reappointed Secretary-General in 1966, U Thant soon lost favour with the United States over his vocal opposition to the war in Vietnam. His secret attempts to broker peace talks between Hanoi and Washington were ultimately rejected by President Johnson. He retired from the United Nations in 1971, glad to be 'liberated' from his global responsibilities.

Long a thorn in the side of Burma's military junta, when U Thant died in New York City in 1974, then President Ne Win, jealous of his international stature, refused him any honours. His coffin was flown back to Burma unmarked. He would have been buried unceremoniously in an ordinary Rangoon cemetery had not incensed student protesters managed to steal the coffin and bury U Thant in the former grounds of the Rangoon University Student Union, destroyed by Ne Win in 1962 following his coup. The students built a makeshift shrine to U Thant on the campus and over several days held rallies calling for democratic reforms. Government troops stormed the campus, killing many of the student demonstrators and removing the coffin. Outrage in the Burmese capital at the killings and at the government's dishonourable treatment of U Thant's remains led to a number of student-led protests on the streets of Rangoon. The protests, like so many that came before and would come afterward, were brutally crushed by government forces.

AUNG SAN SUU KYI

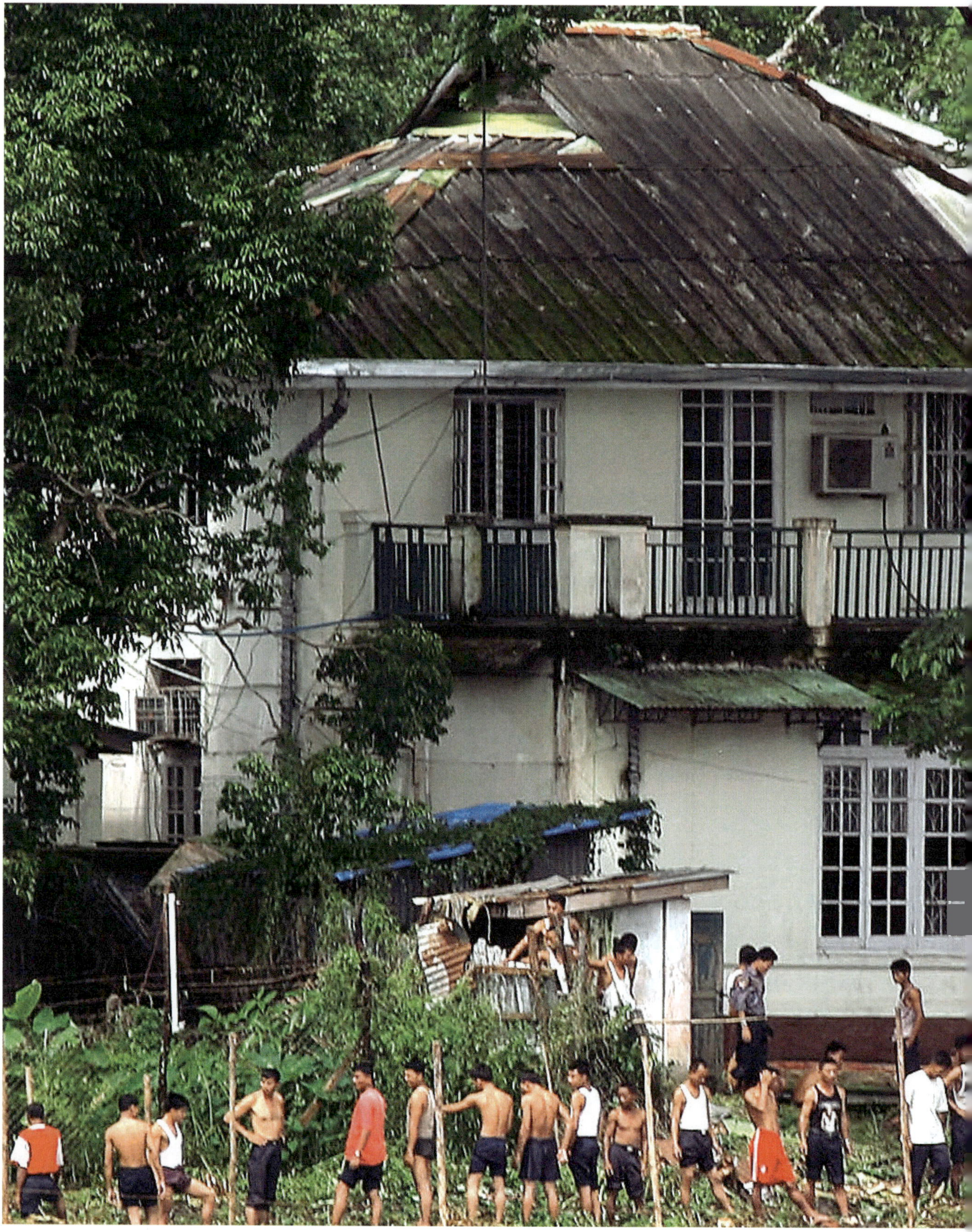

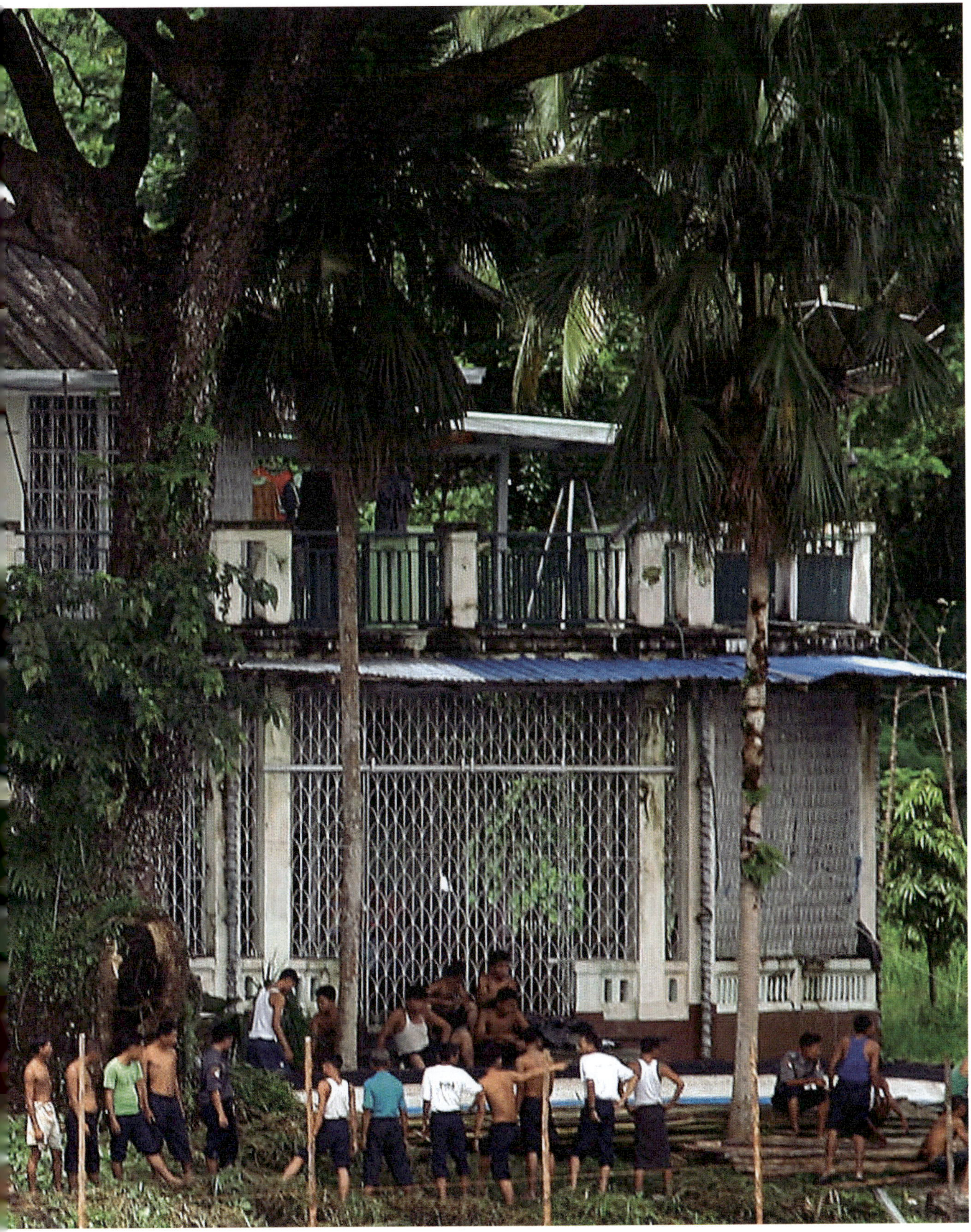

This time the fury of the population could not be contained. The government attempted to stem the unrest by closing all the universities, a tactic they'd used successfully in the past. But many students remained in Rangoon, without classes or work. The spark that lit the fuse took place in a teashop with an argument over the music being played on the establishment's tape deck. Several local boys, apparently drunk, harassed a couple of students over their music. When a fight broke out, all were arrested but the locals were released while the students were held in prison. When it was discovered that one of the locals was related to a government official, more students showed up to lodge a complaint. Refused a hearing, the students returned en masse, to find themselves confronted by armed riot police. As they fled, the police opened fire, killing several and wounding scores more. This brutal response became the tipping point.

Two days later, several thousand peaceful student protesters gathered. Shouting 'Down with Ne Win!', the protesters marched out of Rangoon University but were soon met by a large contingent of riot police and military led by Ne Win's henchman Brigadier-General Sein Lwin. They were herded onto the White Bridge, a narrow overpass along Inya Lake flanked by dilapidated buildings. At the other end, their way was blocked by another detachment of riot police. The students were trapped. Without warning, the military attacked, clubbing, beating and firing directly into the unarmed crowd. Many tried to escape by jumping into the lake, only to be beaten to death in the water or held under until they drowned. Hundreds were killed and many more wounded. The bodies were carted off and destroyed to limit exposure of the atrocity; the injured were eventually taken to Rangoon Hospital. But even as the government tried to clamp down on the spread of information, the brutality of the attack leaked out. Brigadier-General Sein Lwin ordered the White Bridge to be hosed off in an effort to minimise the evidence, but it has been known ever since in the pro-democracy movement as the 'Red Bridge'. Sein Lwin also earned a new name: the Butcher of Rangoon.

❦

## FOUR EIGHTS

DOCTORS AT THE RANGOON HOSPITAL WERE AT FIRST ORDERED NOT TO treat the wounded demonstrators, who were shackled to their beds. Many more students died, even as doctors and nurses secretly tended to the injured. And the violence continued. Days later, 2000 students protested on Rangoon

University's grounds. In the afternoon, military, riot police and security forces stormed the campus with tear gas and batons. Many fled into campus buildings and dormitories but hundreds of others were arrested and packed into waiting trucks. The trucks did not drive off immediately, however; in one truck alone, forty-two students already suffering from beatings and tear gas exposure suffocated to death. The next day, open revolt spread across the city as running bands of students staged strikes against any government target they could hit: office buildings, stores, vehicles. Joined by 18,000 demonstrators from all walks of life, downtown Rangoon was flooded with protesters. By nightfall, Brigadier-General Sein Lwin had brought in thousands of military reinforcements from the outlying areas. They secured all strategic locations within the city and clamped down with orders to shoot and kill any non-military personnel on the streets. Dozens more died throughout the night, but by morning the streets were empty and an unearthly quiet had descended.

Suu Kyi, by force of her mother's illness, found herself in the centre of the action. Due to the sheer number of the injured, Rangoon Hospital had become the hub of revolutionary activity. Amazed that the daughter of the great General Aung San was in their midst, a steady stream of student activists, old-guard leaders, doctors, intellectuals and everyday Burmese sought her out. She listened sympathetically to every story, every ghastly account of brutality and depravity. She said little, but her composure, her sympathy and peaceful attentiveness had a strong impact on everyone who approached her. Internally she roiled, but what exactly could she do? And more importantly, what could she do that would not lead to more bloodshed?

The answers soon presented themselves. After nearly three months it had become clear that Daw Khin Kyi was not going to improve and Suu Kyi made the painful decision to take her home, so that her mother could die peacefully among family and friends. Michael and their sons travelled to Burma to the great comfort of Daw Khin Kyi, any concerns about her English son-in-law now long forgotten. But many other visitors came to the family compound as well, both out of respect for the mother and out of hope for the future from the daughter. The compound became a hive of protest planning. Outside the military still held martial law and brutally enforced a curfew; inside strategies were devised by young activists and the old guard alike. In the centre of it all was Suu Kyi.

But as the pro-democracy movement coalesced, Ne Win dropped a strategic bombshell. In late July 1988, he declared that he would be stepping down as party chairman and commander-in-chief. In addition, in a rambling and

Previous pages: Following American John Yettaw's bizarre lake-side intrusion into Aung San Suu Kyi's house in May 2009 (see page 280), Burmese security guards erected fences on all sides of the compound to prevent further 'rescue' attempts.

AUNG SAN SUU KYI

275

disjointed radio address, he appeared to actually take some small responsibility for the events that had led the nation to the brink of chaos. The country collectively asked could this really be the end of the repressive rule that had sacked Burma for nearly thirty years? But as the days went by, the answer became clear. Ne Win wasn't going anywhere; he had been 'persuaded' by party members not to renounce his membership. His promises of privatising certain businesses were rescinded. And finally he announced his chosen successor: none other than Brigadier-General Sein Lwin, the Butcher of Rangoon.

If there was one man in Burma more detested than Ne Win, it was Sein Lwin. As if the shock of this announcement wasn't enough, Ne Win followed it with a declaration that should demonstrations recur, the military would have standing orders to shoot to kill. Suu Kyi, up until this point still weighing her family obligations, was so aghast at this turn of events that she knew she must now commit herself unflinchingly to Burma's democracy movement. It was time for Michael to make good on his promise: this was her fight now, her people called and she would not leave Burma again until her country and her people were free.

A massive demonstration was called. Organisers, including student demonstrators, Suu Kyi, former Prime Minister U Nu and older stalwarts from her father's generation such as retired Brigadier-General Aung Gyi and General U Tin Oo, called for a general strike and mobilisation throughout the country of workers, students, monks and ethnic groups. They settled on the date of 8 August 1988, or 8-8-88, for its auspicious numerological pattern and because of Ne Win's known paranoia. As preparations were made, Sein Lwin also mobilised his Tatmadaw troops. The strike began at eight minutes after the hour of eight and Burma came to a standstill. Coordinated strikes, demonstrations, rallies and riots took place in all areas, from Rangoon to Mandalay to the jungle provinces. Although amazed at the turnout of hundreds of thousands of protesters, the government forces still responded with brute force. Pitched battles with Molotov cocktail–throwing protesters and machine-gun-wielding soldiers left over 3000 dead within four days; more than 10,000 would die by the end of the month. Even Rangoon General Hospital was fired upon as wounded protesters were treated, killing doctors and nurses.

What would become known as the 8888 Uprising could not be contained. On its fourth day, Sein Lwin resigned; he'd been in office only eighteen days. In his place the BSPP leadership appointed Dr Maung Maung, Ne Win's biographer and the party's first non-military leader. With the lifting of martial law and promises of multi-party elections, the demonstrations subsided. 'The fire of anger can be extinguished with the cool waters of love and compassion,' Dr Maung told a sceptical country in his first radio address. But many remained suspicious that Ne Win was still pulling the strings behind the scenes, especially since his two loyal henchmen had ascended to power. As doubt crept in that the party would ever truly allow fair multi-party elections, protesters returned to the streets across the country.

Following the military attack on Rangoon Hospital, Suu Kyi addressed a demonstration of nearly 50,000 people. She spoke directly and honestly and begged that the protesters remain peaceful. Days later, as hundreds of thousands came out in support of open elections, a massive rally was held at the Shwedagon Pagoda. Though rumours were flying that she would be assassinated there, standing near the mausoleum of her slain father, Aung San Suu Kyi addressed nearly half a million protesters. As witnesses described, the small, demure woman, now in her early forties, was the spitting image of her father, radiating a calm confidence. Speaking in Burmese, she introduced herself to the country and, calling upon her father's example, declared she would now dedicate her life to fighting her country's 'second struggle for national independence'. The crowd went crazy.

She called for a moment of silence to remember the students and monks who had lost their lives in the protests. She promised her complete support for multi-party democracy and begged the people of Burma to remain peaceful and unified. To the roars of the crowd, she said:

> We shall reach our goal of a strong and lasting union only if we are all able to go forward in unity. We have not yet achieved this goal. Let us not be disunited. Therefore let us resolve to march forward in unity towards our cherished goal. In doing so please use peaceful means. If a people or a nation can reach their objectives by disciplined and peaceful means, it would be a most honourable and admirable achievement.

She called for solidarity with the military, and begged all soldiers and police to join their movement. As the din grew to a crescendo of cheers, tears and patriotic songs, Aung San Suu Kyi finished by saying:

> To conclude I would like to reiterate our emphatic demands and protests, namely that we have no desire at all for a referendum, that the one-party system should be dismantled, that a multiparty system of government should

be established, and we call for free and fair elections to be arranged as quickly as possible. These are our demands!

———

## HOUSE ARREST

Following her speech at the Shwedagon Pagoda, Suu Kyi was elevated to the undisputed leader of the pro-democracy movement. And though 75 per cent of the BSPP congressional delegates supported a multi-party government, the leadership declared that they, alone, would organise an election. Protesters again took to the streets, demanding the immediate resignation of all BSPP officials and the establishment of a provisional government to oversee the elections and the transition of power.

Tatmadaw leaders, long plotting in the background, had had enough. On 18 September, under the leadership of General Saw Maung, who had been Sein Lwin's right-hand man, the military retook the country in another coup. Saw Maung declared martial law, repealed the constitution and dissolved the government by establishing the State Law and Order Restoration Council (SLORC), an even more brutal version of Ne Win's despotic BSPP. SLORC crushed all demonstrations with overwhelming force. Up to 5000 more protesters—students, monks, women and children—were indiscriminately slaughtered across the country. Protest leaders were arrested, tortured, killed or chased into the jungles or into exile. By mid-October, the pro-democracy movement had all but collapsed.

Aung San Suu Kyi was placed under house arrest. Michael and the two boys were expelled from the country and returned to England. In December, Daw Khin Kyi died. In a rare show of solidarity, Saw Maung and the leaders of SLORC, activists, the old guard and Suu Kyi agreed on a day of mourning for the wife of the Father of Burma. The country seemed to hold its breath as thousands came out to pay their respects as Daw Khin Kyi was buried at the Shwedagon Pagoda, near her husband. The day passed peacefully, for Suu Kyi's call for non-violence was followed with great discipline, much to the frustration of the Tatmadaw.

Held in her compound, Suu Kyi could now only wait for Saw Maung and SLORC's next moves. These came soon enough, in surprising ways. First, the new government declared that henceforth the country's official name would be changed from the Socialist Republic of the Union of Burma to the Union of Myanmar. The second surprise came when the military junta declared that it would hold national elections in 1990. Apparently confident that it had reined in all opposition groups sufficiently to rig its own victory, the new government wished to provide at least a glint of respectability to its otherwise brutal rise to power.

Suu Kyi's arrest and the latest draconian measures by the junta brought her huge international attention. As the pro-democracy factions organised into the National League for Democracy (NLD), the government disqualified Suu Kyi from running, claiming she had been 'influenced by anti-government opportunistic politicians and insurgent groups'. Still, when election day came in May 1990, 2300 candidates representing ninety-three political parties ran for the 485 seats in the national assembly. An immense number of electoral irregularities were documented, from vote-rigging to outright intimidation. But to the amazement of the country and the utter rage of the junta, the NLD won 392 of the 485 seats, 81 per cent. And though she herself could not run for an assembly seat, as head of the NLD Aung San Suu Kyi had just been elected the Union of Myanmar's new prime minister.

Of course, SLORC was not going to stand for this outcome. They immediately called for a review of the elections and then refused to hand over power to the NLD, using as an excuse that the election had been meant as a referendum on creating a new constitution and promising a transfer of power only after a new constitution was created. Repressive measures increased again and many elected NLD officials fled Burma. International attention increased, helped in part when Suu Kyi was awarded the 1990 Nobel Peace Prize as well as the Sakharov Prize for Freedom of Thought. Her sons Alexander and Kim accepted the Nobel Prize for her and the US$1.3 million award was used to establish a health and education trust for the Burmese people.

Today, the wait for the junta to concede to Burma's voters and transition power is reaching its twentieth year. Aung San Suu Kyi has remained under detention, either in her home compound or in one of Burma's notorious prisons, without being charged with a crime for most of that time. SLORC has refused to relinquish power or recognise the results of the 1990 elections. In 1992, General Than Shwe replaced Saw Maung as head of the junta and in 1997 the government was renamed, with no small irony, the State Peace and Development Council (SPDC).

That same year Michael Aris was diagnosed with terminal prostate cancer. He had not seen his wife since 1995, the last time the junta allowed him and their children an entrance visa. All of his requests, and those of humanitarian organisations and world leaders, would not sway the government, which instead offered Suu Kyi the opportunity to leave the country to tend her dying husband. Knowing full well she would never be allowed to return, Suu Kyi painfully refused the offer. Michael died in 1999, never seeing his beloved wife again.

Anti-government protests have flared up throughout the two decades, most prominently in 2003, following Suu Kyi's brief release from detention. At the time, nearly seventy NLD activists were slaughtered by government forces in what became known as the Depayin Massacre. Following this, Suu Kyi was arrested and taken to an undisclosed prison for three months; many feared she had been killed. But she was returned to her home compound and held under house arrest, where she remains today.

In 2007, following a huge spike in fuel costs and continued government repression, unrest broke out again. Led by Buddhist monks who met briefly with Suu Kyi at the gate of her compound, the protests were fuelled by rumours that Suu Kyi had been carted off to the notorious Insein Prison following the meeting. The rumours were proved to be false when UN representatives confirmed she remained under house arrest. Regardless, this newest disturbance was again brutally put down. With further disorder and protests in 2008, and Suu Kyi's house arrest due to end the following year, pro-democracy advocates in Burma were offered a small glimmer of hope. But even so, many in the country had come to cynically doubt the government would ever allow her to lead the NLD to free elections.

These doubts were proved true in 2009 when a bizarre incident again brought Suu Kyi's plight to the fore and placed Burma's repressive regime in the international spotlight. In May of that year, a semi-delusional American named John William Yettaw—claiming to be driven by a command from God—swam across Inya Lake and stole into Suu Kyi's compound. He remained there for two days, apparently attempting to 'rescue' Suu Kyi before he swam back and was duly arrested by Burmese authorities. Yettaw was charged with criminal trespass and Suu Kyi was charged with breaking the terms of her house arrest. In the ensuing trial, both were found guilty; the Burmese authorities were handed an excuse to reinstate Suu Kyi's house arrest and keep her out of the general elections tentatively scheduled for 2010.

With the intervention of American authorities, Yettaw was released and deported shortly after his conviction. Suu Kyi has not been so lucky. Although the courts have agreed to hear her appeal of the conviction, most agree that she will be barred from participating in any future elections. Still, she remains ever optimistic. 'The future of course is democracy for Burma,' she insists. 'It is going to happen, and I am going to be here when it happens.' To this day, Aung San Suu Kyi stands firm, a prisoner of conscience, who lives minimally in solidarity with her repressed people, waiting for her time to lead. Burma's 'Widow of Rangoon', affectionately known simply as 'The Lady,' waits.

# SOURCE NOTES

### LORD MAHAVIRA: JAINISM AND A RELIGION OF NON-VIOLENCE

I am indebted to several great books on Jainism and the life of Lord Mahavira for the stories of his experiences and his efforts at organising the Jain religion. The quoted descriptions of Mahavira's life come from *Jainism: The World of Conquerors* by Natubhai Shah and *Jainism: A Pictorial Guide to the Religion of Non-Violence* by Kurt Titze. The direct quotes of Lord Mahavira come from *Thus Spake Lord Mahavir*, compiled by Jain Dulichand.

Additional sources of information on Jain cosmology and practice were *Jainism: The World of Conquerors* by Natubhai Shah, 'The Place of Jainism in Indian Thought', an article by Dr Felix Valyi from the Jainism Literature Centre at Harvard University, *Bliss Divine* by Swami Sivananda and *The Building of the Kosmos and Other Lectures* by Annie Besant. *Encyclopedia of Religion and War* by Gabriel Palmer-Fernandez was helpful in learning about the swastika and Adolf Hitler's quote comes from his *Mein Kampf*. Much of the overview of Buddhism was gleaned from Robert E. Buswell's two-volume *Encyclopedia of Buddhism*.

### *LYSISTRATA*: MAKE LOVE, NOT WAR

I used Sarah Ruden's terrific translation and 'topical commentary' *Lysistrata by Aristophanes* for the play's quotes. I also used Alan Sommerstein's translation from his *Lysistrata, The Acharnians, The Clouds*. I am grateful for *Aristophanes: His Plays and His*

*Influence* by Louis E. Lord and *Pericles on Stage: Political Comedy in Aristophanes' Early Plays* by Michael J. Vickers for invaluable information on putting Aristophanes' works into historical context.

The reports of Columbia's gang violence and the 'crossed-leg strike' by their wives and girlfriends comes from the BBC News website and articles in the London *Times* and Scotland's *Sunday Herald International* from 2006. Information about the *Lysistrata Project* comes from their website, www.lysistrataproject.org.

### THE PRINCE OF PEACE: THE SERMON ON THE MOUNT

There is, of course, a broad array of writings on the Sermon on the Mount. The sources I used for background on the sermon were *The Jewish Sources of the Sermon on the Mount* by Gerald Friedlander, *Behind the Gospels* and *Jesus, What Manner of Man* by Henry J. Cadbury and *Who Wrote the Bible?* by Richard Elliott Friedman. For the discussion of the Synoptic Problem, I am indebted to Dennis Bratcher's concise *The Gospels and The Synoptic Problem: The Literary Relationship of Matthew, Mark, and Luke*.

For background on the early Christian church and non-canonical gospels, Ron Cameron's *The Other Gospels: Non-Canonical Gospel Texts*, Hyam MacCoby's *The Mythmaker: Paul and the Invention of Christianity* and Keith Akers' *The Lost Religion of Jesus: Simple Living and Non-violence in Early Christianity* were extremely helpful. Erin Dufault-Hunter's paper 'Pacifism and Just War: Beyond the Stereotypes' from the Center for Christian Ethics at Baylor University was very useful in discussing how Catholicism moved to embracing the concept of 'just war'. I used the New Revised Standard Version of the Bible for all gospel quotes.

### GEORGE FOX: A SEEKER OF PEACE

*The Journal of George Fox*, his autobiography as edited by Rufus M. Jones, was my primary source for this chapter. All of Fox's quoted comments come from his journal and William Penn's excerpts on Fox come from the book's preface. In addition, two biographies were very helpful: *George Fox* by Vernon Noble and *George Fox, Seeker and Friend* by Rufus M. Jones. For background on the evolution of the Quaker philosophy, I found Howard Brinton's *How They Became Friends* and *The Religious Philosophy of Quakerism: The Beliefs of Fox, Barclay, and Penn as Based on the Gospel of John* to be invaluable. Here the Bible quotes come from the King James Version, as Fox used them.

### THE MORIORI: NUNUKU-WHENUA'S LAW

Michael King's *Moriori: A People Rediscovered* has become the definitive history of the Moriori people. It is a meticulously researched and beautifully written book and served as my primary source for this chapter. King also led me to several other useful histories of the Morioroi: *The Morioris* by William Bauke and H. D. Skinner and *The Moriori People of the Chatham Islands* by Alexander Shand. E. Dieffenbach's *Travels in New Zealand* was useful for understanding the Maori and Morioroi dynamic and F.J.W. Gasgoyne's *Soldiering in New Zealand* was essential for understanding the New Zealand wars and the Maori's combat techniques.

I quoted widely from *Koche, King of Pitt* for both the account of Chatham Island's rediscovery and the invasion by the Maori. Interestingly, there remains some confusion about the author. I found an original copy of the story and, through a biography of the Ewing family in the *Catholic Encyclopedia*, found that Koche's story was credited to Hugh Boyle Ewing, a writer of some small note in the late 1800s. However, Michael King credits the book to 'the lawyer' C. Ewing, who I can only deduce must be Hugh Boyle Ewing's younger brother Charles. I believe my reference is correct.

### LEO TOLSTOY: PEACE AND WAR

Although I have drawn from many of Leo Tolstoy's original works, several books of commentary on his life and writings were essential to this chapter, among them Kathryn B. Feuer's *Tolstoy and the Genesis of War and Peace* and Donna T. Orwin's *The Cambridge Companion to Tolstoy*. Regarding Tolstoy's view of war and peace, I found *A Brief History of Pacifism from Jesus to Tolstoy* by Peter Brock and *From Warism to Pacifism: A Moral Continuum* by Duane L. Cady invaluable. The great composer Peter Tchaikovsky's quote comes from Vladimir Volkoff's biography *Tchaikovsky: A Self-portrait*.

### JANE ADDAMS: IDEALS OF PEACE

There have been a number of remarkable biographies of Jane Addams. Essential to this chapter were: *Jane Addams: A Biography* by James Weber Linn, *Waging Peace: The Story of Jane Addams* by Peggy Caravantes, *Jane Addams: Pioneer for Social Justice* by Cornelia Meigs and *Jane Addams, Champion of Democracy* by Judith Bloom Fradin and Dennis Brindell Fradin. Much of this chapter comes from Addams' own writings, including *Newer Ideals of Peace*, *Twenty Years at Hull-House: With Autobiographical Notes* and *Peace and Bread in Time of War*. I gathered much of the material for the story of Henry Ford's pacifistic misadventure from *Henry Ford and His Peace Ship* by Allan Nevins and Frank Ernest Hill.

### BERTRAND RUSSELL: THE PARADOX OF PEACE

Bertrand Russell's exhaustive, three-volume *The Autobiography of Bertrand Russell* was certainly the backbone of this chapter; I quote the book's poetic dedication to his third wife. In addition, *Bertrand Russell: A Political Life* by Alan Ryan and *The Cambridge Companion to Bertrand Russell* by Nicholas Griffin were both extremely useful.

I've cited a number of Russell's own books on pacifism in this chapter. Some additional material on his peace stance comes from 'Russell, Einstein and the Philosophy of Non-Absolute Pacifism' by David Blitz, in volume 20 of *Russell: The Journal of Bertrand Russell Studies,* and *Bertrand Russell on Nuclear War, Peace, and Language: Critical and Historical Essays* by Alan Schwerin from the Bertrand Russell Society.

In addition, some material on Russell's marriages and affairs comes from Dora Russell's memoir *The Tamarisk Tree* and James Edwin Miller's *T.S. Eliot's Personal Waste Land: Exorcism of the Demons.* For the history of the peace symbol, I found the detailed and beautifully illustrated *Peace: 50 Years of Protest* by Barry Miles essential.

## JEAN JAURÈS: ANTI-MILITARY SOCIALIST

Harvey Goldberg's *The Life of Jean Jaurès* was essential to writing this chapter, as was Geoffrey Kurtz 'Jean Jaurès: A Portrait' in volume 5 of the journal *Logos.* For context on French Socialists in the lead-up to World War I, I am indebted to Albert S. Lindemann's *A History of European Socialism.* For an understanding of the general strike, I found Joan Wallace Scott's *The Glassworkers of Carmaux* and Jaurès' own 'The General Strike and Revolution' in his *Studies in Socialism* very useful. Leon Trotsky's quoted comments about Jaurès come from his essay 'Political Profiles in French Socialism: Jean Jaurès'.

## A.J. MUSTE: PACIFIST REVOLUTIONARY

I am grateful to the Archives at the Friends Centre in Philadelphia, Pennsylvania for the original source material on A.J. Muste, the American Friends Service Committee and the Fellowship of Reconciliation. JoAnn Robinson's *Abraham Went Out: A Biography of A.J. Muste* and Nat Hentoff's *Peace Agitator: The Story of A.J. Muste* were also essential to this chapter. For additional information on Muste's pacifist views, I relied on his *Of Holy Disobedience* and *The Essays of A.J. Muste* (edited by Nat Hentoff). In addition, James Tracey's *Direct Action* and Scott Bennett's *Radical Pacifism: The War Resisters League and Gandhian Non-violence in America, 1915–1963* were invaluable for providing background on the peace movement and other peace activists influenced by Muste.

## DOROTHY DAY: CATHOLIC WORKER

Dorothy Day's memoir, *The Long Loneliness: Dorothy Day* was essential to this chapter. In addition, *American Catholic Pacifism: The Influence of Dorothy Day and the Catholic Worker Movement,* edited by Anne Klejment and Nancy L. Roberts, and *The Life You Save May Be Your Own: An American Pilgrimage* by Paul Elie were helpful for understanding Day's influence and writings.

For information on Ammon Hennacy and the Union Eight, I relied on *Direct Action* by James Tracey and *David Dellinger: The Life and Times of a Non-violent*

SOURCE NOTES

285

*Revolutionary* by Andrew Hunt. For background on Day's life in bohemian Greenwich Village I found Ross Wetzsteon's comprehensive *Republic of Dreams, Greenwich Village: The American Bohemia, 1910–1960* invaluable.

## THOMAS MERTON AND THICH NHAT HANH: PACIFIST MONKS

*Thomas Merton and Thich Nhat Hanh: Engaged Spirituality in an Age of Globalization* by Robert H. King was critical to writing this chapter and provided both biographical information and historical context to their brief meeting. Additional biographical information on Merton came from *The Life You Save May Be Your Own: An American Pilgrimage* by Paul Elie and *Practical Pacifism* by Andrew Gordon Fiala. I also used Merton's own writings from *The Seven Storey Mountain*, *The Non-violent Alternative* and *Seeds of Destruction*. The letter to Czeslaw Milosz I quote comes from Merton's *Courage For Truth: The Letters of Thomas Merton to Writers*.

For additional information on Thich Nhat Hanh, I relied on *In Engaged Buddhism, Peace Begins with You* by John Malkin as well as Nhat Hanh's *Creating True Peace*, Sallie B. King's *Being Benevolence* and Daniel Berrigan's *The Raft is Not the Shore: Conversations Toward a Buddhist/Christian Awareness*.

## MOHANDAS K. GANDHI: NON-VIOLENCE FREES A NATION

Mohandas K. Gandhi's *An Autobiography: The Story of My Experiments with Truth* (edited by Mahadev Haribhai Desai) was essential to writing this chapter. I also relied on Vincent Sheean's concise biography *Mahatma Gandhi*, Romain Rolland's early biography *Mahatma Gandhi*, as well as the short *Gandhi Remembered* by Horace G. Alexander. I have also quoted from Leo Tolstoy's 'Letter to a Hindu' and Gandhi's Introduction to the published version as well as Gandhi's *Satyagraha in South Africa*.

*Non-violent Soldier of Islam: Badshah Khan: A Man to Match His Mountains* by Eknath Easwaran was essential for the section on Khan. For the story of Annie Besant I relied on *Annie Besant: Founder of Home Rule Movement* by Raj Rameshwari Devi Kumar and Romila Pruthi, and *Annie Besant: A Biography* by Anne Taylor.

## DR MARTIN LUTHER KING JR: CIVIL DISOBEDIENT

There have been many wonderful books about King's life, but his own memoir, *The Autobiography of Martin Luther King, Jr.* was a primary source for this chapter. In addition, I relied on *The Papers of Martin Luther King, Jr.*, compiled and edited by Clayborne Carson, Peter Holloran, Ralph Luker and Penny A. Russell, and *I May Not Get There With You: The True Martin Luther King, Jr.* by Michael Eric Dyson. Jacqueline Ching's *The Assassination of Martin Luther King, Jr.* was an important source of information about his last days.

For background on Bayard Rustin and the environment that led to King's rise, I'm indebted to Scott H. Bennett's *Radical Pacifism: The War Resisters League and Gandhian Non-violence in America, 1915–1963*. I quote from several of King's most famous speeches, which I have taken from the published version in the 'A.J. Muste Memorial Institute Essay Series'.

### ARCHBISHOP ÓSCAR ROMERO: MARTYR FOR PEACE

*El Salvador, The Face of Revolution* by Robert Armstrong and Janet Shenk provided a great resource for the context of Romero's rise to prominence as a champion of the repressed. James R. Brockman's *Romero: A Life* and *Oscar Romero: Reflections on His Life and Writings* by Marie Dennis, Renny Golden and Scott Wright were of great help. I also used as a source Romero's *The Violence of Love* (translated by James R. Brockman) and Brockman's article 'The Spiritual Journey of Oscar Romero', published in volume 42 of *Spirituality Today*.

I am again grateful for the assistance of the Archives of the Friends Center in Philadelphia, Pennsylvania for their original source material on José Brocca and the efforts of the Fellowship of Reconciliation during Spain's Civil War.

### THE DALAI LAMA: GENTLE EXILE

Tenzin Gyatso, the 14th Dalai Lama's memoir, *Freedom in Exile: The Autobiography of the Dalai Lama* was the primary source for this chapter. In addition, I'm grateful for the insights into the Dalai Lama's life from Thomas Laird's *The Story of Tibet: Conversations With the Dalai Lama*, Kenneth Kraft's *Inner Peace, World Peace* and Catherine Ingram's *In the Footsteps of Gandhi: Conversations with Spiritual Social Activists*. The quoted interview from *Time* magazine was in the issue of 22 March 2008.

### AUNG SAN SUU KYI: PRISONER OF CONSCIENCE

At the time of this writing, Aung San Suu Kyi is again in the news quite frequently, and I have benefited from much of the reporting in writing this chapter. In addition, a primary source was Justin Wintle's comprehensive biography *Perfect Hostage: A Life of Aung San Suu Kyi*. In addition, Whitney Stewart's short biography *Aung San Suu Kyi, Fearless Voice of Burma* was very helpful. Much of the information on the 8888 Uprising came from the All Burma IT Students' Union website, www.abitsu.org.

# BIBLIOGRAPHY

Addams, Jane. *Newer Ideals of Peace*. New York: The Macmillan Company, 1907

Addams, Jane. *Twenty Years at Hull-House: With Autobiographical Notes*. New York: The Macmillan Company, 1912

Addams, Jane. *Peace and Bread in Time of War*. New York: The Macmillan Company, 1922

Akers, Keith. *The Lost Religion of Jesus: Simple Living and Non-violence in Early Christianity*. New York: Lantern Books, 2000

Alexander, Horace G. *Gandhi Remembered*. Wallingford, PA: Pendle Hill Publications, 1969

Armstrong, Robert and Janet Shenk. *El Salvador: The Face of Revolution*. Cambridge, MA: South End Press, 1982

Bauke, William and H.D. Skinner. *The Morioris*. Honolulu, HI: Bishop Museum,1928

Bennett, Scott H. *Radical Pacifism: The War Resisters League and Gandhian Non-violence in America, 1915–1963*. Syracuse, NY: Syracuse University Press, 2003

Besant, Annie. *The Building of the Kosmos and Other Lectures*. Charleston, SC: Bibliolife, 2008.

Brinton, Howard H. *How They Became Friends*. Wallingford, PA: Pendle Hill Publications, 1961

Brinton, Howard H. *The Religious Philosophy of Quakerism: The Beliefs of Fox, Barclay, and Penn as Based on the Gospel of John*. Wallingford, PA: Pendle Hill Publications, 1973

Brock, Peter. *A Brief History of Pacifism from Jesus to Tolstoy*. Syracuse, NY: Syracuse University Press, 1994

Brockman, James R. *Romero: A Life*. Maryknoll, NY: Orbis Books, 2005

Buswell, Robert E. *Encyclopedia of Buddhism*. New York: Macmillan Reference Books, 2003

Cadbury, Henry J. *Jesus, What Manner of Man?*, New York: Macmillan Company, 1947

Cadbury, Henry J. *Behind the Gospels*. Wallingford, PA: Pendle Hill Publications, 1968

Cady, Duane L. *From Warism to Pacifism: A Moral Continuum*. Philadelphia: Temple University Press, 1990

Cameron, Ron. *The Other Gospels: Non-Canonical Gospel Texts*. Philadelphia: The Westminster Press, 1982

Caravantes, Peggy. *Waging Peace: The Story of Jane Addams*. Greensboro, NC: Morgan Reynolds, Inc., 2004

Ching, Jacqueline. *The Assassination of Martin Luther King, Jr.* New York: The Rosen Publishing Group, 2002

Day, Dorothy. *The Long Loneliness: Dorothy Day*. New York: Image Books, Doubleday, 1959

Dennis, Marie, Renny Golden and Scott Wright. *Oscar Romero: Reflections on His Life and Writings*. Maryknoll, NY: Orbis Books, 2000

Dieffenbach, E. *Travels in New Zealand*. London: Murray, 1947

Dulichand, Jain. *Thus Spake Lord Mahavir*. Chennai: Sri Ramakrishna Math, 1998

Dyson, Michael Eric. *I May Not Get There With You: The True Martin Luther King, Jr.* New York: Simon & Schuster, 2000

Easwaran, Eknath. *Non-violent Soldier of Islam: Badshah Khan: A Man to Match His Mountains*. Tomales, CA: Nilgiri Press, 1999

Elie, Paul. *The Life You Save May Be Your Own: An American Pilgrimage*. New York: Farrar, Straus & Giroux, 2003

Ewing, Hugh Boyle. 'Koche, King of Pitt', *Catholic World*, vol. XVII, New York: The Catholic Publication House, 1873

Feuer, Kathryn B. *Tolstoy and the Genesis of War and Peace*. New York: Cornell University Press, 1996

Fiala, Andrew Gordon. *Practical Pacifism*. New York: Algora Publishing, 2004

Fox, George, Rufus M. Jones (ed.). *The Journal of George Fox*. Richmond, IN: Friends United Press, 1976

Fradin, Judith Bloom and Dennis Brindell Fradin. *Jane Addams, Champion of Democracy*. New York: Clarion Books, 2006

Friedlander, Gerald. *The Jewish Sources of the Sermon on the Mount*. Jersey City, NJ: KTAV Publishing House, 1969

Friedman, Richard Elliott. *Who Wrote the Bible?* New York: Harper & Row, 1987

Gandhi, Mohandas K. *An Autobiography: The Story of My Experiments With Truth*. London: Beacon Press, 1993

Gasgoyne, F.J.W. *Soldiering in New Zealand*. London: Guildford, 1916

Goldberg, Harvey. *The Life of Jean Jaurès*. Madison, WI: University of Wisconsin Press, 2003

Griffin, Nicholas. *The Cambridge Companion to Bertrand Russell*. London: Cambridge University Press, 2003

Gyatso, Tenzin, the 14th Dalai Lama. *Freedom in Exile: The Autobiography of the Dalai Lama*. New York: HarperCollins, 1990

Hanh, Thich Nhat. *Creating True Peace*. New York: Simon & Schuster, 2003

Hentoff, Nat. *Peace Agitator: The Story of A.J. Muste*. New York: A.J. Muste Memorial Institute, 1982

Hitler, Adolf. *Mein Kampf* [1925]. New York: Mariner Books, 1998

Hunt, Andrew. *David Dellinger: The Life and Times of a Non-violent Revolutionary*. New York: NYU Press, 2006

Ingram, Catherine. *In the Footsteps of Gandhi: Conversations with Spiritual Social Activists*. Berkeley, CA: Parallax Press, 1990

Jaurès, Jean. *Studies in Socialism*. New York: G.P. Putnam's Sons, 1906

Jones, Rufus M. *George Fox, Seeker and Friend*. New York: Harper & Row, 1928

King, Jr., Martin Luther. *The Measure of a Man*. Minneapolis, MN: Fortress Press, 1988

King, Jr., Martin Luther, Clayborne Carson, Peter Holloran, Ralph Luker and Penny A. Russell. *The Papers of Martin Luther King, Jr.* Los Angeles: University of California Press, 1992

King, Jr., Martin Luther, Clayborne Carson (ed.), *The Autobiography of Martin Luther King, Jr.* New York: Time Warner Book Group, 1998

King, Michael. *Moriori: A People Rediscovered*. Harmondsworth: Penguin Books, 1989

King, Robert H. *Thomas Merton and Thich Nhat Hanh: Engaged Spirituality in an Age of Globalization*. New York: Continuum, 2001

King, Sallie B. *Being Benevolence: The Social Ethics of Engaged Buddhism*. Honolulu: Hawaii University Press, 2006

Klejment, Anne and Nancy L. Roberts. *American Catholic Pacifism: The Influence of Dorothy Day and the Catholic Worker Movement*. New York: Praeger, 1996

Kraft, Kenneth. *Inner Peace, World Peace: Essays on Buddhism and Non-violence*. New York: State University of New York Press, 1992

Kritzman, Lawrence D., Brian J. Reilly and M. B. DeBevoise. *The Columbia History of Twentieth-Century French Thought*. New York: Columbia University Press, 2006

Kumar, Raj Rameshwari Devi and Romila Pruthi. *Annie Besant: Founder of Home Rule Movement*. Jaipur, India: Pointer Publishers, 2003

Laird, Thomas. *The Story of Tibet: Conversations with the Dalai Lama*. New York: Grove Press, 2006

Lindemann, Albert S. *A History of European Socialism*. New Haven, CT: Yale University Press, 1983

Linn, James Weber. *Jane Addams: A Biography*. New York: Appleton-Century, 1935

Livingstone, E.A. (ed.). *The Concise Oxford Dictionary of the Christian Church*. Oxford, UK: Oxford University Press, 1977

Lord, Louis E. *Aristophanes: His Plays and His Influence*. Boston: Marshall Jones, 1925

MacCoby, Hyam. *The Mythmaker: Paul and the Invention of Christianity*. New York: Harper & Row, 1987

Malkin, John. *In Engaged Buddhism, Peace Begins with You*. San Francisco: Shambhala Sun Foundation, 2003

Meigs, Cornelia. *Jane Addams, Pioneer for Social Justice*. New York: Little, Brown & Co., 1970

Merton, Thomas. *Seeds of Destruction*. New York: The Macmillan Company, 1965

Merton, Thomas. *The Non-violent Alternative*. New York: The Macmillan Company, 1981

Merton, Thomas. *Courage for Truth: The Letters of Thomas Merton to Writers*. New York: Harvest Books, 1994

Merton, Thomas. *The Seven Storey Mountain*. New York: Houghton Mifflin Harcourt, 1999

Miles, Barry. *Peace: 50 Years of Protest*. New York: The Reader's Digest Association, Inc., 2008

Miller, James Edwin. *T.S. Eliot's Personal Waste Land: Exorcism of the Demons*, Philadelphia: Penn State Press, 1977

Muste, A.J. *Of Holy Disobedience*. Wallingford, PA: Pendle Hill Publications, 1952

Muste, A.J. *The Essays of A.J. Muste*. New York: Simon & Schuster, 1970

Nevins, Allan and Frank Ernest Hill. *Ford: Expansion and Challenge, 1915–1933*. New York: Charles Scribner's Sons, 1957

Noble, Vernon. *George Fox*. London: Henry Burt & Sons, 1969

Orwin, Donna T. *The Cambridge Companion to Tolstoy*. London: Cambridge University Press, 2002

Palmer-Fernandez, Gabriel. *Encyclopedia of Religion and War*. New York: Routledge, 2003

Robinson, JoAnn. *Abraham Went Out: A Biography of A.J. Muste*. Philadelphia: Temple University Press, 1982.

Romero, Oscar. *The Violence of Love*. Maryknoll, NY: Orbis Books, 2004

Ruden, Sarah. *Lysistrata by Aristophanes: Translation with Notes and Topical Commentaries*. Cambridge, MA: Hackett Publishing, 2003

Russell, Bertrand. *The Principles of Mathematics*. Cambridge, UK: Cambridge University Press, 1903

Russell, Bertrand. *Justice in War-time*. Chicago: Open Court, 1916

Russell, Bertrand. *Why Men Fight: A Method of Abolishing the International Duel*. New York: The Century Co., 1917

Russell, Bertrand. *What I Believe*. London: Kegan Paul, Trench, Trubner, 1925

Russell, Bertrand. *Why I Am Not a Christian*. London: Watts, 1927

Russell, Bertrand. *Marriage and Morals*. London: George Allen & Unwin, 1929

Russell, Bertrand. *Which Way to Peace?* London: Jonathan Cape, 1936

Russell, Bertrand. *History of Western Philosophy and Its Connection with Political and Social Circumstances from the Earliest Times to the Present Day*. New York: Simon & Schuster, 1945

Russell, Bertrand. *Has Man a Future?* London: George Allen & Unwin, 1961

Russell, Bertrand. *Russell's Peace Appeals* (eds Tsutomu Makino and Kazuteru Hitaka). Tokyo, Japan: Eichosha's New Current Books, 1967

Russell, Bertrand. *The Autobiography of Bertrand Russell*. 3 vols. London: George Allen & Unwin, 1967–1969

Russell, Dora. *The Tamarisk Tree*. London: Virago Press Ltd, 1980

Ryan, Alan. *Bertrand Russell: A Political Life*. New York: The Macmillan Company, 1981

Schwerin, Alan. *Bertrand Russell on Nuclear War, Peace, and Language: Critical and Historical Essays*. Santa Barbara, CA: Greenwood Publishing Group, 2002

Scott, Joan Wallace. *The Glassworkers of Carmaux*. Cambridge, MA: Harvard University Press, 1974

Shah, Natubhai. *Jainism: The World of Conquerors*. Eastbourne, UK: Sussex Academic Press, 1998

Shand, Alexander. *The Moriori People of the Chatham Islands*. Wellington, New Zealand: Polynesian Society, 1911

Sheean, Vincent. *Mahatma Gandhi*. New York: Alfred A. Knopf, 1965

Sivananda, Swami. *Bliss Divine*. New Delhi: Divine Life Society, 2006

Sommerstein, Alan. *Lysistrata, The Acharnians, The Clouds*. New York: Penguin Books, 1973

Stewart, Whitney. *Aung San Suu Kyi, Fearless Voice of Burma*. Minneapolis, MN: Lerner Publications Company, 1997

Taylor, Anne. *Annie Besant: A Biography*. Oxford, UK: Oxford University Press, 1991

Titze, Kurt. *Jainism: A Pictorial Guide to the Religion of Non-Violence*. New Delhi: Motilal Banarsidass Publishers, 2001

Tolstoy, Leo. *War and Peace* [1865–1869]. New York: Modern Library Classics, 2004

Tolstoy, Leo. *Anna Karenina* [1875–1877]. New York: Penguin Classics, 2004

Tolstoy, Leo. *A Confession and Other Religious Writings* [1882]. New York: Penguin Classics, 1988

Tolstoy, Leo. *What I Believe* [1884]. New York: Cosimo Classics, 2007

Tolstoy, Leo. *Collected Shorter Fiction: Volume 1*. London: Everyman's Library, 2001

Tolstoy, Leo. *The Kingdom of God is Within You* [1894]. London: Oxford University Press, 1936

Tracey, James. *Direct Action*. Chicago: University of Chicago Press, 1996

Trotsky, Leon. *Political Profiles*, London: Index Books, 1972

Vickers, Michael J. *Pericles on Stage: Political Comedy in Aristophanes' Early Plays*. Austin, TX: University of Texas Press, 1997

Volkoff, Vladimir. *Tchaikovsky: A Self-portrait*. Boston: Crescendo, 1975

Wetzsteon, Ross. *Republic of Dreams, Greenwich Village: The American Bohemia, 1910–1960*. New York: Simon & Schuster, 2002

Wintle, Justin. *Perfect Hostage: A Life of Aung San Suu Kyi*. London: Hutchinson, 2007

## PICTURE CREDITS

AKG images: p. 48

Bellarmine University; Photograph of Thomas Merton by John Howard Griffin. Used with permission of the Merton Legacy Trust and the Thomas Merton Center: p. 178

Corbis: cover (top middle and right), pp. 2, 18, 24, 108, 122, 213, 220–221, 244, 272, 273

Getty Images: cover (top left, bottom), pp. 116, 148, 159, 181, 194, 208–209, 230, 246, 258, 260

Library of Congress: pp. 84, 98

Milwauke Journal photo 1968, courtesy of the Marquette University Archives: p. 164

National Library of New Zealand — Alexander Turnbull Library: pp. 68, 75

Photolibrary: pp. 8–9, 33, 36–37, 52–53, 134, 145

# ACKNOWLEDGEMENTS

I would like to thank Murdoch Books' Publisher Diana Hill for believing in this book and for her encouragement at every step of the way. I'm grateful to editors Paul O'Beirne and Anne Savage for their care in trimming the fat and checking the facts. Thanks also to Peter Long for his terrific layout and design.

Special thanks to Joe Cummins for making introductions, reading drafts, offering suggestions, giving excellent advice, and for being such a great friend. I couldn't have written this book without the assistance of my brother Richard Sanders, librarian extraordinaire, who tracked down a number of essential publications and opened up his own extensive library to me. Kristen Richardson and Donald Davis were of immense help with the archives at the American Friends Service Committee in Philadelphia. Thanks also to Jotham and Nathalie Bailey.

I am so grateful to the spirit of my parents Edwin and Marian Sanders whose lifelong dedication to peace activism helped guide this book. Thanks also to my blessedly not-so-peaceful children Nellie and Yoshi for being such good sports and for always professing interest. And of course very special thanks to Priscilla Alvarado for the million things she does every day, including keeping the peace.

# INDEX

Published in 2010 by Pier 9, an imprint of Murdoch Books Pty Limited

Murdoch Books Australia
Pier 8/9
23 Hickson Road
Millers Point NSW 2000
Phone: +61 (0) 2 8220 2000
Fax: +61 (0) 2 8220 2558
www.murdochbooks.com.au

Murdoch Books UK Limited
Erico House, 6th Floor
93–99 Upper Richmond Road
Putney, London SW15 2TG
Phone: +44 (0) 20 8785 5995
Fax: +44 (0) 20 8785 5985
www.murdochbooks.co.uk

Publisher: Diana Hill
Project Editor: Paul O'Beirne
Designer: Peter Long

Text copyright © Erin Ladd Sanders 2010
Design copyright © Murdoch Books Pty Limited 2010

National Library of Australia Cataloguing-in-Publication Data:

| | |
|---|---|
| Author: | Sanders, Erin. |
| Title: | In the Name of Peace: how history's great pacifists changed the world / Erin Sanders. |
| ISBN: | 978-1-74196-567-4 (pbk.) |
| Notes: | Includes index. |
| | Bibliography. |
| Subjects: | Pacifism—History. |
| | Pacifism—Social aspects. |
| | Pacifists. |
| | Non-violence—Social aspects. |
| | Social change—History. |
| Dewey Number: | 303.66 |

A catalogue record for this book is available from the British Library.

PRINTED IN HONG KONG.